## Get a FREE eBook

To register this book, scan the code or go to
**www.manning.com/freebook/papp**

### By registering you get

- **FREE eBook copy**
  download in PDF and ePub

- **FREE online access**
  to Manning's liveBook platform

- **FREE audio**
  read and listen online in liveBook

- **FREE AI Assistant**
  it knows the contents (and your exact location) when it answers

- **FREE in-book testing**
  fun tests to lock in your knowledge

In Manning's liveBook platform you can share discussions and comments with other readers, add your own bookmarks and highlights, insert personal notes anywhere on the page, see color versions of all the book's graphics, download source code and other resources, and more!
To register, scan the code or go to www.manning.com/freebook/papp

# Investing for Programmers

STEFAN PAPP

MANNING

SHELTER ISLAND

For online information and ordering of this and other Manning books, please visit www.manning.com. The publisher offers discounts on this book when ordered in quantity. For more information, please contact

    Special Sales Department
    Manning Publications Co.
    20 Baldwin Road
    PO Box 761
    Shelter Island, NY 11964
    Email: orders@manning.com

©2026 by Manning Publications Co. All rights reserved.

No part of this publication may be reproduced, stored in a retrieval system, or transmitted, in any form or by means electronic, mechanical, photocopying, or otherwise, without prior written permission of the publisher.

Many of the designations used by manufacturers and sellers to distinguish their products are claimed as trademarks. Where those designations appear in the book, and Manning Publications was aware of a trademark claim, the designations have been printed in initial caps or all caps.

♾ Recognizing the importance of preserving what has been written, it is Manning's policy to have the books we publish printed on acid-free paper, and we exert our best efforts to that end. Recognizing also our responsibility to conserve the resources of our planet, Manning books are printed on paper that is at least 15 percent recycled and processed without the use of elemental chlorine.

The authors and publisher have made every effort to ensure that the information in this book was correct at press time. The authors and publisher do not assume and hereby disclaim any liability to any party for any loss, damage, or disruption caused by errors or omissions, whether such errors or omissions result from negligence, accident, or any other cause, or from any usage of the information herein.

| | |
|---|---|
| Manning Publications Co.<br>20 Baldwin Road<br>PO Box 761<br>Shelter Island, NY 11964 | Development editor: Connor O'Brien<br>Technical editor: Anirudha Singh Bhadoriya<br>Review editor: Angelina Lazukić<br>Production editor: Kathy Rossland<br>Copy editor: Julie McNamee<br>Proofreader: Jason Everett<br>Technical proofreader: Ignacio Beltran Torres<br>Typesetter: Dennis Dalinnik<br>Cover designer: Marija Tudor |

ISBN: 9781633435803
Printed in the United States of America

*To all the entrepreneurs and innovators who dare to make a difference!*

## brief contents

1. The analytical investor  1
2. Investment essentials  19
3. Collecting data  52
4. Growth portfolios  78
5. Income portfolios  105
6. Building an asset monitor  123
7. Risk management  143
8. AI for financial research  181
9. AI agents  216
10. Charts and technical analysis  239
11. Algorithmic trading  273
12. Private equity: Investing in start-ups  297
13. The road goes ever on and on  321

appendix  Setting up the environment  330

# contents

*preface xiii*
*acknowledgments xv*
*about this book xvii*
*about the author xx*
*about the cover illustration xxi*

## 1 The analytical investor 1

1.1 Your investment journey 2

1.2 Assets 2

*Stocks 3 ▪ Bonds 4 ▪ Exchange-traded funds 4
Other funds 5 ▪ Foreign exchange market 5 ▪ Crypto 5
Derivatives 6 ▪ Private equity 6 ▪ Other assets 7
Choosing assets 8*

1.3 Investment approaches 8

*Quantitative research 10 ▪ Qualitative research 11
Algorithmic trading and asset monitors 12 ▪ Portfolios
and investing strategies 13*

1.4 Risks and rewards 15

1.5 A programmer's unfair advantage 16

*You think in systems and data 16 ▪ Your mindset is built for
the market 16 ▪ Define your parameters 17*

## 2 Investment essentials   19

- 2.1 Accounting in a nutshell   20
  - *Income statement   21 • Balance sheet   25 • Free cash flow   26*
- 2.2 Industry classification   28
  - *Influences on GICS sectors   28 • Sectors and economic cycles   30*
- 2.3 Capitalization   32
- 2.4 Metrics and ratios   33
  - *Liquidity   34 • Debt   36 • Earnings   36 • Valuation   37 Profitability   40 • Dividends   40 • Ownership   44 Sustainability   45*
- 2.5 External assessments   46
  - *Ratings   47 • Target prices   48*

## 3 Collecting data   52

- 3.1 Financial data   53
- 3.2 Financial analysis platforms   54
- 3.3 Data science notebooks   57
- 3.4 yfinance   57
  - *Fundamental analysis   58 • Technical analysis   61 Limitations of yfinance   66*
- 3.5 Commercial libraries   67
  - *Finviz   69 • EODHD   71 • Alpha Vantage   73 OpenBB   75*
- 3.6 Other libraries   76

## 4 Growth portfolios   78

- 4.1 Investment thesis   79
  - *Starting with an idea   79 • Challenging the idea   81 Your investment thesis   84*
- 4.2 LiDAR market   85
  - *Picking candidates   86 • Price development   88 • Debt   91 Management   92 • Technology and partnership   92 Projected earnings   94*
- 4.3 Risks   95
  - *Falling into obsolescence   96 • Squashed by industry giants   96 Globalization and conflicts   97*

4.4 Ongoing analysis 97

*Media 97 ▪ Trend analysis 98 ▪ News sentiment analysis 100 ▪ Measuring success 101*

4.5 What is next 101

## 5 Income portfolios 105

5.1 Dividends 106

5.2 Bonds 112

5.3 Crypto staking 117

*Ledgers and exchanges 117 ▪ Mining and staking 118 Affordable staking options 119*

5.4 Early retirement 120

## 6 Building an asset monitor 123

6.1 Architecture 124

6.2 The spreadsheet 126

6.3 Extracting data 127

*Alpaca: A developer-first broker 128 ▪ Interactive Brokers: A legacy powerhouse with a modern twist 129*

6.4 Enriching data 130

6.5 Processing assets 131

*Stocks 131 ▪ Exchange-traded funds 135 ▪ Bonds 137 Cryptocurrencies 138*

6.6 Outlook 141

## 7 Risk management 143

7.1 Ukemi 144

*Stop-loss 144 ▪ Risk classification 146 ▪ Risk measurement 148*

7.2 Generating risk profiles for individual stocks 150

*Value at risk (VaR) 150 ▪ Correlation 153*

7.3 The human factor 156

*Negligence 157 ▪ Risk avoidance 157 ▪ Resilience 159*

7.4 Hedging 160

*Derivatives 160 ▪ Diversification 163 ▪ Pair trading 163 Risk pairing 164*

### 7.5 Nonfinancial risk 165
*Markets 166 • Economic data 166 • Assessing nonfinancial risk 168*

### 7.6 Portfolio optimization 169
*Markowitz-efficient portfolio 169 • Shiller P/E ratio 174 Rebalancing 176*

## 8 AI for financial research 181

### 8.1 From code to machine learning 182
*Unsupervised learning example 184 • Supervised learning example 187 • Market challenges 192 • Technical challenges 195 • Narrowing the scope 197*

### 8.2 From machine learning to generative AI 198
*Comparing LLMs 199 • Complementing ML with GenAI 200 • Challenges 200 • Final judgement on ML and GenAI 200*

### 8.3 Practical use of GenAI 201
*Using LLMs as research assistants 201 • Integrating LLMs into code 203*

### 8.4 Prompt engineering 208
*An investor's profile 208 • Using prompts to find companies to invest in 211*

## 9 AI agents 216

### 9.1 Requirements 217
*Successful communication 217 • Agentic design patterns 218*

### 9.2 Agentic workflows without frameworks 222
*Prompt repository 222 • Export results 224*

### 9.3 Framework for AI agents 228
*From one-shot prompting to agents 229 • Retrieval-augmented generation 231*

## 10 Charts and technical analysis 239

### 10.1 Charts 240
*Reading charts 246 • Patterns 247 • Interpreting a chart 249 • Alternative chart types 250*

10.2 Using charts to interpret price changes 253

*Candlesticks 254 ▪ Charts based on averages 257 Ichimoku Cloud 264*

10.3 Visualization with Streamlit 267

## 11 Algorithmic trading 273

11.1 Nonfinancial data 274

*Big data by example 276*

11.2 Catalysts 278

*Mergers and acquisitions 278 ▪ Companies in distress 279 Earnings calls 280 ▪ Disasters 281 ▪ Interest rate changes 282*

11.3 Trading algorithms 282

*Backtesting 283 ▪ Complex trading signals 287*

11.4 Orders 289

*Exchanges vs. brokers 289 ▪ Order modifiers 291 Executing orders 292*

## 12 Private equity: Investing in start-ups 297

12.1 From idea to initial public offering 298

*The first minimum viable product (pre-seed) 298 ▪ Validating the business model (seed) 301 ▪ Scaling a start-up: The shift to institutional investment 303 ▪ Exits: The final transition 304*

12.2 Investment vehicles 306

*Venture capital 308 ▪ Angel networks 309 ▪ Sovereign wealth funds 311*

12.3 Assessing start-ups 312

*Valuation 312 ▪ Dilution 314 ▪ Scoring 316*

## 13 The road goes ever on and on 321

13.1 Getting advice 322

13.2 Stay curious 323

13.3 Alpha hunter 323

13.4 Nomadism 324

13.5 Activist investing 325

13.6 Measures of control  326
*Checks and balances  326 ▪ Gain distance  327 ▪ Programmer's journey  327 ▪ Playing it safe  328*

appendix  *Setting up the environment  330*

*index  339*

## *preface*

Imagine this: a 50-year-old is approached by a genie with an intriguing offer. They can receive staggering wealth to never work again or be rejuvenated to age 20. The allure of reliving life with youth and wisdom is strong. But from a purely financial standpoint, which is the wiser choice?

I grew up believing everyone must work until their mid-60s to retire. Stopping work at 50 seemed like pure luck. Over time, investing became my passion. I've learned that starting early and making informed investment decisions can make financial independence by 50 achievable, especially if you know how to code. Programming sharpens the skills needed for better investment choices.

I've always believed that work should serve a higher purpose, but meaningful work is often not the highest-paid. I wrote the book I wish I had at 20—to accelerate my path to financial freedom and independence from a paycheck. After reading it, all you'll need is to find a genie who could send you back to age 20—armed with the knowledge to retire early. But even without the genie, what you learn here can transform how you invest, helping you move toward financial freedom with purpose and precision.

I also want to convince you that investing can be fun. I love using programming to analyze companies and form data-backed investment theses. There's nothing quite like seeing a company you believed in multiply in value fivefold or more.

Of course, no path to wealth is guaranteed. You can pick the wrong horse. Picture the late 1990s: a friend tells you about a failing tech company whose ousted founder just returned and about a thriving American energy company riding the wave of deregulation. If you chose the second, you picked Enron over Apple, and lost your investment. Diversification helps mitigate such risks, but the larger lesson is this: hubris and impatience are dangerous. Mindset matters most.

In the early 2010s, I pivoted to big data. It wasn't just about using more data but transforming entire businesses. I noticed some companies outsmarted others. If I invested in the smarter ones, I could ride their success. It was a natural progression: from using data to understand customer behavior to using data to predict which companies would thrive.

Through this journey, I've found four key traits for investment success: critical thinking, patience, dedication, and curiosity. Programmers excel at these, and I believe they can shine as investors.

Happy reading and coding! I wish you sharp insights and smarter investing.

## *acknowledgments*

I want to thank the following individuals, in chronological order, for their invaluable contributions to this book.

When I first approached acquisition editor Jonathan Gennick with a proposal for a book that didn't fit the typical mold at Manning, I knew approval wouldn't come easily. However, Jonathan believed in the project, and I'm convinced this book would have been impossible without his advocacy.

I am also profoundly grateful to Connor O'Brien, an exceptional development editor. His unwavering support and insightful feedback were instrumental in shaping the quality of this work.

Technical editor Anirudha Bhadoriya provided an excellent review of the manuscript. His thoughtful questions and genuine engagement added valuable perspectives to the book. Anirudha is a staff software engineer specializing in distributed systems at Snowflake. He has been actively investing his own money in the equity markets for more than 20 years, combining deep technical expertise with personal financial acumen.

Many thanks to Julie McNamee for copy editing and Azra Dedic for the support with the visualizations. Their input significantly improved the fine details of this book

To all the reviewers—Amarjit Bhandal, Arun Kumar Rajamandrapu, Bin Li, Charles Lam, Chris Heneghan, Gary Bake, Ian Long, James Carella, Jeremy Chen, Juan Pablo Duque, Kevin Orr, Koushik Sundar, Marco Seguri, Nikhil Kassetty, Oscar Cao, Patrick Grütter, Pierre Boutquin, Piti Champeethong, Prateek Punj, Raghuram Katakam, Sahithi Donkina, Saketh Patibandla, Sneha Thangaraja, Sofiia Shvets,

Thomas Heiman, Vijay Pahuja, Vinicios Wentz, and William Dealtry—your suggestions helped make this a better book.

I want to thank all contributors through the Manning liveBook who provided feedback on the book. I incorporated every piece of advice I received up to the production release, and I'll also look at comments after the production release for new editions.

Finally, a special thanks to Warren Buffett. Though he does not know me, he has served as an enduring role model for the kind of investor I strive to become.

# about this book

*Investing for Programmers* introduces tools and techniques for analyzing investment opportunities using Python and modern analytical methods. This book does not offer financial advice but shows you how to explore financial assets and make more informed investment decisions.

After reading this book, you'll be able to analyze financial assets with Python, build AI agents, and use LLMs to gain deeper insights into your investment options. Keep in mind that there are no guaranteed paths to wealth. This book may help you improve your odds of long-term financial success and increase your skills to gain insights for better decision-making. Be skeptical of anyone claiming risk-free riches.

## Who should read this book

You should have basic programming skills. However, if you have only minimal experience, you can still benefit from using large language models (LLMs) to help set up the environment and fill in any gaps in your Python knowledge.

## How this book is organized: A road map

This book has 13 chapters. The book begins by teaching the basics, including interpreting financial ratios and collecting data. As you progress, the topics become increasingly complex. You can always jump to later chapters if you're experienced with the basics.

- Chapter 1 introduces you to the investment domain and how programmers can excel.

- Chapter 2 teaches financial basics and introduces you to key metrics for exploration.
- Chapter 3 demonstrates collecting financial data using Python libraries, including Yahoo Finance and alternative libraries.
- Chapter 4 teaches you how to create an investment thesis to look for growth portfolios.
- Chapter 5 explains how to look for portfolios to create passive income.
- Chapter 6 demonstrates how to collect data from brokers and exchanges, centralize all holdings in one place, and facilitate their analysis.
- Chapter 7 explains how to investigate risks and learn ways to hedge them. We look at Sharpe ratios and other methods.
- Chapter 8 introduces AI for investment analysis. We introduce machine learning use cases and explore the application of generative AI in investment research.
- Chapter 9 demonstrates how to use AI agents for more advanced use cases, enabling data exploration and the integration of additional data sources.
- Chapter 10 shows how to display charts and technical analysis. You learn how to create charts using Bollinger Bands and other frameworks.
- Chapter 11 explores algorithmic trading and the application of nonfinancial data in financial analysis.
- Chapter 12 explores private equity as a form of ownership in startups and how to make informed investment decisions.
- Chapter 13 summarizes what you learned and provides some final thoughts for the path ahead.

## About the code

This book heavily uses source code, primarily in numbered listings throughout the chapters. The source code is formatted in a `fixed-width font like this` to distinguish it from ordinary text. Sometimes, code is also bold to highlight changes from previous steps in the chapter, such as when a new feature is added to an existing line of code.

In many cases, the source code has been reformatted, with line breaks and reworked indentation added to accommodate the available page space in the book. Additionally, comments in the source code have often been removed from the listing when the code is described in the text. Code annotations accompany many of the listings, highlighting important concepts.

You can get executable code snippets from this book's liveBook (online) version at https://livebook.manning.com/book/investing-for-programmers. The source code for the examples in this book is available for download on the publisher's website at www.manning.com/books/investing-for-programmers. The code is also available on GitHub at https://github.com/StefanPapp/investing-for-programmers.

### *liveBook discussion forum*

Purchase of *Investing for Programmers* includes free access to liveBook, Manning's online reading platform. Using liveBook's exclusive discussion features, you can attach global comments to the book or specific sections or paragraphs. It's a snap to make notes for yourself, ask and answer technical questions, and receive help from the author and other users. To access the forum, go to https://livebook.manning.com/book/investing-for-programmers/discussion.

Manning's commitment to our readers is to provide a venue for meaningful dialogue between individual readers and between readers and the author. It isn't a commitment to a specific amount of participation by the author, whose contributions to the forum remain voluntary and unpaid. We suggest you ask the author some challenging questions lest his interest stray! The forum and archives of previous discussions will be accessible on the publisher's website as long as the book remains in print.

## *about the author*

**STEFAN PAPP** is a trailblazer at the intersection of AI and investment strategy. With a career that spans decades as a data engineer, architect, and consultant for top-tier clients, Stefan has mastered the art of using data to solve complex problems. His thought leadership is reflected in his published technical books and his role as a university educator, where he inspires the next generation of tech innovators.

As a seasoned investor with more than 20 years of experience in stocks, cryptocurrency, and bonds, Stefan brings a data-driven approach to portfolio optimization that few can replicate. By combining cutting-edge AI techniques, including generative AI, with deep market insights, he has consistently outperformed traditional investment strategies.

In this book, Stefan demystifies the application of programming skills to financial analysis, sharing practical tools and real-world examples from his journey. Readers will learn how to harness data, adapt evolving best practices, and use AI to uncover opportunities, optimize research, and gain a decisive edge in the market.

## *about the cover illustration*

The figure on the cover of *Investing for Programmers*, titled "Arméniennes à Erzeroum," or "Armenian Girls from Erzurum," is taken from *The Nations. Album of Costumes From All Countries* by Alexandre Lacauchie, published in 1847. Each illustration is finely drawn and colored by hand.

In those days, it was easy to identify where people lived and what their trade or station in life was just by their dress. Manning celebrates the inventiveness and initiative of the computer business with book covers based on the rich diversity of regional culture centuries ago, brought back to life by pictures from collections such as this one.

# The analytical investor

**This chapter covers**
- An overview of securities and the market
- Investment strategies for managing risk and maximizing gains
- Tools and techniques for the data-driven investor
- Programmers' traits that can be an advantage

A tough work environment often marks the beginning of the journey to financial independence. Formal education rarely prepares people for the sometimes harsh realities of the workplace: the micromanaging boss, a difficult coworker, a cutthroat culture, or the client who secretly rewrites your code and blames you if things go wrong. At some point, many programmers dream of escaping—maybe as a sheep herder in a remote forest or the captain of a starship in galaxies far, far away.

Finding a new job often proves to be a temporary fix. Starting your own company usually means trading a 40-hour week for an 80-hour one, with less pay and only a slim chance of long-term success. If the start-up fails, you can land right back where you started, only to find that the toxic former colleague who had teased you got promoted and is now your boss.

But what if the solution isn't another job, but greater independence *from* any job through gradually building passive income? The timeline to financial freedom varies depending on your circumstances—a family, a mortgage, or even just residing with Her Majesty, the cat—creating a different scenario for everyone. Freedom can begin with the first realization that some of your essential expenses are covered by passive income . . . forever. And if you keep going, the number of things you don't have to work for to pay for increases. Knowing that you *can* leave a high-paying, soul-crushing job for a more fulfilling one, even if it pays less, is a powerful relief for a developer who has endured hell on earth.

This book serves as a step-by-step guide to achieving greater independence. It emphasizes rational thinking and patience; no miracles are guaranteed. Be wary of anyone claiming you can get rich in 24 hours. Following such advice often depends on luck, a good lawyer, or both.

## 1.1 Your investment journey

Diving into the financial world can feel like stepping onto the road, and if you don't keep your feet, there's no knowing where you might be swept off to. To avoid straying off the beaten track, we need to understand the essentials of what we want to explore.

Sooner or later, financial planning becomes a necessity. Perhaps we saw our dream house, met the person we want to start a family with, heard the demands for more comfort from Her Majesty the cat, or wanted to achieve financial independence. Every journey begins the same way. You assess what you already have and explore and optimize your expenses to determine how much surplus money you can accumulate on average each month.

With your carefully estimated monthly surplus, friends might approach you with ideas on how to invest it. Some of your "expert advisors" may try to charm you with stocks and their alleged high *returns*. The conservative camp prefers bonds instead, reasoning that they offer lower *risk*. A third group of finance aficionados may suggest that you put everything into an index fund and refrain from thinking about your investments until you need the money.

Risk and return are the pillars of any investment strategy. However, simply estimating potential outcomes under normal market conditions isn't enough. Without a fundamental understanding of what you're investing in, it's unwise to risk your capital based on a casual tip from a friend.

This book aims to guide you toward becoming a data-driven investor. You'll learn both the basics of investing and, in parallel, how to make smarter decisions based on data, research, rational thinking, and analysis.

## 1.2 Assets

To get started with investing, we must understand the basics of assets. In its simplest form, an *asset* is something we can purchase to monetize. We use the term *securities* to refer to a group of assets in the financial domain, such as stocks and bonds. In general, assets are monetized in two ways:

- *Capital appreciation*—For example, buy low and sell high.
- *Passive income*—For example, getting regular payments (interest payments on savings accounts or receiving rent from a tenant).

Investors should begin by understanding their risk tolerance—the amount of potential loss they can handle without stress—and their financial goals, which outline how much they hope to earn within a specific time frame. A third critical factor, often overlooked in books for professional investors but vital for individuals, is the time required to manage an investment strategy. If monitoring your portfolio consumes time you'd rather spend on other activities, it's a clear signal that you need to rethink your approach. The more aware you are of your risk appetite, desired returns, and maximum time commitment, the better prepared you are to develop an investment strategy that helps you meet your life goals.

### 1.2.1 Stocks

Stock represents ownership, also known as *equity*. When you buy stocks, you acquire a small part of a company. As of June 2025, Apple has 15,509,763,000 shares outstanding. Purchasing one *share* of Apple means you own 0.000000006447552% of the company.

Supply and demand affect stock prices. Investors typically buy more shares of successful companies, which causes their share prices to rise. However, a stock's value depends on more than just its company's performance. The entire market is also significantly influenced by larger factors, including global politics and economic news.

> **Terminology**
> Through a brokerage account, investors buy *shares* (referring to a countable amount) of the company's *stock* (representing the total assets of a company. A *portfolio* is a collection of *securities* (stocks, bonds, options, etc.) that you own. If a position in your portfolio is higher than its purchase price, you have an unrealized gain until you sell it to realize the gain. The same logic applies to unrealized and realized losses.

Some stocks offer income to investors through a small payment per share, known as a *dividend*. As of June 2025, Apple trades at about $213.55 per share, and the company pays a quarterly dividend of roughly $0.26 per share. These payments result in a dividend yield of approximately 0.49%, representing the return before taxes that an investor gains from dividends relative to the share's price.

To put this into perspective, we can compare a company's dividend yield to the yield on a 10-year US Treasury bond, which is often used as a benchmark for a "risk-free" return. As of June 2025, these bonds offer a yield of around 4.3%—considerably higher than Apple's current dividend payout.

Considering the treasury yield, investing in Apple solely for its dividend income is a poor choice. Because inflation usually exceeds its ~0.5% yield, an investor would lose buying power if they don't account for potential capital gains from the stock's growth.

If you're passionate about identifying companies that can outperform the market, chapter 4 provides all the details you need to build an investment thesis and develop a growth portfolio in a structured way.

### 1.2.2 Bonds

A *bond* is an IOU. When you buy a bond, you lend money (the *principal*) to an entity, such as a government or a company. In return, you receive periodic interest payments, known as *coupons*. With few exceptions, bonds have a maturity date—a specific date in the future when the issuer repays your original principal in full.

All bonds are equal, but some are more equal than others. Because many issuers exist, each bond has a different level of risk:

- *Credit risk*—Some issuers are more likely to default on their debt obligations. To help investors evaluate this risk for other issuers, credit rating agencies such as Moody's and Standard & Poor's (S&P's) provide independent assessments.
- *Yield*—Typically, the more risk you accept, the greater your potential return or yield.

When holding a bond, you can either wait until maturity to receive its full face value or sell it on the open market earlier. Choosing to sell before maturity means the price you receive will be determined by the market, which could result in a gain or a loss on your initial investment.

> **NOTE** The basic assumption behind considering US government bonds *risk-free* is the belief that the US government will always honor its debt obligations and won't default. This convention has become standard practice in finance. However, describing such assets as *extremely low risk* would be more accurate because, theoretically, even the US government could default.

Chapter 5 discusses how to build dependable passive income, offering a way to cover everyday expenses and boost your financial independence. It emphasizes practical methods, including a detailed comparison of bonds and dividend stocks as primary sources of income.

### 1.2.3 Exchange-traded funds

Savvy investors diversify their risk by not putting all their eggs in one basket. Investment companies help with this by bundling multiple securities into a single fund. Exchange-traded funds (ETFs) are a popular type of investment that trades on an exchange, making them easily accessible for purchase and sale through any online broker.

Buying an ETF is a simple way to diversify your investments. Instead of analyzing and purchasing hundreds of individual stocks, you can hold a small stake in carefully chosen assets with just one transaction. Most ETFs are *passively managed*, meaning they track a market index automatically, such as the S&P 500. Algorithms are used to rebalance the fund's holdings, keeping it aligned with its index. In *actively managed* ETFs, a portfolio manager selects specific investments to buy.

ETFs aren't free, and ETF issuers charge a small annual management fee (expense ratio). Still, they are highly cost-effective. For an individual, buying all the underlying stocks directly in separate transactions would cost more due to transaction fees. Because ETFs are collections of assets, all sections that discuss the underlying assets also include ETFs.

### 1.2.4 Other funds

Other common pooled funds are mutual funds and hedge funds. These funds are described here:

- *Mutual funds*—These funds are similar to ETFs in that they provide diversification and are highly regulated. The primary operational difference is that mutual funds only trade once a day at a price determined *after* the market closes, known as the net asset value (NAV).
- *Hedge funds*—These funds are typically less regulated, require a substantial minimum investment, and are generally accessible only to wealthy investors.

While ETFs and mutual funds target retail investors, hedge funds operate at a different level. They use more aggressive and complex strategies and are only available to *accredited investors*, which include high-net-worth individuals and institutions that meet specific wealth requirements.

Other funds are outside the scope of this book; however, we explore hedging techniques used by professional hedge funds in chapter 7. Investors can use these techniques to optimize their portfolios.

### 1.2.5 Foreign exchange market

Beyond owning equity or lending money, investors can also speculate on currency exchange rates in the *foreign exchange (forex) market*. Every country has its currency, and the value of these currencies fluctuates against each other in pairs (e.g., the EUR/USD). For example, one day, the euro might strengthen against the US dollar, and the next day it might weaken. Forex traders analyze economic indicators and market trends to predict these movements, aiming to make a profit by buying a currency before it appreciates or selling it before it depreciates.

Currency risk is discussed in chapter 7. Additionally, all aspects of technical analysis, as outlined in chapter 10, apply to all assets, including forex.

### 1.2.6 Crypto

For many, cryptocurrency is a complex asset class that can be hard to understand. To clarify, it's essential first to separate the underlying technology from its most well-known application:

- *Blockchain*—This is the core technology. Think of it as a secure, decentralized digital ledger—a growing list of records (blocks) linked and protected by

cryptography. Although it's best known for digital currency, blockchain technology has uses in many other areas.
- *Cryptocurrency*—This refers to a digital asset built on blockchain technology.

The primary value of cryptocurrency lies in its ability to facilitate peer-to-peer transactions without requiring a trusted third party. Unlike traditional financial systems, which rely on intermediaries such as banks, cryptocurrency networks enable direct transfers between individuals.

The technology that secures these networks also presents unique investment opportunities. Chapter 5 explores one such method—*staking*—which allows you to earn rewards by helping validate transactions. It also offers a vital overview of the common risks and criticisms associated with this volatile asset class.

### 1.2.7 Derivatives

Think of a derivative as a contract whose value is *derived* from an underlying asset, such as a stock or a commodity. It establishes rules for future transactions, helping you manage risk or speculate on price movements.

For most investors, options are the most useful derivatives. An *option* grants you the *right, but not the obligation*, to buy or sell an asset at a set price before a certain expiration date.

Think of it this way: you pay a small fee (the *premium*) to get an API key. This key grants you access to a function—either `buy()` or `sell()`—that you can execute under specific conditions. If the conditions aren't met, you let the key expire. Your only loss is the premium you paid.

- A *put option* gives the buyer the right, but not the obligation, to *sell* an asset at a set price (the *strike price*). It's a type of insurance.
- A *call option* gives the buyer the right, but not the obligation, to *buy* an asset at a specified strike price. It's a way to bet on a price increase with limited risk.

You can also be on the other side of the transaction and *sell* (or, as it's also called, *write*) options. You receive the premium as income, but you assume an *obligation*.

Selling a put option means you're obligated to buy the stock at the strike price if the buyer chooses to exercise it. If the stock drops to zero, you're still required to buy it at the high strike price, which could lead to a potentially disastrous outcome.

Options are powerful tools, but they're complex instruments with significant risk. That's why they are covered in chapter 7, which focuses on risk.

### 1.2.8 Private equity

After purchasing shares on an exchange, you become a shareholder of a publicly traded company. One advantage of being publicly traded is that it makes buying shares easy. Investors worldwide can become shareholders within seconds if they are logged in to their brokerage account and decide to buy shares.

Start-ups present the most significant profit potential. They are ideal for investors willing to accept more risk in exchange for the opportunity to achieve wealth more quickly. Because private companies aren't traded on public stock exchanges, you need to take a different approach:

- *Direct investment*—You can invest directly in companies. Start-ups that seek single private investors are usually in their earliest stages, typically pre-seed or seed stage.
- *Angel or venture capital investments*—These involve funds created to invest in start-ups. As a private investor, you can become a limited partner in such a fund. If the start-up achieves a successful exit, you can expect high multiple returns on your investment.

Chapter 12 examines opportunities to invest in private equity and highlights the main differences between this type of investment and investing in stocks.

### 1.2.9 Other assets

Investing involves acquiring assets and monetizing them, either through *capital gains* or *passive income*. We might not always recognize every asset as such. For example, a patent can be valued and licensed for royalties, but not everyone considers it part of their assets.

Commodities are raw materials, such as gold, oil, and wheat, that investors can trade. Because their value is linked to real-world supply and demand, their prices often move independently of the stock and bond markets. While investors can gain exposure through futures contracts or ETFs, they should be aware that these markets can be very volatile. This volatility is caused by a variety of complex factors, including geopolitical events, weather conditions, and global economic growth.

Some investors view real estate as a safe investment, but it comes with challenges. For one, it's a highly illiquid asset, meaning that selling a property can be a slow and tedious process. Additionally, landlords face the risk of difficult tenants who might damage the property or fail to pay rent.

An asset is considered non-fungible if it's unique and can't be easily replaced by another identical item. In contrast, fungible assets are interchangeable, which makes them a good starting point for new investors. This interchangeability allows them to be traded easily and efficiently. While you can still make a good living from non-fungible assets, investing in securities simplifies your life for several reasons:

- *Lower capital requirements*—You can buy shares for just a few dollars, whereas non-fungible assets such as real estate or art may cost millions.
- *Lower maintenance*—Physical objects require secure storage, insurance, and preservation, resulting in significant overhead and maintenance costs. Securities don't have these drawbacks.
- *Liquidity*—Shares can be sold at any time, while owners of non-fungible items must find a buyer. Converting them into cash at a fair price can take months or even years.

- *Scalability*—Investors who find a well-performing company can keep purchasing shares, whereas investors of non-fungible assets can't buy assets twice.

For these reasons, this book concentrates on securities and other assets not included here.

### 1.2.10 Choosing assets

Before you begin exploring which assets to purchase, consider these four questions about your investment goals, and answer them as honestly as possible:

- How much money do I need to live a happy life?
- How much money do I have that I don't need right now and can use for investments?
- How much risk am I willing to take for possible bigger gains?
- How much time am I willing to dedicate to the investment process itself, such as researching potential investments and monitoring my portfolios?

Besides some universal principles of investing, such as investing only in businesses you understand, there is no one-size-fits-all strategy. Still, every investor can find an approach that best suits their expectations and goals. Now that we know the asset types, we can explore further and examine investment strategies that align with our needs.

## 1.3 Investment approaches

Having covered the fundamentals of financial assets, we'll now focus on how to create value from them. We can classify methods of monetizing assets into three main categories:

- *Gambling*—A surprising number of people rely on gut feelings or perceived signs from the universe when deciding to buy or sell. Even experienced investors can fall victim to cognitive biases, such as noticing patterns in random events and believing "no coincidence" has led them to a life-changing investment.
- *Investing*—We'll avoid gambling-like speculation to focus on more structured ways to build wealth. Disciplined investing views building wealth as a long-term goal. It depends on careful analysis and critical thinking, aiming to reduce impulsive decisions.
- *Trading*—While investing focuses on long-term success, trading centers on capitalizing on short-term price fluctuations. Due to its higher frequency and shorter time horizons, trading carries more risk than long-term investing.

Let's explore some strategies that can help us become better traders or investors and, in turn, help us avoid gambling. Figure 1.1 illustrates the entire investment process and highlights all chapters where relevant topics are discussed in detail.

We use financial platforms and publicly available information to collect data on securities. We can generate more insights about the securities using various analytical

## 1.3 Investment approaches

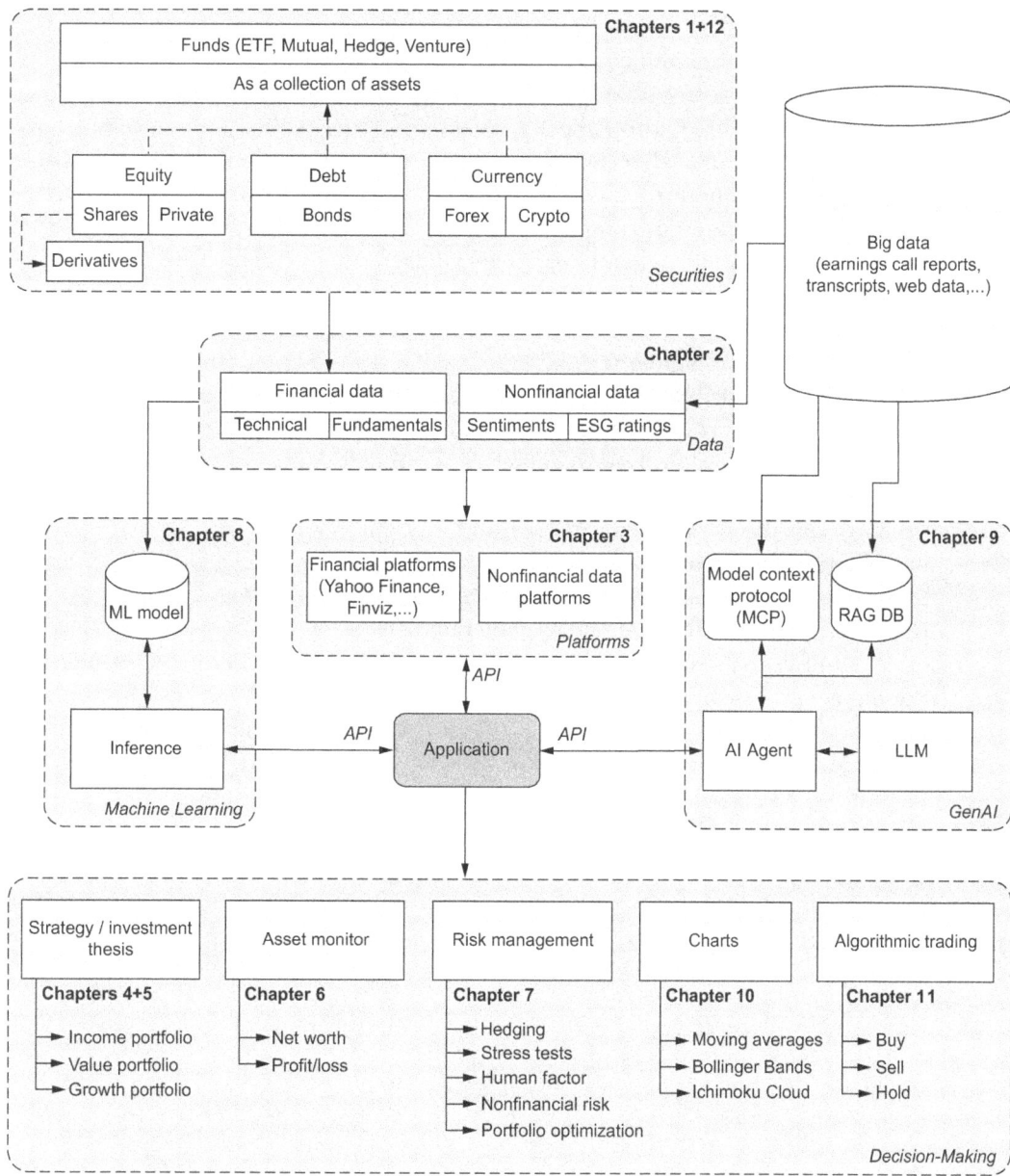

**Figure 1.1** A survey of the tools and techniques covered in this book, including pointers to the chapters that focus on the relevant domains

methods, including machine learning and AI. We can then apply these new insights to our decision-making processes.

### 1.3.1 Quantitative research

*Quantitative* refers to numbers, counts, and averages that provide information about what is happening. The goal is to gather as much financial data as possible across many companies and compare these "factors" that may influence the future development of share prices. You can analyze a company's performance from multiple angles. Historical data shows how performance has changed over time. You can compare the current performance of numerous companies.

Thanks to accounting standards, financial data is highly standardized. As we'll see in this book, nonfinancial data can also be quantifiable and incorporated into investment research.

In chapter 2, we highlight the financial data that could be especially relevant for quantitative analysis, such as revenues, profit margins, and price-to-earnings (P/E) ratios. Quantitative research begins with data collection and aggregation.

In chapter 3, we show how to gather data relevant to investment analysis. We can use Python libraries designed to provide financial data in a structured format. Alternatively, we can also scrape data from websites.

Having quantitative data allows us to use a machine learning algorithm to forecast future price movements based on historical data. Chapter 8 offers a detailed overview of how machine learning models are generated.

Technical analysis involves assessing assets by examining statistical trends from trading activity, such as price changes and volume. Technical analysts use historical price charts and various indicators to identify patterns and forecast potential future price movements. For example, figure 1.2 shows a price chart for NVIDIA, which a technical analyst would analyze to make informed trading decisions.

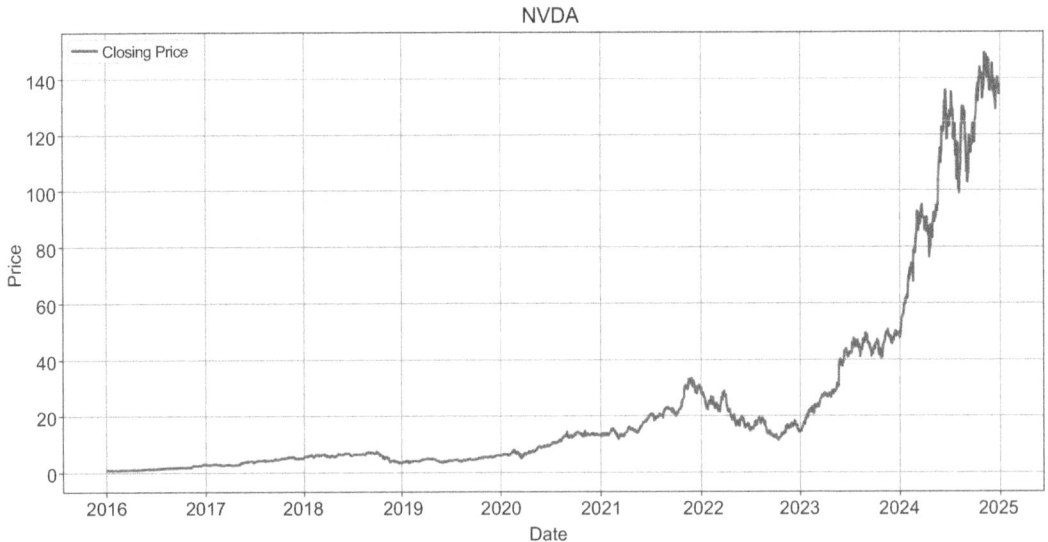

Figure 1.2 The price development of NVIDIA from 2016 to 2025. Notice the sharp rise in recent years; this is a typical example of the growth that attracts many traders and investors. Keep in mind that such growth rates are rare.

## 1.3 Investment approaches

While a line chart of share price development is one of the easier charts to create, we also have charts that calculate indicators to help with deciding when to buy or sell. In figure 1.3, we present a candlestick chart for NVIDIA for July 2025, which we created using the code introduced in chapter 10.

**Candlestick chart for NVIDIA for July 2025**

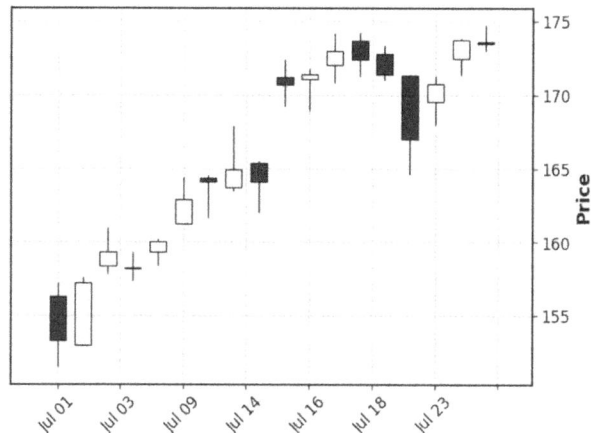

Figure 1.3 Candlestick charts help us evaluate stock performance over multiple days. Black (or red) shows that a stock's price decreased, while white (or green) shows that it increased during the day.

### 1.3.2 Qualitative research

*Qualitative* data includes user feedback from a bug report—the context, feelings, and reasons that explain *why* the issue is happening. The financial aspects involve the strength of that company's brand, the quality of its management, and the risk of a new competitor disrupting its market.

Some of the qualitative data can also be converted into quantitative data. Think of scraping data from earnings reports, conducting sentiment analysis on the transcripts, and comparing the scores of all earnings calls. A key part of analyzing qualitative data is the use of GenAI and AI agents, as summarized here:

- *Generative AI (GenAI)*—This is a newer type of AI that can produce new content and insights. In finance, GenAI is used to summarize large datasets (e.g., earnings reports and news articles), analyze market sentiment from social media, and even simulate market scenarios to stress-test investment strategies. We discuss GenAI in chapter 8.
- *AI agents*—These are advanced AI systems designed to perform complex, multistep tasks independently. An AI agent can be tasked with conducting thorough research on an asset by collecting data from the web, analyzing financial statements, assessing recent news, and generating a comprehensive report. This process automates the entire analytical workflow. We dedicate chapter 9 to AI agents.

To illustrate these concepts, chapter 4 will examine companies in the autonomous driving field as a case study for growth investing, while chapter 5 will focus on income investment strategies. Both chapters will highlight opportunities for programmers to gather data about various opportunities more efficiently and to develop better methods for creating scorecards for investability.

### 1.3.3 Algorithmic trading and asset monitors

While an investor focuses on a company's long-term health and intrinsic value, a trader mainly cares about an asset's price movement and market conditions. This focus enables traders to employ strategies that are uncommon in traditional investment portfolios. We can divide trading approaches into two main categories:

- *Going long (long position)*—This is a common strategy that involves buying an asset with the expectation that its price will rise. This method follows the traditional "buy low, sell high" principle.
- *Going short (short selling)*—This strategy aims to profit from a decline in an asset's price. A trader borrows an asset (e.g., shares of stock), sells it on the open market at the current price, and plans to repurchase it later at a lower cost.

With this understanding, let's examine several key categories of trading. These styles are characterized by their time frames, methods, and dependence on technology:

- *Short-term trading*—This is a broad category of trading that involves buying and selling assets over a short period, from minutes to weeks. A trader typically executes these trades manually, based on a predetermined strategy. The specific time frame often determines the name of the trading style:
  - *Day trading*—This style involves opening and closing all trading positions within the same trading day. A day trader seeks to profit from intraday price movements and avoids holding any positions overnight.
  - *Swing trading*—This strategy involves holding positions for more than a day but usually no longer than a few weeks. A swing trader aims to capture larger price swings or short-term trends that develop over several days.
- *Automated trading (algorithmic trading)*—Traders use algorithms to execute buy and sell orders based on predefined indicators such as price changes or trading volatility. Automation enforces disciplined execution of a strategy, removing emotion from the decision-making process. For example, a day trader could automate their specific plan. Chapter 11 explains how to identify potential alpha factors.
- *High-frequency trading (HFT)*—This is an advanced form of automated trading that operates at breakneck speeds with large volumes of orders. HFT firms use powerful computers and sophisticated algorithms to capitalize on minute, fleeting price differences or arbitrage opportunities, frequently executing trades in microseconds. Being faster than competitors is the primary focus of HFT, a field led by specialized quantitative firms.

Effective asset management starts with a unified view of all holdings. Chapter 6 lays the groundwork for this by showing how to gather data from multiple brokers and exchanges into a single Google Sheet. We'll use Python to connect to two global brokers, Interactive Brokers and Alpaca. If you aren't comfortable connecting directly to brokers, you can use database tables to store their holdings instead.

Building on that, chapters 8 and 9 explore how to use AI-driven algorithms to analyze stock performance and identify market trends. This then leads to chapter 11, which explains the principles of algorithmic trading—techniques that automatically execute trades when specific parameters or factors are met.

A key part of any such strategy is backtesting. Like unit testing in software development, backtesting assesses an algorithm by testing it against historical market data. This process illustrates how the strategy would have performed in the past, offering essential insights into its potential effectiveness before any capital is risked.

### 1.3.4 Portfolios and investing strategies

We can classify investment styles into three main categories: value, growth, and income investing. These categories sometimes overlap. One approach is called *Growth at a Reasonable Price (GARP)*, which combines value and growth investing. Let's look at these three types of investing next.

#### VALUE INVESTING

A value investor seeks to identify companies trading below their intrinsic value. These opportunities often arise when the market overreacts to temporary setbacks, negative news, or poor earnings reports, overlooking a company's long-term potential. To spot these deals, the investor carefully examines financial data, comparing key metrics and ratios to identify genuine undervaluation. Chapter 2 covers the basics of applying value investing.

#### GROWTH INVESTING

A growth investor focuses on companies with the potential for rapid expansion, often innovators in emerging sectors such as quantum computing and autonomous driving. Success in these complex fields relies on a key principle popularized by legendary investor Peter Lynch: your personal or professional knowledge of a domain can give you a strong investment advantage.

He famously argued that an amateur with specialized insight can often outperform a professional without it. Chapter 4 is dedicated to this very idea, guiding you on how to use your unique expertise to identify and analyze growth opportunities.

#### INCOME INVESTING

An income investor focuses on assets that provide a consistent stream of passive income. An income portfolio usually includes dividend-paying stocks, bonds that offer regular interest payments, or real estate investment trusts (REITs). Chapter 5 centers on income investments.

Table 1.1 compares these three strategies, enabling readers to identify the approach that best aligns with their risk profile, return goals, and time investment.

Table 1.1  Comparing growth, value, and income investing

| Attribute | Growth investing | Value investing | Income investing |
|---|---|---|---|
| **Primary goal** | Capital appreciation | Capital appreciation | Regular income |
| **Investor focus** | Future potential, innovation | Undervalued "bargains" | Consistent cash payouts |
| **Typical company** | Young, innovative, rapidly expanding | Mature, stable, temporarily unpopular | Established, predictable, high cash flow |
| **Dividends** | Low or none (profits are reinvested) | Often pays dividends | High and stable dividends key |
| **Key metrics** | High revenue growth, High P/E | Low P/E, Low P/B* | High dividend yield, stable cash flow |
| **Risk profile** | High | Low to moderate | Low |
| **Time horizon** | Long-term | Medium to long term | Any, but often for immediate needs |

* P/E = price-to-earnings; P/B = price-to-booking.

Many individuals employ a hybrid approach, carefully combining various methods to achieve multiple financial goals. This approach may also include trading strategies in conjunction with the investment strategies mentioned earlier. Often, this blended method takes the form of a "core and satellite" portfolio:

- *The core*—This is the foundation of the portfolio, focused on long-term investing. These assets are held with patience, allowing wealth to grow through compounding and enabling primary growth goals to develop over time.
- *The satellites*—Surrounding the core are more minor, more tactical divisions. Investors can design these satellites for various purposes:
  - A portion of the capital may be allocated for short-term trading to capitalize on market fluctuations actively.
  - Another portion can be invested in income-producing assets to generate a steady stream of passive income, adding stability and cash flow to the overall financial picture.
  - This balanced structure enables individuals to maintain a disciplined, long-term plan while also capitalizing on short-term opportunities and securing a steady income.

## 1.4 Risks and rewards

This book will also examine strategies that support investment and trading decisions. *Hedging* is a risk management tactic used to offset potential losses in an investment. By taking an opposing position in a related asset, an investor can safeguard their portfolio from adverse price movements. Essentially, hedging is akin to buying insurance; it involves a tradeoff where you may sacrifice some potential gains to mitigate the risk of a significant loss. Chapter 7 covers risk management, including hedging strategies.

Figure 1.4 shows the returns of different assets. Should we simply choose the top performers and move forward?

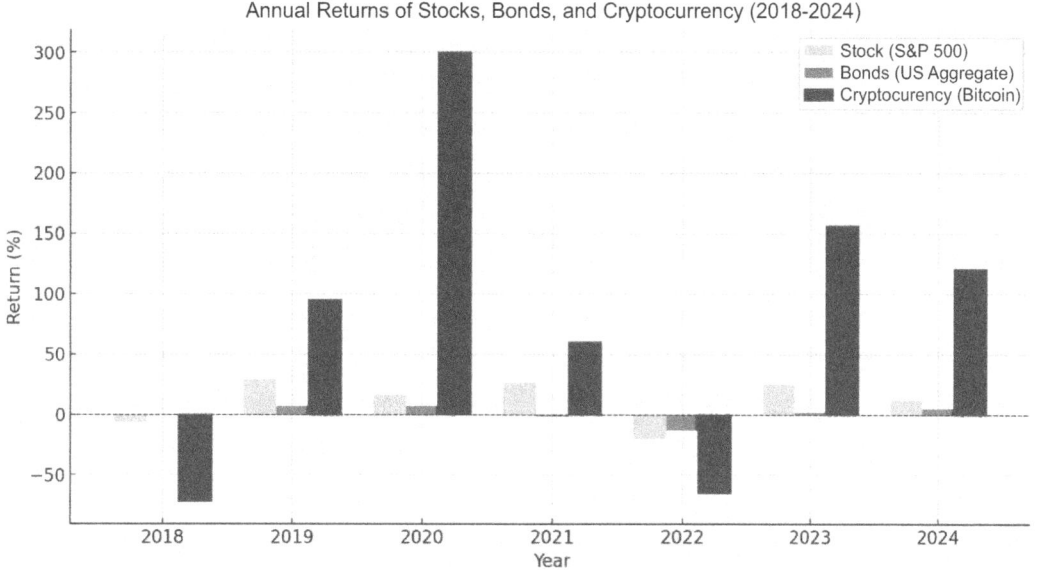

Figure 1.4 Comparison of returns of stocks, bonds, and cryptocurrency (generated by ChatGPT)

Past results don't guarantee future outcomes. The market is unpredictable, and no set of tools, techniques, or strategies guarantees success. As explained in chapter 12, startups can return much more than other assets, but they are also the riskiest. As of June 2025, Bitcoin is valued at around $118,000. While an investor buying now might benefit if the price increases from this point, they also face a realistic risk that it could drop sharply and lose a significant portion of its value.

Especially in recent years, it has become increasingly clear how fragile the stock market is and how social media can sometimes have a more significant effect on share prices than earnings reports. We've often seen the unpredictable actions of public figures causing overnight gains to disappear, only to rebound later.

Warren Buffett once said, "Be fearful when others are greedy, and greedy when others are fearful." This principle advises caution during a rising bull market, especially when experienced investors begin to warn of underlying risks, such as high federal debt or economic instability. In such times, it's wise to resist the temptation to invest aggressively.

## 1.5 A programmer's unfair advantage

Forget stereotypes from pop culture and movies. Slick traders don't run the modern market in boardrooms; it's a complex system of data, logic, and algorithms. It's an environment where you, as a programmer, have a natural and powerful advantage. The skills you use every day to build software are the same skills that can create wealth.

### 1.5.1 You think in systems and data

Your job is to turn raw data into logical decisions. Whether you're debugging from a log file or analyzing performance metrics, you follow evidence, not emotion. Investing is the same. A company's financial statements are just datasets waiting for analysis. Stock charts are patterns waiting to be recognized. While others rely on gut feelings, you can do the following:

- *Perform fundamental analysis.* Similar to debugging a program by inspecting its core components, you can assess a company's financial health (income, balance sheets) to determine its intrinsic value.
- *Use quantitative tools.* The skills needed to analyze data or run scripts are directly applicable to backtesting trading strategies and automating your research.
- *Build a system.* Programming involves developing rule-based systems. This skill is essential for crafting a disciplined investment plan that steers clear of common biases, such as panic selling or chasing hype.

### 1.5.2 Your mindset is built for the market

Beyond technical skills, your mindset has been prepared for the realities of investing. Here are some mindset traits you can use to your advantage:

- *Patience and discipline*—You understand the frustration of a tough bug and the satisfaction that comes with finally fixing it. Successful investing is the highest form of delayed gratification, requiring the same resilience to see a strategy through to its conclusion.
- *Abstract thinking*—You're comfortable with abstractions, from APIs to complex data structures. This helps in understanding intangible assets, such as stocks, bonds, and derivatives, more easily. You can see the system, not just its parts.
- *Visionary thinking*—You operate at the forefront of technology. You're not just a user of emerging trends in AI, virtual reality (VR), or biotech—you're often a creator. This domain knowledge provides you with a unique perspective on which companies are set to shape the future.

### 1.5.3 Define your parameters

As a programmer, you can align your investment strategy with your life choices. Some programmers choose a career that offers a high income, allowing them to retire early with a solid financial plan.

Other programmers might choose workplace flexibility over a fixed location and become part of the growing community of digital nomads. Sometimes, the benefit isn't more money but lower expenses and taxes.

The key to investment success is understanding your environment and goals. You shape your investment philosophy, just as you would define the specs for a project: How much risk can you handle? How much time will you dedicate? What are your ethical boundaries?

Answering these questions will help you develop a strong, personal strategy you can follow, turning your natural advantages as a programmer into real-world results. Note that this book doesn't provide financial advice or recommend the purchase of specific assets. It guides you in using your existing analytical skills to analyze securities, ultimately supporting your decision-making process.

## *Summary*

- An investment is an asset or item acquired to generate income or appreciation.
- Assets aren't restricted to financial products. Each asset follows different rules and principles to generate value. Nonfinancial assets can be complex for new investors to trade as they are non-fungible (not interchangeable).
- Unlike most other assets, financial assets are fungible, a feature that makes them significantly easier to trade.
- A share is a partial ownership of a publicly listed company. Therefore, every investor could purchase a majority in publicly traded companies. Stocks are usually purchased through stockbrokers.
- Private equity is ownership in privately held companies that aren't available on a public stock exchange.
- Derivatives are investments that are created from an underlying asset. A stock option offers an investor the right to buy or sell a stock under predefined conditions. You can also trade options, which means you can acquire or sell the right to trade.
- Selling stock options can provide you with a small income, but you might face significant risks in some scenarios.
- Dividends are payments made by a company to its shareholders in proportion to the number of shares they hold. Not every company pays dividends. Coupon payments, in contrast, are payments received for bonds.
- Unlike stocks, bonds are associated with debt. Bondholders don't own parts of the organization to which they lend money; instead, they receive interest payments as compensation for their investment.

- ETFs are pooled investments that are mostly passively managed and contain multiple assets. Holding ETFs is generally considered less risky for investors than holding stocks.
- A hedge fund is a riskier investment vehicle that employs more advanced investment strategies, typically sold to a limited number of accredited investors and institutions.
- Cryptocurrency is an asset that enables people to transfer value without requiring third-party involvement in transactions.
- Although some assets are called risk-free, no asset is entirely without risk.
- Programmers may possess a range of skills that enable them to make data-driven investment decisions.
- New investors benefit from defining investment goals before exploring investment strategies, as each strategy requires a different level of investment, risk tolerance, and time commitment.
- This book doesn't give financial advice. It aims to teach best practices for using programming skills and AI to gain deeper insights and make more informed investment decisions.

# Investment essentials

**This chapter covers**
- Core understanding of the investment domain
- Metrics that help us find profitable investments
- What to look for in financial reports

In chapter 1, we claimed that programmers' traits can often make these wizards of bits and bytes into outstanding investors. But traits (and brains) alone won't do. Take the following statement that you might find in any financial analysis of a share price: "With a P/E ratio of over 25, this stock seems overvalued." For someone new to investing, sentences like that or dialogs between investors in movies such as *Wall Street* or *The Big Short* might sound like a foreign language. In 2003, Eric Evans published his book, *Domain-Driven Design*, which contains principles for creating software in unfamiliar domains for software engineers. One cornerstone of these principles is the use of ubiquitous language. This principle asserts that each domain has developed its specialized language using terminology exclusive to domain experts. An essential part of software engineering is learning to understand and communicate effectively in this language. So, let's start the next part of our journey by getting deeper into the domain language of investment.

Once we understand the domain language, we can easily interpret the previous P/E ratio statement. A *share* is a share of ownership in a company. As a tradable asset, a share may trade at a price below or above its intrinsic value. To assess a stock's valuation, we may investigate multiple metrics or ratios related to a company's performance. The price-to-earnings (P/E) ratio is a key financial metric related to a company's earnings.

Finance is a complex domain; if one universal strategy led to guaranteed incredible riches in a short time, hedge funds wouldn't compete for the best performance. However, intelligent value investors have demonstrated that finding undervalued stocks, when studying fundamentals, is possible. If you're solely interested in the code, feel free to proceed to the next chapter, where we demonstrate how to collect the ratios and metrics introduced in this chapter using Python.

## 2.1 Accounting in a nutshell

Think of financial statements as a company's source code. While they may seem cryptic at first, once you learn to read them, they reveal precisely how a business is performing. In this section, we explore the basics of reading the financial code because investing without understanding at least the basics of accounting is like trying to create a software application with zero programming skills.

Companies follow global accounting standards. If one company reports numbers in one way and another company in a different way, we would end up in chaos. One powerful entity can compel companies to report data in a standardized manner: the government, which requires these reports as a basis for taxation.

> **NOTE** Just as programmers can misjudge a colleague's source code at a glance, investors can misinterpret financial statements. In both cases, context is crucial, and a seemingly simple number may be misleading without it. Admitting you were wrong is difficult, but making the initial mistake of judging code or numbers too quickly is a costly one.

Accounting standards haven't existed since the beginning of stock exchanges. The prevailing economic philosophy of laissez-faire capitalism in the roaring twenties extended to corporate reporting. There were no federal laws compelling companies to disclose financial information to the public. While the New York Stock Exchange had some listing requirements, they weren't rigorously enforced, and there was no uniform standard for the information that needed to be provided. The stock market crash of 1929, which led to the Great Depression and caused widespread pain, had multiple root causes. Missing accounting standards exacerbated the problem, and, not surprisingly, the *Generally Accepted Accounting Principles (GAAP)* were established in response to the crash.

These accounting standards establish a stable baseline by mandating a consistent method for companies to report their financial information. Violating them can be costly, sometimes even threatening a company's existence. In addition to GAAP, there's a second standard, the *International Financial Reporting Standards (IFRS)*, which is used in the international market. These standards differ in detail, but these differences are irrelevant to a programmer's book on investments. What counts is that all companies are required to report their findings in three documents that are the basis for all key financial metrics that investors discuss:

- *Income statement*—How much revenue a business makes and how much it spends
- *Balance sheet*—What assets a business owns and what it owes
- *Cashflow statement*—How much cash the business generates

We can safely assume that every public company provides these three documents. Whether it's Apple, Walmart, Coca-Cola, or a non-US company such as Rolls-Royce or Deutsche Bank, they similarly calculate revenue and expenses, although the numbers in the sheets might differ according to the business model. Every company reports all three statements quarterly.

> **NOTE** As this is a book for programmers, we keep the description of accounting statements to a minimum; however, some basic knowledge is necessary to perform a financial analysis. Sites such as Investopedia (www.investopedia.com/) can provide you with more detailed information on monetary terms.

### 2.1.1 Income statement

An income statement shows the company's performance over a year or a quarter. Figure 2.1 also shows the relationship of the income statement to other statements.

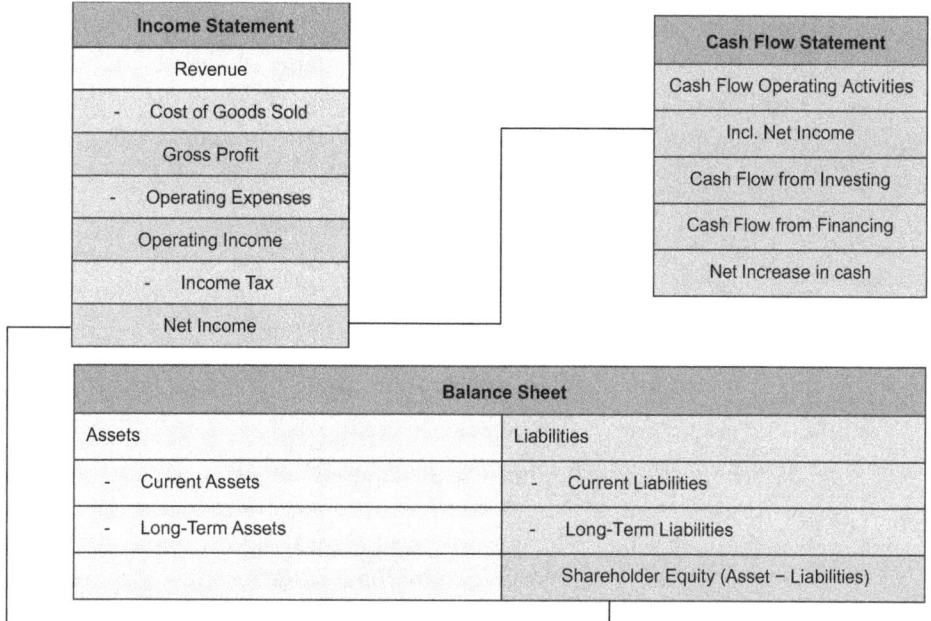

Figure 2.1 This illustrates a simplified relationship between the accounting statement and its interconnection.

Investors typically compare a given quarter with the same quarter from previous years, as many business conditions fluctuate on an annual cycle. Consider how much retail companies are affected by Christmas sales or the holiday season. Therefore, for some companies, Q4—the quarter of the Christmas season—might be decisive for their overall success.

The main components of an income statement are as follows:

- *Revenue*—Total income from sales or services
- *Expenses*—Costs incurred to generate revenues
- *Net income*—Revenue minus expenses, indicating profit or loss

If I receive $1 today, it's worth more than $1 I receive in a year. This concept is called the *time value of money*. I can invest this dollar today and earn interest on it. At a 5% annual interest rate, $1 becomes $1.05 in one year. Inflation also affects the time value of money, meaning I can buy less with one uninvested dollar in a year than I can today, as consumer prices tend to rise on average.

Imagine a company that consistently generates the same net income over 10 years. Over this period, the real value generated decreases each year. Investors typically expect a successful company to increase both revenue and net income over time.

Analyzing a company's accounting statements over time helps in formulating hypotheses about its performance and operations. Let's explore this using a simplified financial model of a fictional consulting firm, which is based on aggregated accounting data. This model has the following characteristics, as shown in figure 2.2:

- Revenue is generated by selling services.
- Research and development (R&D) investments encompass training, personnel certification, and new skill development.
- Service costs are primarily the salaries of employees performing billable work.

We continue to monitor the company's financial statements over time and are interested in seeing if these numbers change significantly. Let's imagine after studying their latest income statement, we discover that R&D expenses increased enormously. The company finances this increase in research with foreign capital, as shown in figure 2.3.

Just by looking at the increased R&D expenses without any further details, we can take a guess at what's going on here to come up with theories and create a bullish (optimistic) and a bearish (pessimistic) hypothesis:

- *Bullish hypothesis*—They must have acquired new projects that will start soon for which they train new consultants, or they are preparing to sell new services to existing customers. The company will see a significant increase in its earnings soon. If investors panic due to additional foreign capital acquired by the company to finance further research, causing the share price to drop, this company is a perfect buying opportunity.

## 2.1 Accounting in a nutshell

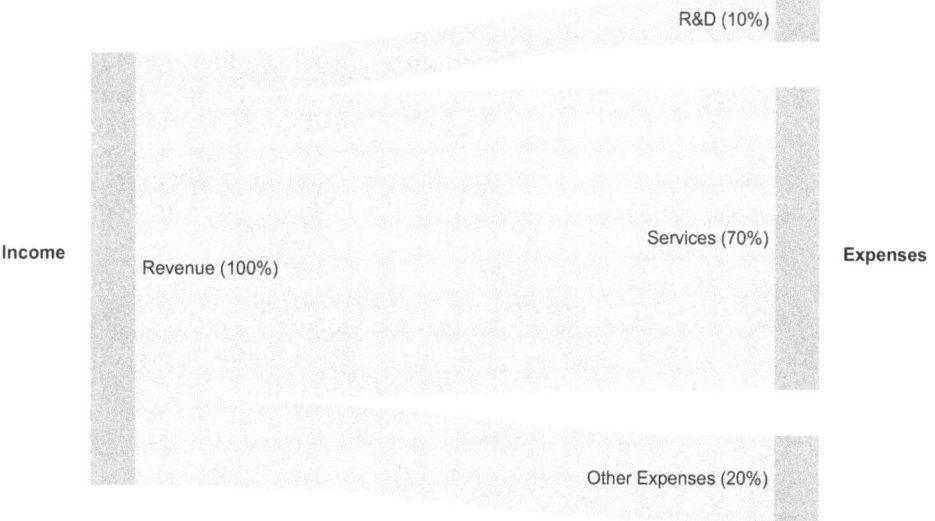

**Figure 2.2** A simplified model of a consulting company that makes its money on selling services and spends most of it on employee salaries

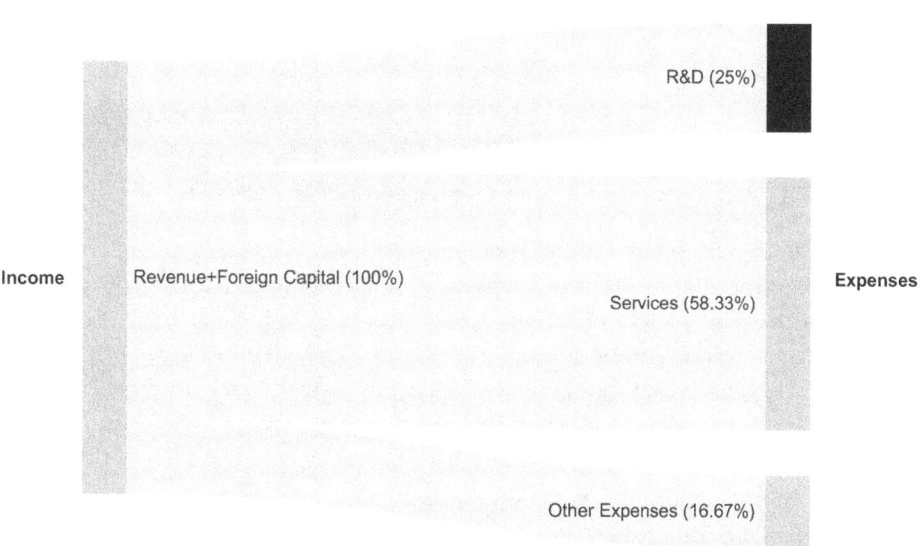

**Figure 2.3** Here, the R&D expenses have increased, and the additional expenses are covered with foreign capital.

- *Bearish hypothesis*—The company had to attract foreign capital to continue operating. Maybe they are in trouble. If their business goes bad, we might not see the effect right away on their accounting sheets. We need to monitor the next income statements to see if their income goes down and if they start cutting expenses. If they plan to roll out new services and fail, they will incur additional debt and may run into liquidity problems. It may be better not to invest in that company.

Consider an alternative scenario in which the company reduces its spending on services and R&D, while the revenue is unaffected. Figure 2.4 outlines this scenario.

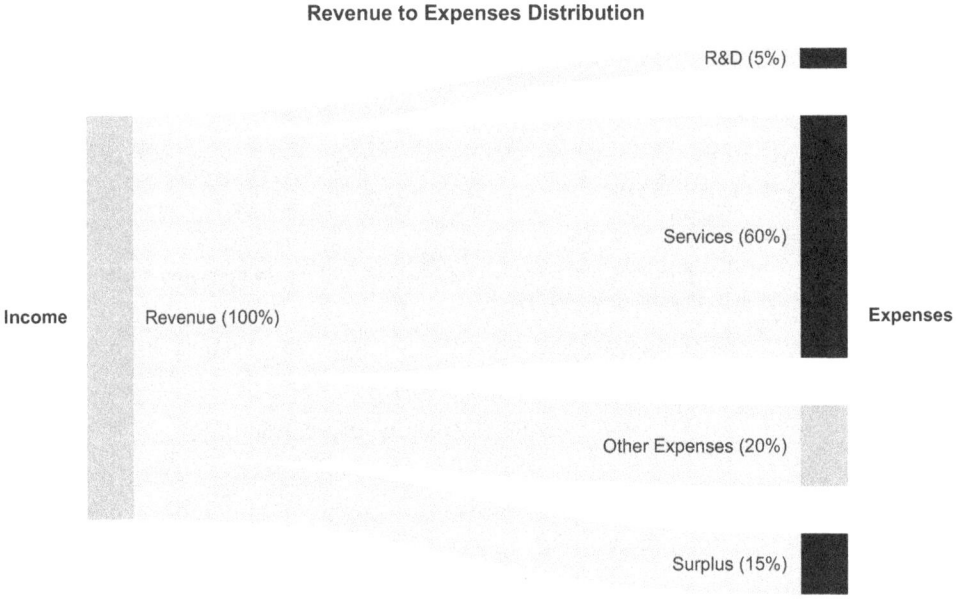

Figure 2.4  Here, the company reduces spending on research and services.

This scenario suggests that the company may see little room for growth. Instead of trying to increase profits by selling more, they monetize existing revenues. Financial experts may examine the interest rate set by the Federal Reserve or the central bank to determine whether that company's strategy is tied to an economic cycle. Many companies prefer to invest less when interest rates are high and the economy is in a recession. But still, all we can do is create hypotheses about what's happening:

- *Bullish hypothesis*—The company still provides the same number of services for existing clients for less expense costs, which indicates they do more work for the same money. Maybe the company became more efficient thanks to AI and automated its processes. As it creates a surplus, the company might become a dividend-paying stock. This is an opportunity to generate passive income.

- *Bearish hypothesis*—A company's value increases if it grows. If the company cuts down on research, it will likely not grow. Having a surplus is fine, but if we don't know what the company is planning to do, it's better not to invest.

This was a simplified model, used for demonstration purposes, for a type of company that is relatively easy to model. Consulting companies can be relatively straightforward, as expenses are often linked to income. Consultants work on client projects. The company makes a profit by selling consultancy services at a higher price than their salary expenses. Other companies are far more challenging to model. For example, think of a conglomerate such as Alphabet, for which you need to consider subsidiaries (e.g., Waymo) that operate in multiple domains from advertising to cloud computing.

Another challenge is that we reduced our model to a minimum of parameters for demonstration purposes. The reality is more complex. At the same time, if you analyze concrete companies, you have more resources, such as media reports on the company and interviews with analysts who know the company well. Data-driven investors can build models of companies and create their own priorities regarding what they consider to be essential for a company's value. The essentials might vary from business to business as well.

**NOTE** Companies in different industries operate on vastly different business models. A tech firm such as Apple spends enormous sums on R&D to create a few high-revenue products. In contrast, supermarket chain Walmart focuses on selling a high volume of products from many suppliers. For Walmart, innovation isn't about creating new products, but about optimizing storage and supply chains while maintaining quality service. Therefore, comparing metrics such as R&D spending between Apple and Walmart would be misleading—it's like comparing apples and oranges. An investor can achieve a far more insightful analysis by comparing companies within the same industry, such as evaluating Walmart against direct competitor Costco.

The income statement reveals how much a company earns and how it allocates its expenses, which helps us evaluate a company's strategy. To complete our tour of financial statements and gain a comprehensive picture, we must now determine what the company already owns. We get this information from the balance sheet.

## 2.1.2 Balance sheet

The income sheet tells us what a company made in a period by listing the revenue generated and the expenses. The information that a company already owns or owes still needs to be added. The essence of a balance sheet can be reduced to this simple formula:

$$\text{Assets} = \text{Liabilities} + \text{Shareholders' equity}$$

*Assets* are what a company owns, *liabilities* are what it owes, and *shareholder equity* is the amount shareholders would get paid if all assets were liquidated and the debts were paid. A company may be in serious trouble when its liabilities exceed its assets.

*Liquidity* is a metric that tells how easily an asset can be converted to cash. Imagine a manufacturing company that puts one of its factories, along with all of its machinery, up for sale. It may take some time to find a potential buyer. Other assets, such as inventory goods, may have better liquidity.

> **NOTE** Do you think like an economist? Consider everything you own—computers, cars, or clothing—would you list these items as nonliquid assets? Or do you count only your financial assets as part of your net value? Thinking as an economist, you might list all of your belongings as part of your wealth.

Programmers often work on projects to reduce capital expenses (CapEx) for their clients or employers. Cloud migration may be the best reference for such projects, as companies decide that they prefer renting over owning hardware with such a move. Some investors also claim that software companies are popular investments because they aren't capital-intensive. Low CapEx is often considered low risk, as it requires less initial investment, even though operating expenses (OpEx) may be higher.

> **NOTE** Engineers sometimes perceive economic soundness differently than business administrators. Think of an on-premise platform that solves business problems with minimal OpEx. While engineers might view the investment as sound, if costs are reduced permanently and a return on investment is achieved over time, business administrators may be more cautious. Among other things, they might argue that higher up-front CapEx may lead to lower liquidity, and he raises the question of opportunity costs and the real total cost of ownership.

The balance sheet might differ significantly between industries. Software companies may have almost no assets listed as inventory, whereas supermarket chains must maintain a large inventory to quickly supply customers with goods. Additionally, you'll find inventory listed under current assets in companies such as NVIDIA, which sell hardware.

The balance sheet already indicated that having more liabilities than assets is an alarm signal. However, there's another detail to analyze after we understand that the accounts payable and accounts receivable entries on a balance sheet indicate that we might have some incoming or outgoing money in our books, but not yet in our possession. It's possible that a company can't pay its bills, even if its books show a positive balance. A third financial statement—the cash flow statement—can give us more details on a company's solvency.

### 2.1.3 Free cash flow

Obviously, we can't pay bills with all forms of assets. *Free cash flow (FCF)* is the amount of cash remaining after a company has covered its operational costs and CapEx. Here's the simplified formula of FCF:

$$\text{Free cash flow} = \text{Operating cash flow} - \text{Capital expenditures}$$

Operating cash flow refers to the cash a company generates through its normal business operations. More than any other document, this statement reveals whether the company is financially stable, can afford new investments, and can pay its bills without incurring additional debt.

> **Why cash flow matters**
>
> Imagine Eugene owns a prestigious antique car business that purchases, renovates, and sells these vintage beauties to car enthusiasts. He has invested a lot of money in a garage and a small factory hall, where he also stores a vast inventory of rare replacement parts. You're transported to a different era in the garage when you see all the Studebakers, Packards, and classic Chevy Impalas.
>
> One day, Eugene looks at his books and realizes he has run out of cash. He had previously found a treasure trove. A wealthy collector of old cars had passed away, and Eugene acquired a vast collection of rare old vehicles from the heirs at a significantly reduced price. Eugene knows that he can sell all those cars with a huge profit margin, but buying all these cars required him to use all of his cash reserves, and he must even take a loan from his local bank.
>
> Some salary and other payments are due soon, so he can only keep his business in operation by borrowing more money. His local bank, which had already given him the first loan, is hesitant to give him a second one and is inquiring about securities.
>
> Eugene's cars and equipment might be worth millions; some clients might even owe him money. However, he can't pay the plumber who fixes his restrooms in the shop by giving away a car or a client's debt. Therefore, a vehicle in Eugene's inventory isn't a liquid asset.
>
> If Eugene proves that his business outlook is good, he'll most likely get a loan from the bank. Still, this example suggests one idea we can explore with algorithms: the risk that a company may be insolvent.

Each accounting statement will still contain many unfamiliar terms if you don't have a degree in business administration. Explaining each term in this book isn't possible, so be sure to look up and research terms as you run across any you're unsure of.

As a programmer, you've seen code written for web applications, data processing, or embedded systems, and each domain requires different best practices, depending on the resources available. This same principle applies to companies. Only some of the best practices are effective for certain companies. Companies are distinct, and understanding this difference is crucial if you want to invest in them.

## 2.2 Industry classification

Before discussing financial metrics and ratios, let's examine the possible sectors and industries to understand potential differences in how companies generate revenues and allocate their expenditures. Figure 2.5 outlines a categorization of sectors according to the Global Industry Classification Standard (GICS) of S&P (www.spglobal.com/spdji/en/landing/topic/gics/), a standard used to categorize companies based on their business models.

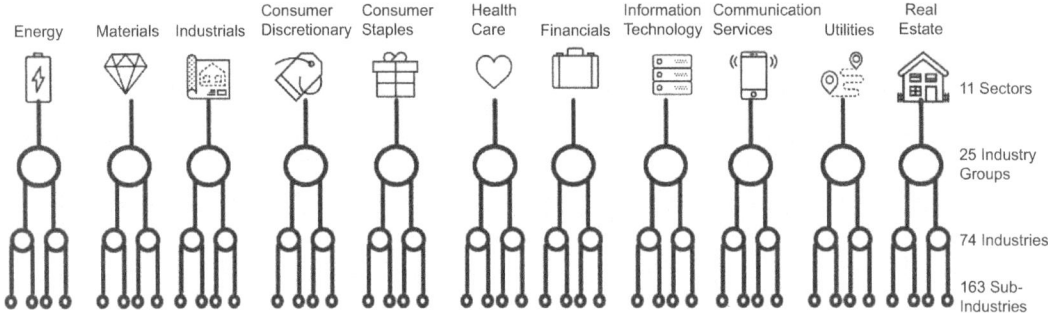

Figure 2.5 All sectors with icons based on the GICS standard used in many financial platforms (Source: www.msci.com/our-solutions/indexes/gics)

**NOTE** GICS is one standard among multiple official industry classification standards. Investors, such as Peter Lynch, have created their own unofficial systems. Be sure to explore these standards independently, as they offer different perspectives on companies that can help you better understand them. We use GICS in this book due to its widespread global use and recognition.

GICS groups companies on four levels. The sector (e.g., Utilities) represents the highest level, and subindustries are at the most detailed level. Different categorizations of businesses help to separate them by business models. Each business model may affect the financial metrics and ratios to watch. Governments regulate specific sectors more heavily, and changes in law have a greater effect on companies in these sectors than on others. Other sectors might be more affected by increased interest rates or economic cycles than others.

### 2.2.1 Influences on GICS sectors

In this chapter, we aim to identify factors that can influence a company, enabling us to build models later. If we know, for instance, that a sector is influenced by interest rates, economic cycles, and raw material costs, we can try to build a machine learning (ML) model that predicts stock prices based on these input factors as features of the ML model. In table 2.1, we introduce the GICS sectors and the key factors that may influence the price of an asset in each sector.

## 2.2 Industry classification

**Table 2.1 GICS sectors and their influences**

| Sector | What it does | Influenced by |
|---|---|---|
| Utilities | Companies that provide essential services such as electricity, water, and natural gas | Interest rates, energy prices, regulation, and bond yields |
| Consumer Staples | Companies that produce essential products such as food, beverages, and household items | Interest rates, inflation, consumer confidence, and raw material costs |
| Consumer Discretionary | Companies that produce nonessential goods and services, including automobiles, apparel, and leisure | Consumer spending, unemployment rates, and disposable income |
| Communication Services | Companies that provide communication services, including telecom and media | Government regulation, intense competition, technology changes, general economic conditions, consumer and business confidence, spending, and changes in consumer and business preferences |
| Real Estate | Companies involved in the development, management, and operation of real properties | Demographic changes, interest rates, economic cycle, government policies, housing demand, and economic growth |
| Information Technology | Companies that produce software, hardware, or semiconductor equipment, and companies that provide internet or related services | Innovation, cybersecurity threats, and regulatory changes |
| Energy | Companies that play a role in extracting, refining, or supplying consumable fuels | Oil prices, geopolitical stability, and renewable energy trends |
| Health Care | Companies that provide medical services, manufacture medical equipment, or develop pharmaceuticals | Pandemics, regulation, drug pricing, and demographic changes |
| Financials | Companies that provide financial services, including banking, insurance, and investment | Interest rates, economic cycles, and regulatory changes |
| Industrials | Companies that produce goods used in construction and manufacturing, including machinery and equipment | Manufacturing output, trade policies, and commodity prices |
| Materials | Companies that provide raw materials used in the manufacturing process, including metals and chemicals | Commodity prices, supply chain stability, and environmental regulations |

Some categorizations of companies might be misleading. Many would consider Amazon, Tesla, and Google to be companies in the information technology sector. GICS categorizes Amazon and Tesla in the Consumer Discretionary sector, and Google in the Communication Services sector. Still, when looking up ratios, it makes sense to look up the company's sector to add context.

> **Investing only in companies whose business you understand**
>
> Warren Buffett recommends investing only in businesses that you understand. A supermarket chain such as Walmart is different from a tech company. If a tech company launches a successful product, it may be reflected in its yearly results (think of the effect of the iPhone on Apple's business). However, the best-selling product of a supermarket chain won't have a visible effect on an accounting statement.
>
> Reading accounting statements of a company and understanding what they mean, as well as being able to interpret changes in numbers, may not make you an accountant, yet. However, being able to interpret the numbers and connect them to the company's business model provides a foundation for making wise investment decisions.

### 2.2.2 Sectors and economic cycles

In an economic crisis with unpleasant side effects, such as high unemployment rates or high inflation, it makes sense that some businesses are more affected than others. To demonstrate the effect of economic cycles on share prices, let's pick four suspects—Microsoft, Coca-Cola, Walmart, and Ford—and check their share prices during the 2008 financial crisis, when the housing market collapsed. For table 2.2, we used an interval from January 1, 2008, to January 1, 2010.

Table 2.2 Highs and lows of selected share prices from 2008 to 2010

|      | Microsoft (MSFT) | Coca-Cola (KO) | Walmart (WMT) | Ford (F) |
| --- | --- | --- | --- | --- |
| High | 35.95 | 32.79 | 21.28 | 10.37 |
| Low  | 14.87 | 18.72 | 14.37 | 1.01 |
| Avg. | 24.82 | 25.65 | 17.60 | 5.42 |

Even if we only look at the numbers, it's evident that Ford's value declined far more steeply than Walmart's, falling to just one-tenth of its previous value at its lowest point. A bar chart accentuates the changes even more clearly in figure 2.6.

This chart makes sense because Ford and Microsoft produce products that consumers can drop more easily. If resources are scarce, postponing the purchase of a new car may be a viable option, but choosing not to go to the supermarket, even in a crisis, isn't possible; we still have to eat. Let's examine how various sectors performed during the 2008 financial crisis.

One way to improve this exploration is to compare sector indices. A sector index is a collection of multiple companies within a single sector, which can also be referred to by their respective tickers. In figure 2.7, we look at XLK (Technology sector), XLP (Consumer Staples), and XLY (Consumer Discretionary). The graph shows what common sense has already told us: companies producing goods for everyday needs are less affected by crises.

## 2.2 Industry classification

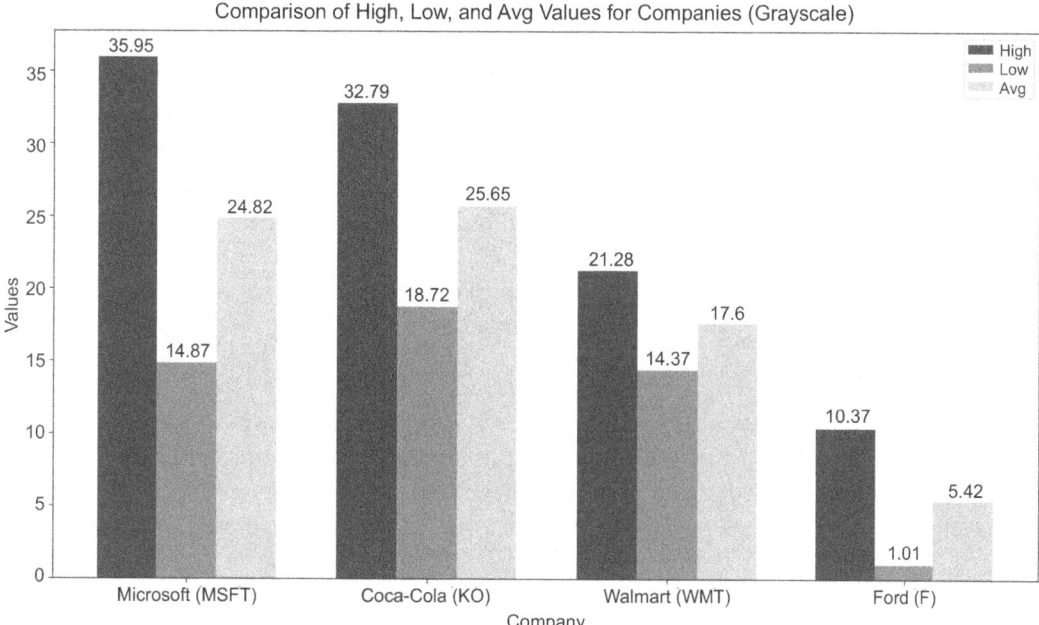

Figure 2.6 Data from the table shown in a bar chart makes the drop in value of some companies more obvious.

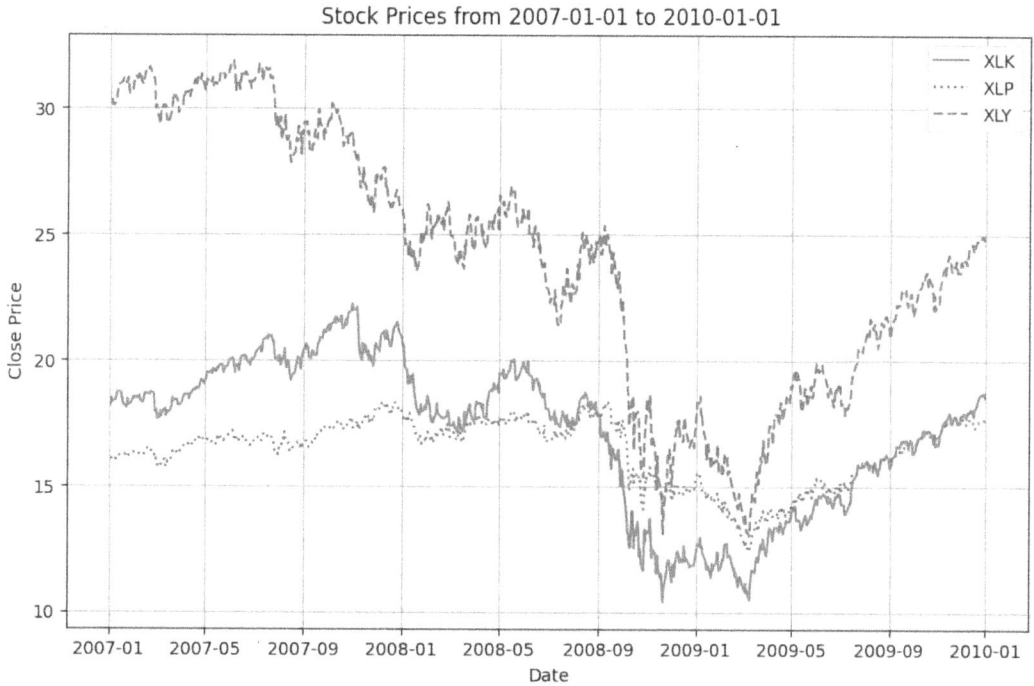

Figure 2.7 The effect of the 2008 housing market crisis on selected indices XLK (Technology), XLP (Consumer Staples), and XLY (Consumer Discretionary)

A company's performance is fundamentally linked to the economic cycle, which consists of four stages: expansion, peak, contraction, and trough. During an economic expansion, rising employment and disposable income boost spending on nonessential goods. Conversely, during a contraction, consumers prioritize essentials and cut back on discretionary items. This dynamic reveals that some companies are highly *cyclical*, with their success directly tied to the health of the economy. In contrast, others are *noncyclical* or *defensive*, remaining stable during economic downturns. This sensitivity extends beyond business cycles, as other macroeconomic forces—such as government fiscal policy, interest rates, inflation, commodity prices, and currency exchange rates—also affect industries in vastly different ways.

## 2.3 Capitalization

As we now understand that companies in different industries and sectors may react differently to market conditions, we might develop an "invest in too-big-to-fail companies" investment hypothesis. While smaller companies might perish in a crisis and lose their invested money permanently, we can bet on big companies that will survive all crises and consistently grow over the years, on average.

Before we challenge this idea, let's first define what *larger* or *smaller* means in this context. The number of employees at a company can be a misleading indicator of size. A more suitable metric for investors to consider is capitalization. In short, *capitalization* refers to the value that people are willing to pay for the company at the current time. Investors calculate a public company's capitalization by multiplying the total amount of outstanding shares of a stock by the current stock price.

Although many companies with a small market capitalization (e.g., start-ups and small and midsize enterprises [SMEs]) are private and so not listed on stock exchanges, the difference between companies on the stock market can still be vast. We can group companies as follows (with some slight variations in different markets):

- *Mega-cap*—Market value of $200 billion or more
- *Large-cap*—Market value between $10 billion and $200 billion
- *Mid-cap*—Market value between $2 billion and $10 billion
- *Small-cap*—Market value between $250 million and $2 billion
- *Micro-cap*—Market value of less than $250 million

A mega-cap company's bankruptcy risk is lower than that of companies with a lower market capitalization. At the same time, finding *tenbaggers*—a term coined by Peter Lynch for an investment that returns 10 times its initial purchase price—is much more likely with a micro-cap stock. They have far more room to grow.

> **NOTE** Intrinsic value reflects an asset's true worth, which can be estimated using various methods, such as discounted cash flow analysis or other fundamental valuation techniques. Even with rigorous analysis, every intrinsic value estimate carries a degree of uncertainty. The greater the gap between an asset's market capitalization and its estimated intrinsic value, the larger the potential investment opportunity.

Mega-cap companies, such as NVIDIA, Apple, or Microsoft, differ significantly from those with a considerably lower market value. Investors who own shares in mega-cap companies may sit out crises, as the likelihood of bankruptcy is low. Companies with a viable business model will eventually return to their earlier, higher share prices. Shareholders of smaller companies may be more concerned about worst-case scenarios. The smaller the company, the higher the risk, but also the higher the chance for gains. Many experienced investors, for this reason, love to explore smaller companies and mitigate risks by conducting more thorough due diligence and in-depth research.

If we look back in time and examine the fate of companies with the highest market capitalization over the decades, we'll see that some past winners have lost their significance or disappeared. Even Jeff Bezos claims that Amazon might fail at some point in the future (https://mng.bz/pZR0). Trusting that giants on the stock market will always survive might end up like betting during the Jurassic era that some large reptiles are too big to go extinct. Instead, the stock market is akin to the survival of the fittest, and it makes sense to investigate the fundamentals of companies.

## 2.4 Metrics and ratios

With knowledge of a company's classification and capitalization, we have a basis to go on. We might pick companies in a sector we understand and choose companies to invest in. Now, we need to learn more about a company's fitness. A *metric* is a statement about a company's performance. One example is the dividend yield, which indicates the amount of dividends per share. We get most metrics from the accounting statements. A *ratio* is a statement about a relationship between two *independent* metrics. The price-to-earnings ratio (P/E) measures the share price relative to the earnings per share (EPS).

Understanding financial metrics is much like evaluating software quality. In software development, metrics such as code readability are essential; however, a catastrophic score in one area—such as a high crash rate—demands immediate action from team leaders, regardless of how elegant the code may be. Similarly, in finance, a company might appear strong. Still, a critical red flag from a single ratio, such as an inability to pay its bills, signals serious trouble that forces management to take action.

Conversely, just as no single metric can guarantee a high-quality product, a few good financial ratios alone don't confirm a company's health or future success. A common investment mistake is to fixate on one impressive number while ignoring potential weaknesses elsewhere. The key in both fields is a holistic evaluation. By analyzing multiple metrics and comparing them to those of industry peers, we can develop a strong and reliable indicator of a company's overall performance.

> **NOTE** It's impossible to cover all ratios used in the financial industry. Therefore, this subset of possible ratios might be interesting when assessing potential investments. Web pages such as the Terms page from FullRatio (https://fullratio.com/terms) give more context to what each ratio could mean for an industry.

To assess a company's overall status, we must consider multiple factors. As we'll demonstrate in chapter 3, platforms with stock screeners, such as Finviz, provide an excellent overview of company data. Let's examine some ratios for NVIDIA and Walmart in table 2.3. The Beta column refers to a measure of a stock's volatility—or systematic risk—in relation to the overall market.

Table 2.3  Selected ratios of NVIDIA and Walmart

| Company | Market cap | Sales | Employees | P/E | Beta |
|---|---|---|---|---|---|
| NVIDIA | 3457.97B | 148.51B | 36,000 | 45.65 | 2.12 |
| Walmart | 779.85B | 685.09B | 2,100,000 | 41.81 | 0.69 |

Data from the Finviz platform on June 8, 2025 (for the latest data, go to https://finviz.com/quote.ashx?t=NVDA&p=d or https://finviz.com/quote.ashx?t=WMT&p=d)

We find some noteworthy differences in the numbers. Walmart's revenue is significantly higher. However, the supermarket chain also has approximately 60 times the number of NVIDIA's employees. Having lots of employees also means high expenses. A supermarket chain also needs to maintain a lot of infrastructure and inventory. However, as mentioned already in the section on sectors and economic cycles, during economic downturns, customers will still visit supermarkets to buy food.

In contrast, some individuals and companies will delay technology purchases if they don't have sufficient funds. A low beta value of a stock—Walmart has a beta of 0.69, and NVIDIA has a beta of 2.12—reflects its resilience against market risks. We observe considerable differences in expected values across GICS sectors, as well as in other ratios.

## 2.4.1 Liquidity

In the simplest terms, *liquidity* measures a company's ability to pay bills. If you collect information on multiple companies in a DataFrame, you might find problematic outliers. In this chapter, we explore two ratios: the current ratio and the quick ratio.

The *current ratio* measures a company's ability to pay its short-term liabilities with its assets. This is calculated by dividing the current assets by the current liabilities. We can collect both values from the balance sheet.

The *quick ratio* is more stringent. It only considers assets, such as cash, marketable securities, and receivables, that the company can use to pay short-term debts today and omits assets such as inventory. The liquidity ratios as of June 8, 2025, for Walmart, Altria, NVIDIA, and Salesforce are shown in table 2.4.

Table 2.4  Liquidity ratios for Walmart, Altria, NVIDIA, and Salesforce

| Company | Sector | Industry | Current ratio | Quick ratio |
|---|---|---|---|---|
| Walmart (WMT) | Consumer Defensive | Discount Stores | 0.780 | 0.185 |
| Atria (MO) | Consumer Defensive | Tobacco | 0.571 | 0.468 |

Table 2.4 Liquidity ratios for Walmart, Altria, NVIDIA, and Salesforce *(continued)*

| Company | Sector | Industry | Current ratio | Quick ratio |
|---|---|---|---|---|
| NVIDIA (NVDA) | Technology | Semiconductors | 3.388 | 2.857 |
| Salesforce (CRM) | Technology | Software - Application | 1.069 | 0.899 |

Data collected from the yfinance library on June 8, 2025

The table provides insights about sectors. Technology companies tend to have higher liquidity ratios, which can also be explained by their business models. If we consider discount stores such as Walmart, we can imagine the amount of capital these companies have in inventory or goods still to be sold. Nobody wants to go into a store and find only a minimum of products on the shelves, as supermarket chains want to improve their liquidity ratios and only buy new products once the old ones are out of stock.

Again, this statement shows that we can't compare the ratios between different sectors. Table 2.5 is more interesting for a financial analysis, as it compares Walmart, Costco, Target, and Dollar Tree, which are peer companies. We can compare the companies based on these returns and have a basis for discussing which one is performing better.

Table 2.5 Liquidity ratios for Walmart, Costco, Target, and Dollar Tree

| Company | Sector | Industry | Current ratio | Quick ratio |
|---|---|---|---|---|
| Walmart (WMT) | Consumer Defensive | Discount Stores | 0.780 | 0.185 |
| Costco (COST) | Consumer Defensive | Discount Stores | 1.015 | 0.472 |
| Target (TGT) | Consumer Defensive | Discount Stores | 0.935 | 0.152 |
| Dollar Tree (DLTR) | Consumer Defensive | Discount Stores | 1.044 | 0.122 |

Data collected using yfinance on June 8, 2025

As we delve into the numbers at the micro level for the same sector, we need to take a deeper dive into them with a different mindset to make key decisions. Perhaps the insight from one category alone isn't enough for an investment decision, but it can still influence that decision. An investor knowledgeable in discount stores might examine all of these numbers and deduce that Costco has a better ratio than Walmart.

> **NOTE** Value investors know what makes businesses in the sectors they understand successful and look for confirmation in numbers. They often spend a considerable amount of time comparing metrics they have selected based on their understanding of the business. For value investors, sophisticated scorecards of carefully chosen metrics and ratios can be key decision-making factors.

## 2.4.2 Debt

In a financial sense, *debt* is all liabilities with interest-bearing obligations. The debt-to-equity (D/E) ratio is calculated by dividing a company's total liabilities by its total shareholders' equity. This ratio is a key indicator of a company's financial leverage, showing the proportion of debt used to finance its assets compared to equity. A higher ratio indicates a greater reliance on debt financing, which can increase financial risk. Let's look again at some examples in table 2.6.

Table 2.6 Liquidity ratios for Apple, Walmart, and NVIDIA

| Company | Sector | Industry | Debt-to-equity |
|---|---|---|---|
| Apple (AAPL) | Technology | Consumer Electronics | 146.994 |
| Walmart (WMT) | Consumer Defensive | Discount Stores | 74.138 |
| NVIDIA (NVDA) | Technology | Semiconductors | 12.267 |

Data collected using yfinance on June 8, 2025

This chart highlights the need to look beyond surface-level metrics. While Apple's debt-to-equity ratio seems 10 times worse than NVIDIA's, the number reflects a deliberate financial strategy, not necessarily poor health.

Apple strategically issues highly rated corporate bonds at very low interest rates to finance its research, development, and other growth initiatives. For investors, this debt isn't a red flag if the interest rates are close to or below the rate of inflation. In that scenario, the company is using low-cost leverage as a powerful tool to fund growth, turning a seemingly poor ratio into a sign of sophisticated capital management.

The interest coverage ratio, not shown in the table but a key metric to explore in an analysis focused on debt, is a crucial indicator used to assess a company's ability to pay the interest on its outstanding debt easily. It's calculated by dividing a company's Earnings Before Interest and Taxes (EBIT) by its interest expenses for a given period. A result below 1.0 is a universal red flag, indicating that the company's current profits are insufficient to cover its interest obligations, which signals significant financial distress regardless of the industry.

## 2.4.3 Earnings

We collect the raw earnings data from the income statements to calculate ratios. The *earnings per share (EPS)* metric mentioned earlier serves as the basis for many key ratios. This metric measures the company's profits for each outstanding share. The EPS is calculated with the following formula:

$$(\text{Profit} - \text{Preferred dividends}) \div \text{Shares outstanding}$$

In earnings calls, companies inform their shareholders about quarterly results. Companies retrospectively assess past earnings from previous quarters and estimate their earnings for the following quarters. Whether the numbers are above or below expectations can affect the stock price.

*Free cash flow per share* is a profitability metric that measures the total amount of FCF generated by the company attributed to each share over one year. A good ratio of FCF underlines that a company can expand business operations, pay down debt, or return capital to shareholders. The formula follows:

$$\text{Free cash flow per share} = \text{Free cash flow (FCF)} \div \text{Shares outstanding}$$

FCF is calculated by the following:

$$\text{Operating cash flow} - \text{CapEx}$$

The earnings ratios are mostly interesting for valuation purposes, as earnings are often used as a basis to evaluate the company. So, it makes sense to continue there.

### 2.4.4 Valuation

Suppose a start-up claims to be valued at $100 million. What does this mean? A third party believes that $100 million could be a fair price for acquiring a specific start-up. However, if a potential buyer is willing to pay this amount, that's another story. These valuations are often rough estimates based on data provided by the start-up. Companies considering a purchase of that start-up may come up with entirely different numbers after a more detailed assessment. In the worst case, buyers aren't interested in buying the start-up at all, even close to its valuation.

Start-up valuation can be tricky. Proper valuation, such as with the *discounted cash flow (DCF) method*, requires sound accounting practices over multiple years. This demand raises questions: Has the start-up reported enough years with all the thoroughness necessary for a sound assessment? What if the third party doing the valuation benefits from giving a high rating? (They might attract other start-ups by giving high valuations in general.)

Start-up valuations are often rough estimates of a start-up's worth, assuming everything goes as planned and there are no hidden problems. According to the efficient market theory, the share price on a stock exchange reflects all available market information, causing the valuation of public companies to be more accurate. We multiply the stock price by the number of shares outstanding and obtain the company's *market capitalization*. Some investors challenge this assumption and try to use valuation metrics to find undervalued companies. We can do the same: let's learn valuation ratios quickly and complement our knowledge by comparing ratios using practice examples.

We observed that EPS is a crucial metric. If an EPS diverges strongly from the previous report, it's a strong buy or sell signal for investors.

> **NOTE** The exact formula for EPS also subtracts a metric of preferred dividends from the net income, which can be ignored for this example.

We've defined EPS earlier. We calculate the price for $1 of earnings (price-to-earnings) by dividing the share price by EPS. The P/E ratio is essential for determining whether a stock is overvalued or undervalued.

If we take the time to explore the P/E ratios of multiple companies, we'll soon learn that they vary significantly. If NVIDIA has a P/E ratio of 47.61 and Pfizer one of 10.43, as of January 31, does this mean NVIDIA is overvalued, and Pfizer is undervalued? The reality is not so simple. We need to compare the P/E ratio of a company with a baseline. One baseline could be the S&P 500 index. At the time of writing, the P/E ratio of the S&P 500 was around 30. However, this is still vague. The average P/E ratios vary by sector, so it may be more effective to compare a company's P/E value with that of its peers. In this example, the sector median is 25.31, which indicates that NVIDIA is overvalued. But there's still one problem. The P/E ratio doesn't include projected growth. By dividing the P/E ratio by EPS growth, we get another standard ratio, the price/earnings-to-growth ratio (PEG). Let's take a snapshot of NVIDIA's valuation as of June 8, 2025, shown in table 2.7.

Table 2.7  A snapshot of NVIDIA's valuation

|  | Sector relative grade | NVIDIA | Sector median | % diff. to sector | NVIDIA 5Y avg. | % diff. to 5Y avg. |
| --- | --- | --- | --- | --- | --- | --- |
| P/E Non-GAAP (TTM) | D | 44.43 | 22.20 | 100.10 | 63.09 | 29.59 |
| P/E Non-GAAP (FWD) | C- | 33.14 | 22.64 | 46.38 | 47.38 | 30.05 |
| P/E GAAP (TTM) | C- | 45.71 | 28.17 | 62.22 | 83.84 | 45.49 |
| P/E GAAP (FWD) | C | 35.04 | 29.14 | 20.24 | 62.08 | 43.56 |
| PEG GAAP (TTM) | B | 0.56 | 0.91 | -38.45 | — | NM |
| PEG Non-GAAP (FWD) | B+ | 1.15 | 1.73 | -33.48 | 1.80 | 36.21 |

FWD, forward (future financial performance); TTM, trailing 12 months (most recent 12-month period); NM, nonmeaningful value

Data taken from Seeking Alpha on June 8, 2025 (for the latest data, go to https://mng.bz/Gwm8)

### Which story do you want to tell?

In June 2024, NVIDIA became the most valuable company in the world, with a total valuation of over $3 trillion. The snapshot of NVIDIA shows that it's up to us to decide which story to tell with the data.

The P/E ratio, as of January 31, 2025, is calculated using a share price of $124.65, resulting in a P/E ratio of 47.61. The sector median is 25. In addition, NVIDIA's P/E ratio is far above its peers. We could stop here and conclude that it's unwise to buy shares in a company where you pay more than double for each earnings compared to similar companies.

> If we look at future earnings, things start to look more promising. NVIDIA had great past earnings, but future earnings look even better. The P/E GAAP (FWD) brings us closer to the sector peers. However, we can reason differently than before with the PEG GAAP (TTM) and PEG Non-GAAP (FWD). First, we must highlight that there has been a substantial increase in earnings. Projecting these earnings into the future gives us a ratio—PEG GAAP (TTM)—that beats the sector by 81.27%. We can reason that NVIDIA remains a bargain, considering its P/E ratios have consistently been higher than those of its peers in the past, and its share price has still increased significantly.

The *price-to-sales* ratio reflects the price per $1 of sales. Sales figures are generally considered relatively reliable, whereas other income statement items, such as earnings, can be manipulated by various accounting rules. For early-stage companies that aren't yet profitable, sales growth, as represented by this metric, can be a good indicator of future success. The *price-to-book* ratio is how much you pay for $1 of equity. It reflects the market's valuation of the company's net assets on its balance sheet and is particularly attractive for capital-intensive companies.

After this brief introduction to ratios, we can make them more meaningful by looking at some examples. For this, we select two technology companies (Apple and NVIDIA), one utility company (Sempra), a supermarket chain (Walmart), and a beverages company (Coca-Cola), as depicted in table 2.8.

Table 2.8 Earnings ratios for NVIDIA, Apple, Sempra, Walmart, and Coca-Cola

| Company | Forward P/E | Trailing P/E | PEG ratio | Price-to-sales | Price-to-book | Beta |
|---|---|---|---|---|---|---|
| NVIDIA (NVDA) | 34.40 | 45.72 | 1.76 | 23.27 | 41.22 | 2.122 |
| Apple (AAPL) | 24.54 | 31.76 | 1.85 | 7.61 | 45.10 | 1.211 |
| Sempra (SRE) | 14.95 | 16.89 | 2.03 | 3.76 | 1.63 | 0.656 |
| Walmart (WMT) | 35.83 | 41.65 | 3.72 | 1.14 | 9.32 | 0.693 |
| Coca-Cola (KO) | 24.02 | 28.65 | 4.41 | 6.55 | 11.72 | 0.46 |

Data taken from Seeking Alpha on June 8, 2025 (https://seekingalpha.com)

Let's try to interpret the numbers of two companies. NVIDIA has a high P/E ratio and a low PEG ratio. These numbers indicate that NVIDIA is still experiencing massive growth, and we expect continued earnings growth in the future.

> **NOTE** Investors might also consider whether outstanding PEG ratios are sustainable over multiple years. The holy grail of many investors is companies that show constant earnings growth over the years and whose further growth can't be challenged by competitors.

In contrast, Coca-Cola's PEG ratio indicates lower growth potential. This maturity makes it a perfect candidate for a dividend-paying company, which we'll explore in section 2.4.6.

As shown earlier in section 2.4.1 when discussing liquidity, comparing different sectors may help us see common knowledge reflected in numbers. Coca-Cola has been in existence since 1892; its soft drinks are already widely distributed worldwide. With that, it's improbable that this company would face an existential crisis. It's hard to imagine that a vast percentage of consumers who are used to drinking Coca-Cola would stop drinking it. NVIDIA is the market leader in a competitive market. In recent years, the company has gained success after success, and their growth continues as the market expands significantly (a trend not observed in the soft drinks market). At the same time, it's more conceivable than with Coca-Cola that the semiconductor market could be disrupted by a competitor, making NVIDIA less resilient than Coca-Cola. Comparing NVIDIA with tech company AMD (trailing PE of 81.81 and PEG ratio of 0.59) would be more interesting, as we could hypothesize that while AMD is overvalued compared to NVIDIA, its growth potential is bigger.

### 2.4.5 Profitability

We calculate *profitability* by subtracting expenses from earnings, and we can calculate profitability ratios. Having data about profit (or loss), we need to understand its relationship to other parameters, such as assets or equity. In some cases, we may find that we make a profit, but compared to the amount of money invested, the investment can still be considered a questionable decision.

*Return on assets (ROA)* is calculated by dividing net income by total assets. It reflects how effectively the company uses its assets to generate revenue. If Company A reported $10,000 of net income and owns $100,000 in assets, its ROA is 10%. Every $1 of assets generates $0.10 cents in profits yearly. It takes 10 years to pay off all the asset investments.

*Return on equity (ROE)* is calculated by dividing net income by shareholder equity. It indicates how effectively a company compensates its shareholders for their investment. If Company B reported $10,000 in net income and its shareholders have $2 million in equity, its ROE is 0.5%. For every $1 of equity that shareholders own, the company generates $0.05 cents in annual profits.

We calculate the *profit margin* by dividing the net income by the revenue. This metric often varies significantly across different industries. Supermarkets sell a lot, but their margin per sale is low.

### 2.4.6 Dividends

Some new investors may wonder why some companies pay dividends at all. After all, companies would retain more profits without dividend payments, and more cash means having more opportunities to invest in the company's growth.

## 2.4 Metrics and ratios

Let's think about Coca-Cola. Almost everyone is familiar with the brand and has tried its flagship product. Even with the highest imaginable marketing budget, the company couldn't make the brand more widely known to the global population, and it's challenging to convert those who don't drink Coca-Cola already into customers. Even the most eloquent advertisement campaign won't convert those who have tried it and who prefer other beverages to fans of Coke.

If the company didn't spend its profits due to missing growth opportunities in a mature market, it would need to hoard them. Consequently, inflation would decrease these savings. Returning money to investors makes sense, especially because this plan makes the stock more attractive for investment strategies that rely on returning cash to their investors, such as retirement funds.

> **What if a company starts using its money to invest?**
> Companies can also use profits to invest in other companies. Coca-Cola is a good example of such a move, as it owned subsidiaries in the entertainment industry, such as Coca-Cola Telecommunications. If you're from the UK, you'll be familiar with several bank divisions, in addition to two of the largest supermarket chains—Tesco and Sainsbury's—that both attempted to establish virtual network operators for mobile services.
>
> Companies with strong brand recognition and financial power have many opportunities to enter new markets. Whether this strategy is good or not is debatable. Some may argue that it risks damaging the brand's reputation and might be hindered by bureaucracy. Others may think that these companies already have established structures and can use their capital to expand into other industries as a conglomerate. History shows that not all spin-offs of successful companies met their expectations, and they have good reasons to stick to their core business.

Let's explore the details of creating passive income with stocks. Passive income investors buy X shares of a company with higher dividend yields, such as Coca-Cola, on day Y. For their stock ownership, they get dividends paid in intervals. Dividend payouts are a provided amount of money per share. This payout is taken from the share price. In other words, an investor who buys shares before a dividend payout to sell them again after the dividend payout won't benefit from such a move.

Dividend stock investors may also benefit from capital appreciation. Examining many high-dividend-paying companies, we observe that they also tend to grow in share price. Let's look at table 2.9 where we've highlighted some growth companies (those that invest their surplus more in growth) and value companies (those that prefer to pay dividends rather than invest in further scaling the company). We observe this in the *payout ratio,* which is the percentage of profits distributed as dividends, and the dividend yield. Someone who buys Apple stock purely for dividend yield picked the wrong strategy to invest in Apple. The interest rate of treasury bonds, which reflects the risk-free rate of capital, is mostly around 5%. Altria (MO) is the only stock in the table with a dividend yield above the interest rate of Treasury bonds, at 6.89%.

Table 2.9  Dividends of Apple, Altria, Microsoft, NVIDIA, Sempra, Walmart, and Coca-Cola highlighting different payout strategies

| Company | Yield FWD % | Payout ratio % | Div growth 5Y % | Consecutive years of growth | Consecutive years of dividend payments |
|---|---|---|---|---|---|
| Apple (AAPL) | 0.51 | 14.10 | 5.24 | 12 | 12 |
| Altria (MO) | 6.89 | 77.54 | 4.00 | 55 | 55 |
| Microsoft (MSFT) | 0.71 | 25.04 | 10.24 | 20 | 20 |
| NVIDIA (NVDA) | 0.03 | 1.25 | 20.11 | 1 | 12 |
| Sempra (SRE) | 3.36 | 53.18 | 4.88 | 14 | 26 |
| Walmart (WMT) | 0.96 | 34.03 | 4.41 | 51 | 51 |
| Coca-Cola (KO) | 2.86 | 67.99 | 4.20 | 62 | 62 |

Data from Seeking Alpha on June 8, 2025 (https://seekingalpha.com)

Let's say 10 years ago, someone bought stock in Coca-Cola. Did they benefit from this purchase? Or would it have been wiser to invest in a fixed-income asset, such as a treasury bond, at a rate of around 5%? In July 2025, Coca-Cola's share price was $71.01. As of July 2015, the share price was $41.25. The stock price grew by more than 5% per year. Add this capital increase to the dividend, and you'll see a higher yield than with safe treasury bonds, which don't provide capital appreciation.

An individual who bought Coca-Cola stocks worth $100,000 in 2015 can sell them 10 years later for more than $150,000. As of this writing, Coca-Cola pays $2.04 per share annually, representing a yield of 2.86%. If we calculated the yield with the price of 10 years ago, we would get 4.6%.

> **NOTE** Companies try to increase annual payouts per share over time. As of June 2025, Coca-Cola pays $2.04 per share in annual dividends. The further back in time you go, the less money you would have received per share, while, on average, the share price was lower. It's often a bad sign for investors if companies reduce annual payouts per share. Investors can interpret a reduction as a sign that the company is under pressure and needs to allocate more resources to sustain its business.

You calculate the dividend yield by dividing the dividend per share by the share price. Apple has an annual payout per share of 1.04, and the share price is $203.95 (as of June 2025): 1.04 ÷ 203.95 yields a dividend of 0.51%. Many investors will conclude that most tech stocks are growth-oriented companies that typically pay only a small dividend.

**NOTE** The height of a company's dividend yield depends on the share price, and its value can be misleading. As of June 2025, AT&T offers a dividend yield of 3.95%, but it will only pay $1.11 per share. At the beginning of 2014, Apple had a share value of approximately $20, similar to AT&T in 2024. Anyone who purchased 1,000 Apple shares in 2014 for $20,000 not only increased the value of the shares by more than 10 times but also received a $1,000 dividend payment each year.

We also add some high-paying dividend examples in table 2.10. Adding the sector and industry as parameters will help us identify specific industries with higher dividends.

Table 2.10 Looking at a dividend scorecard from data collected via Python

| Company | Sector | Industry | Dividend yield | Payout ratio |
|---|---|---|---|---|
| Microsoft (MSFT) | Technology | Software - Infrastructure | 0.71 | 0.2442 |
| Walmart (WMT) | Consumer Defensive | Discount Stores | 0.96 | 0.3665 |
| NVIDIA (NVDA) | Technology | Semiconductors | 0.03 | 0.0129 |
| Sempra (SRE) | Utilities | Utilities - Diversified | 3.36 | 0.4404 |
| Apple (AAPL) | Technology | Consumer Electronics | 0.51 | 0.1558 |
| Altria (MO) | Consumer Defensive | Tobacco | 6.89 | 0.6779 |
| VICI Properties (VICI) | Real Estate | REIT - Diversified | 5.50 | 0.650 |
| Restaurant Brands International (RBI.VI) | Financial Services | Banks - Regional | 4.06 | 0.4297 |

Data collected using yfinance

Each company sets its dividend policy according to what it thinks is in the best interest of its shareholders. Some asset types, such as *real estate investment trusts (REITs)*, are required by law to have high payout ratios. If a stock's payout ratio is low, it's a good sign because it can still experience significant growth. The longer a company increases its dividend payment per year, the more likely it is that this trend will continue. Another attractive attribute is the dividend growth rate. When researching dividend yield, it's also important to consider historical growth.

Companies have different payment schedules (annual, semi-annual, quarterly, monthly). A few companies also pay dividends at irregular intervals. If you plan to use income from dividends for a specific purpose, such as paying for a summer vacation, carefully consider whether the dividend payment date aligns with your travel plans.

One related aspect is stock buybacks. In a buyback, a company purchases its shares from the market, thereby reducing the number of outstanding shares. Although this action may sound illogical to a newcomer, remember that the fewer shares there are on the market, the more valuable the remaining shares will be. A stock buyback is, therefore, an alternative way to reward existing shareholders without distributing cash. While dividend payments are a recurring commitment—some investors rely on companies to keep paying the same amount per year or slightly more each year as a dividend—buybacks aren't, giving companies more flexibility.

> **Dividend yields or coupon payments**
>
> Some critics argue that using dividends to generate passive income is unwise, preferring fixed-income assets, such as bonds, as a more reliable source of income.
>
> Many investors are unaware that the amount paid per share to shareholders is also deducted from the share price. If you own 10 shares of Apple and receive $0.251 per share in a quarterly payment, you'll receive $2.51 in cash, excluding taxes. At the same time, the share price decreases by $0.251 on the payment date. This calculation makes dividend payments appear to be a zero-sum game compared to bond coupon payments, where the amount received is guaranteed. If you receive 5% interest on bonds, the value of your bond position isn't affected.
>
> Taxation can even result in *theoretical losses* when dividends are paid. For instance, nonresident aliens may be subject to a withholding tax of up to 30% on dividends from US companies. Based on the numbers just given, when the dividend is paid, the Apple share price would drop by $0.251. An investor subject to a 30% withholding tax would lose $0.753 that day. This example highlights the importance of consulting a tax advisor to understand how taxes can affect your investment returns.

## 2.4.7 Ownership

A company's ownership structure isn't static and provides key insights into its valuation. The total number of a company's shares held by all of its shareholders is known as its outstanding shares. A related metric, the *float*, refines this number by excluding shares held by insiders and large institutions, representing the shares available for public trading.

Just as a central bank can influence a currency's value by adjusting the money supply, a public company can alter its share value by changing the number of outstanding shares. Following are two ways this is done:

- *Issuing new shares*—When a company issues additional stock, it increases the total supply, thereby diluting the ownership stake of existing shareholders.
- *Repurchasing shares (buybacks)*—Conversely, when a company repurchases its stock, it reduces the number of outstanding shares, thereby concentrating ownership and potentially increasing the value of the remaining shares.

Monitoring these changes is crucial for understanding the dynamics of a company's equity.

Analyzing the trading activity of a company's executives, often referred to as *insider transactions*, can provide valuable insights into their confidence in the business. It's crucial to monitor whether key figures are buying or selling their own company's shares.

Table 2.11, for example, details this activity for NVIDIA. The data indicates that over the past six months, more insiders have sold shares than have purchased them.

Table 2.11 Looking at insider trading

| Insider purchases last 6 months | Shares | Transactions |
|---|---|---|
| Purchases | 3,914,505.0 | 17 |
| Sales | 2,564,508.0 | 14 |
| Net shares purchases (sold) | 1,349,997.0 | 31 |
| Total insider shares held | 1,057,007,872.0 | <NA> |
| % net shares purchases (sold) | 0.001 | <NA> |
| % buy shares | 0.004 | <NA> |
| % sell shares | 0.002 | <NA> |

Data from the yfinance library on June 8, 2025

As of this writing, NVIDIA's stock rally is a well-known success story. This success can explain why many NVIDIA employees might have sold stocks. It might have been just an opportunity to reap some benefits of success, knowing that the share price might decrease. If more insiders sell shares than buy them, it can be a warning, but it's not yet a single indicator of a problem.

> **Stock-based compensation and dilution**
>
> Many developers have received stock-based compensation (SBC) as part of their overall package. This incentive allows companies, especially tech firms and start-ups, to attract and retain talent and keep salary payments lower while reducing the *burn rate*, which indicates how fast an unprofitable company consumes its cash reserves.
>
> While SBC can be a wealth-building tool for employees, it can be a source of dilution as it increases the number of outstanding shares over time. More shares mean that each existing share represents a smaller slice of the company.
>
> The smaller the company, the more effect an SBC has. In chapter 12, we'll examine private equity and start-ups because everyone investing in start-ups must be aware of the effect of SBC.

### 2.4.8 Sustainability

Some investors think beyond potential profits and aim to back companies with solid social responsibility. Many ethically motivated investors exclude companies with poor environmental, social, and governance (ESG) ratings, as investing in a company can also be seen as supporting its practices.

Sustainability data, such as that available on Yahoo Finance, enables this analysis. These datasets include various metrics, such as flags indicating a company's involvement in controversial industries, including gambling, animal testing, or tobacco. They also provide detailed scores across different ESG categories, which are typically rated on a scale of 0 to 100, where a lower score indicates better performance.

Table 2.12 shows these ESG ratings for NVIDIA. A key analytical step is to compare a company to its peers. In this case, the data reveals that NVIDIA's ESG performance is better than the average for its peer group (other semiconductor companies), as shown by its lower overall score.

Table 2.12  Selected sustainability ratings of NVIDIA

| Sustainability metrics | esgScores |
| --- | --- |
| totalEsg | 12.46 |
| environmentScore | 2.73 |
| socialScore | 4.08 |
| governanceScore | 5.65 |
| peerEsgScorePerformance | min: 8.87, avg: 23.06, max: 40.69 |
| peerGovernancePerformance | min: 2.14, avg: 5.32, max: 9.27 |
| peerSocialPerformance | min: 2.41, avg: 5.80, max: 10.28 |
| peerEnvironmentPerformance | min: 2.6, avg: 7.89, max: 16.95 |

Data collected from yfinance on June 8, 2025. Each score (E, S, G) is based on a rating from 0 to 100. The total ESG score is the sum of all individual scores.

We can also compare NVIDIA's score with that of other companies on platforms like Sustainalytics (www.sustainalytics.com/esg-ratings). Investors who care about sustainability can also review the ESG reports that companies regularly publish (https://mng.bz/Dwag). In these pages and reports, companies periodically share their views on ESG topics and how they address them.

## 2.5 *External assessments*

Investment firms, such as Goldman Sachs, Morgan Stanley, and JPMorgan Chase, exist because they can generate profits with the money of other people. Their analysts may incorporate many of the discussed ratios into algorithms to assess companies. Programmers may notice a slight resemblance to open source at large software companies when these investment firms share some of their insights with the public. They benefit when some of their work is publicly available, allowing them to upsell more professional services.

In this section, we examine some of the insights they offer us. In the next chapter, we'll also demonstrate how to collect this data using Python libraries. The following list compares ratings and estimated target prices, two parameters commonly used in investment analysis:

- *Ratings*—Analysts from reputable investment firms evaluate companies and assign ratings based on their potential for investment. A relatively new trend is crowdsourced financial analysis, in which any investor, including those with minimal experience, can share their investment ideas on a platform.
- *Estimated target prices*—Based on available financial data, some analysts even estimate target prices for individual companies after one year using statistical analysis and ML. However, as many future events are unforeseeable, these estimates are often highly inaccurate.

### 2.5.1 Ratings

Analysts give buy, hold, or sell recommendations to other investors. Table 2.13 shows a list of ratings, which can be found on the investment platform Seeking Alpha (https://seekingalpha.com/). This data was collected on June 8, 2025, and you can find updated information at the platform. This table shows aggregated ratings of the following:

- *SA Analyst Rating*—An aggregation of crowdsourced ratings by platform users
- *Wall Street Rating*—An aggregation of ratings by professional Wall Street analysts
- *Quant Rating*—A rating calculated by a Seeking Alpha algorithm

Table 2.13 Company ratings based on the Seeking Alpha platform

| Company | SA analyst rating | Wall Street rating | Quant rating |
|---|---|---|---|
| NVIDIA (NVDA) | 3.83 | 4.56 | 3.38 |
| Pfizer (PFE) | 3.18 | 3.56 | 3.40 |
| Aeva Technologies (AEVA) | 2.50 | 4.40 | 4.99 |
| Innoviz (INVZ) | — | 4.25 | 3.35 |
| Ouster (OUST) | 3.33 | 5.00 | 4.50 |
| Luminar Technologies (LAZR) | 3.25 | 2.75 | 2.63 |
| Sumitomo Mitsui Financial Group (SMR) | 2.60 | 4.00 | 3.47 |

For the latest numbers, go to https://seekingalpha.com/.

The analysis of Wall Street analysts can also be queried using Python, which is a topic covered in the next chapter. Table 2.14 presents the results of data collection for NVIDIA on June 8, 2025.

**Table 2.14  Ratings for NVIDIA**

| Period | Strong buy | Buy | Hold | Sell | Strong sell |
|---|---|---|---|---|---|
| 0m | 12 | 45 | 6 | 1 | 0 |
| −1m | 12 | 44 | 6 | 1 | 0 |
| −2m | 12 | 44 | 7 | 1 | 0 |
| −3m | 11 | 27 | 5 | 0 | 0 |

Data taken from the yfinance library on June 8, 2025

The result shows that the ratings decreased over time. Some investors will explore why analysts are gradually losing confidence. Still, the rating overall is excellent and could convince some investors to buy shares.

### 2.5.2 Target prices

Table 2.15 also provides 12-month analyst price targets, which are estimates of a stock's future value. The data for Apple, for example, reflects an average high target of $300 and a low of $164. Analysts typically derive these figures using fundamental analysis, such as DCF models discussed earlier, although their specific methods are often proprietary.

However, investors must approach these targets with caution. Price targets are estimates, not guarantees, and they inherently assume stable market conditions while failing to account for unpredictable events. As history has repeatedly shown, even the most astute analysts can be wrong. In the next chapter, we'll demonstrate how to collect this type of data programmatically using Python.

**Table 2.15  Target prices of selected companies**

| Company | Price ($) | Mean price ($) | Median price ($) | High price ($) | Low price ($) | Recommended mean | Recommended key | No. of analysts |
|---|---|---|---|---|---|---|---|---|
| Apple (AAPL) | 203.92 | 228.85 | 232.5 | 300.0 | 170.62 | 2.1 | Buy | 40 |
| Microsoft (MSFT) | 470.38 | 509.11 | 500.0 | 650.0 | 429.86 | 1.4 | Strong buy | 50 |
| NVIDIA (NVDA) | 141.72 | 172.02 | 175.0 | 220.0 | 100.0 | 1.44 | Strong buy | 55 |
| Salesforce (CRM) | 274.51 | 354.25 | 360.0 | 442.0 | 225.0 | 1.7 | Buy | 52 |

Data taken from the yfinance library on June 8, 2025

## 2.5 External assessments

Analyst ratings are provided by reputable firms, including Goldman Sachs, Morgan Stanley, and JPMorgan Chase.

While target prices are useful, studying the history of rating changes can be even more insightful for understanding the evolution of market sentiment. Table 2.16 shows an excerpt of this data for NVIDIA, transcribed from Yahoo Finance on June 8, 2025.

Table 2.16  Upgrades and downgrades of ratings of NVIDIA

| Action | Analyst: rating | Date |
| --- | --- | --- |
| Maintains | Truist Securities: Buy to Buy | 5/29/2025 |
| Maintains | Raymond James: Strong Buy to Strong Buy | 5/29/2025 |
| Maintains | Piper Sandler: Overweight to Overweight | 5/29/2025 |
| Maintains | Mizuho: Outperform to Outperform | 5/29/2025 |

Data from June 8, 2025. Updated data is available at https://finance.yahoo.com/quote/NVDA/analysis.

Should we trust the judgment of professional analysts for our decision-making? Critics view the favorable ratings of junk bonds by investment firms in 2007 as a crucial root cause of the mortgage crisis. US taxpayers will also remember who had to bail out large investment firms after it was revealed they had been wrong in their assessments. There's no silver bullet to get guaranteed high returns. Financial investment can be challenging for people who prefer to think in binary terms, such as right and wrong, or good and evil. Instead, good investors believe in probabilities.

> **Treating statements of experts as opinions, not as predictions**
>
> At the beginning of 2024, influential newspapers, such as *The Economist*, predicted that stock prices would decline that year (https://mng.bz/YZnQ). However, looking at the share prices of some companies, the opposite happened.
>
> Even with all the data in the world, no analyst can predict the future, a fact best illustrated by the recent history of high-growth stocks. Many investors deemed companies such as Tesla, NVIDIA, and Palantir to be overvalued and ripe for a major correction. Yet, instead of crashing, their share prices often defied these predictions, either continuing their ascent or entering a prolonged period of consolidation.
>
> This highlights a fundamental principle of investing: success isn't about being right every time, but about being right more often than wrong. Because certainty is impossible, investors rely on diversification to manage probabilities and build a portfolio that can thrive despite inevitable prediction errors.

## Summary

- The three accounting documents (income statement, balance sheet, and free cash flow [FCF]) follow accounting standards that help us compare companies.
- Industry classification standards group companies into different sectors (higher granularity) and industries (lower granularity) to facilitate classification and identify peers among companies.
- Investors may interpret ratios differently depending on the company's sector and industry. They often select ratios for their assessment based on their industry knowledge.
- While it's possible to compare companies across different industries, we obtain the most reliable results through comparisons of companies within the same industry.
- Some metrics help us determine a company's status independently of its industry, especially those related to solvency, as the question of whether a company can pay its bills is a universal concern for all companies.
- Income statements provide insight into what companies earn during a period.
- The balance sheet provides insight into a company's assets and liabilities. We can calculate shareholder equity by subtracting the total liabilities from the total assets.
- A FCF statement provides insight into a company's liquidity and is often the basis for calculating liquidity ratios.
- Liquidity ratios are calculated mainly from the cash flow statement and reflect a company's ability to pay bills with its assets. As some assets aren't liquid, some companies may have a positive balance sheet but still be unable to pay their bills.
- Debt ratios provide insight into a company's leverage by comparing its debt and assets. In some extreme cases, these ratios may indicate a pending bankruptcy.
- Earnings ratios measure the company's profits per share, and we can use them in various ratio calculations, such as the price-to-earnings (P/E) ratio.
- Profitability ratios assess a business's ability to generate earnings relative to its revenue, operating costs, balance sheet assets, or shareholders' equity over time.
- Dividend ratios indicate a company's commitment to return money to its shareholders in small amounts over various periods.
- Ownership metrics examine changes in a company's ownership, including insider trading, and can be informative for valuing the company.
- Sustainability metrics evaluate a company's commitment to causes beyond profit-making, encompassing environmental, social, and governance (ESG) considerations.
- We can collect analyst recommendations. However, following the recommendations of third parties without due diligence is a risky approach.

- Ratings are scorecards given by outside organizations to companies. They indicate the potential risks and gains of investing in those companies. Ratings might contradict each other and don't guarantee that the companies' share prices will rise or fall.
- Target prices are forecasts provided by accredited financial analysts of potential stock prices. These estimates are highly speculative.

# Collecting data

**This chapter covers**
- Data collection from financial platforms
- The types of data used for financial assessments
- Selecting Python libraries for financial analysis
- Comparing free Python libraries and commercial libraries
- Fundamental and technical analysis using Python

Chapter 2 focused on *what* we can analyze to make sound investment decisions. With that knowledge, it's time to show *how* to collect and explore data. Some data analysts claim that financial data is cleaner than data from other domains. Still, even with superb data, we need to invest time in preparing it for analytical algorithms and determining how to extract insights most efficiently.

This chapter teaches you how to gather financial data using Python. We'll focus on yfinance, a powerful open source library for scraping data from sources such as Yahoo Finance, Google Finance, and Finviz.

While yfinance is excellent for our initial data exploration, we'll also discuss its limitations and explore more robust, production-ready alternatives. All the libraries we cover are either free or offer a freemium model.

We'll start by examining the unique characteristics of financial data. Then, you'll learn to use these Python libraries to collect it. With this knowledge, you'll be ready for the first use case in chapter 4.

## 3.1 Financial data

Many data projects, independent of a specific domain, often raise data quality issues, making it difficult to predict whether the provided facts and numbers lead to insights that enable better investment decisions. One advantage of financial data is that it's regularly audited, and financial statements are required to meet predefined accounting standards. Whether data analysts receive data from free or paid sources, the information in the data represents the information that a company's accountants have officially reported.

This high-quality data is unavailable to analysts working with data in other fields. Data scientists working with machine data from factories are more likely to face issues where defective sensors can mismeasure data or multiple unforeseen environmental conditions might affect results.

Still, people working with financial data may face different challenges in interpreting data. The purpose of the obligatory accounting statements is to provide insights about a company's economic situation. However, different accounting strategies may conceal corporate problems or exaggerate profits. How accountants present numbers in detail can lead to varying interpretations of a company's results.

But before we collect the data, let's try to classify it first. To analyze financial assets, we can divide the data into three categories:

- *Fundamental data*—Fundamental data doesn't change regularly within short time frames. Consider regularly published quarterly financial documents, such as income statements, balance sheets, or cash flow statements. They are updated in intervals, such as with quarterly reports. We expect public companies to follow accounting standards, as their reports may be subject to audit. However, the reported data may still contain accounting tricks that make a company's balance sheet appear more favorable.

- *Technical data*—As a prominent example of technical data, share prices of company stocks change continuously during the open hours of stock exchanges. Many traders try to predict trends from these price movements. As many people depend on this data to earn money as day traders, we can also assume that the data is usually reported correctly. While data delivery speed isn't crucial for fundamental data, traders who focus on making decisions based on technical data may benefit from receiving data more quickly and executing orders faster. Besides historical share prices of companies, examples of other technical data are trading volume and short interest rates.

- *Nonfinancial data*—In the 2010s, big data became a buzzword for all data sources—primarily in unstructured form—that store information that can be mined to find hidden insights. We can analyze data from social media to determine the frequency of mentions of a stock ticker and to identify whether the conversations tend to be positive or negative. Machine learning (ML) engineers may use algorithms to analyze executives' emotions when presenting their company's earnings reports to detect potential discrepancies in their statements.

> **NOTE** AI algorithms that analyze human emotions in video and audio streams demonstrate a potential future for investment analysis. For instance, by processing footage of a company's general assembly, these AI tools could detect whether employee morale is more positive or negative than anticipated. Most people will likely agree that this also raises ethical questions.

Fundamental, technical, and nonfinancial data differ fundamentally (no pun intended). While fundamental analysis is primarily based on comparing financial data between companies within an industry to identify good investment opportunities, technical analysis is used to make quick trading decisions that benefit from bullish or bearish market trends. The next step is to look at the origins of the data.

---

**All roads lead to Rome**

This chapter introduces many platforms and libraries, although they solve the same generic problems (providing financial information and interpretations to allow clients to make better investment decisions). It's fair to ask whether focusing only on one library is sufficient.

Different open source and commercial platforms may offer varying quality standards and perspectives on financial data. One framework might meet the demands of one group of users, but another framework better suits the needs of others. Investment decisions can significantly affect our lives; the more diverse sources we have backing our decision-making, the lower the risk we face.

---

Before we process data with Python, let's explore some financial platforms that provide data through a user interface (UI). Although we could load everything into Python data structures right away, it often helps to use these platforms to preselect what to explore in depth.

## 3.2 Financial analysis platforms

Many financial analysis platforms help investors make better decisions by providing insights into various assets. The scope of these platforms can differ significantly: some focus on a single asset class, such as stocks or cryptocurrencies, while others limit their coverage to specific geographic regions.

> **NOTE** We'll focus on stocks in this chapter and address bonds and crypto in later chapters.

According to various sources, globally, there are between 47,000 and 58,000 publicly listed companies. Given this vast universe, one of the primary functions of financial platforms is to help users narrow down choices efficiently. This is where stock screeners come in. A *stock screener* is a tool that allows investors to filter listed stocks based on customizable criteria and displays relevant information onscreen to support informed decision-making.

Imagine you're an investor with a strong understanding of software companies. While you already hold many US stocks, you're considering diversifying internationally. To reduce risk, you focus on companies that are "too big to fail"—industry giants with massive market capitalizations. Your strategy is to identify potential candidates and then conduct a more in-depth analysis of their software offerings and market opportunities.

Many financial analysis platforms offer screeners that allow investors to filter stocks based on specific criteria. While these tools often share similar features, investors typically choose based on personal preferences. In this book, we demonstrate how to create a preselection using the Finviz platform (https://finviz.com).

In the example shown in figure 3.1, we screen for technology companies outside the United States with a market capitalization of more than $200 billion, matching the "mega-cap" category. You can access this filter directly at https://mng.bz/0zJW. The results may vary slightly from those captured in the screenshot on June 16, 2025.

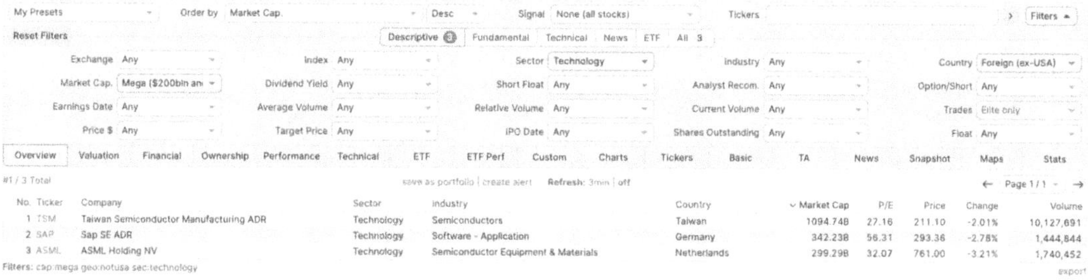

Figure 3.1 Finviz (https://finviz.com) is one of many financial services platforms that offer a stock screener to help users find companies through various filters. In this screenshot, we selected non-US technology companies with a market capitalization of more than $200 billion and received three results.

As shown in the figure, stock screeners allow users to filter by various criteria, functioning like data mining tools. Investors can drill down into individual companies to explore detailed information. For example, clicking on the link for SAP provides access to the company's key financials and other relevant data. Figure 3.2 shows SAP's fundamentals, illustrating just one example of what can be uncovered during the screening process. Of course, the level of detail and presentation varies across different financial platforms.

A stock screener is like a landing zone or home base for investors. When individual investors seek specific information about stocks, the platform might offer advisory services or a more refined analysis as a paid subscription feature. Table 3.1 categorizes financial platforms.

Peers MSFT AMZN ORCL CRM IBM NOW ADBE CSCO INTU WDAY Held by EAGL BAI SKYY AVDE APIE IDVO FFLC FTHI FBCG DFIC Scroll to Statements

| | | | | | | | | | | | |
|---|---|---|---|---|---|---|---|---|---|---|---|
| Index | - | P/E | 56.31 | EPS (ttm) | 5.21 | Insider Own | 0.01% | Shs Outstand | 1.17B | Perf Week | -5.31% |
| Market Cap | 342.23B | Forward P/E | 35.65 | EPS next Y | 8.23 | Insider Trans | 0.00% | Shs Float | 1.17B | Perf Month | 1.70% |
| Income | 6.14B | PEG | 2.02 | EPS next Q | 1.65 | Inst Own | 6.28% | Short Float | 0.16% | Perf Quarter | 11.17% |
| Sales | 37.72B | P/S | 9.07 | EPS this Y | 49.26% | Inst Trans | 2.59% | Short Ratio | 1.33 | Perf Half Y | 16.72% |
| Book/sh | 42.33 | P/B | 6.93 | EPS next Y | 16.76% | ROA | 7.66% | Short Interest | 1.92M | Perf Year | 55.43% |
| Cash/sh | 12.02 | P/C | 24.40 | EPS next 5Y | 27.83% | ROE | 12.81% | 52W Range | 186.50 - 311.40 | Perf YTD | 19.15% |
| Dividend Est. | 2.69 (0.92%) | P/FCF | 60.54 | EPS past 5Y | -1.42% | ROIC | 10.85% | 52W High | -5.79% | Beta | 1.32 |
| Dividend TTM | 2.54 (0.87%) | Quick Ratio | 1.17 | Sales past 5Y | 3.69% | Gross Margin | 73.60% | 52W Low | 57.30% | ATR (14) | 5.65 |
| Dividend Ex-Date | May 13, 2025 | Current Ratio | 1.17 | EPS Y/Y TTM | 201.10% | Oper. Margin | 26.10% | RSI (14) | 45.01 | Volatility | 1.60% 1.27% |
| Employees | 109121 | Debt/Eq | 0.22 | Sales Y/Y TTM | 9.39% | Profit Margin | 16.29% | Recom | 1.43 | Target Price | 337.64 |
| Option/Short | Yes / Yes | LT Debt/Eq | 0.15 | EPS Q/Q | 306.69% | Payout | 65.77% | Rel Volume | 1.00 | Prev Close | 301.74 |
| Sales Surprise | 2.35% | EPS Surprise | 11.69% | Sales Q/Q | 8.69% | Earnings | Apr 22 AMC | Avg Volume | 1.45M | Price | 293.36 |
| SMA20 | -2.71% | SMA50 | 2.73% | SMA200 | 13.48% | Trades | | Volume | 1,444,844 | Change | -2.78% |

**Figure 3.2 Looking at the fundamental data of SAP on Finviz**

**Table 3.1 Categorization of financial platforms for developers**

| Platform category | Examples | Summary |
|---|---|---|
| Finance pages of a search engine provider | Yahoo Finance, Google Finance, or MSN Money | They provide financial data and insights without asking users to pay for a subscription (except for Yahoo Finance, which offers a premium subscription).<br>In many cases, open source developers create libraries to scrape data from the platforms to provide that data to programmers. The yfinance library is a good example of such a library. |
| Financial advisory platform for private investors | Seeking Alpha, The Motley Fool, Morningstar, Ziggma, Zacks, Koyfin, Stock Rover, Empower, Simply Wall St, TipRanks | They provide insights about financial assets on a tiered subscription model.<br>With yearly subscription packages, typically ranging from $10 to $350 for standard plans, you gain access to more in-depth insights.<br>Only a few advisory platforms provide an API to programmers. |
| Financial data providers for fintech start-ups | EODHD, Alpha Vantage, OpenBB | They provide financial data through APIs. Most of them also offer a freemium version, providing limited access to economic data.<br>Prices for commercial packages, which include more data, more requests, and faster access, vary but are often in the range of $240 to $1,200 per year. |
| Commercial products for large investment firms | Bloomberg Terminal, Refinitiv, MSCI | These products normally exceed the budget of individual investors. They provide an immense amount of data and insights for analysts and fund managers. |

We could use libraries for web scraping and collect financial information from these platforms if they don't offer an API. However, using a web scraper means cleaning data and facing the risk of unpredictable errors, so we want to load the data into our environment using an API. Before doing that, we should address some basics about how we want to process financial data.

## 3.3 Data science notebooks

Pythonistas and data scientists have worked with Jupyter, Databricks, and similar platforms that provide notebooks to users. A *notebook* is an environment where you can run code in single cells and use the results from those cells in other cells, providing an interactive environment for engineers.

The appendix includes a section explaining how to install the relevant tools necessary for working with data, including Python libraries. However, addressing "application versus notebook" in advance makes sense. Many software engineers may consider themselves app-centric. If they know they can collect and process data, they might also be tempted to build a UI to display everything to users. In a later chapter, we demonstrate how to do this using Streamlit; however, this is often not the primary approach to exploring financial data for personal investment decisions.

For personal financial research, creating frontends might be an unnecessary overhead. Each investment assessment is a unique research project that may require research in different data sources. As the goal of a personal investment decision is to buy, sell, or hold based on data, numbers in a console are good enough. All programmers might need are data science notebooks, in which they can write down an investment hypothesis and start exploring data to prove or disprove their theses. Occasionally, they might rerun some cells with different data, or they might copy and adjust them for alternative analyses.

In this chapter, we'll introduce libraries and code snippets to analyze some core investment aspects of companies. In chapter 4, we'll continue to apply this knowledge to identify concrete investment opportunities. Until then, become familiar with the development environment of your choice and become accustomed to working with data science notebooks. The code presented in this chapter can also be found in the book's downloads and the Git repository.

## 3.4 yfinance

Pick a random book covering financial data exploration with Python or look for relevant code snippets online, and, most likely, you'll find code that collects data through the yfinance library. This library is the perfect starting point for exploring financial data by experimentation.

The yfinance library enables developers to load a wide range of data from the Yahoo Finance platform into Python data structures, making yfinance the best choice for programmers getting started with exploring financial data. We can use yfinance for technical and fundamental analysis.

> **NOTE** As you know, a stock ticker is a unique company identifier on a stock exchange. In chapter 2, for example, you saw NVDA for Nvidia, AAPL for Apple, and so on. For international exchanges, platforms add an acronym for the stock exchange. So, if we use Yahoo Finance, we find Rolls-Royce listed as RR.L on the London Stock Exchange (LSE), or Allianz SE as ALV.DE on the

Frankfurt Stock Exchange. We need to watch out for mismatches, as there is, for instance, a ticker ALV registered on the New York Stock Exchange (NYSE). Unfortunately, the acronyms to identify stock exchanges may differ between APIs. We'll show in a later example that another library, EODHD, uses the logical LSE as an identifier for the London Stock Exchange.

### 3.4.1 Fundamental analysis

Programmers can retrieve a company's accounting data, introduced in chapter 2, using yfinance and the code snippets shown here. This DataFrame contains all the information a company provides when reporting this data, such as aggregated sales figures over time. In this example, we used Microsoft (MSFT is Microsoft's stock ticker, a unique identifier for the company on the NASDAQ stock exchange, where Microsoft is listed):

```
import yfinance as yf
microsoft = yf.Ticker('MSFT')
microsoft.income_stmt
microsoft.balance_sheet
microsoft.cash_flow
```

For each of the fetched properties of the `microsoft` object, the returned object is a DataFrame representing an accounting statement with the reporting dates as columns and the metric for each report as a row. Table 3.2 shows the output of the DataFrame returned by the property `income_stmt`. The properties `balance_sheet` and `cash_flow` would return data in the same data structure, but with different values representing the accounting statements.

Table 3.2  Microsoft's income statement in a DataFrame

|  | 2024-06-30 | 2023-06-30 | 2022-06-30 | 2021-06-30 |
|---|---|---|---|---|
| Tax effect of unusual items | -99918000.0 | -2850000.0 | 43754000.0 | 180160797.164637 |
| Tax rate for calcs | 0.182 | 0.19 | 0.131 | 0.138266 |
| Normalized EBITDA | 133558000000.0 | 105155000000.0 | 99905000000.0 | 83031000000.0 |
| Total unusual item | -549000000.0 | -15000000.0 | 334000000.0 | 1303000000.0 |
| Total unusual item excluding goodwill | -549000000.0 | -15000000.0 | 334000000.0 | 1303000000.0 |
| Net income from continuing operational net | 88136000000.0 | 72361000000.0 | 72738000000.0 | 61271000000.0 |

**Table 3.2** Microsoft's income statement in a DataFrame *(continued)*

|  | 2024-06-30 | 2023-06-30 | 2022-06-30 | 2021-06-30 |
|---|---|---|---|---|
| Reconciled depreciation | 22287000000.0 | 13861000000.0 | 14461000000.0 | 11686000000.0 |
| Reconciled cost of revenue | 74114000000.0 | 65863000000.0 | 62650000000.0 | 52232000000.0 |
| EBITDA | 133009000000.0 | 105140000000.0 | 100239000000.0 | 85134000000.0 |
| EBIT | 110722000000.0 | 91279000000.0 | 85779000000.0 | 73448000000.0 |

Source: yfinance

We can access the specific information in financial account statements by referring to the data and the specific identifier of the information we're looking for, as shown in the following:

```
microsoft.income_stmt["2024-06-30"]["EBITDA"]
```

Users who explore the content of an object's attribute can iterate through columns representing report filing dates. Programmers interested in the quarterly results of the three account statements can also use the same approach by calling an attribute with the identifier `quarterly_` followed by the identifier of the accounting statement, as shown here:

```
microsoft.quarterly_income_stmt
microsoft.quarterly_balance_sheet
microsoft.quarterly_cash_flow
```

In chapter 2, we introduced several financial ratios. Collecting financial ratios of companies with Python is easy, as most ratios can be obtained through attributes from simple objects populated using the yfinance functionality. We continue with the object `microsoft`. The `microsoft.info` property is an object of the type dictionary. Converting it into a Pandas Series allows us to access the information referenced by the dictionary's keys as attributes of the newly generated object:

```
import pandas as pd
info = pd.Series(microsoft.info)
```

This `info` object contains numerous attributes related to corporate information, including headquarters address and financial ratios, such as the P/E value. When writing this book, the library offered 132 attributes to explore. The following code returns the details of what can be queried:

```
print(', '.join(info.keys()))
```

Accessing that one attribute is a one-liner. Next, we collect Microsoft's current share price:

```
info.currentPrice
```

We define a small helper function to collect the company's ratios. The following snippet returns a DataFrame containing a list of ratios we pass as identifiers:

```
import pandas as pd
import yfinance as yf

def collect_ratios(tickers: list, ratios: list):
    rows = []

    for ticker in tickers:
        info = yf.Ticker(ticker).info
        row = [ticker] + [info.get(ratio, None) for ratio in ratios]
        rows.append(row)

    return pd.DataFrame(rows, columns=["Ticker"] + ratios)
```

In chapter 2, we presented various query results in tables. The `collect_ratios` method makes it easy to get multiple `ratios`. In the following code, we collect the current and quick ratios of four companies: Walmart (WMT), Altria (MO), NVIDIA (NVDA), and Salesforce (CRM). We also add the sector and industry to the output:

```
collect_ratios(["WMT", "MO", "NVDA", "CRM"], ["sector", "industry",
"currentRatio", "quickRatio"])
```

The output of these methods can be reviewed in chapter 2, as we've used this method to collect all the data for the ratios that have been introduced there. Using this method, we can collect more ratios and analysis using attributes, such as `debtToEquity`, `forwardPE`, `trailingPE`, `pegRatio`, `priceToSalesTrailing12Months`, `priceToBook`, `beta`, or `recommendations_summary`. The book contains a data science notebook called Ratios, which includes a set of reference commands to generate the results for the ratios shown in chapter 2. Feel free to explore them and choose companies that interest you.

It's time to discuss some ratios we introduced in chapter 2 that aren't provided as attributes. First, we need to collect a ticker. We'll also collect references to the latest accounting statements as they are returned to us, in a DataFrame where columns represent the reporting dates:

```
import yfinance as yf
company = yf.Ticker("MSFT")
col_latest_inc_stmt = company.income_stmt.columns[0]
col_latest_bs = company.balance_sheet.columns[0]
```

As shown in table 3.3, we can use code to collect the information. Note that we reference specific financial accounting documents at a particular date, and you may need to adjust the dates accordingly.

Table 3.3 How to collect specific ratios using the collected object and helper functions

| Ratio | Code |
|---|---|
| Return on assets | company.income_stmt[col_latest_inc_stmt]["Net Income"]/company.balance_sheet[col_latest_bs]["Total Assets"] * 100 |
| Return on equity | company.income_stmt[col_latest_inc_stmt]["Net Income"]/company.balance_sheet[col_latest_bs]["Stockholders Equity"] * 100 |
| Profit margin | company.income_stmt[col_latest_inc_stmt]["Net Income"]/company.income_stmt[col_latest_inc_stmt]["Total Revenue"] * 100 |
| Asset turnover ratio | company.income_stmt[col_latest_inc_stmt]["Total Revenue"]/company.balance_sheet[col_latest_bs]["Total Assets"] |
| Debt-to-equity | company.balance_sheet[col_latest_bs]['Total Debt']/company.balance_sheet[col_latest_bs] ['Stockholders Equity'] |

Another interesting fact is the development of ratios over time. Apple has a higher debt-to-equity (D/E) ratio than its peers, which is likely related to accounting practices. However, it could be a bad sign if the last value suddenly rises significantly. The following code indicates that this ratio fluctuates within years (in 2021, 2.16; in 2022, 2.61; in 2023, 1.78; and in 2024, 1.87), and we can conclude that this D/E ratio won't prevent us from making an investment decision:

```
company = yf.Ticker("AAPL")
for i in range(0,4):
    print(f"{company.balance_sheet.iloc[:,i].name}: {company.balance_sheet.iloc[:,i]['Total Debt']/company.balance_sheet.iloc[:,i]['Stockholders Equity']}")
```

### 3.4.2 Technical analysis

We can use yfinance to examine time series data. In the following example, we load Microsoft's historical stock data into a DataFrame for one year, as shown in table 3.4. In the following code, we load the data for one year by executing this query:

```
import yfinance as yf
historical_data = yf.Ticker("MSFT").history(start="2024-05-08", end="2025-05-08
historical_data
```

Table 3.4 Microsoft's historical price data showing open, high, low, and close prices, as well as trading volume

| Date | Open price ($) | High price ($) | Low price ($) | Close price ($) | Volume |
|---|---|---|---|---|---|
| 2025-05-07 00:00:00-04:00 | 433.05 | 437.32 | 430.32 | 432.56 | 23,295,300 |
| 2025-05-06 00:00:00-04:00 | 431.41 | 436.93 | 430.38 | 432.52 | 15,104,200 |
| 2025-05-05 00:00:00-04:00 | 432.08 | 438.69 | 431.32 | 435.37 | 20,136,100 |
| 2025-05-02 00:00:00-04:00 | 430.95 | 438.63 | 429.20 | 434.48 | 30,757,400 |
| 2025-05-01 00:00:00-04:00 | 430.32 | 436.19 | 424.12 | 424.62 | 58,938,100 |

Source: yfinance data from June 8, 2025

Occasionally, we prefer to have exact time intervals; in the following code, we show how to collect data for 2023. The source code output here would return the same data structure as in table 3.4, with different dates and values:

```
import yfinance as yf
hd_msft_2023 = yf.Ticker("MSFT").history(start="2023-01-01",
end="2023-12-31")
hd_msft_2023
```

The everyday use case uses technical data to explore how stock prices evolve: What is the spread between highs and lows, and how volatile is the stock? The more volatile the share price has been in the past, the higher the likelihood that it will continue to be erratic.

> **NOTE** Past performance doesn't guarantee future results. However, if you take several stocks with stable past performance and put them in a portfolio, you can absorb single stocks performing below expectations. Providing risk-optimized portfolios is often the domain of exchange-traded funds (ETFs).

In chapter 2, we concluded that the share prices of companies from the consumer staples sector, such as Coca-Cola, are likely more stable. This sector represents goods for everyday needs, but consumers will also purchase during crises. If we compare Coca-Cola with a start-up, we can see this difference in the numbers. Let's load the required data and compare Coca-Cola with NuScale (SMR), a company focusing on building small modular reactors. We also add Apple (AAPL) to the portfolio to diversify our baseline with a third company:

```
import yfinance as yf
hist_prices_2023 = yf.Tickers(["AAPL", "SMR", "KO"]).history
(start= "2023-01-01", end= "2023-12-31")
```

The share prices of different stocks don't give us a basis for comparing stocks. Company A might be traded at $1,000 per share, and Company B at $10. The price is just a number without the number of shares outstanding. Companies with high share prices often consider a share split to reduce the cost of purchasing a single share. If Company A decided to split the shares in a 1:10 ratio, and you held 1 share, after the split, you would have 10 shares of stock with a share price of $100. Therefore, we need to set a starting date for our comparison and assume the price of each company starts at 100%, from which we track the price changes in percentage terms.

NuScale's share price could have been better in 2023. We'll plot the share prices as a percentage over time to illustrate this. The following code extracts the closing prices and creates a DataFrame with the percentage changes for each ticker at the beginning of the period (you may need to install the Matplotlib library):

```
def plot_closing_prices(data):
    import matplotlib.pyplot as plt
    close_prices = data["Close"]
    price_change_in_percentage = (close_prices / close_prices.iloc[0] * 100)
    price_change_in_percentage.plot(figsize = (12,8), fontsize = 12)
    plt.ylabel("Percentage")
    plt.title(f"Price Chart", fontsize = 15)
    plt.show()
```

By calling this method with the DataFrame as a parameter, such as by `plot_closing_prices(hist_prices)`, we can generate a plot, as shown in figure 3.3.

Figure 3.3  **The share price development of Apple (AAPL), Coca-Cola (KO), and NuScale (SMR)**

If you looked purely at 2023, you might be tempted to say that it would be wise to invest in Apple and short sell NuScale. However, if you look at the results of 2024, in which the share price of NuScale soared, this would have been a disastrous decision. Figure 3.4 shows the results if we picked the stock starting from November 22 and one year back. We collect the data using the stock tickers as identifiers and then call the method to plot the graph:

```
import yfinance as yf
hd_nvda_smr_aapl_1yr = yf.Tickers(["AAPL", "SMR", "KO"]).history
(start= "2023-11-22", end= "2024-11-22")
plot_closing_prices(hd_nvda_smr_aapl_1yr)
```

Figure 3.4  The share price development of Apple (AAPL), Coca-Cola (KO) and NuScale (SMR) in 2024

In chapter 4, we'll explore more details on how to identify other companies, such as NuScale, that can grow stronger than the market. Let's begin by exploring the market returns. We have the closing price of a share and can compare it with the previous day's price. With that, we can calculate daily returns:

```
simple_returns = hist_prices_24 ["Close"].pct_change
(fill_method=None).dropna()
simple_returns
```

Returns calculated this way are called *simple returns*. A second method for calculating returns is using *logarithmic returns*. Instead of subtracting the end price from the starting price, we use log functions:

```
import numpy as np
log_rets = hist_prices_24["Close"].apply(lambda x: np.log(x /
x.shift())).dropna()
log_rets
```

Logarithmic returns have found broad application in calculating returns compared to simple returns, which we would obtain if we simply subtracted the previous day's closing price from the current day's closing price. Logarithmic returns differ in that they measure the continuous compounded rate of returns, which is more beneficial for statistical analysis. We can also plot the returns in a histogram to discover how often we had outliers (see figure 3.5 for the results):

```
log_rets_2023 = hist_prices_2023["Close"].apply(lambda x: np.log(x /
x.shift())).dropna()
log_rets_2023.hist(bins=35, figsize=(10, 6))
```

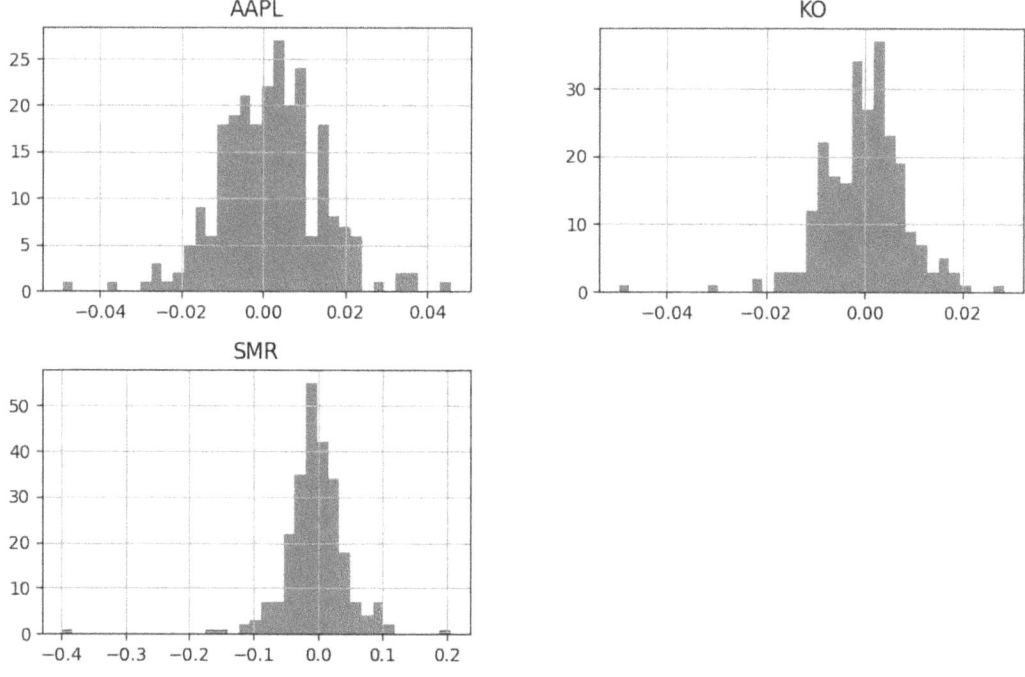

Figure 3.5 The histogram of the returns for Apple (AAPL), Coca-Cola (KO), and NuScale (SMR)

To finalize our primer on technical analysis, let's look at three standard metrics: mean, standard deviation, and variance. Again, we use a snippet here to visualize the differences between these statistical methods (see the results in table 3.5):

```
summary = log_rets_2023.agg(["mean", "std", "var"]).T
summary.columns = ["Mean", "Std", "Var"]
summary
```

Table 3.5  Statistics for Apple, Coca-Cola, and NuScale

| Company | mean | std | var |
|---|---|---|---|
| Coca-Cola | -0.035349 | 0.134959 | 0.018214 |
| Apple | 0.442217 | 0.199222 | 0.039690 |
| NuScale | -1.149094 | 0.799615 | 0.639385 |

Source: yfinance 2023 data

The *mean* is the average stock price over the given period, representing the "central" value of the dataset. *Variance* measures how far each price deviates from the mean in squared units. The *standard deviation* is the square root of the variance, bringing the measure back to the same units as the prices.

The data shows that NuScale exhibits significant fluctuations. However, someone who in 2023 made a short-term bet on Coca-Cola would have been disappointed as well. These metrics already give us an idea about the performance of stocks. In later chapters, we'll delve into more detail and demonstrate how to determine if stocks in a portfolio correlate.

### 3.4.3  Limitations of yfinance

Digging into the source code of the yfinance code on GitHub, we see that it uses web scraping frameworks, such as Beautiful Soup. On the landing page, the author introduces this library as a wrapper for Yahoo's internal API, highlighting that Yahoo doesn't maintain the yfinance library. For developers who rely on getting valid results, this scenario poses a risk. Yahoo is unlikely to inform the maintainers of an open source product that scrapes its data about upcoming changes. In the worst case, Yahoo might even decide, at some point, to implement anti-scraping methods to restrict access to its financial data at any time.

As shown in figure 3.6, sustainability data wasn't supported with a version of yfinance in the middle of 2024. Programmers who wanted to incorporate sustainability data into their analysis would have to use a different library.

The good news is that with the latest version of yfinance, this problem disappeared. Still, yfinance depends on Yahoo's benevolence, so it's essential to know alternative products.

```
[1]  1  import yfinance as yf
     2
     3  info = yf.Ticker("MSFT")
     4  info.sustainability
```
Executed at 2024.06.26 06:37:17 in 1s 34ms

> Traceback...
YFNotImplementedError: Have not implemented fetching 'sustainability' from Yahoo API

**Figure 3.6** Initial limitations of yfinance with sustainability data. Note that this problem is gone with newer versions.

## 3.5 Commercial libraries

For many personal investment assessments, yfinance is just fine. While commercial libraries primarily target companies seeking to develop their financial products, there are still compelling reasons for private investors to collaborate with these libraries.

The freemium model of commercial libraries encompasses certain aspects of analysis for personal use. If, for instance, the limitation of a free plan is that some data arrives delayed or you have a limited quota of API calls, you might still run some algorithms on stocks in your portfolio. In this book, we primarily use yfinance, but in some examples later, we'll use some of these commercial libraries in their freemium versions, where it makes sense.

> **NOTE** Commercial libraries require you to create API keys. In the appendix, we show a general approach to working with API keys.

Before we explore commercial libraries, let's see how the ideal data provision works. Scraping data from a UI, as in yfinance, adds risks and overhead. The moment the UI structure changes, we may need to adjust our code to scrape the platform. One risk that users of yfinance face is that Yahoo could change its policy to allow an open source library to scrape its data. While we can transition as private investors to a different library, some of us prefer not to make that effort and are ready to pay a small sum for a commercial product, especially if it helps us generate better returns.

The root for technical data is the exchange that lists the stocks we're interested in. As we have many exchanges, various entities provide data from different sources. Don't forget that we also have international exchanges, in addition to US exchanges, and collect data from all over the world. Each of these exchanges may provide different APIs and standards. We need to dedicate some effort to maintaining the data collection process if we aim to build a commercial library that provides data from all exchanges.

> **Financial providers and their data providers**
>
> Yahoo Finance statistics (https://mng.bz/z2Dg) confirm that Yahoo Finance uses data providers such as Refinitiv, Edgar Online, and Morningstar to collect information. The provider EODHD (https://eodhd.com/) claims in its FAQ that it collects data through direct contracts with various exchanges. They also collect fundamental data from financial news providers, corporate websites, and annual reports, with direct extraction from www.sec.gov for the US and www.sedarplus.ca/landingpage/ for Canada.

Fundamental data is extracted from accounting statements; the best source is to load data from those entities where the data is filed. This information should be available to the public anyway. Let's examine figure 3.7, which illustrates a reference process.

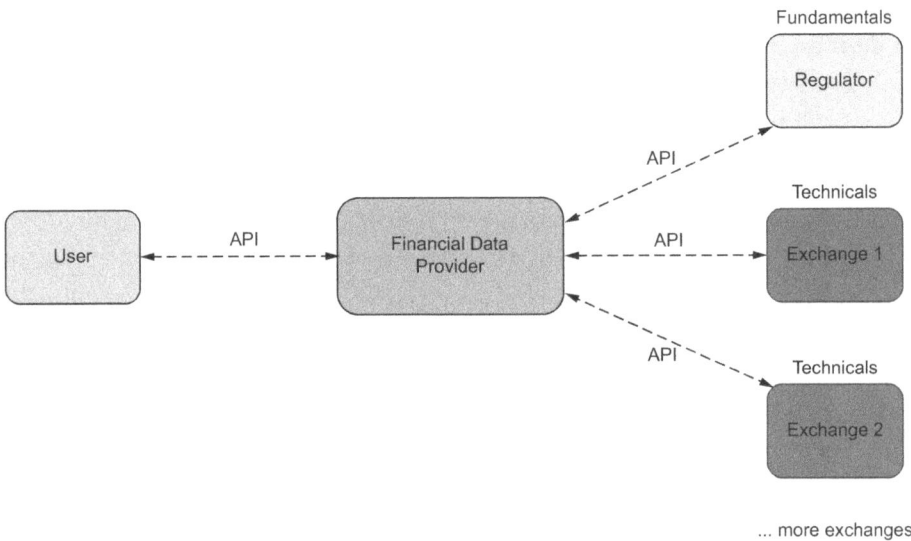

Figure 3.7 In a slightly simplified way, users can collect data from financial data providers, who collect technical data from one or more exchanges per country and one regulator per country.

Data providers collect data from exchanges and government agencies. While accounting statements are filed quarterly, share prices change frequently during an exchange's opening times, so data from exchanges is likely a streaming source.

> **NOTE** We can integrate generative AI (GenAI) platforms into our source code, submit prompts, and interpret results using frameworks such as LangChain. Large language models (LLMs) and AI agents will eventually transform the way we analyze investments. For now, being able to collect data to obtain reproducible results deterministically is a use case that GenAI hasn't yet replaced.

## 3.5 Commercial libraries

Many companies provide financial data to consumers. Some, such as Refinitiv and Morgan Stanley, are focused on business-to-business (B2B) companies. In this book, we focus on four providers that may be of interest to start-ups, as listed in table 3.6.

Table 3.6 APIs and their packages

| Platform | Packages |
| --- | --- |
| Finviz | Elite subscription costs $24.96 per month. |
| EODHD | Packages range from $0 to $199.00 per month. |
| Alpha Vantage | Packages range from $0 to $249.99 per month. |
| OpenBB | Pricing isn't disclosed. |

### 3.5.1 Finviz

Finviz is a popular financial platform best known for its feature-rich stock screener on the platform's webpage, as shown in figure 3.8. The major downside of this platform is that it only provides data for companies listed on US exchanges. Because Finviz is popular among investors and often featured in finance training videos, it still makes sense to introduce the API to users who plan to invest only in the United States and appreciate the stock screener's richness. However, we won't use this API for samples in the book.

Figure 3.8 Finviz stock screener home page showing various tickers

Finviz offers a paid subscription called Finviz Elite, which offers an API. You can set up an authentication token to parse the screener, as shown in figure 3.9.

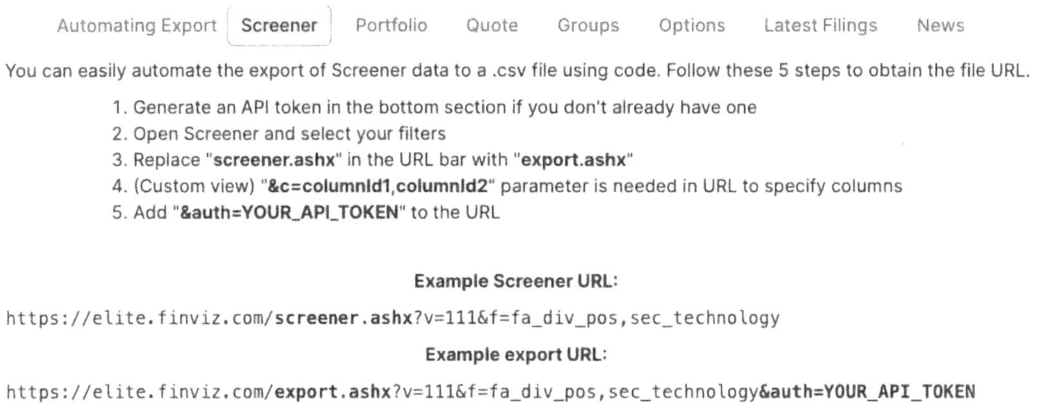

Automating Export | **Screener** | Portfolio | Quote | Groups | Options | Latest Filings | News

You can easily automate the export of Screener data to a .csv file using code. Follow these 5 steps to obtain the file URL.

1. Generate an API token in the bottom section if you don't already have one
2. Open Screener and select your filters
3. Replace "**screener.ashx**" in the URL bar with "**export.ashx**"
4. (Custom view) "**&c=columnId1,columnId2**" parameter is needed in URL to specify columns
5. Add "**&auth=YOUR_API_TOKEN**" to the URL

**Example Screener URL:**
https://elite.finviz.com/**screener.ashx**?v=111&f=fa_div_pos,sec_technology

**Example export URL:**
https://elite.finviz.com/**export.ashx**?v=111&f=fa_div_pos,sec_technology&**auth=YOUR_API_TOKEN**

**Figure 3.9** Finviz screen that explains how to use the API

After generating a token, we can access stock data. In this example, we can use the following code to access Finviz and export data to a CSV file. We use a REST API to collect information about the stock. It exports all data based on predefined filters, allowing us to collect fundamental data. Note that to execute the following code, you need to define a variable token that contains your access token. This token is required for multiple requests to collect data from Finviz:

```
import requests
URL = f"https://elite.finviz.com/export.ashx?[allYourFilters]&auth={token}"
response = requests.get(URL)
open("export.csv", "wb").write(response.content)
```

The commercial Finviz API also lets users collect data for the portfolios they create on the platform. Figure 3.10 shows a sample portfolio in Finviz. A portfolio is a list of stocks a user tracks to which they can add the number of shares they own. With that, you can quickly run a personalized portfolio analysis if you've already tracked your portfolio on Finviz.

A unique ID identifies every user portfolio. Using the paid Finviz API, users can collect data via the following URL by passing the portfolio ID as a variable:

```
https://elite.finviz.com/portfolio_export.ashx?
pid={pid}&o=price&auth={token}
```

Python Package Index (PyPI) lists alternative and free libraries that scrape Finviz data without using Finviz's paid service. These libraries follow the same strategy as yfinance: They scrape data from the web and return data in Pandas DataFrames. These

| | | | | | | | |
|---|---|---|---|---|---|---|---|
| Climate Change ▾ ⋮ | | | Open in Screener | Edit | Delete | Create New | Set Alerts |
| AAPL, MSFT, $CASH, ... **Add Tickers** | | | | | | | |
| ✓ Ticker | Company | Shares | Avg. Cost | Total Cost | Price | Change % | Volume |
| ✓ NKLA | Nikola Corp | | | | 9.37 | -10.94% | 4,088,967 |
| | Date Transaction | Shares | Cost / Share | Total Cost | | | |
| | 06-26-2024 Buy ▾ | | | Today's price | **Save** Cancel | | |
| METC | Ramaco Resources Inc | + Trade | | | 11.69 | -3.71% | 660,162 |
| MVST | Microvast Holdings Inc | + Trade | | | 0.47 | -0.67% | 2,754,764 |
| NEE | NextEra Energy Inc | + Trade | | | 72.98 | -1.18% | 11,011,132 |
| SMR | NuScale Power Corporation | + Trade | | | 10.97 | +9.48% | 8,701,581 |
| OXY | Occidental Petroleum Corp. | + Trade | | | 63.10 | -0.24% | 6,207,704 |
| | Summary: 6 Tickers / 0 Transactions | | | 0.00 | | 0.00% | |

Figure 3.10 Example portfolio with Finviz containing assets associated with climate change

libraries also share the same risks as yfinance. If the financial platform deploys anti-scraping methods, the libraries become unusable.

> **NOTE** Finviz users might observe that stocks of companies with a headquarters outside the United States are displayed, even though Finviz only supports US stock markets. For example, users may be able to explore a Danish company that produces weight loss drugs (Novo Nordisk), but they don't see a large windmill producer from Denmark (Ørsted A/S). The reason is American Depositary Receipts (ADRs), which mirror a stock from a foreign exchange to the US exchange. However, this vehicle has downsides, including dividend custody fees and other risks.

The paid Finviz API may be a suitable alternative for investors who primarily use US stock exchanges and want to avoid potential long-term risks associated with incompatibilities with open source libraries. Still, we must continue our search, as we need a library that covers a wide range of stock exchanges.

### 3.5.2 EODHD

Finviz and yfinance, the libraries we've explored so far, attract users with powerful UIs that provide stock screening functionality and add libraries to collect data as an additional feature. EODHD, in contrast, is a platform where data provision is the primary business model.

EODHD offers a freemium model that provides historical data from the previous year. It's limited to 20 API calls per day, which may be helpful to private investors who run analyses on their data infrequently. The paid subscription helps programmers build a product that expects many API calls from clients, as their pricing data includes features such as 100,000 API calls per day or 1,000 API requests per minute.

The first part of the following code is self-explanatory. We instantiate a client object using an API key as a parameter that identifies us:

```
from eodhd import APIClient
client = APIClient(api_key)
```

The platform then determines whether we're authorized to use specific features based on our subscription model (see the appendix for more information on API keys). The biggest challenge with the Finviz library is that it only supported US exchanges. Let's confirm that we aren't limited in such a way using EODHD. We run code to collect the number of exchanges and obtain 77 exchanges connected to this platform, as shown in table 3.7:

```
client.get_exchanges()
```

Table 3.7  A query that returns 77 possible exchanges for EODHD

|   | Name | Code | OperatingMIC | Country | Currency | CountryISO02 | CountryISO03 |
|---|------|------|--------------|---------|----------|--------------|--------------|
| 0 | USA Stocks | US | XNAS, XNYS, OTCM | US | USD | US | US |
| 1 | London Stock Exchange | LSE | XLON | UK | GBP | GB | GBR |
| 2 | Toronto Exchange | TO | XTSE | Canada | CAD | CA | CAN |
| 3 | TSX Venture Exchange | V | XTSX | Canada | CAD | CA | CAN |
| 4 | NEO Exchange | NEO | NEOE | Canada | CAD | CA | CAN |

Source: Data is from the DataFrame.

With 77 exchanges, we can build a product that caters to the international market. Let's load some historical data from Rolls-Royce on the LSE and display the results in table 3.8.

```
resp = client.get_eod_historical_stock_market_data(symbol = 'RR.LSE',
 period='d', from_date = '2024-06-01', to_date - '2024 06-17', order='a')
df = pd.DataFrame(resp)
df
```

Table 3.8  EODHD showing the data for Rolls-Royce

| Date | Open | High | Low | Close | Adjusted close | Volume |
|------|------|------|-----|-------|----------------|--------|
| 2024-06-03 | 459.30000000 | 468.10000000 | 458.60000000 | 460.90000000 | 460.90000000 | 51,917,078 |
| 2024-06-04 | 460.20000000 | 462.70000000 | 448.00000000 | 448.00000000 | 448.00000000 | 31,952,811 |

**Table 3.8  EODHD showing the data for Rolls-Royce** *(continued)*

| Date | Open | High | Low | Close | Adjusted close | Volume |
|---|---|---|---|---|---|---|
| 2024-06-05 | 450.70000000 | 458.00000000 | 448.80000000 | 453.30000000 | 453.30000000 | 19,116,760 |
| 2024-06-06 | 458.00000000 | 463.10000000 | 450.50000000 | 458.20000000 | 458.20000000 | 19,410,820 |
| 2024-06-07 | 458.20000000 | 462.30000000 | 451.00000000 | 456.90000000 | 456.90000000 | 15,420,780 |

Source: London Stock Exchange

Comparing the results of this DataFrame with the yfinance DataFrame reveals that both have a similar column structure. If we're willing to pay for EODHD as a data provider, we would eliminate these limitations and be able to switch from yfinance to EODHD without having to rewrite a lot of code, as the interfaces are similar.

### 3.5.3  Alpha Vantage

Like EODHD, Alpha Vantage's primary business model is to provide financial data via an API. The provider offers a free package and advanced services through a paid subscription.

Let's collect some time series data. In this example, we load data from Apple. As with EODHD, we need a key that authenticates us. We'll get access to more data if we upgrade our key with a paid subscription:

```
from alpha_vantage.timeseries import TimeSeries
import pandas as pd

symbol = 'AAPL'
ts = TimeSeries(key)
data, meta_data = ts.get_daily(symbol=symbol)
df = pd.DataFrame(data)
df
```

The result is again a DataFrame, as shown in table 3.9. However, the columns and rows are displayed transposed by default in EODHD and yfinance.

**Table 3.9  The results of querying data from Alpha Vantage (inverted compared to yfinance or EODHD)**

| Type | 2025-06-06 | 2025-06-05 | 2025-06-04 | 2025-06-03 | 2025-06-02 | 2025-05-30 | 2025-05-29 | 2025-05-28 |
|---|---|---|---|---|---|---|---|---|
| Open | 203.0000 | 203.5000 | 202.9100 | 201.3500 | 200.2800 | 199.3700 | 203.5750 | 200.5900 |
| High | 205.7000 | 204.7500 | 206.2400 | 203.7700 | 202.1300 | 201.9600 | 203.8100 | 202.7300 |
| Low | 202.0500 | 200.1500 | 202.1000 | 200.9550 | 200.1200 | 196.7800 | 198.5100 | 199.9000 |
| Close | 203.9200 | 200.6300 | 202.8200 | 203.2700 | 201.7000 | 200.8500 | 199.9500 | 200.4200 |
| Volume | 46,607,693 | 55,221,235 | 43,603,985 | 46,381,567 | 35,423,294 | 70,819,942 | 51,477,938 | 45,339,678 |

Source: yfinance

Luckily, transforming to the style of yfinance and EODHD requires only one command, `df.T`, and the results are shown in table 3.10.

Table 3.10 Data from Alpha Vantage after a transpose operation to match the structure of yfinance and EODHD

| Date | Open | High | Low | Close | Volume |
|---|---|---|---|---|---|
| 2025-06-06 | 203.0000 | 205.7000 | 202.0500 | 203.9200 | 46,607,693 |
| 2025-06-05 | 203.5000 | 203.5000 | 200.1500 | 200.6300 | 55,221,235 |
| 2025-06-04 | 202.9100 | 206.2400 | 202.1000 | 202.8200 | 43,603,985 |

Source: yfinance

There's one hidden limitation. Many platforms return two different datasets for the closing price: the adjusted close and the close price. The adjusted close price returns data is adjusted for stock splits and dividend payouts. The good news is that we can obtain the adjusted close price using an alternative method. However, this method is part of a premium service. Calling the following method without a subscription would only return a message that tells us to subscribe to a premium service:

```
data, meta_data = ts.get_daily_adjusted(symbol, outputsize='full')
```

The free package includes another feature that may be of interest to programmers. The following code collects news sentiments through the REST API from Alpha Vantage and stores them in a DataFrame. For this code example, we use the ticker SMR, which we used earlier to represent the stock of NuScale Power, a nuclear energy company that builds Small Modular Reactors (SMRs). Figure 3.11 shows the output of the following query:

```
import requests
import pandas as pd

ticker = 'SMR'
url = f'https://www.alphavantage.co/query?function=NEWS_SENTIMENT&tickers={ticker}&apikey={key}'
r = requests.get(url)
data = r.json()['feed']
df = pd.DataFrame.from_dict(data)
df
```

## 3.5 Commercial libraries

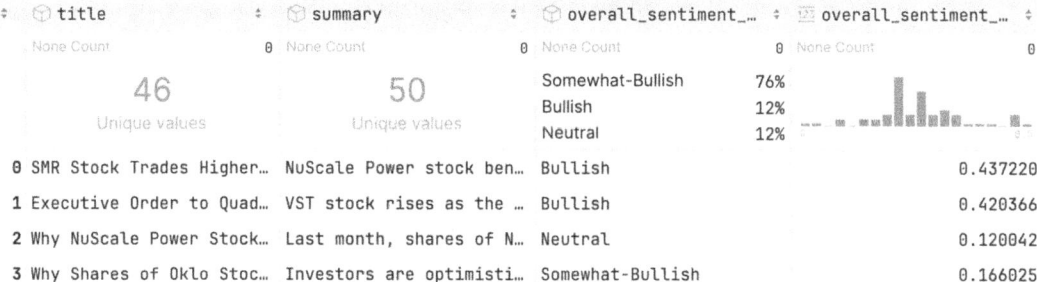

Figure 3.11  The sentiment analysis results for the nuclear energy company NuScale

### 3.5.4  OpenBB

OpenBB integrates various asset classes beyond stocks. However, first, let's demonstrate how to collect data using methods similar to those employed by other libraries. Using two lines, we collect technical data on a stock:

```
from openbb import obb
obb.equity.price.historical("NVDA").to_df().head()
```

As shown in table 3.11, our output is like that of other libraries that load technical data for stocks.

> **NOTE**  At the time of writing this book, the OpenBB library didn't yet support the latest available Python version (3.13). Users who want to explore this library can use Python version 3.12.

Table 3.11  Retrieving technical data through OpenBB

| Date | Open | High | Low | Close | Volume |
|---|---|---|---|---|---|
| 2023-06-26 | 42.460999 | 42.76400 | 40.099998 | 40.632000 | 594,322,000 |
| 2023-06-27 | 40.799000 | 41.93999 | 40.448002 | 41.875999 | 4,621,750,000 |
| 2023-06-28 | 40.660000 | 41.845001 | 40.518002 | 41.117001 | 582,639,000 |
| 2023-06-29 | 41.557999 | 41.599998 | 40.599998 | 40.821999 | 380,514,000 |
| 2023-06-30 | 41.680000 | 42.549999 | 41.500999 | 42.301998 | 501,148,000 |

Source: OpenBB

Let's focus on this API's differentiator. The following code shows how to integrate multiple data providers into this API. We can work with various providers in theory, which increases our possibilities by allowing us to switch from one provider to another without requiring any code changes:

```
obb.equity.price.historical("NVDA", provider="yfinance").to_df().head()
```

But this doesn't end here. So far, we've been focused on stock information, but as we learned in chapter 1, the financial universe consists of many assets. Let's look at the following self-explanatory snippets:

```
obb.currency.price.historical("USDGBP").to_df().head()
obb.fixedincome.government.treasury_rates(
start_date="2024-01-02").to_df().dropna()
obb.crypto.price.historical("SOLUSD").to_df().tail()
```

Using this library, we also get access to other assets. OpenBB might be the best library for programmers who want to explore markets other than stocks; they could choose this library.

## 3.6  Other libraries

The Awesome Quant GitHub page at https://github.com/wilsonfreitas/awesome-quant provides a comprehensive list of alternatives for collecting financial data. However, rewriting the code can be time-consuming if we choose libraries and later find out that they don't meet our expectations.

One parameter to see if the library meets today's standards is the day of its last update. The PyPi web page is a commonly used repository for Python libraries and provides this information. All we need to do is look at the library's page, as shown with yfinance here: https://pypi.org/project/yfinance/. We can see regular releases in the PyPI release History page.

Another source of information is a library's GitHub repository, where the library's source code is hosted. We can look for the dates of the most recent commits. Following is the link to the yfinance repository: https://github.com/ranaroussi/yfinance.

One rule of thumb is to use a library that has been updated within the past year. New Python versions are being released, and financial platforms are changing their interfaces. At some point, a library may become incompatible if nobody is left to maintain it. For that reason, we want libraries with multiple contributors. We should also compare libraries by the number of stars and forks and select more popular libraries, as this indicates a substantial likelihood of attracting new contributors.

We aim to filter the existing library repository to identify further possible limitations. Let's set some further criteria:

- Some libraries require system-specific software and may only support specific operating systems. We want libraries that run on most platforms.
- Some APIs are designed specifically for stock exchanges in a single country. We look for libraries that support as many stock exchanges as possible.
- Although English is the default language for most projects, we may encounter projects that use a different documentation language. We want to exclude these projects.

For this book, we'll focus as much as possible on yfinance. It's the best-known API for investment analysis, and you'll find tons of snippets and advice to extend the code you write.

## Summary

- We can categorize data into three groups: fundamental, technical, and nonfinancial.
- Data science notebooks are ideal for analyzing individual stocks, as their interactive nature allows you to explore data and discover insights rapidly.
- Fundamental analysis involves examining financial reports and ratios.
- Technical analysis involves analyzing asset prices to inform sound investment decisions.
- Nonfinancial analysis encompasses all data unrelated to technical and fundamental analysis and may, for instance, include sentiment analysis about a company.
- Different libraries offer different advantages and have other constraints. It's good to know more than one library to load financial data.
- yfinance is the best library for beginners experimenting with financial data because it's free and provides stock data from numerous exchanges (both US and non-US) for fundamental and technical analysis.
- Using the yfinance library for professional financial products is risky because Yahoo doesn't officially support it. Any changes to the Yahoo Finance platform can cause the library to break without warning.
- To build a commercial product using financial data, you need libraries that offer a paid subscription and provide service guarantees. EODHD, Finviz, Alpha Vantage, and OpenBB are candidates that could be explored further.
- Finviz provides an API on a paid subscription basis and supports only stocks listed on US exchanges. It can be a good option for investors who plan to invest only in the US market.
- EODHD is a commercial data provider that offers a free version with limited API calls, supporting many exchanges. If you have a limited number of daily calls, use the free EODHD version.
- Alpha Vantage is a commercial data provider with a limited free version. One challenge with the free API is that it doesn't provide adjusted close prices. Alpha Vantage allows you to collect news sentiments through its library, making it unique among similar libraries.
- OpenBB is a commercial data provider that offers access to a wide range of assets beyond stocks, including bonds, cryptocurrencies, and foreign exchange markets. Use this library if you're interested in more generic investment strategies and aren't limited to investing in stocks.

# Growth portfolios

**This chapter covers**
- Using an investment thesis to predict growth companies
- Creating a portfolio that reflects an investment thesis
- Finding specific assets that reflect your thesis for your portfolio
- Taking the required risks to pursue potential gains

This chapter explores the process of building an asset portfolio designed to outperform the market. Finding these winners, or alphas as they are often called, is the holy grail of investing. A stock picker who consistently is just slightly more right than wrong may have already gained the Midas touch.

Many investors distinguish between gambling and investing when making decisions about trading assets. We're excited about potential investment ideas that could make us wealthy. And as these dreams of joining the Warren Buffett club are overly pleasant, we tend to downplay doubts that threaten to undermine this endearing feeling of getting rich soon. Gambling begins when we rely more on feelings than on critical thinking when making investment decisions. With only a little research, we find suitable candidates for investments. The tricky part is conducting the required deep research to identify those candidates for an investment that truly yields a return.

I first learned how important a well-considered strategy can be at the age of 10 in chess club. As I had started playing chess earlier than my peers, I was more skilled at seeing combinations, such as forks, to capture my opponents' pieces, which allowed me to win most of my games. My chess teacher saw me moving around and waiting for my opponent to make a mistake. He took me aside and told me: "If you just rely on someone else to make a mistake to win, you'll lose against better players. You need a strategy to win a game. Even a bad plan is better than no plan." He turned out to be right. Better players with a strategy roasted me on the chessboard. I quickly learned an indispensable principle of learning that can also be applied in investing: research, plan, execute, reflect, and adjust. With that strategy, learning from mistakes and coming out stronger is a necessary part of achieving long-term success. Let's explore how we can invest with a plan. We begin with a case study for a specific domain, and then we extract the lessons learned from that case study to create a generic approach to researching investments.

## 4.1 Investment thesis

An *investment thesis* is a researched theory about a stock's predicted performance. We face many possible scenarios. Some share prices have performed poorly, and we consider them undervalued, betting on a turnaround. Other stocks may provide a solid income through steadily growing dividends, and we believe this trend will continue. And, of course, we might also bet against companies and short-sell assets that we consider overvalued. In this chapter, we aim to showcase one of these many possible scenarios, focusing on companies poised for growth and expansion.

Creators of an investment thesis must be able to defend their reasoning and allow, or even better, invite others to challenge their ideas. The more unbiased experts who peer-review the thesis, the better. Let's start this investigation with the idea that we'll refine until we identify a group of assets to purchase. One essential aspect of buying assets is defining goals to understand from the start and having a guideline for holding or selling the asset in the future.

> **NOTE** The chapter's focus is to outline a process for finding stocks, not to promote a specific set of stocks for you to purchase. You may continue to conduct your own extended research based on insights from this chapter. What remains crucial is that you only invest in businesses *you* understand.

### 4.1.1 Starting with an idea

Chapter 2, section 2.2, covering industry classification, outlines how businesses can vary significantly from one another. Different business models pose different challenges, and if you don't know what can go wrong in a specific domain, you risk a lot by investing in it.

The Dunning-Kruger effect is a cognitive bias where people with low ability in a specific area tend to overestimate their competence, while those with high ability tend to underestimate theirs. When we encounter individuals who are new to a field we've already mastered, the consequences of that bias often become apparent to us. We often see the extent of misery when inexperienced persons take bold actions, and we frequently can predict where they fail and when. But how can we guarantee that we're not victims of the Dunning-Kruger effect ourselves when we pick companies to invest in? The brutal answer is that we can never be 100% sure if we're too confident. Undetected overconfidence is likely one of the primary root causes why so many people fail in their investment journey.

Still, we can reduce the chances of being overconfident by picking a field where there is evidence that we understand one thing or two, such as through a track record of work experience. That's why I picked an industry I've worked in for a while.

Evolving an idea into a thesis is accomplished through iterative steps. We must gradually refine our thoughts and challenge them until we arrive at a refined concept. The path to a good thesis can be rocky. We sometimes must accept that we're on the wrong path and need to start over. This process is similar to designing a product for a start-up: occasionally, you need to pivot, but eventually, you learn what the market needs. One advantage of an investor over a founder is that an investor doesn't have to bring all the entrepreneurial skills to the table to launch products or services.

When it becomes clear that we can defend our theory about a profitable business through reasoning and receive feedback, we're on to something. We can start calling our idea a thesis.

> **Investment idea: Autonomous driving will pay off**
>
> The market for autonomous driving is growing. Numerous statistics support this assertion: at some point in the future, self-driving vehicles will become the norm, not the exception. Waymo claims to deliver 250,000 driverless robotaxi rides a week (https://waymo.com/sustainability/). Various sources predict that this market will grow exponentially worldwide.
>
> Assuming that this market keeps growing, we can foresee the following effects:
>
> - Fewer individuals will own cars. Instead, people will gradually switch to robotaxis to get to their destinations.
> - For logistics companies, trucks without drivers will expand their reach, as algorithms require no rest, unlike human drivers.
> - As the demand for self-driving cars grows, so will the demand for the required hardware, such as sensors.
> - A complete transition to autonomous driving will affect infrastructure. With robotaxis, the demand for parking slots in city centers will be minimized, allowing a considerable amount of space below concrete to be repurposed for other uses.

> When people discuss autonomous driving, experts refer to it as level 5—full automation. Under the term Advanced Driver-Assistance System (ADAS), we summarize many more technologies in greater detail that will eventually lead to full automation, such as parking sensors or collision warnings. Each category in ADAS may be a valuable investment opportunity.
>
> Just as digitalization has created new tech giants that didn't exist before, the field of autonomous driving can provide an environment for new start-ups to grow and become significant players. Other companies may lose business due to the emergence of autonomous driving.

### 4.1.2 Challenging the idea

Conducting a strengths, weaknesses, opportunities, and threats (SWOT) analysis of this investment idea enables a more in-depth examination, leading to a more detailed exploration. We can use large language models (LLMs) to learn about them or engage in discussions with domain experts within our network. Many experts raise ethical questions about self-driving cars. Suppose an autonomous vehicle can't prevent an accident. An algorithm must decide whether to drive into a meadow, where it will hit a person standing there, or hit a wall that will hurt the person in the car. A lengthy discussion about possible priorities, which go far beyond this simple example, and about other safety requirements, such as protection standards against hacking, can slow down or halt the adoption of self-driving vehicles.

> **Sub-thesis: Ethics and security may slow down, but not halt**
> A nation serious about its AI strategy can't afford to prohibit the development of self-driving cars due to concerns over ethics and security. Any country that halts its research while others advance will quickly face a significant competitive disadvantage.
>
> Additional bureaucracy, due to ethical and security concerns, may still deter some contenders, and autocratic governments might have an advantage in enforcing innovation compared to democracies. This presents a dilemma for investors, who must weigh their preference for societies that value human rights against a nation's sheer "ability to execute."

Think like a science fiction author and imagine a world where autonomous driving is fully adopted. Robotaxis follow a ride-hailing business model similar to Uber's. You order, you get in at your origin, leave the car at your destination, and the car picks up the next passenger. Owning a car will be like owning a horse today; it will merely be a status symbol. The moment autonomous driving is proven to be safer, expect insurance companies to insist on higher premiums if people still choose to drive themselves, which may accelerate the adoption of autonomous driving.

In such a world, we can envision the vast amount of concrete in parking spaces being pulverized into dust and replaced with fertile earth on which trees and gardens can grow. We can imagine start-ups creating a business model by buying cars and leasing them to companies that orchestrate rides, such as Uber. Of course, we can also consider all the companies that build hardware for these cars. Let's group potential growth assets for autonomous driving:

- *Ride-hailing services*—Companies that offer ride-hailing services can benefit from cost reduction by replacing drivers with autonomous systems.
- *Car manufacturers with a level-5 system*—Leaders in the field of autonomous driving may increase sales if clients trust them more than their competitors.
- *Truck manufacturers with a level-5 system*—Driverless trucks can be operated 24/7 with only brief breaks for loading, unloading, and refueling.
- *Appliance providers*—Some companies offer complete autonomous driving systems to car manufacturers, but they don't manufacture cars themselves.
- *Component providers*—Some companies produce components for autonomous driving systems, encompassing both hardware and software at a high level.

We also need to consider countries where companies reside, as they create the space for them to evolve. Without a doubt, the United States is the leader in the robotaxi field. However, we can't exclude other countries with a firm bid on technologies enabling this transition, such as China, Israel, and Germany.

> **Sub-thesis: Known brands are already valued highly**
> Known brands working on solutions for robotaxis include Google (Waymo), Amazon (Zoox), and Tesla. Their capabilities to innovate are already reflected in their stock prices, so buying these shares means we're not purchasing undervalued stocks. Although these companies may be excellent investment opportunities otherwise (Note: the author holds shares of two of these companies), we decide to focus on smaller, lesser-known companies that have more substantial growth potential.

One way to move forward is to explore car manufacturers that haven't yet established a strong reputation in their robotaxi program but are performing better than is publicly known. However, we need access to recent insider knowledge of employees working for these companies.

Let's explore suppliers whose products enable the development of autonomous cars. A self-driving car relies on a combination of several key components to operate autonomously. Following is a list of various additional components an autonomous car needs:

- *Sensors:*
  - *Light Detection and Ranging (LiDAR)*—Measures distances using laser light to create a 3D map of the environment.

- *Radar*—Uses radio waves to detect objects and their speeds, especially in poor visibility conditions.
- *Cameras*—Provide visual information about the surroundings for object recognition and lane detection.
- *Ultrasonic sensors*—Detect objects close to the vehicle, which is helpful for parking and low-speed maneuvers.

- *Processing unit:*
  - *Car processing units*—Handle data from sensors, run machine learning models, and perform complex calculations to make real-time decisions.

- *Software:*
  - *Perception algorithms*—Interpret sensor data to recognize objects, pedestrians, and road signs.
  - *Localization software*—Determines the car's precise location using GPS and detailed maps.
  - *Planning and decision-making algorithms*—Determine the best course of action based on current and anticipated traffic situations.
  - *Control systems*—Manage the vehicle's speed, steering, and braking based on the planned route.

- *Connectivity:*
  - *Vehicle-to-everything (V2X) communication*—Enables communication with other vehicles, infrastructure, and network services for enhanced situational awareness and coordination.

- *Mapping:*
  - *High-definition maps*—Provide detailed information about road geometry, traffic signals, and lane markings, which are crucial for accurate navigation.

- *Power supply:*
  - *Battery and power management*—Ensures all electronic components and sensors are adequately powered.

Researching the potential change in demand for each of these components requires considerable effort. We need to understand the industry and assess its specific details. Some industries may depend heavily on raw materials and be vulnerable to shortages, while others may face a market with a high number of competitors.

If we were to write a book about investing in companies for autonomous driving, we could dedicate a chapter to each component in the supply chain and analyze it in detail, including individual SWOT analyses and a thorough technical study. Comparing serious investing with gambling—picking a potentially promising company without thorough research—highlights the significant effort required to make informed decisions. This book aims to outline a research process. Therefore, we need to narrow our focus and skip detailed research on every component. Instead, we'll illustrate the process within a specific domain and select LiDAR systems as a likely candidate for research.

> **Refined investment idea: LiDAR will rebound**
>
> While investing in AI and car manufacturers such as Tesla has been booming, the share prices of companies that provide sensors and other types of hardware are undervalued. As the LiDAR market is capital-intensive, many investors may be hesitant, primarily due to the high interest rates of recent years. However, if the number of robotaxi drives increases, demand for hardware will rise, and these companies will see a corresponding rise in valuation.
>
> LiDAR may also have applications beyond autonomous driving. The world is facing significant demographic shifts, and the number of workers is expected to decline in the upcoming years. LiDAR systems are part of factory automation, reducing the demand for human workers. This reduction in worker demand is also highly beneficial in mining, as some areas are inaccessible to human workers.
>
> We see examples of many stocks that have successfully rebounded after unfavorable times, and LiDAR wouldn't be the first industry to be resurrected. If the market for these sensors is down in 2025 and we expect demand to increase in the upcoming years, we might consider buying low today and selling high later.

The methodology for identifying concrete assets to invest in becomes more apparent with each step, and we define what we're looking for more precisely. However, we're still proceeding. Let's explore LiDAR further before selecting our first assets to investigate.

### 4.1.3 Your investment thesis

We've demonstrated how to explore ideas to arrive at a thesis. Given that autonomous driving is a game-changer, our theory is that the market for LiDAR systems will rebound.

We can now begin with an in-depth analysis and collect as much information about the market as possible. You can use note-taking apps such as Notion and OneNote to structure your research. Some of us may collect all the notes in the data science notebooks we use for analysis. Just keep in mind that a significant amount of research occurs outside of code environments.

We gradually need to pick investment candidates and keep researching them. With every research, here are the main questions:

- Can the company generate immense cash in the upcoming years, outperforming potential competitors?
- How well can the company protect these profits from copycats? (Buffett calls the ability of a company to wall itself from competitors an *economic moat*.)
- How large is the margin of safety to protect oneself against risks?

Let's explore this showcase further and examine the LiDAR market.

## 4.2 LiDAR market

The global LiDAR market was valued at approximately $2–$2.5 billion in 2023. With a compound annual growth rate (CAGR) of 20%–25%—the mean annual growth rate of an investment over a period longer than one year—it's expected to reach $6 to $8 billion within seven years. This growth rate appears promising, but further exploration is needed to determine whether to invest in this market. Let's examine the key information that could influence our decision to invest in LiDAR:

- *Technology differentiation*—LiDAR technologies can be divided into several types, including time-of-flight, frequency-modulated continuous wave (FMCW), and solid-state LiDAR. I spoke with an autonomous driving expert who highlighted that moving parts in hardware components lead to wear and tear, which makes them more costly. He therefore sees an advantage in solid-state LiDAR systems, which are also smaller than other LiDAR systems.
- *Cost efficiency and scalability*—Different vendors offer systems with varying ranges, resolutions, and accuracies. Superior performance often comes at a cost, which is reflected in the total price of the system.

  Some manufacturers may achieve a satisfactory performance with less costly systems. Some of them may even attempt to find alternatives to expensive LiDAR systems by relying solely on cameras.
- *Strategic partnerships*—Some LiDAR manufacturers have partnered with automotive, robotics, or industrial automation players. New deals with prominent companies, such as Tesla and Ford, as well as tech giants Google and Amazon, could indicate that LiDAR companies will become increasingly valuable.
- *Regulatory environment and market adoption*—The LiDAR market covers autonomous driving, drones, and smart city initiatives. In addition, architects and engineers (not to mention research scientists such as geologists, geographers, and archaeologists) use LiDAR heavily. Companies with products that meet evolving safety and regulatory standards (especially in automotive) will have an edge. To cover this topic, we must discuss geopolitical challenges. As Chinese companies, such as Huawei, have been banned by the United States, we must explore whether Chinese LiDAR makers might face similar challenges.
- *Patent portfolio*—Companies with a solid intellectual property portfolio in sensor design, signal processing, or AI integration may have a sustainable competitive advantage. This section will delve into considerable detail and may require a deep technical understanding of the components of LiDAR systems. We need to assess whether specific scanning technologies patented by companies provide them with a competitive advantage.
- *Competition*—Smaller companies that innovate faster or disrupt traditional business models may offer higher growth potential. In one of the interviews, an expert expressed a strong opinion that he believes LiDAR start-ups lack the

power to compete against existing giants in the industry, which have been on the market for years.
- *Financials and leadership*—Strong balance sheets, low debt, and competent leadership, along with a clear road map for growth, are essential. However, given that LiDAR is capital-intensive, we must be vigilant for excessive cash burn rates that don't generate clear revenue.

> **Patience: A success factor**
>
> One likely outcome of an investment research sprint is that you end up with inconclusive results. You may have spoken to many experts who contradict each other. You examine the data of specific companies; the numbers are satisfactory, but more is needed to convince you to invest a reasonable sum. Investors often also learn that the biggest enemy of the best investment opportunity is the abundance of good enough opportunities. If you purchase every asset you get excited about, you might end up with a vast portfolio of many small- to medium-sized holdings. While diversification itself is beneficial, losing track of what you've invested in and why is not.
>
> Occasionally, the best course of action is to document all the research and take no further action. Refrain from falling prey to the temptation of quick riches; instead, staying risk-aware and keeping a clear head are often the basis for long-term success. As a programmer, you know that you can rerun algorithms with new and better data at a later stage. So, why rush when you can proceed with confidence?

### 4.2.1 Picking candidates

It's time to select our first investment candidates. Although they may not yet be the companies we invest in, we use them to learn more about what we're looking for until we can make final decisions. After conducting web research and reading articles on various platforms, we selected four LiDAR manufacturers for an initial investigation. A GenAI chat also supported the results of this initial research.

An initial list of investment candidates is not finite. We can add new companies to this list later or remove some as needed. However, we must find a way to determine which assets are good investments, and we need to start somewhere. These are the four candidates, listed by stock ticker in brackets.

- Luminar Technologies (LAZR)
- Innoviz Technologies (INVZ)
- Ouster (OUST)
- Aeva Technologies (AEVA)

We're first interested in their market capitalization and earnings growth. The following market capitalization code reuses the method to collect ratios from earlier chapters:

```
import yfinance as yf
import pandas as pd
def collect_ratios(tickers: list, ratios: list):
```

## 4.2 LiDAR market

```
    rows = []

    for ticker in tickers:
        info = yf.Ticker(ticker).info
        row = [ticker] + [info.get(ratio, None) for ratio in ratios]
        rows.append(row)
    return pd.DataFrame(rows, columns=["Ticker"] + ratios)
objects = ["AEVA", "LAZR", "INVZ", "OUST"]
for o in objects:
    ticker = yf.Ticker(o)
    print(f"ticker {o}: {ticker.info['marketCap']}")
```

Examining the results, we obtain the following market capitalization as of 2024:

- LAZR: $449,100,640
- OUST: $308,347,328
- AEVA: $175,966,752
- INVZ: $136,608,288

These numbers also indicate that these companies still need to become mid-cap stocks, which typically start with a valuation of $2 billion. The risk associated with a lower valuation is significantly higher, as the "too big to fail" clause may still be applicable for some companies.

Let's examine these companies' earnings to see their performance over the past few years. The following code uses the Alpha Vantage library introduced in chapter 3 to explore this information:

```
from alpha_vantage.fundamentaldata import FundamentalData
objects = ["AEVA", "LAZR", "INVZ", "OUST"]
fd = FundamentalData(key=key, output_format='pandas')
for o in objects:
    df_earnings = fd.get_earnings_annual(o)[0].set_index('fiscalDateEnding')
    print(f"ticker {o}: {df_earnings}")
```

We obtain the results shown in table 4.1 by ticker and reported earnings per share (EPS).

**Table 4.1  EPS score of four LiDAR producers**

|  | AEVA | LAZR | INVZ | OUST |
|---|---|---|---|---|
| 2024-06-30 | -1.13 | -0.37 | -0.31 | -1.08 |
| 2023-12-31 | -0.65 | -0.86 | -0.85 | -7.68 |
| 2022-12-31 | -0.68 | -0.78 | -0.94 | -0.74 |
| 2021-12-31 | -0.51 | -0.56 | -2.34 | -0.83 |
| 2020-12-31 | -0.0185 | -2.2127 | -1.2487 | -8.2332 |
| 2019-12-31 | 0.05 | 0.0585 | -2.4782 | N/A |

The numbers suggest that COVID-19 may have affected industries, as their EPS scores during the COVID years were lower than in other years. Nevertheless, the results show a general tendency toward negative earnings.

If you approach finance conservatively, you might object to investing in companies without profits. Personal finance teaches us that spending more than earning eventually leads to high debts and misery. Entrepreneurs, however, understand that personal and corporate finance sometimes follow different rules. It takes some start-ups years to become profitable. When evaluating start-ups, investors focus on what a start-up is projected to earn. If the outlook is substantial enough, banks and investors will continue to invest in these companies, even if they aren't yet profitable.

### 4.2.2 Price development

Let's examine how stock prices have developed in recent years, and we'll get the same picture with all four of them (see figures 4.1, 4.2, 4.3, 4.4). They started somewhere, then there was hype about the stock, and they all fell. The obvious question, therefore, is whether they can rebound.

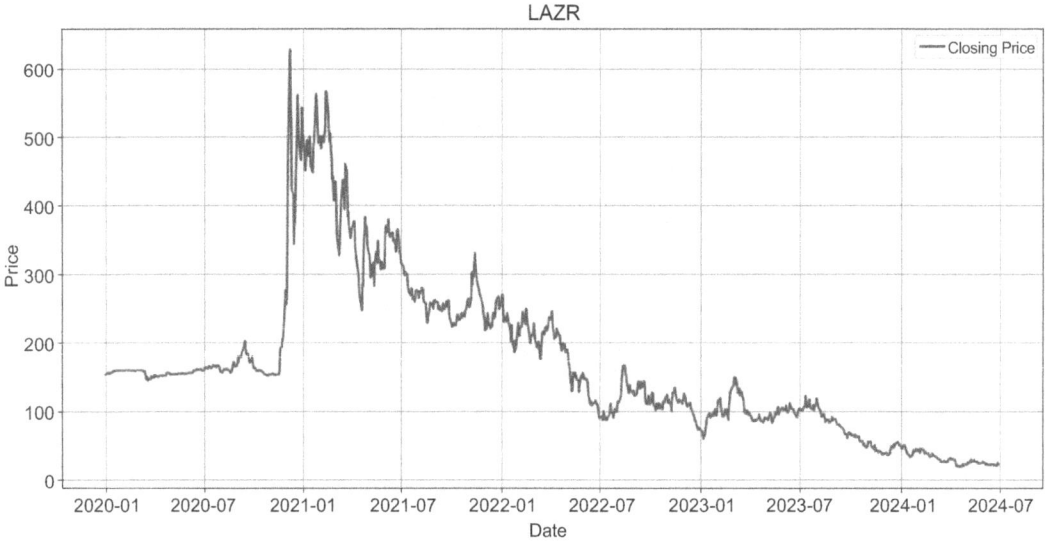

Figure 4.1 Price development of Luminar Technologies (LAZR)

All four companies experienced a decline in share price. At the beginning of the decade, there was hype surrounding autonomous vehicles. Interestingly, share prices increased during the COVID-19 pandemic. Driverless cars may have sounded appealing to many during times of social distancing. Additionally, it's worth noting that LiDAR is used to automate factory work, which means a reduced dependency on human labor.

**Figure 4.2  Price development of Innoviz Technologies Ltd (INVZ)**

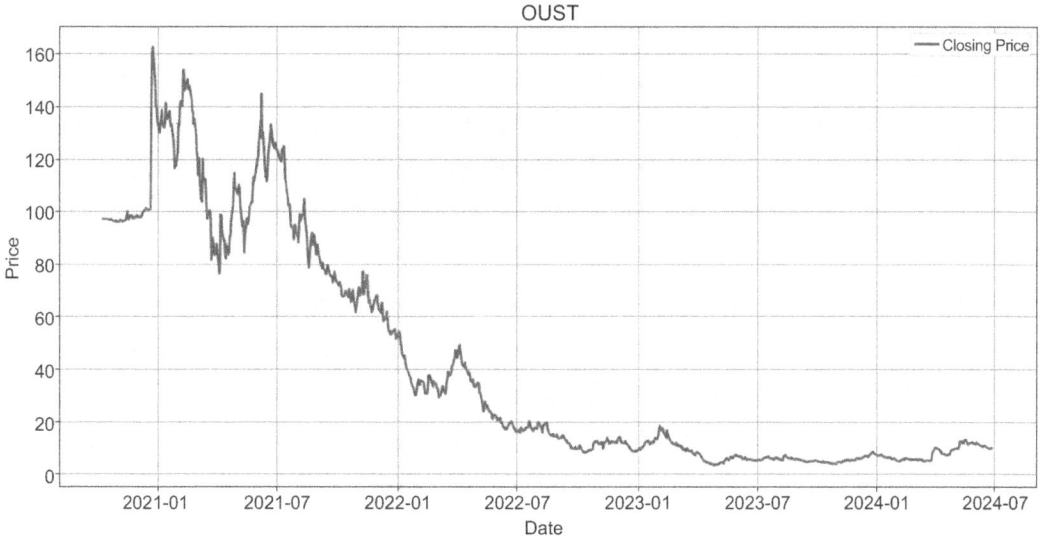

**Figure 4.3  Price development of Ouster (OUST)**

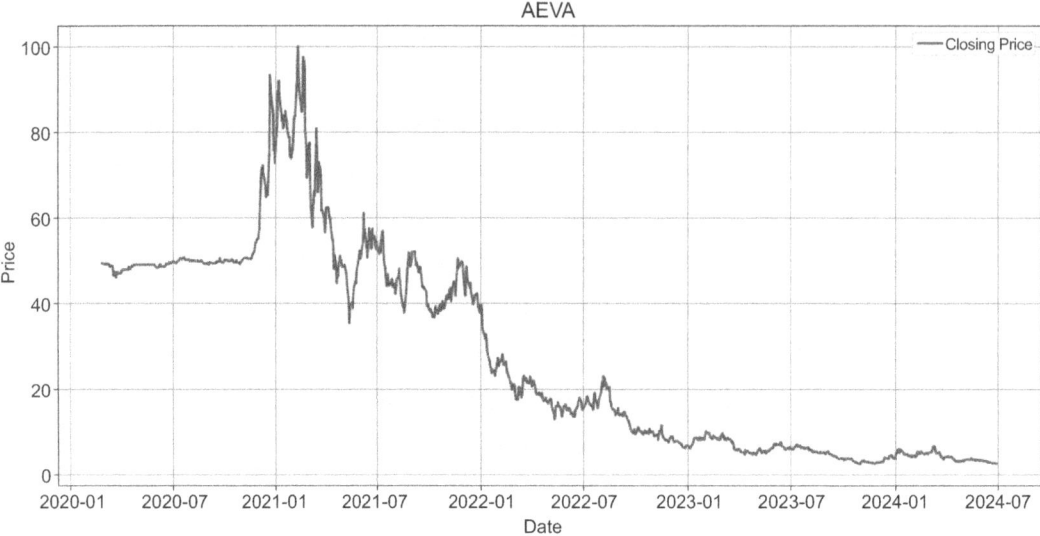

Figure 4.4  Price development of Aeva Technologies (AEVA)

Following the COVID-19 pandemic, the shares declined. This decline can be attributed to the notion that the market was overhyped and that inflation fears, arising from the pandemic, particularly affected a capital-intensive industry with significant cash burn. Starting in 2022, the Fed increased its interest rate to combat inflation, as shown in figure 4.5. As it became more expensive to lend money, investors may have lost interest in capital-intensive LiDAR stocks.

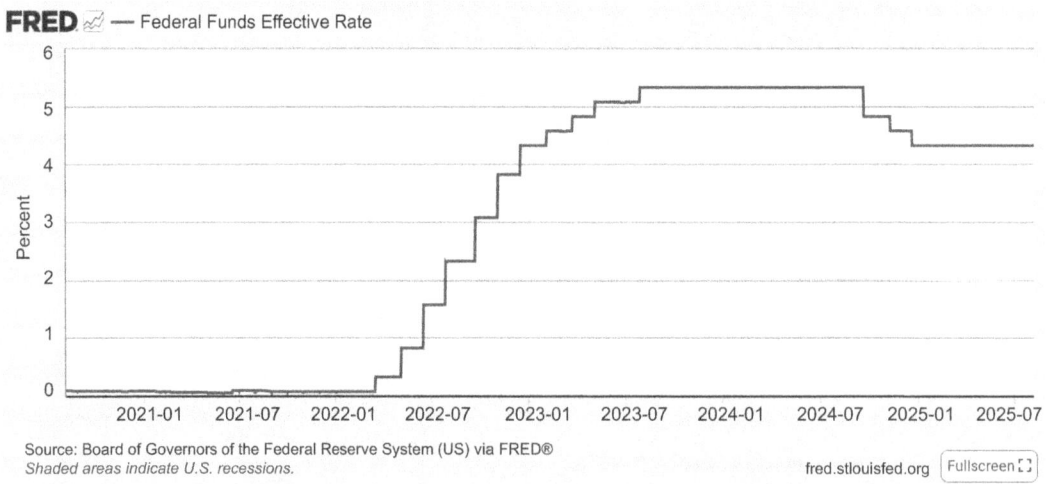

Figure 4.5  The interest rate at which depository institutions trade federal funds (Source: https://fred.stlouisfed.org/series/DFF)

Let's explore the highs and lows of all stocks in table 4.2 to gain a deeper understanding of their price movements.

Table 4.2  Down from the all-time high

| Ticker | High | Low | Down |
|--------|------|-----|------|
| AEVA | $100.00 | $3.33 | 96.67% |
| LAZR | $41.80 | $0.91 | 97.82% |
| OUST | $162.50 | $6.36 | 96.09% |
| INVZ | $16.00 | $0.79 | 95.06% |

As these four companies are so far below their peak, let's consider scenarios in which they get back on track. Let's explore a scenario that sounds like a path to riches and will give us the necessary drive to keep researching.

> **Speculative scenario: LiDAR stocks rebounding**
>
> Suppose we invested $40,000 equally among four assets, and all of these stocks return to their former heights. We would receive approximately 3,003 shares of AEVA, 10,989 shares of LAZR, 1,572 shares of OUST, and 12,658 shares of INVZ. Multiplying these by the high value would result in $1,217,675.75. An investment of $40,000 would make us millionaires. However, we must also note that if all four companies go bankrupt (obviously we don't want that to happen), we may lose $40,000. Nevertheless, if three go bankrupt and only one returns to its former glory, we would still make a profit.
>
> We can formulate a speculative hypothesis: once federal interest rates decrease, the share prices of capital-intensive LiDAR companies are likely to rebound. Even if they don't return to their former heights, we can still make a profit by buying low and selling high.

We must now determine the likelihood of these four companies returning to their former levels. Investors had already been enthusiastic about the stock, and those who had invested after the IPO—when the stock went public—were already heavily disappointed. The question is whether it's even possible to recoup the initial investment. Let's examine the debt.

### 4.2.3 Debt

As LiDAR companies are capital-intensive, debt is a viable option to consider. If we call the method collect ratios with the parameters having the signature `collect_ratios(objects, ["sector", "industry", "debtToEquity"])`, we obtain the results in table 4.3.

**Table 4.3 Debt-to-equity results for LiDAR companies**

| Ticker | sector | industry | debtToEquity |
|---|---|---|---|
| AEVA | Technology | Software - Infrastructure | 3.504 |
| LAZR | Consumer Cyclical | Auto Parts | NaN |
| OUST | Consumer Cyclical | Auto Parts | 26.658 |
| INVZ | Technology | Electronic Components | 39.549 |

NaN = not a number.

Based on the financial data, AEVA and LAZR might be more troubled than the others. LAZR has a higher total debt than its market cap. Looking at the news, we also see that LAZR has announced a workforce reduction. Additionally, being listed among the most shorted stocks on Wall Street isn't a positive sign (https://mng.bz/WwXd). This doesn't mean that these companies are on the verge of bankruptcy. According to the SEC filings, Austin Russell, the founder of Luminar, holds 104.5 million shares, which comprise approximately 35% of Luminar's total outstanding shares. This high ownership could mean significant room for equity investments. Additionally, according to Crunchbase, the last equity investment in Luminar was made in December 2022. A viable business with growing potential offers ample investment opportunities. At the same time, it's also clear that executives might want to wait before bringing in additional investors if there's room for the company to increase its valuation on its own.

### 4.2.4 Management

Many investors look at management to understand the potential. All companies are led by their founders. Austin Russel is the founder of Luminar. Omer David Keilaf cofounded and is the CEO of Innoviz. Cofounder Soroush Salehian leads Aeva, and Angus Pacala is the cofounder and CEO of Ouster.

We can continue to monitor the market; a leadership change could be a strong signal in the market, but we can disregard this aspect for now. If founders leave these companies, it's a warning sign. Investment decisions are often based on monitoring companies and reacting to events. For instance, if founders leave, it could be a signal to short-sell the company.

### 4.2.5 Technology and partnership

We can also explore these companies' LiDAR systems to determine whether they offer better or worse performance:

- *AEVA*—FMCW
- *LAZR*—Hybrid solid-state (with emphasis on long-range 1550 nm lasers)
- *INVZ*—MEMS-Based Solid-State
- *OUST*—Digital Solid-State (VCSEL-based)

LLMs are great research assistants. You can ask them to rank companies and highlight their value propositions. ChatGPT returned the following ranking in response to a simple prompt to rank them:

1. Aeva (AEVA) for its unique FMCW technology and velocity measurement
2. Luminar (LAZR) for its long-range, cost-effective LiDAR solution
3. Innoviz (INVZ) for solid-state LiDAR and automotive partnerships
4. Ouster (OUST) for affordable digital LiDAR and scalability

All companies have product road maps. For instance, Luminar Halo is designed for mainstream consumer vehicles. In addition, all the manufacturers have partnerships with existing car manufacturers. Luminar is deploying its LiDAR system in a Volvo car, a brand known for its maximum robustness. BMW uses Innoviz solid-state LiDAR systems, and AEVA sells its products to Daimler Trucks. Ouster lists Zoox, the Amazon-owned autonomous vehicle company, as a client. Ouster might differentiate itself from the others in the market. The company aims for broader adoption of LiDAR, such as in smart cities.

Experts tend to disagree on the time that we'll be fully autonomous. The pessimists still consider decades rather than a few years as realistic. When discussing full automation, we highlight a scenario in which an autonomous car manages all possible scenarios. Imagine you've been using robotaxi rides for years, but then your ride unexpectedly crashes because the system becomes confused by a specific combination of conditions. Considering all the details a vehicle might have to manage, it becomes clear that covering the edge cases is the real challenge.

You encounter scenarios where a car performs one functionality well (e.g., automated parking) but needs time to master other cases (driving in historically grown cities with all their narrow alleys and facing human drivers who don't always follow rules). The term *operational design domain* addresses this by placing automation within a specific context. Waymo doesn't build cars for the consumer market. It provides taxi services in the city and doesn't sell vehicles to individuals, as the car ownership business model is becoming obsolete. Eyeing another use case, the German Autobahn doesn't have speed limits. Traveling at 200 mph or more from Berlin to Munich in an autonomous vehicle is one use case that residents of Germany would love to have. A use case that supports cars at this speed is uninteresting for the US market without regulatory changes in maximum speed limits. Therefore, companies targeting the German market may prioritize their capabilities to be fast and autonomous, while others focus on excelling in other areas, such as city driving.

Another consideration is limitations and poor capabilities. Lousy driving conditions, such as fog, can hinder even the best drivers. However, most sensors are superior to the human eye, and autonomous cars are less limited by visual conditions.

You spend significant research time exploring companies in complex technical domains. To be effective, you must structure and continuously deepen your knowledge base. In technology, seemingly minor features—often overlooked without domain-specific expertise—can be game changers. You don't need to master every technical detail, but you must understand how components interact, know which questions to ask, and know whom to ask.

### 4.2.6 Projected earnings

Let's examine the projected earnings for the four companies on the market. Their earnings per share and projected revenue growth, as of November 2024, are listed in table 4.4, based on data from the investment platform Seeking Alpha.

Table 4.4  Projected earnings in millions

| Ticker | Dec 2024 | Dec 2027 | Growth |
|---|---|---|---|
| AEVA | 6.63 | 32 (in 2026) | 382.65% |
| INVZ | 24.30 | 670 | 2660.49% |
| LAZR | 70.28 | 851 | 1110.8% |
| OUST | 111.00 | 311.80 | 180.9% |

Source: Seeking Alpha

Examining these projections, it would be irrational not to invest if they could be guaranteed. Several details in these projections require validation. LAZR is expected to grow revenues by more than 10 times in three years; this sounds ambitious. Let's see if we can gather different data from other sources.

We can explore whether we get similar data from Python using financial libraries. We can run this code, which fetches and interprets earnings estimates collected with the yfinance library:

```
objects = ["AEVA", "LAZR", "INVZ", "OUST"]
for o in objects:
    stock = yf.Ticker(o)
    print(f"{o}: {stock.earnings_estimate}")
```

The results of this query yield different outcomes. Table 4.5 displays the transcribed earnings estimates of Luminar, with the timespan on the left and expected average, low, and high results. The `yearsAgoEps` column refers to the value in the last epoch. Examining the first row, `yearsAgoEps` of -3 corresponds to the result of the quarter preceding it.

Table 4.5  Earnings estimates of Luminar Technologies

|  | avg | low | high | yearsAgoEps | NrOfAnalysts | growth |
|---|---|---|---|---|---|---|
| 0q | -1.99971 | -2.25 | -1.71885 | -3 | 4 | 0.3334 |
| +1q | -1.82250 | -2.10 | -1.50000 | -2.85 | 4 | 0.3605 |

Table 4.5 Earnings estimates of Luminar Technologies *(continued)*

|  | avg | low | high | yearsAgoEps | NrOfAnalysts | growth |
|---|---|---|---|---|---|---|
| 0y | -9.94375 | -10.20 | -9.62 | -13.05 | 4 | 0.2380 |
| +1y | -6.53799 | -7.60 | -5.85 | -9.94 | 4 | 0.3425 |

This data indicates that Luminar is still expected to post no profits. On the positive side, losses are expected to narrow significantly compared to prior periods. From last year's EPS of –13.05, we expect an EPS of –9.94 for that year, representing a 24% improvement. The company is improving and burning less cash. If the trend doesn't change, it's a matter of time before a profit is achieved. However, as there's no profit yet in sight, risk is involved.

Earnings of start-ups may be the most difficult items to project. To forecast the future, we often need to rely on past data. Ouster was founded in 2015, Luminar in 2012, and Innoviz and Aeva in 2016. We can assume that these companies were waiting for autonomous driving to become mainstream so they could monetize the idea that, at some point, every car in the world would need "eyes." Using the number of past earnings for these companies may not be a reliable source. One of the companies might land a big deal that suddenly becomes a game changer. This may be the time to stop and wait for market signals: a large contract with a major player, some information that the project is progressing well, or that the car is exceeding expectations.

> **Analyzing other fields**
>
> The purpose of this chapter is to outline the process of identifying growth companies. This research process often becomes far more extensive and iterative, with cycles of building up theses, learning from new events or insights, and refining knowledge to adjust the investment strategy.
>
> Select the domains you're familiar with. If you're knowledgeable in biotech, research companies working on mRNA vaccines. If you're skeptical about this approach, consider weight loss drugs as a strong alternative to explore. Continue researching until you find the equivalent of a start-up's unfair advantage (https://mng.bz/8XEW).

## 4.3 Risks

Suppose we become obsessed with making millions by buying shares of undervalued LiDAR companies and selling them at high prices. We might lose objectivity—too many individuals who sank money into dreams ended up in nightmares.

Exploring risks may be even more important than analyzing potential benefits. If you miss a good investment opportunity, it might hurt your pride, but losing money can be even more devastating, especially if you later discover that a loss could have been prevented with better risk management.

Hedge funds often split the roles of analysts between those who research risks and those who research returns. This creates checks and balances to prevent overly optimistic investments.

If we invest alone, we can switch viewpoints. One day, you let yourself get excited and explore all the good things that can happen. Another day, you switch roles and analyze the opportunity from a pessimist's perspective. Seeing this opportunity from multiple angles will increase your chances of making the right decisions.

Let's imagine we're approached by an overly excited investor who claims that "LiDAR stocks will rebound once the federal interest rates go down." Our job is now to explore reasons why this optimist might be wrong and what we need to analyze to reduce uncertainties.

### 4.3.1 Falling into obsolescence

Tesla Vision is a program that explores an autonomous driving future in which better computer vision algorithms replace LiDAR sensors. Many experts debate whether Elon Musk's bet on a future without LiDAR systems is a good move. Many believe that level-5 autonomous driving without laser sensors that measure the distance to objects is impossible. However, what if Tesla's strategy pays off?

LiDAR systems are costly components. If automakers can achieve a good enough level of performance without these sensors, they'll likely eliminate them to make cars more affordable for their customers.

In the worst-case scenario, LiDAR companies focusing mainly on the automotive market could lose their very existence. Before investing seriously in LiDAR, a deeper understanding of LiDAR alternatives is helpful.

### 4.3.2 Squashed by industry giants

Waymo's business model is to offer robotaxi rides to consumers. They don't manufacture cars on their own. Let's consider a scenario in which Waymo management decides to sell appliances to other car manufacturers, enabling them to reach level-5 automation. Competing with Alphabet, which offers a comprehensive platform as one of the pioneering companies in the field of autonomous driving, might be challenging. The bad news for those interested in investing in LiDAR start-ups is that Waymo builds its own hardware.

The four companies we investigated are start-ups that try to gain a larger market share with their hardware. Many existing larger corporations have been providing LiDAR systems to their automotive clients for years. One example is Valeo, a company headquartered in France. Suppose you are a car manufacturer who is deciding on new LiDAR systems for an upcoming model. You've tested the hardware of various suppliers. Let's assume the hardware of both a new start-up and a large supplier you've been working with for many years scored equally. Would you pick the smaller supplier, whom you don't know well yet, and take on more risk due to their small size?

### 4.3.3 Globalization and conflicts

Innoviz Technologies is headquartered in Israel. At the time of writing this chapter, Israel is involved in ongoing conflicts. Forecasting how existing conflicts evolve is beyond the scope of this book; however, we must acknowledge that companies headquartered in a country facing conflict are at risk.

We've also seen trade wars between the United States and China. The United States has already banned Huawei, so why couldn't the American government investigate banning Chinese LiDAR companies from the US market? Hesai Group, the leading Chinese manufacturer, might face challenges in the US market. Looking at recent news, they had already been blacklisted at the Pentagon, which was reversed after the company sued (https://mng.bz/KwzE).

In the late 1990s and early 2000s, Germany's companies were among the leading producers of solar panels. More than 20 years later, China is responsible for over 80% of the world's photovoltaics manufacturing capacity across the supply chain. Some experts argue that China's economic model of state intervention can give Chinese companies an unfair advantage. To understand this risk better, we would have to explore scenarios in which state-controlled interventions affect the market and assess their likelihood.

## 4.4 Ongoing analysis

We can compare looking for investment opportunities to a hunter waiting for their prey. If they strike too soon or too late, they miss the target. Finding the right moment is also crucial when hunting for investments.

Like a real hunter, an investor also has limited shots. If you lock in your money too early in investment opportunities, you may lack the capital when a better opportunity arises. Therefore, an investment analysis might lead to a "let's wait and see!" approach, keeping an eye out for a more favorable opportunity. In this section, we explore how to maintain continuous market screening.

### 4.4.1 Media

Investment platforms provide articles by analysts, for example, "LiDAR Quarterly Insights Q3 2024 Summary" at https://mng.bz/jZDV. An investor can subscribe to newsletters to understand what other investors think. Additionally, platforms such as Reddit often feature subreddits dedicated to specific stocks, and you can follow companies on social media. High-quality content comes from reputable newspapers, such as *The Wall Street Journal*, *The Financial Times*, or *Bloomberg*. For domains such as LiDAR systems, there are notable magazines for experts who delve into the details about the technology.

One key challenge is to extract truthful content. LLMs might hallucinate, and content from a company's social media or investor relations department may not always be objective. A specific event for every public company is the earnings report assembly. No executive will ever say something like, "This quarter was horrible; we completely failed in everything we set out to do." Instead, the art is to read between the lines. Sometimes, analysts need a solid domain understanding to interpret a CEO's words correctly.

### 4.4.2 Trend analysis

Trends can be foreseen by analyzing Google searches or hashtags on social media. Examining the LiDAR searches in figure 4.6, we observe that this topic has become increasingly popular over time.

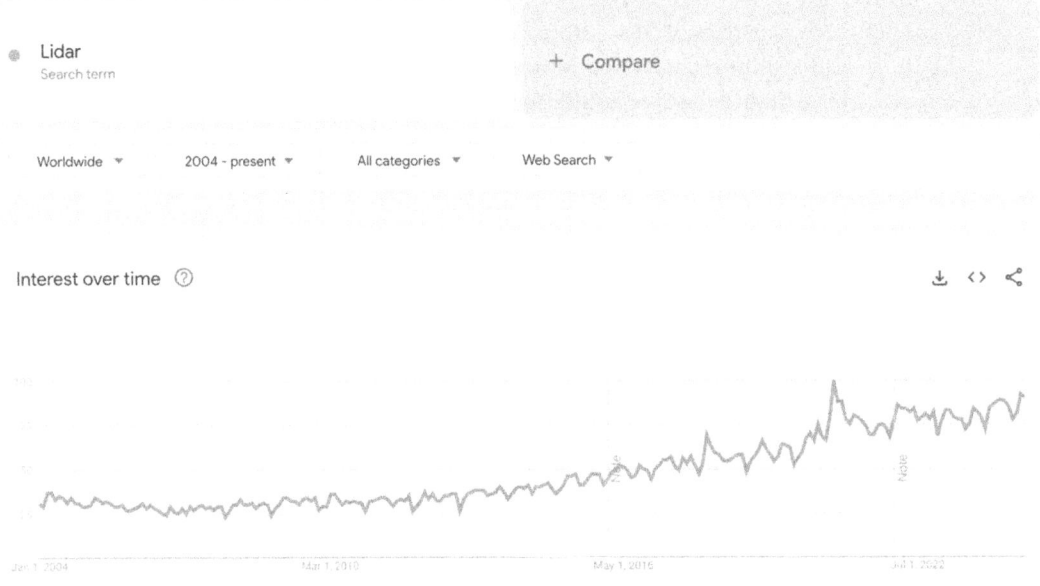

Figure 4.6 LiDAR in Google Trends

Let's also explore the four companies we chose and examine how often they are searched on Google. We can experiment by adjusting stock tickers and changing names. After all, "ouster" also has a different meaning in English, and using the stock ticker OUST doesn't help. Figure 4.7 shows the results of a Google Trends investigation for the company names in 2024.

## 4.4 Ongoing analysis

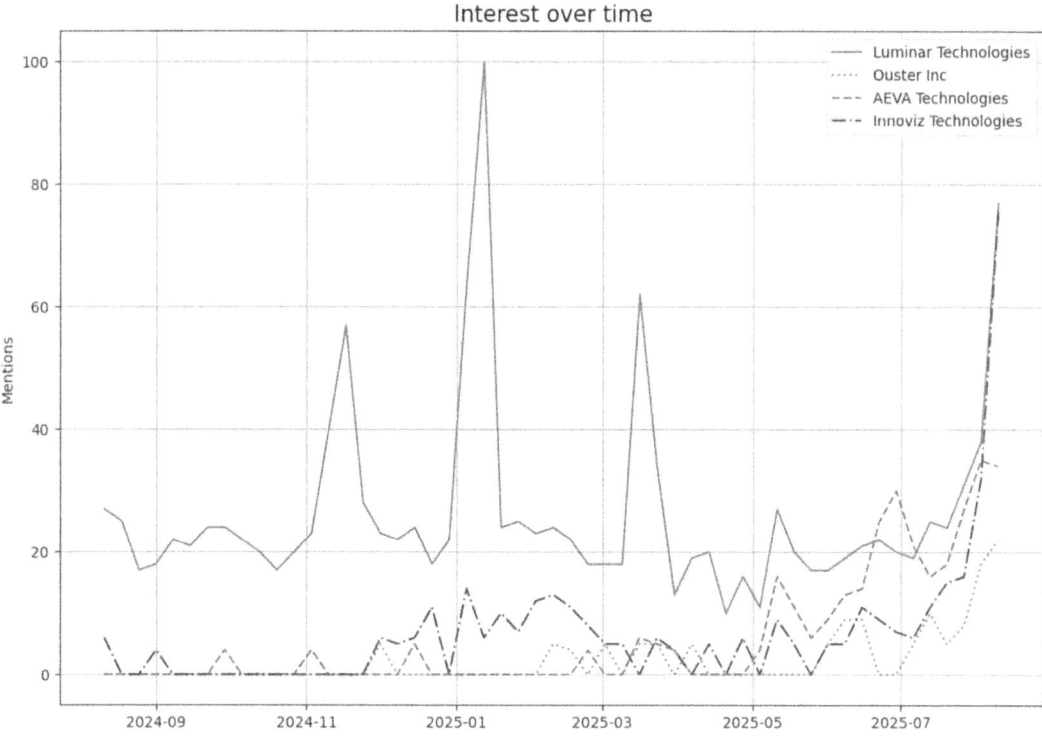

**Figure 4.7** Google Trends on Ouster, Luminar, AEVA Technologies, and Innoviz

We can also use Python code to collect information on trends. One library to accomplish this step is Pytrends. Let's examine the following code, which collects historical trend data from Google:

```
from pytrends.request import TrendReq
import pandas as pd
pytrend = TrendReq(hl='en-US', tz=360)
keywords = ["Luminar Technologies", "Ouster Inc",
    "AEVA Technologies", "Innoviz Technologies"]
pytrend.build_payload(keywords, cat=0, timeframe='today 12-m',
    geo='', gprop='')
interest_over_time_df = pytrend.interest_over_time()
print(interest_over_time_df
.head())
interest_over_time_df.to_csv('google_trends_data.csv')
```

Examining the results allows us to continue screening for trends and observe if anything changes. Table 4.6 shows the results.

**Table 4.6  Trends in Google search for LiDAR companies**

| Date | Luminar | Ouster | AEVA | Innoviz | isPartial |
|---|---|---|---|---|---|
| 2024-10-13 | 33 | 5 | 3 | 3 | True |
| 2024-10-06 | 43 | 5 | 4 | 3 | False |
| 2024-09-29 | 42 | 2 | 2 | 2 | False |
| 2024-09-22 | 48 | 0 | 0 | 0 | False |
| 2024-09-15 | 39 | 0 | 0 | 0 | False |

Trends indicate how often users search for a keyword, but we need to conduct a news sentiment analysis to examine the sentiments.

### 4.4.3  News sentiment analysis

We can collect news and comments from any form of media and analyze them with algorithms. The Alpha Vantage library, introduced in chapter 3, provides methods to collect reaggregated data. Let's use the following code to examine the news sentiment score:

```
def collect_sentiments(ticker):
    import requests
    r = requests.get(f'https://www.alphavantage.co/query?
        function=NEWS_SENTIMENT&tickers={ticker}&apikey={key}')
    return pd.DataFrame.from_dict(r.json()['feed'])


def summarize_sentiments(df, ticker):
    from collections import Counter

    ticker_sentiment = df['ticker_sentiment']
    label_string = ""
    score = 0
    for record in ticker_sentiment:
        if record[0]['ticker'] == ticker:
            if label_string != "":
                label_string += ","
            label_string += record[0]['ticker_sentiment_label']
            score += float(record[0]['ticker_sentiment_score'])

    print(score)
    word_count = Counter(label_string.split(","))
    word_count_df = pd.DataFrame(word_count.items(),
        columns=['Word', 'Count'])
    print(word_count_df)
```

Calling the method `collect_sentiments` with the tickers of four start-ups will provide us with a sentiment score, and we categorize news results from November 2024 as bullish (BU), somewhat bullish (SW BU), neutral (NEU), somewhat bearish (SW BE), or bearish (BE) in table 4.7.

Table 4.7 The sentiment score of selected LiDAR companies

| Ticker | Score | BU | SW BU | NEU | SW BE | BE |
|---|---|---|---|---|---|---|
| INVZ | 1.197801 | 0 | 6 | 16 | 1 | 0 |
| OUST | 6.714778 | 10 | 10 | 4 | 0 | 0 |
| LAZR | 4.497577 | 5 | 9 | 11 | 1 | 0 |
| AEVA | 1.623819 | 1 | 5 | 22 | 1 | 0 |

The news tends to be positive. We still want to be cautious. What if most of the sources are from investors who plan to invest? Therefore, it's helpful to continue analyzing trends, exploring shifts when they occur, and checking the sources carefully.

### 4.4.4 Measuring success

Whatever thesis you follow, always ask yourself how to measure success. Some breakthroughs aren't immediately visible in revenues or profits. The best sources are often insiders, such as company employees. Experts working on crucial projects are commonly prohibited from disclosing their insights publicly.

In the reference example of autonomous driving, we can count the number of robotaxis on the street and monitor the media for upcoming deals and contracts. One way to assess whether you've done proper work in creating your investment thesis is to evaluate how easily you can find the metrics to measure its success. If you're unsure what to look for, you should take more time to refine your thesis.

## 4.5 What is next

Many analysts who carefully read our LiDAR study may agree that there are still many details that require further research before a decision can be made. This exploration of LiDAR can be concluded in a "wait and see" scenario. Some bolder investors might choose to invest. One detail that every investor needs to decide for themselves is how much time they want to spend on analysis before making a decision. Even though LLMs can speed up the research process, thorough analysis may still take time.

We've outlined many risks. One day, we might discover that Tesla Vision is on the right track and that the market for LiDAR in the automotive sector is being disrupted. However, we could also find that Tesla's approach without LiDAR is failing. Other market signals can influence the future of LiDAR stocks. While investigating start-ups, we found that one of them is likely to be acquired by a larger company, which would probably boost share prices.

The definition of an ideal company to invest in is one that is poised to generate substantial cash flow for several years while maintaining a strong economic moat. Based on the existing analysis, we've identified candidates with a promising future. However, we must acknowledge that there's still considerable uncertainty. The decision-making process depends significantly on the individual investor's strategy:

- Some bold investors might see enough evidence to invest money.
- Cautious investors may spend more time researching the company. Some may conclude that the risks aren't worth the potential gains and pick more conservative choices.
- Some investors may also employ a mixed strategy. They start investing a small amount and keep researching.

> **Some speculative ideas to explore**
> Lastly, if you don't come up with ideas for researching investment areas, here are some ideas that could be interesting for you to explore:
>
> - With the COVID-19 pandemic, we've witnessed a significant advancement in mRNA technology. Vaccine providers now have access to numerous resources for researching new applications of mRNA. What would happen if one of these providers were to discover a vaccine against cancer?
> - Climate change is having an increasingly significant effect on the world. What measures are necessary to mitigate its effects, and which technologies could help mitigate it? Consider renewable energy or carbon sequestration.
> - Obesity is affecting the health of many people in the world, and many consumers still believe in traditional beauty standards. What are the criteria that a weight loss drug must provide so it can become popular globally?
> - Vegan products are often cheaper than meat. However, carnivores claim that meat alternatives still don't taste like real meat. What if a food producer created a vegan product that tastes as good as meat?
> - Every day, we face new threats in geopolitical challenges. Which solutions are needed to overcome these threats?
> - While many AI companies are already highly valued, consider also those firms that indirectly contribute to the adoption of AI. Take energy as a reference. Data centers require a substantial amount of energy constantly. Which energy sources can provide that and ideally don't emit too much carbon dioxide?

## *Summary*

- Gambling is often guided by instinct, whereas investing is led by critical thinking. Success isn't guaranteed, but investors can continually reflect on the outcomes of past decisions and learn from them for the future.
- We tend to overestimate our skills in areas that are new to us. This tendency is perilous, as it can lead to taking unnecessary risks. Stick to what you know and invest in businesses that you understand.
- An investment thesis highlights why you believe an investment will be profitable. It requires structured research that may take some time.

- Peer reviews are invaluable for refining a thesis. Invite others to question your assumptions and test your reasoning.
- Investing in what you know is key to success. Violate this principle, and you may as well be throwing darts blindfolded. There are many different influences on a market, and understanding them often requires extensive experience. Therefore, it's better to invest in something that you know well.
- Explore innovations such as autonomous driving to stay ahead of the market. To find investments, you must explore possible investments within that industry that solve a specific problem better than others.
- Investors and founders share the same challenge: they need to find a successful business idea. The investor, however, doesn't need to operate the business.
- We need to consider potential risks, such as ethical risks or risks of obsolescence, as illustrated in the case study.
- One way to find good investments is to look for undervalued companies, which are often those that already receive little attention from investors. Therefore, we might look for players in a niche who can contribute a significant amount of unseen value.
- Try to find companies that will generate a significant amount of cash for an extended period with a new business model. If their business model can't be easily copied or challenged by competitors, you have a candidate for a high-performing growth stock. Finding these companies takes work and patience.
- Seeing an opportunity's potential isn't enough; we must thoroughly challenge and assess ideas.
- Start-ups may take years to produce profits; however, if the business model is strong, we can benefit significantly from investing in a not-yet-profitable company in an emerging market. Start-ups and small companies also might run into liquidity problems more easily than larger companies.
- Hardly anyone invests more time and energy into a company as a founder. It's often a sign of strength if they remain part of the management team; we must be vigilant to learn about founders who are leaving.
- Technology might make a difference. However, we must also consider the cost factors and other aspects that may determine whether a product penetrates the market. There's no guarantee that the best product will become the market leader.
- Missing an investment opportunity might hurt your pride; however, ignoring it may result in financial loss.
- Knowledge is profit. Always know what you're buying.
- Be aware that every product might become obsolete. Keep an eye on the competition and the market.
- When betting on start-ups, you risk more to aim for higher returns. However, start-ups often must prevail against larger corporations in the markets.

- Geopolitics will increasingly affect the performance of companies in the global market.
- In doubt, don't invest, but keep your ears open for changes that allow you to revisit your analysis.
- An investor can analyze trends and news sentiments for investment areas.
- When possible, seek the advice or analysis of an expert in the domain you're considering investing in.
- Be always skeptical. Hear all, but trust nothing until you have enough evidence.
- Investigate partnerships and connections with other industries, including potential partnerships that aren't yet formal.
- Some investors look for companies where they believe their value is artificially or temporarily suppressed (value investing). Others look for companies that might disrupt markets with a game-changing product or service (growth investing). Both approaches can overlap.
- When exploring companies to invest in, also study industry- and product-specific risks. For instance, some companies may be capital-intensive and face risks when interest rates are high. Others may face the risk of a product-market fit mismatch.

# Income portfolios

**This chapter covers**
- Strategies to create passive income
- Finding stocks that pay solid dividends
- When to choose bonds over stocks for income portfolios
- Using cryptocurrency staking to generate passive income

Chapter 4 explored how identifying outliers can give you an edge in beating the market. We use these techniques to identify undervalued stocks (*value investing*) or look for companies with new technologies or business models that will outperform others (*growth investing*). This approach, however, also means settling for delayed gratification. We might have to wait years until our shares have gained enough capital appreciation to sell them again for enough profit.

For many who have experienced challenging jobs or projects, just seeing the rewards of investment portfolios on a cash account and mapping them with existing recurring expenses triggers a strong feeling of freedom and assurance. The more you rely on your salary, the more permanent your job feels. The moment you stop needing it, every job feels temporary.

This chapter will focus on passive income—investments with recurring payouts. While the previous chapter focused exclusively on stocks, this chapter will also explore two other asset types: bonds and cryptocurrency. Let's begin by examining how to maximize recurring payments through stock dividends.

**NOTE** *Fixed income* refers to an investment that pays the investor a fixed amount on a fixed schedule. However, many typical fixed-income investments have variants where we get varying payments on a fixed schedule (e.g., bonds with a floating rate or crypto staking rewards). For that reason, the term *passive income* is broader as it considers these fluctuations.

## 5.1 Dividends

A *dividend* is a portion of a company's profit that is paid to its shareholders. To understand the purpose of dividends, let's consider how companies evolve after they are incorporated.

In their early stages, companies focus on growth and establishing a foothold in their markets. Revenue is reinvested into expansion, whether by hiring new employees, developing improved products or services, or increasing operational capacity. During this phase, companies typically don't pay dividends. Instead, shareholders of startups benefit primarily from the potential for exponential growth—the transformation of a small garage-based enterprise into a thriving, steady business. Investing in these evolving companies often follows the high-risk, high-reward principle.

As a company matures and establishes itself in the market, its growth rate slows. At this stage, companies generate consistent profits, and investing all of their earnings in an even more aggressive campaign to grow further would no longer pay off, as they have already established themselves as leaders in the most profitable markets. Instead, this stability allows them to pay a portion of their profits to shareholders as dividends, making them attractive to investors seeking passive income. Mature companies paying regular dividends often represent lower-risk investment opportunities.

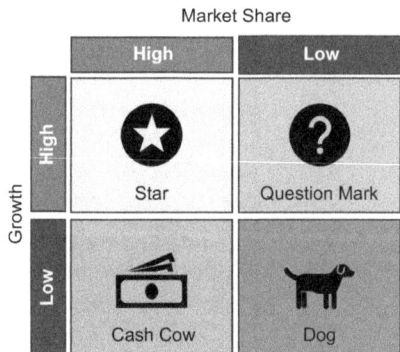

Figure 5.1 The BCG Growth-Share Matrix as a reference for picking dividend-paying companies that are likely cash cows (© https://productfolio.com/growth-share-matrix/)

This lifecycle of company evolution aligns with the Boston Consulting Group (BCG) Growth-Share Matrix. As illustrated in figure 5.1, the ideal dividend-paying stock is a "cash cow"—a business that generates stable profits with minimal reinvestment requirements, allowing surplus funds to be distributed to shareholders.

## 5.1 Dividends

We must first clarify our criteria for using data to identify dividend stocks. It's not just larger companies with higher market capitalizations that are more likely to pay dividends; the type of industry also plays a crucial role. For example, companies in the utilities sector tend to pay higher dividends than those in the technology industry. Consider a utility company that supplies water or electricity to homes. Their business model is stable and supported by extensive infrastructure, such as pipelines and cables. This infrastructure acts as an economic moat—a competitive advantage that makes it difficult for rivals to encroach on their market share. At the same time, these companies face challenges in driving competitors out of other regions, as those rivals possess similar infrastructure elsewhere.

While the risks of losses are minimized in such industries, the growth potential is also limited. Figure 5.2 outlines examples of economic moats, highlighting how a long profit history in a saturated market and minimal competitive threats create the perfect conditions for a stable, dividend-paying company.

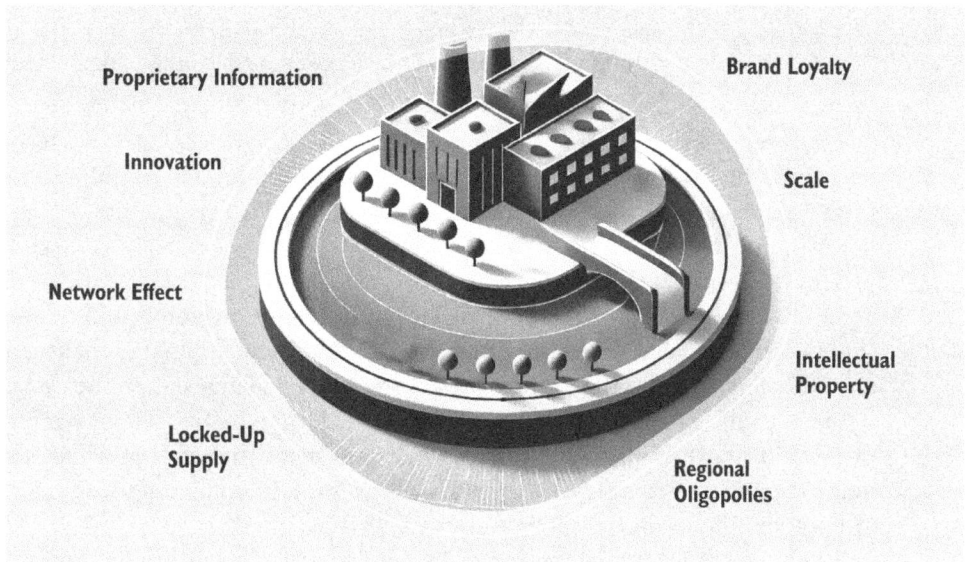

**Figure 5.2 Examples of economic moats**

Conversely, most tech companies must continuously invest in R&D to stay in business and find the next big thing in the market. Apple, Microsoft, NVIDIA, and other major tech firms would cease to thrive if they stopped investing in research or acquiring innovative startups that bring new products and ideas to them. For these companies, it makes sense to keep dividend payments small to allocate more funds toward innovation and research initiatives.

> **Examples of economic moats**
>
> Here are some examples of economic moats per category:
>
> - *Proprietary information*—Coca-Cola's secret formula gives it a competitive advantage by making its product difficult to replicate.
> - *Brand loyalty*—Apple customers are highly loyal and willing to pay premium prices for iPhones despite alternatives with similar or better specs.
> - *Innovation*—Tesla disrupted the auto industry by pioneering electric vehicle technology, battery efficiency, and self-driving capabilities.
> - *Scale*—Amazon benefits from economies of scale, offering lower prices and faster shipping than smaller competitors.
> - *Network effect*—Facebook (Meta) becomes more valuable as more people join, making it difficult for competitors to attract users.
> - *Locked-up supply*—De Beers historically controlled the diamond supply, restricting access and maintaining high prices.
> - *Intellectual property*—Pfizer's patents on drugs such as Viagra and COVID-19 vaccines prevent competitors from replicating their products.
> - *Regional oligopolies*—Utilities such as electricity providers in many regions operate as regulated monopolies or oligopolies, facing little to no competition.

One reference example of a dividend stock is the Coca-Cola Company. Its economic moat is its brand recognition. Supermarkets and restaurants are unlikely to remove Coca-Cola from their shelves or menus, making it hard to imagine the company's cash flow running dry.

However, detecting long-term cash flow risks is essential. Take the tobacco industry as an example. Many tobacco companies pay excellent dividends, but as an investor, you must decide what future you foresee for them. Some argue that tobacco products are in decline and that the industry will face severe challenges when the percentage of smokers in the population becomes negligible. Others believe these companies will successfully transform to provide alternative products with better prospects than traditional cigarettes. Regardless of your belief, investing in companies within an industry without confidence in their long-term success is unwise.

In chapter 2, we partially covered dividend metrics and ratios, but now we need to go deeper. Applying the algorithm becomes trivial if we know what to look for. The following parameters can be essential for finding suitable dividend investments:

- *Annual payout*—The total amount paid out per share per year.
- *Dividend payout frequency*—How often dividends are paid out per year, which is usually monthly, quarterly, semi-annually, annually, or irregularly. In most cases, yearly payouts are distributed equally. For example, a $1 annual payout per share results in $0.25 per quarter if paid quarterly.
- *Dividend yield*—Calculated by dividing the annual payout per share by the share price. A high dividend yield isn't always a positive indicator; it can also signal a falling share price, which increases the risk of a reduced annual payout.

- *Dividend growth*—This metric tracks how many years a company has consistently increased its dividends. Companies with long histories of raising dividends, such as Coca-Cola with 62 years of increases, are considered reliable long-term income stocks.
- *Dividend growth rate*—The rate at which a company grows its dividends. Some companies grow their dividends faster than others, but larger companies may take a slower approach to increases.
- *Payout ratio*—The fraction of a company's net income paid to shareholders. A smaller payout ratio suggests more room for growth and reinvestment.
- *Residence of the company*—Your residency can affect taxation. For example, non-US investors may face additional taxes when investing in US-based companies compared to those headquartered elsewhere.

The script in listing 5.1 calculates the dividend growth per year. To do this, we calculate the sum of dividends paid in the first and last year, and then we can determine the average yearly increase. Next, we calculate the payouts per year by counting the frequency of dividend payments and deducting the payment frequency.

Listing 5.1 Calculating dividend growth

```python
def calc_div_growth_rate (stock):
    try:
        dividends = stock.dividends

        if dividends.empty:
            return None, None

        dividends_by_year = dividends.resample('YE').sum()      # Gets the dividend sum by years

        if len(dividends_by_year) > 1:
            first_year = dividends_by_year.index[0].year         # Calculates growth rate (CAGR)
            last_year = dividends_by_year.index[-1].year
            first_dividend = dividends_by_year.iloc[0]
            last_dividend = dividends_by_year.iloc[-1]
            num_years = last_year - first_year
            cagr = ((last_dividend / first_dividend)
                ** (1 / num_years)) - 1
        else:
            cagr = None

        payouts_per_year = dividends.resample('YE').
            count().mean()
        if payouts_per_year > 3.5:                               # Determines payout frequency
            payout_frequency = "Quarterly"
        elif payouts_per_year > 1.5:
            payout_frequency = "Semi-Annual"
        elif payouts_per_year > 0.5:
            payout_frequency = "Annual"
        else:
            payout_frequency = "Irregular"
```

```
        return cagr, payout_frequency
    except Exception as e:
        print(f"Error processing {stock}: {e}")
        return None, None
```

Executing listing 5.2 loads companies from the S&P 500 index and extracts their dividend metrics. As the results of executing the code will vary depending on the execution time, we'll look at some results we got during the execution while writing this book.

In the second method, we collect ticker data through the tickers and filter by dividend-paying companies and those whose market cap exceeds a minimum threshold. This threshold is passed to the function as a parameter.

Listing 5.2 Executing code

```
import requests
import pandas as pd
import yfinance as yf
from io import StringIO


def get_sp500_tickers():
    url = "https://en.wikipedia.org/wiki/" \
        "List_of_S%26P_500_companies"
    response = requests.get(url)                                    ──┐ Collects all
    tables = pd.read_html(StringIO(response.text))                    │ tickers from S&P
    sp500_table = tables[0]                                           │ 500 companies
    return sp500_table["Symbol"].tolist()                           ──┘

def get_stocks_with_dividends_and_high_market_cap\
    (tickers, market_cap_threshold):
    data = []
    for ticker in tickers:
        try:                                                        ──┐
            stock = yf.Ticker(ticker)                                 │ Collects company
            info = stock.info                                         │ data from all tickers
            if info.get("dividendYield") and                        ──┘
                    info.get("marketCap") >= market_cap_threshold:
                cagr, payout_frequency = (
                    calc_div_growth_rate(stock))
                data.append({
                    "Ticker": ticker,
                    "Name": info.get("longName", "N/A"),
                    "Market Cap": info.get("marketCap"),
                    "Dividend Yield": info.
                    get("dividendYield"),                           ──┐ Gets dividend data
                    "Sector": info.get("sector", "N/A"),              │
                    "payoutRatio": info.                              │
                    get("payoutRatio", "N/A"),                        │
                    "dividendRate": info.                             │
                    get("dividendRate", "N/A"),                       │
                    "cagr": cagr,                                     │
                    "payout_frequency": payout_frequency,             │
                })
```

```
    except Exception as e:
        print(f"Error processing {ticker}: {e}")

return pd.DataFrame(data)
```

Running this code, we can review various companies in the DataFrame and form investment theses. Let's look at some outliers. Thermo Fisher Scientific (TMO) has a low payout ratio—at the time of writing, it's 7.09%. At the same time, dividend payments have grown for some years. Therefore, an investor could assess this company now based on the theory that TMO has a lot of room to grow if we compare the payout ratios to those of other companies. An investor who believes in the long-term business model of TMO could see an investment in this company as a long-term investment.

> **Real estate investment trusts**
>
> Real estate investment trusts (REITs) can be viewed as a distinct category among dividend-paying stocks. If you're seeking steady cash flow and diversification in your income portfolio, REITs are a compelling option. They offer several advantages for building an income portfolio:
>
> - *High dividend yields*—REITs are required by law to distribute at least 90% of their taxable income to shareholders as dividends, resulting in consistent and often higher-than-average yields compared to traditional dividend stocks.
> - *Portfolio diversification*—Adding REITs introduces real estate exposure to your portfolio, diversifying away from equities and bonds. Real estate tends to have low correlation with other asset classes, providing stability.
> - *Hedge against inflation*—Real estate assets typically appreciate over time, and rental income often rises with inflation, making REITs a good inflation hedge.
> - *Liquidity*—Unlike directly owning property, publicly traded REITs can be bought and sold on stock exchanges, offering liquidity without the complexities of managing real estate.
> - *Professional management*—Professionals manage REITs, meaning you benefit from their expertise in property acquisition, development, and leasing without needing to handle them yourself.
> - *Accessibility*—REITs allow small investors to gain exposure to real estate without requiring significant capital investments. You can invest in a wide range of property types (e.g., residential, commercial, industrial) with minimal cost.
> - *Tax benefits*—While dividends from REITs are typically taxed as ordinary income, some REIT dividends may qualify for the 20% pass-through deduction under US tax laws, reducing your effective tax rate.
> - *A variety of options*—REITs span different sectors, including health care, retail, residential, and data centers, allowing you to tailor your portfolio to specific real estate trends or needs.
> - *Steady income streams*—Many REITs generate predictable cash flows from long-term leases or stable tenant relationships, making them a reliable source of income.

We can also examine another company from our DataFrame, Exxon Mobil (XOM). At the time of writing, Exxon has a high dividend yield (3.70%), and its dividend payments have grown over the years. A dividend investor might consider buying Exxon with the idea that this company will keep growing, and, at the same time, the investors will harvest solid dividend payments from the start that can grow above bond yields, which we'll look at next.

## 5.2 Bonds

If you own a share of a company, you can brag at parties that it's partly yours. However, those who are literate about investing won't be impressed with your ownership of Apple, NVIDIA, or any other company unless your portfolio has beaten the market and you can be considered a master of capital appreciation.

While dealing with stocks involves equity, the bond business model relates to debt. In other words, bonds follow an IOU model: you lend money to someone, and the borrower pays interest until they return the borrowed money in full. The basic principle of bonds is outlined in figure 5.3.

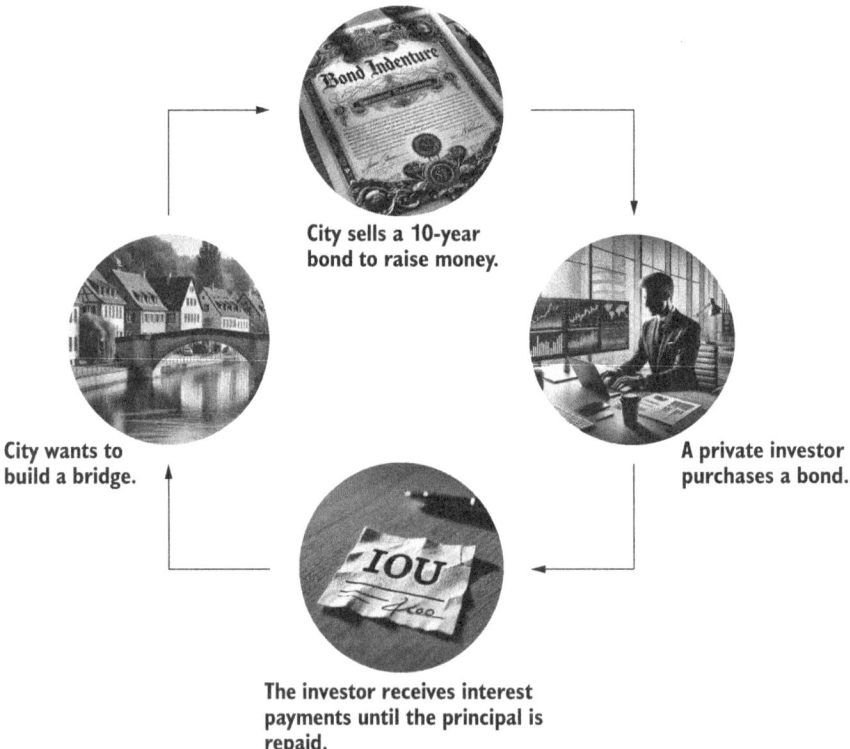

Figure 5.3  A plain vanilla bond

Many attributes define a bond's details, also called the *indenture*. Let's look at the particulars affecting how you can lend money and benefit from that:

- *Borrower*—The borrower refers to the party who receives the money. You can lend money, for instance, to the federal government, municipalities, or companies.
- *Maturation date*—This parameter defines the day the borrower must repay the *principal* (the total amount of borrowed money) to the lender. The time to maturity of a bond at its emission can vary from months to decades.
- *Coupon payments*—Eventually, a coupon rate is an investor's annual payment while holding a particular bond. Rates can also be floating or fixed, meaning coupon rates may change over time for some bonds.
- *Risk rating*—A bond's interest rate depends strongly on the borrower's default risk. The higher the risk, the higher the rate. Therefore, a third party needs to evaluate the default risk. Figure 5.4 outlines the rating structure of Moody's and Standard & Poor (S&P), two rating agencies in the United States.
- *Payment modalities*—For cash flow planning, investors must also know when they get their payments. The payment modalities define, among other things, how often and when the lender receives money. In many cases, coupon payments are made quarterly.

In its simplest form, a *vanilla bond* is an IOU with fixed coupon payment intervals and a set maturation date. However, there are many variations. For instance, some bonds allow borrowers to repay the principal in intervals alongside coupon payments, similar to how mortgage payments work. Bonds can also be collateralized, meaning that if the borrower defaults, an asset can be liquidated to repay the lender. This is akin to real estate foreclosures, where a property is seized if the owner can't keep up with payments.

While this book focuses on basic scenarios, it's worth noting that more complex variations of bonds are the subject of advanced certifications, such as the Chartered Financial Analyst (CFA). The job of a rating agency is to evaluate bonds offered on the bond market and to rate them. The higher the risk, the higher the returns an issuer offers to attract possible lenders. Table 5.1 shows the rating categories of the three big rating agencies in the United States.

**Table 5.1  Rating of bonds**

| Rating tier | Moody's | S&P | Fitch | Meaning |
|---|---|---|---|---|
| **Investment Grade** | | | | |
| Highest quality | Aaa | AAA | AAA | Prime credit quality, lowest risk |
| High quality | Aa1, Aa2, Aa3 | AA+, AA, AA- | AA+, AA, AA- | Very high credit quality |
| Upper medium grade | A1, A2, A3 | A+, A, A- | A+, A, A- | Strong capacity to meet financial commitments |

Table 5.1  Rating of bonds (continued)

| Rating tier | Moody's | S&P | Fitch | Meaning |
|---|---|---|---|---|
| Lower medium grade | Baa1, Baa2, Baa3 | BBB+, BBB, BBB- | BBB+, BBB, BBB- | Adequate capacity, some susceptibility to conditions |
| **Speculative grade** | | | | |
| Upper speculative | Ba, Ba, Ba3 | BB+, BB, BB- | BB+, BB, BB- | Higher risk of default, but financial commitment met |
| Highly speculative | B1, B2, B3 | B+, B, B- | B+, B, B- | Material default risk, but financial obligations still met |
| Substantial risk | Caa1, Caa2, Caa3 | CCC+, CCC, CCC- | CCC+, CCC, CCC- | Very high risk, substantial vulnerability to default |
| Near default | Ca | CC, C | CC, C | Highly vulnerable to default |
| Default | C | D | RD, D | In default |

Chapter 1 highlights two standard ways to earn money through investment: passive income and capital appreciation. As shown with bonds, coupon payments generate passive income. Bonds also offer the potential for capital appreciation. When issued, investors buy them on the primary market, where financial institutions act as intermediaries between the borrower and lender, setting an initial price (known as the *face value* or *par value*). Before the maturation date, bonds can be traded on the secondary market, where their price fluctuates. If the price rises above the face value, the bond trades above par; if it falls below, it trades below par. Buying a bond at a 5% discount to its face value means that 5% contributes to your yield upon maturity when the principal is repaid.

> **Why selling bonds before the maturation date may not always be unwise**
>
> Common sense tells us that if we lend $10,000 to someone, selling the debt to a third party for a smaller amount would be unwise. If we get our regular interest payments and principal back in full at maturity, why should we sell something for a loss?
>
> Contemplating such scenarios brings us closer to thinking like economists and forecasting. Investors might sell bonds as the market changes, and the possible capital appreciation of investing the money received by selling the bond below $10,000 might be higher than $10,000 plus all the coupon payments until then. Chapter 11 goes into detail about forecasting and making decisions based on forecasts.

Let's explore fixed-income assets from the US Treasury as a reference example. Depending on their durations, they are categorized as Treasury bills (maturing in up to one year), Treasury notes (maturing in up to 10 years), or Treasury bonds (maturing in more than 10 years). For further details, see https://mng.bz/lZPR.

Data can help identify bonds with projected yields higher than alternative investments. The Federal Reserve's interest rate policies directly influence bond prices and yields. When the Fed raises rates, new bonds are issued with higher yields to match prevailing rates, making existing bonds with lower yields less attractive and causing their prices to drop. Conversely, when the Fed lowers rates, existing bonds with higher yields become more appealing. Additionally, high interest rates increase default risks for weaker borrowers. Understanding interest rate trends is crucial when deciding between investing in stocks or bonds. The following code demonstrates how to collect bond interest rates using the EODHD platform introduced in chapter 3:

```
import requests
def fetch(country_code):
    url = f'https://eodhd.com/api/eod/{country_code}.GBOND?api_token={eod_api_key}&fmt=json'
    return requests.get(url).json()

import pandas as pd
us = pd.DataFrame(data=fetch("US10Y"))
```

We can now plot the results and explore the outcome. Looking at the rates when plotting the graph, we can reason that investing in a bond would have been a better decision than in previous times, as shown in figure 5.4:

```
import matplotlib.pyplot as plt
p = us[["date", "adjusted_close"]]
p.set_index("date", inplace=True)

p.plot(figsize = (12,8), fontsize = 12)
plt.ylabel("Price (USD)")
plt.title("yield Price Chart", fontsize = 15)
plt.show()
```

Alternatively, we can analyze high-risk bonds, often referred to as junk bonds, and use data to determine if some are undervalued relative to their ratings. Unfortunately, the free EODHD version is limited and doesn't provide corporate data. The following code uses an alternative open platform to load data from an International Securities Identification Number (ISIN), a bond identifier. The REST API returns the metadata for the bond based on the input:

```
import requests

headers = {
    "Content-Type": "application/json",
    "X-OPENFIGI-APIKEY": OPEN_FIGI_KEY
}

isin = "US36166NAJ28"  # Example ISIN

data = [{"idType": "ID_ISIN", "idValue": isin}]

response = requests.post("https://api.openfigi.com/v3/mapping",
                         headers=headers, json=data)
print(response.json())
```

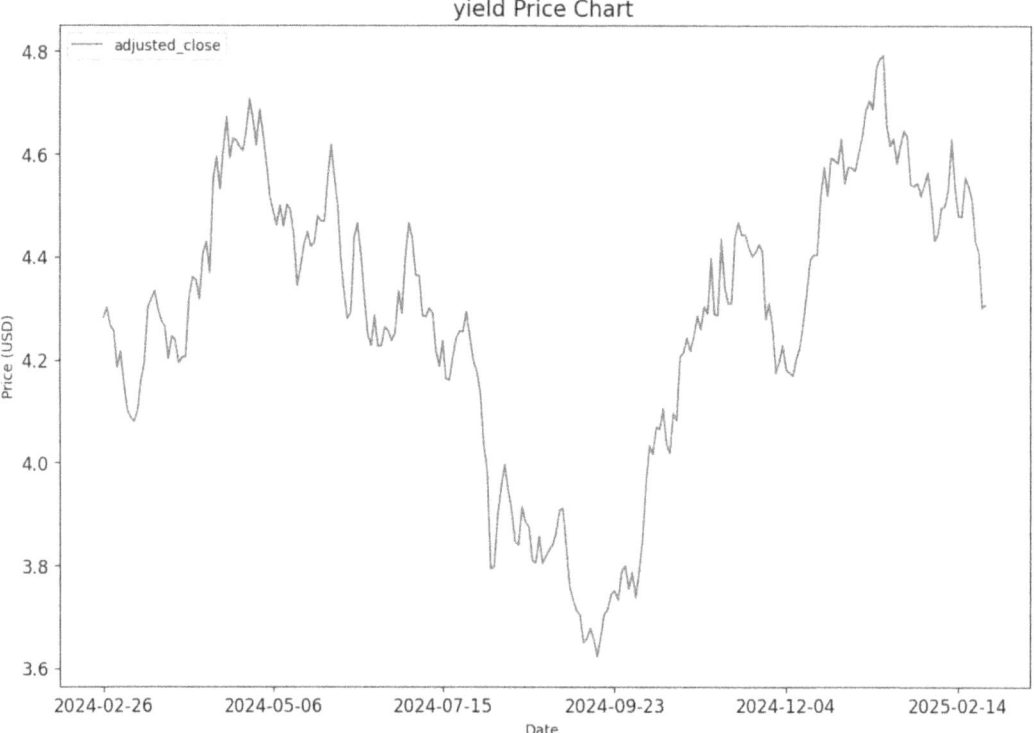

**Figure 5.4** Return of US Treasury bonds

This approach is highly speculative and may require insider knowledge. Another speculative tool is the *credit default swap* (CDS), which some readers may recognize from the movie *The Big Short*. A CDS acts as an insurance contract against bond default: you pay an ongoing premium, and if the debtor defaults, the insurer compensates you for the bond's full value. Interestingly, CDS can be detached from the original lender. For example, if A borrows money from B, C can purchase an insurance from D that is paid to C when B defaults.

Michael Burry famously used data to predict the 2007 financial crisis, betting on the defaults of various collateralized debt obligations (CDOs)—packages of bundled bonds. His foresight proved correct, showcasing how deep data analysis can uncover opportunities and risks.

While these advanced strategies offer potential, they are complex and risky. For simplicity, bonds can still provide steady yields with lower risk than stocks. Data can help determine whether dividend-paying stocks or bonds are better suited for passive income. Next, we explore a third passive income option: cryptocurrency.

## 5.3 Crypto staking

Most individuals who accumulated significant wealth through cryptocurrency did so via capital appreciation. They invested in cryptocurrency at low prices during its nascent stages or after one of its crashes and reaped substantial gains as its value soared. Crypto enthusiasts argue that cryptocurrencies, with a few exceptions, have a constant capital appreciation as a scarce resource. As there can never be more than 21 million BTC, the idea is that the value of Bitcoin will always increase. Consequently, if you believe in the long-term value of crypto, there isn't much more to say, as all you need to do is wait for the right time to sell.

This chapter focuses on strategies to generate passive income with cryptocurrency, as there is still much to learn. But before that, we need to recap some crypto basics to be able to invest.

### 5.3.1 Ledgers and exchanges

One thing enthusiasts and critics may agree on is the number of scams and the potential risks of losing money with crypto if you don't know what you're doing. Even if we don't go into speculative actions in this book, exploring some risk management basics is necessary.

> **WARNING** Knowledge of cryptocurrency reduces your risk of being a victim of fraud or scam. However, the cryptocurrency industry is highly unregulated, and even experienced crypto traders have lost considerable amounts of money. Cryptocurrency is likely to remain a risky investment.

The term "lost cryptocurrencies," as used by the media, can lead to misconceptions because cryptocurrencies can't be lost. However, crypto holders can lose their keys, confirming their cryptocurrency ownership. We'll explain this in detail by illustrating how cryptocurrency works, as depicted in figure 5.5.

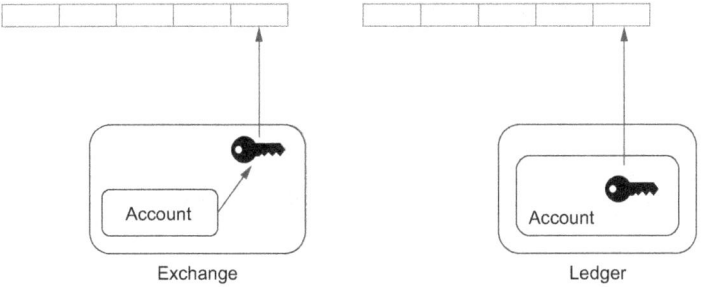

Figure 5.5 If you hold cryptocurrency on an exchange, the exchange owns the keys signing the transactions on the blockchain. Ledgers, such as cold wallets, provide ways to store the keys that signed the last transaction in a safe place. Be aware that cryptocurrency, a distributed transaction log, is a public blockchain and therefore never stored on your device or account.

In its simplest technical terms, blockchain is all about private keys that sign blocks of an immutable, distributed transaction log during a transaction. Cryptocurrency monetizes this principle. The more blocks are signed with your key, the more ownership you have.

We can use accounts on exchanges, such as Binance or OKX. For investors working with brokers, using an exchange seems like having a brokerage account from a bird's-eye view. Exchanges invest to ensure that your account on their platform is as safe as possible from attacks by hackers. They will encourage—or even enforce—all kinds of account protection mechanisms, such as multifactor authentication. Their user interfaces are user-friendly, aiming to make it easy to buy and sell cryptocurrency.

However, we need to go into more detail to understand the problems many investors see with an exchange. Exchanges enable you to trigger transactions using your user account; however, the exchanges sign the transaction with *their* keys, which is the source of the slogan "Not your keys, not your coins." Most cryptocurrency exchanges reside in countries where it's difficult to regulate them. The risks of this lack of regulation have become apparent with the FTX scandal, in which the company misused the investments of private investors, and its principal founder, Sam Bankman-Fried, became a symbol of crypto fraud.

To completely control your crypto investments, you need to be in control of the keys that are used for transactions. You can store your keys on your physical devices (a hardware ledger or cold wallet) or on software service providers who provide you with the keys (a software ledger or warm wallet). The concept is the same: crypto transactions are signed, but in the case of a ledger, transactions are signed with your key. You still need to protect your keys, but you've vastly reduced your exposure to market risks (namely, that the value of your cryptocurrency might go down) and cyberattacks on the blockchain.

### 5.3.2 Mining and staking

Crypto user forums are flooded with offers on how to get rich with crypto, and many scams lure people into highly speculative and risky ways to make money. Mining and staking are two forms of passive income that can also appeal to risk-aware investors. Let's explore these two options.

*Mining* involves using computational power to validate transactions on a blockchain network. This approach is also called a Proof-of-Work (PoW) consensus mechanism. If the machines in your mining farms solve a complex mathematical problem, you receive some cryptocurrency. While it can be lucrative, mining requires significant up-front investment in hardware and incurs ongoing electricity costs. The profitability depends on factors such as the cryptocurrency mined, mining difficulty, and local electricity rates.

*Staking* allows crypto holders to lock up their assets in a blockchain network to support its operations, such as validating transactions. In return, stakers earn rewards, often as additional tokens. This method, also called the Proof-of-Stake (PoS) consensus mechanism, is energy-efficient compared to mining using the previously mentioned PoW mechanism. However, it requires holding a certain minimum amount of cryptocurrency. It involves the risk of token devaluation, which can be roughly compared with inflation: the more tokens are created, the more the worth of existing tokens will be reduced.

Becoming a crypto entrepreneur may sound appealing to engineers. After all, they can use their core strengths to build a moneymaking business. However, in many cases, a substantial up-front investment is needed. Without investment in strong hardware, there's no mining, and mining is still expensive if your hardware is in a region with high electricity prices. Staking can also be costly, but there are still some forms in which you can create revenue while you hold your cryptocurrency for the long term. Let's look at these options.

### 5.3.3 *Affordable staking options*

Staking and validation mean your cryptocurrency is used to validate network transactions with a PoS consensus mechanism. A validator node is a computer on the internet representing existing cryptocurrency stakeholders. During a transaction, validators are chosen randomly, based on stake size or other factors. Validators confirm transactions, propose blocks, and add them to the blockchain. For this service, validators earn rewards in the form of a minimal share of the transaction.

In this process, individual investors can generate passive income with cryptocurrency. They can set up a validator node to validate transactions. Being in control of a validator often means a significant investment. To provide a validator for Ethereum, you need to stake at least 32 ETH (https://ethereum.org/en/staking/). This is a substantial up-front investment. If ETH is priced above $3,000, the initial investment exceeds $100,000.

The easier alternative is to delegate your cryptocurrency to a third-party validator. The validator will provide you with rewards but will take a commission, reducing your rewards compared to running your node; this approach avoids the substantial time and financial commitments of setting up and maintaining validator hardware and software. Hardware ledgers typically offer software to manage positions, such as Ledger Live or Trezor Suite. To stake your cryptocurrency on a hardware ledger, simply follow the instructions as shown in the supplier's software to manage your crypto investments. Please be aware that cryptocurrency is largely unregulated, and there are fraud risks when you stake coins.

> **Are stable coins the safest way to passive income using cryptocurrency?**
> When considering staking rewards, some cryptocurrencies offer exceptionally high returns. For example, networks such as Cosmos (ATOM) and Polkadot (DOT), which act as bridges between blockchains, can provide staking rewards of up to 20%. However, calling this a guaranteed income is misleading. Tokens that provide high-stakes

> *(continued)*
>
> rewards often have a high rate of devaluation. Consider the following common scenario: Pierre buys 100 tokens at $7 each for $700 and earns 20% staking rewards. If the token's price drops to $5, Pierre's 120 tokens, after collecting the rewards, would only be worth $600, resulting in a $100 loss if sold.
>
> Stablecoins present an alternative for staking, as their value is pegged to government-issued currencies such as the US dollar. For instance, someone purchasing 100 USD Coin tokens at $1 each and earning a 10% staking reward would end up with 110 tokens worth $110, potentially outperforming traditional bonds. However, staking rewards are often volatile, and high returns aren't guaranteed if the interest rate fluctuates. Evaluating the risks and potential fluctuations in token value is essential for anyone considering staking as an income strategy.

So, how much can you earn through staking? One challenge is that staking rewards vary significantly depending on transaction value. It differs from interest payments of bonds, where there are constant interest payments. Table 5.2. shows average staking rewards over time.

Table 5.2  Staking rewards

| Cryptocurrency | Average staking rewards (APY) in % |
|---|---|
| Ethereum (ETH) | 4–6 |
| Cardano (ADA) | 4–6 |
| Solana (SOL) | 6–8 |
| Polkadot (DOT) | ~14 |
| Avalanche (AVAX) | 8–12 |

Chapter 6 will show how to access your assets—stocks, ETFs, bonds, and crypto—through a Python API. One specific challenge with using cold wallets is that they are designed to limit access to protect you from hackers. Providing Python APIs to access information related to cryptocurrency isn't the primary use case for a hardware ledger provider. Therefore, we'll explain how to access Binance, although we want to emphasize that many crypto investors advise against using exchanges to hold cryptocurrency.

> **NOTE** As staking means providing cryptocurrencies for transactions, they can also be locked for specific periods. Keep that in mind if you, in parallel, desire to make money using day trading.

## 5.4 Early retirement

We can approach financial independence in two ways. One way is to accumulate enough money to live off these reserves for the remainder of your life. For most, the more likely path is to create a high enough passive income stream. By knowing your total annual expenses, you can calculate the money needed for financial independence using a simple formula: divide your yearly costs by your expected return rate. While this formula ignores factors such as inflation and safety margin, a reasonable estimate for a low-risk yield is around 5%.

> **NOTE** If you plan to retire through passive income by investing all of your money in an account that returns a 5% interest rate per year, which covers exactly your yearly expenses, please consider the inflation and other factors that may affect your spending. The average inflation rate in the United States from 1975 to 2024 was 3.5%.

Many financial advisors recommend adjusting your investment strategy with age. As you age, shifting toward assets that provide passive income becomes more common. This is partly because growth portfolios yield higher long-term returns than fixed-income investments. For example, the Vanguard S&P 500 ETF (VOO) has demonstrated a 10-year growth rate of 192.20% as of January 2025. Similarly, the iShares MSCI World ETF (URTH), which invests globally, achieved a return of 123.40% over the same period. Both outperform most high-fixed-income portfolios and offer dividends in addition to growth.

This underscores a timeless principle emphasized by value investors such as Charlie Munger and Warren Buffett: patience is one of the greatest virtues in investing. Through the power of compounding, those who adhere to sound principles and maintain a disciplined approach can achieve significant wealth over time.

Still, even if you're the most patient person on earth, remember that there's no universal investment strategy for everyone. If you consider retiring, whether at a younger or older age, projected long-term returns that have yet to materialize won't pay your bills. In the worst-case scenario, growth assets with the potential for high returns might even evaporate. Even if you bet on stable companies, it's a problem if you need money in a bear market and must sell at a lower price than in a bull market.

## *Summary*

- Some companies pay dividends to shareholders, making them a potential source of passive income.
- Typically, larger, more mature companies with limited growth opportunities offer higher dividends. These companies are often classified as "cash cows" in the BSG Growth-Share Matrix.
- Investors can evaluate dividend-paying stocks using metrics such as payout ratio, dividend growth rate, annual payment, and dividend yield.
- Real Estate Investment Trusts (REITs) are specialized investment vehicles that generate passive income, primarily through property-related investments.
- Bonds are fixed-income assets where investors lend money to an entity (e.g., government, municipality, or corporation) in exchange for interest payments. At maturity, the principal is returned to the lender.

- Payment modalities, such as interest rates and payout frequencies, might vary per bond, and investors must carefully study them when making investment decisions.
- Bond classifications specifically for US Treasury bonds include Treasury bills, which mature in under 1 year; Treasury notes, which mature between 1 and 10 years; and Treasury bonds, which mature in over 10 years.
- Central bank interest rates, like those set by the Federal Reserve, significantly affect bond values. Riskier bonds offer higher yields, as assessed by rating agencies.
- In a very simplified view, cryptocurrency works based on signing blocks during a transaction with a private key. If you don't own that key, you don't own the cryptocurrency.
- Cryptocurrency is controversial and has sparked many debates. The best way for a newbie to understand the arguments of both sides is to research the details first before forming an opinion.
- Whether you're an enthusiast or a critic, be aware of many scams involving crypto.
- Cryptocurrency offers several passive income opportunities, with staking being among the most accessible. By staking, your cryptocurrency supports transaction validation.
- Staking rewards can fluctuate, and cryptocurrencies are susceptible to scams and fraud. Avoid holding assets on exchanges to minimize risks and use secure cold storage options such as hardware wallets.
- While passive income strategies offer stability, growth stocks typically outperform them over time due to compounding returns and capital appreciation.
- Many see 5% as a realistic value for a passive income. Still, if you have high inflation and other unexpected expenses, it might take longer to retire early and say goodbye to corporate life forever.

# Building an asset monitor

**This chapter covers**

- Collecting portfolio data from online and offline sources
- Analyzing asset performance in a portfolio
- Projecting future returns from assets and portfolios
- Creating monthly reports on passive income and gains
- Collecting data in a Google Sheets document

In the previous chapters, we showed how to select assets for possible investments. Assuming you might have already bought assets, it's time to show you how to monitor existing portfolios. This chapter is about staying in control, staying informed, and maximizing the potential returns of your assets.

First, we'll walk you through collecting your holdings from various brokers. Next, we'll aggregate this data into clear, actionable insights: tracking your total passive income, identifying standout performers (both positive and negative), and uncovering areas for improvement. Finally, we'll project your future earnings and growth to answer the big question: When will you hit your financial milestones?

We gather data using Google Sheets, enabling us to visualize our information, filter it, and delve deeper into the details. Let's uncover the secrets to managing your stock portfolio like a pro. Ready to level up? Let's get started.

> **NOTE** The Git repository and the download sections contain a full-functioning Jupyter Notebook. The code snippets in this book help to understand the code, but not every helper variable is declared in the listings in the book. You can also refer to the appendix to learn about the required Python libraries.

## 6.1 Architecture

In this chapter, we'll build a data science notebook to consolidate information about your holdings from various sources into a central repository. We aim to track key metrics, including the current portfolio value and projected annual returns from capital appreciation and passive income. As illustrated in figure 6.1, we'll extract data for each asset category and export it to dedicated worksheets, allowing you to view stocks, crypto, bonds, and other asset types in separate spreadsheet tabs.

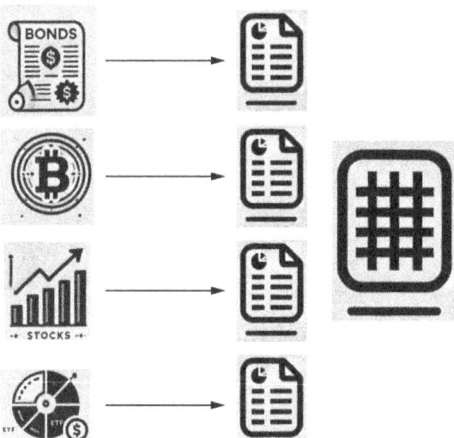

Figure 6.1 Data Flow from asset data to worksheets in a Google Sheets document

This chapter will gather data from two stockbrokers and one cryptocurrency exchange as a demonstration portfolio. Even if you use different platforms, the provided code samples can serve as templates for building custom data pipelines to collect information from your broker.

Hundreds of institutions and products, such as banks, brokers, exchanges, and crypto wallets, offer you the ability to store assets worldwide. Unfortunately, they don't use a single standard to provide you with access to your portfolio using code. Some of them may not offer access at all that supports automated data retrieval.

Figure 6.2 illustrates the data extraction challenge: while some assets can be retrieved from multiple platforms, others may not be accessible via API. To address this, we merge online data with manually tracked holdings. An exception arises with an asset with no digital footprint, such as real estate. Entering these details manually into a spreadsheet may be the most practical approach.

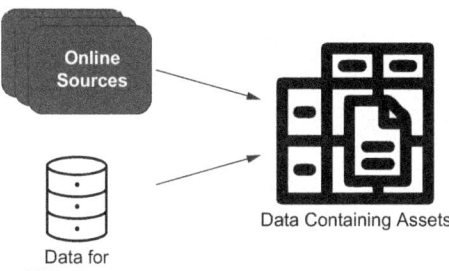

**Figure 6.2  Collecting online sources into DataFrames**

Let's create a table to track all holdings without automated data retrieval, named offline_asset. The Jupyter Notebook, available for download at the publisher's website, uses an SQLite database as file-based storage, which is ideal for demonstration and exploration. These notebooks may declare some variables that aren't listed in the examples.

Following is the Data Definition Language (DDL) statement for the database table you need to execute in a SQL console connected to the database. In the appendix, we'll provide some guidelines for those who aren't familiar with SQLite. In the code repository, we also have a small reference database with some prefilled datasets. If you start working with your data, you also need to fill in these tables with additional entries that reflect your portfolio.

```
create table main.offline_asset
(
    ticker          TEXT
        constraint InterestTable_pk
            primary key,
    yield           REAL,
    avg_price       REAL,
    exchange        TEXT,
    amount          REAL,
    asset_type      TEXT
);
```

We use the ticker as a unique identifier. Even if we occasionally forget the company name behind that ticker, we can collect all the required data once we uniquely identify the asset. We use the yield column for passive income from assets such as bonds, stocks with dividend payments, or cryptos with staking options. The avg_price column reflects the weighted average price of all past purchases.

We also track where we hold an asset in the exchange column and record the shares we own in the amount column. Finally, we need the asset_type column to identify the asset type, such as stock, exchange-traded funds (ETFs), crypto, or bond.

Once the table is created, we must add our position as a dataset. The following command loads the offline data into a DataFrame with a one-liner. We'll later merge the content of this DataFrame with the data collected from brokers and exchanges:

```
all_offline_assets = pd.read_sql('offline_asset', engine, index_col='ticker')
```

This chapter's complete notebook can be downloaded from the publisher's website. The chapter will explain essential data extraction, transformation, and export code.

## 6.2 The spreadsheet

Before describing the logic, let's look at the expected outcome. We export data into a spreadsheet, and you can download a template from https://mng.bz/Bzyl. Clone this template, and set up the appropriate permissions to access the spreadsheet. Afterward, you can download a JSON file containing all the required parameters to access the Google Sheet document online. Once you've set this up correctly, including references to this file in your source code, you can export the financial data into the worksheets using the code we'll introduce in this chapter. Alternatively, you can download a Microsoft Excel file from the download section and convert it to a Google Sheets document. The file is also available in the book's GitHub repository (https://github.com/StefanPapp/investing-for-programmers).

Let's explore what the worksheets will look like. Figure 6.3 shows a screenshot featuring reference data on stocks. Note that each ticker is part of a portfolio, and you can filter by each column. We display the number of shares we own for a ticker, the total value, and the expected yearly yield. We also calculated potential losses or gains in two columns. The Live column represents real-time data gathered through cell formulas that pull information from Google Finance. While the Value column represents the total value of a position at the time of export, we can also track changes since the last update with live data.

| ticker | portfolio | value | Yield | # amount | Proj. Gains | Past Gains | live | chg_since_last_update |
|---|---|---|---|---|---|---|---|---|
| INVZ | DI | $1.120,00 | $0,00 | 700,00 | $798,00 | 595,00 | $644,00 | -$476,00 |
| LAZR | DI | $37,90 | $0,00 | 7,00 | $151,68 | -56,53 | $23,24 | -$14,66 |
| OUST | DI | $9.061,00 | $0,00 | 820,00 | $1.599,00 | 754,40 | $11.283,20 | $2.222,20 |
| AEVA | DI | $890,34 | $0,00 | 209,00 | $252,37 | 177,65 | $3.981,45 | $3.091,11 |
| GOOGL | AI | $21.076,00 | $88,00 | 110,00 | $2.816,44 | 3.136,10 | $18.503,10 | -$2.572,90 |

Figure 6.3  A reference example of the Google Sheets worksheet with stock information

Figure 6.4 shows the overview page of this spreadsheet template called "assets," which also contains some reference data. On this worksheet, we sum up the value and yields of all assets. The graph shows the asset type distribution, giving you a good overview of your distribution. You can see right away, for instance, that this reference dataset

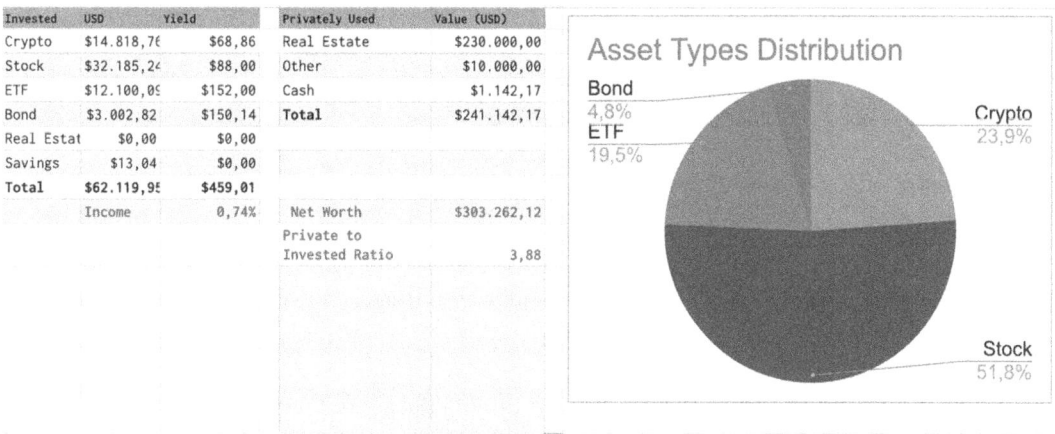

Figure 6.4  Overview worksheet with assets grouped by value (USD column) and passive income (Yield column)

represents a perilous portfolio as most risk-averse investors would prefer to have a far higher distribution on index funds, which are held as ETFs.

We'll now demonstrate how to collect data, extract essential metrics, convert all values to a single currency (in case we hold assets in different currencies), and export that data to a Google Sheet. Let's get started!

## 6.3 Extracting data

Stockbrokers facilitate the trading and holding of assets for investors. This book examines two brokers that offer Python APIs for accessing account balances: Alpaca and Interactive Brokers. Unlike many brokers restricted to specific countries, both provide services internationally, making them accessible to readers around the globe. Remember that registering with a broker requires identification, such as a passport, as well as information about your tax residency. This procedure is known as Know Your Customer (KYC) and is mandatory for the investment services industry. In the appendix, we'll provide more insights about brokers.

> **NOTE**  Take time to research a broker. Many brokers restrict their services to a few countries. Higher or lower order and transfer fees may affect gains and losses. If you want to automate, be aware that not every broker offers APIs to their clients. Validate that every broker is serious. If you're in doubt, inquire about the broker with a financial advisor.

To process data from various sources, we need to store it in a unified format and merge it. Therefore, we must define the target data structure for our DataFrames. Let's examine the required attributes:

- *Ticker*—The stock symbol that serves as a unique identifier.
- *Number of shares*—The total number of shares currently held.

- *Average price*—The average purchase price aggregated for all transactions.
- *Exchange*—The exchange on which the asset is traded.
- *Broker*—A constant value to identify the data source. In our case, this will be either INTERACTIVE_BROKER or ALPACA.

### 6.3.1 Alpaca: A developer-first broker

Alpaca markets itself as a developer-first broker, offering modern APIs designed for seamless integration into your workflows. To use the Alpaca platform, you'll need an account, and you must generate access keys on this account. These keys enable programmatic access to your account for tasks such as retrieving balances or executing trades.

For this book's showcase, we use the dotenv library to load the keys securely from a plain text *.env* file. Be cautious if you use this library!

> **WARNING** Avoid storing sensitive information on shared or unsecured computers. Stolen keys can lead to unauthorized actions that could compromise your account.

Ensure the .env file contains your keys in this format:

```
ALPACA_API_KEY=your_api_key_here
ALPACA_SECRET_KEY=your_secret_key_here
```

Once your environment is correctly configured, listing 6.1 demonstrates how to connect to Alpaca using the py-alpaca library. After creating the `trading_client` object, we call the `get_all_position()` method to load every dataset into the DataFrame. We also select the columns to create a data structure that can be merged with the data from other brokers. Install the Python package for Alpaca via `pip install alpaca-py`.

#### Listing 6.1 Extracting data from Alpaca

```
from alpaca.trading.client import TradingClient
ALPACA_KEY = os.getenv("ALPACA_API_KEY")               ◁── Collects the secrets
ALPACA_SECRET = os.getenv("ALPACA_SECRET_KEY")             from a local .env file

trading_client = TradingClient(ALPACA_KEY, ALPACA_SECRET, paper=False)

positions_data = [
    [position.symbol, position.qty,
     position.avg_entry_price,
     position.exchange.value, 'ALPACA']
    for position in trading_client.get_all_positions()
]                                                       ◁── Collects data
alpaca_balances = pd.DataFrame(                             through the method
    positions_data,                                         get_all_positions()
    columns=[COL_TICKER, COL_AMOUNT, COL_PRICE_INIT,
             COL_EXCHANGE, COL_BROKER])
```

If you don't want to invest real money and want to experiment, you can also use Alpaca's paper accounts by setting the parameter `paper` to `true`. You can see a paper account as a test environment for investing.

> **NOTE** Alpaca only supports US dollars as currency. Although transferring money in any currency to Alpaca is possible, remember that international transfers that convert currency can be expensive. Investors often must also wait days for the funds to arrive. You can transfer cryptocurrency to bypass currency conversion and convert your crypto tokens to USD on Alpaca.

### 6.3.2 *Interactive Brokers: A legacy powerhouse with a modern twist*

Founded in 1978, Interactive Brokers has built a reputation as a feature-rich platform for investors. However, some programmers find its approach to integrating APIs a bit old-school. Unlike modern cloud-based brokers, Interactive Brokers requires installing a local application, the Trader Workstation (TWS), to access data through a Python API. APIs connect to this workstation, adding complexity for developers building cloud-based investment solutions.

That said, once set up correctly, Interactive Brokers offers powerful tools for retrieving and managing investment data. With the ib_insync library, you can connect to the TWS programmatically. Note that, depending on your configuration, you must adjust some settings in the TWS. We'll add more details in the appendix. Listing 6.2 shows how to retrieve data using this library. We collect the data for our positions by calling the `positions()` method. We unwrap the data from the returned data structure and ensure that we have all the data in the same structure as the data from Alpaca.

**Listing 6.2 Extracting data from Interactive Brokers**

```
from ib_insync import *
util.startLoop()                          Connects to the local
ib = IB()                                 TraderWorkstation
ib.connect()

ibr = util.df(ib.positions())
ibr[COL_TICKER] = (ibr.contract.apply
                    (lambda x: x.symbol))
ibr["exchange"] = (ibr.contract.apply      Collects data through
                    (lambda x: x.exchange))  ib.positions()
ibr["broker"] = "INTERACTIVE_BROKER"

IB_balances = (ibr[[COL_TICKER, 'position', 'avgCost',
                COL_EXCHANGE, COL_BROKER]].
            rename(columns={'position': COL_AMOUNT,
                            'avgCost': COL_PRICE_INIT}))
```

## 6.4 Enriching data

We now have data in two DataFrames containing information from two brokers arranged in the same data structures. Additionally, we have a DataFrame that includes offline assets. We can merge them as shown here:

```
all_positions_raw = pd.concat([alpaca_balances, IB_balances, offline_assets])
```

All the information from our data sources is now consolidated into one DataFrame. We've completed the data extraction.

We aim to use the tickers in the `all_positions_raw` DataFrame as identifiers to obtain financial data from Yahoo Finance and Google Finance. We must complete one remaining task before merging the data from our holdings with information from this platform. In most instances, the tickers that brokers provide align with those found on financial platforms. However, exceptions do exist. For example, shares of Berkshire Hathaway with the ticker BRK.B are identified as BRK-B on Yahoo Finance. We can create a lookup table that maps broker tickers to those used on financial platforms to prevent issues arising from mismatched tickers.

We'll also use this table to map each asset to a portfolio. This allows an investor to group similar assets, which can be crucial when filtering and comparing performances on a more abstract level. Following is a list of the five columns we need for this lookup table:

- *Ticker*—The broker's unique identifier for a stock
- *Asset type*—The type of asset (here, stocks; different types of assets will be collected later)
- *Portfolio*—The portfolio the asset belongs to
- *Yahoo*—The ticker name on Yahoo Finance
- *Google*—The ticker name on Google Finance

One of the simplest techniques for demonstration purposes is again using SQLite to store these values. We can create a table for the asset lookup using DDL and SQL commands:

```
create table main.asset_lookup
(
    ticker     TEXT not null
        constraint base_security_pk
            primary key,
    asset_type TEXT not null,
    portfolio  TEXT,
    yahoo      TEXT,
    google     TEXT
);
```

When we populate this table with data from our holdings, we can retain NULL values for the `yahoo` and `google` columns if there are no discrepancies between the data from brokers and the corresponding financial platform. Listing 6.3 illustrates how to load data from a local SQLite database. Once loaded, these columns are combined with `all_positions_raw`, which contains our positions in memory. We also populate all identifiers with the `ticker` column value if there is no mismatch between tickers. In other words, assuming we've stored "BRK-B" for Yahoo Finance, we end up with a mapping between BRK.B (for the `ticker` column) and BRK-B (for the `yahoo` column). If the `yahoo` or `google` columns are null, we populate them with the value in the `ticker` column. Note that you must fill in all the rows with data representing your portfolios to work with this lookup table for your positions.

### Listing 6.3 Loading metadata

```
from sqlalchemy import create_engine
engine = create_engine('sqlite:///portfolio.sqlite')
asset_lookup = pd.read_sql('asset_lookup',
                           engine,                         ◁─── Loads data
                           index_col=COL_TICKER)                from SQLite

all_positions = all_positions_raw.merge(asset_lookup, on=COL_TICKER)

all_positions[COL_YAHOO] = (all_positions[COL_YAHOO].
                            fillna(
    all_positions[COL_TICKER]))
all_positions[COL_GOOGLE] = (all_positions[COL_GOOGLE].fillna(    ◁─── Fills NULL values
    all_positions[COL_TICKER]))                                        with ticker data
```

Finally, we can start processing data. The function `collect_fin_data`, as shown here, expects a list of tickers and returns an object with all company information for the assets:

```
def collect_fin_data(tickers):
    return {ticker: yf.Ticker(ticker).info for ticker in tickers}
```

If you pass a long list, the query might run for a couple seconds as the `Ticker` function in the loop downloads data from Yahoo Finance for multiple assets.

## 6.5 Processing assets

Now that we've enriched data, it's time to go into further detail and show how to aggregate data for assets. The section on stocks will also show you how to convert assets held in different currencies to a unified currency, which can also be applied to other assets.

### 6.5.1 Stocks

The following code extracts stocks and collects all information using the `collect_fin_data` method. We filter the stocks from our data collection for all our assets and collect the data for the companies:

```
shares = all_positions[all_positions[COL_ASSET_TYPE].isin(["STOCK"])]
unique_stock_tickers = shares[COL_YAHOO].unique().tolist()
yfin_data_stocks = collect_fin_info(unique_stock_tickers)
```

We now have Yahoo data for all of our stocks in the DataFrame `yfin_data`, which allows us to merge relevant attributes into the DataFrame holding our shares. The function `merge_fin_data`, shown in listing 6.4, extracts the desired metrics we pass as a parameter.

##### Listing 6.4 Merging Yahoo Finance data into DataFrames

```
def merge_fin_data (df_orig, ticker_data, metrics):
    df = df_orig.copy(deep=True)
    for m in metrics:
        df[m] = None

    for ind in df.index:
        ticker_symbol = df.loc[ind, "yahoo"]         ⎤ Gets the symbol
        company = ticker_data.get(ticker_symbol, {}) ⎦ from the DataFrame

        for m in metrics:                            ⎤ Adds desired metrics
            df.loc[ind, m] = company.get(m, None)    ⎦ to the DataFrame

    return df

ratios = ["currentPrice", "targetMeanPrice", "dividendRate"]

stocks = merge_fin_data(shares, yfin_data_stocks, ratios)
```

One challenge can be different currencies. For example, an individual investor might hold Microsoft shares, listed on NASDAQ, in US dollars; in parallel, he might hold BMW shares, listed on the Frankfurt Stock Exchange (FSE), in euros. Converting all positions into a single currency helps sum up the total value of our assets. The code in listing 6.5 provides us with a method for conversion using the Python library CurrencyConverter. Note that we need to agree on a target currency. In the code, we map the exchange—each exchange trades money in its country's currency—to the US dollar as the target currency by default.

> **NOTE** Some investors try to avoid different currencies as they add additional risks through fluctuations in exchange rates. There are also special types of stocks called American Depositary Receipts (ADR) that allow a foreign company to list on a local exchange. However, this isn't available for all assets.

A showcase mapping can only contain a minimum set of exchanges, such as Euronext Amsterdam (AEB) or Vienna Stock Exchange (VSE). Extend this list to include any exchanges you might be using that aren't covered by the mapping.

##### Listing 6.5 Converting currency

```
from currency_converter import CurrencyConverter

def get_conversion(target_currency = "USD"):
    c = CurrencyConverter()                ⎤ Sets up the
    mapping_exchange_currency = {          ⎦ mapping
```

```
        'ARCA': c.convert(1, 'USD', target_currency),
        'NASDAQ': c.convert(1, 'USD', target_currency),
        'NYSE': c.convert(1, 'USD', target_currency),
        'BATS': c.convert(1, 'USD', target_currency),
        'PINK': c.convert(1, 'USD', target_currency),
        'IBIS': c.convert(1, 'EUR', target_currency),
        'AEB': c.convert(1, 'EUR', target_currency),
        'VSE': c.convert(1, 'EUR', target_currency),
        'AMEX': c.convert(1, 'USD', target_currency),
        'BVME': c.convert(1, 'EUR', target_currency),
        'SBF': c.convert(1, 'EUR', target_currency),
        'EBS': c.convert(1, 'CHF', target_currency),
        'CPH': c.convert(1, 'DKK', target_currency),
        'PRA': c.convert(1, 'CZK', target_currency)
    }
    return mapping_exchange_currency
conversion = get_conversion()      ◁──  Specifies USD as the target currency
```

Once this is set up, we can convert all columns with different currencies into one standardized currency. The code in listing 6.6 converts the following parameters of an asset into a single currency:

- Current price
- Average price
- Dividend rate

Let's examine the code in the listing to perform the conversion. We pass the column name containing values in different currencies as a parameter for this conversion. In this code sample, we convert the initial price, current price, and yield into US dollars.

**Listing 6.6 Executing conversion**

```
def convert(row, column_name):
    return (row[column_name] *
            conversion[row[COL_EXCHANGE]])                      ◁──  Maps the conversion to the exchange column

df[COL_PRICE_INIT_USD] = df.apply(convert,
                                  column_name=COL_PRICE_INIT,
                                  axis=1)                       ◁──
df[COL_PRICE_USD] = df.apply(convert,
                             column_name=col_price,
                             axis=1)                            ◁──  Gets a single currency from a field
df[COL_YIELD_USD] = df.apply(convert,
                             column_name=col_yield,
                             axis=1)                            ◁──
```

The information in the DataFrame is per single share. Listing 6.7 shows how to aggregate values based on the number of shares we own. As we likely have more than one share for each position, we must multiply the values, such as price or yield, by the number of shares to get a position's total value and yield. Based on the price estimations, we can also calculate past and potential future gains and losses.

#### Listing 6.7 Aggregating values

```
df[COL_TOT_INIT_VALUE] = (df[COL_AMOUNT] * df[COL_PRICE_INIT_USD]).round(2)
df[COL_TOT_VALUE] = (df[COL_AMOUNT] * df[COL_PRICE_USD]).round(2)
df[COL_TOT_YIELD] = df[COL_AMOUNT] * df[COL_YIELD_USD]
df[COL_PAST_GAIN] = df[COL_TOT_VALUE] - df[COL_TOT_INIT_VALUE]
df[COL_PROJ_GAIN] = ((df[COL_TARGET_PRICE] - df[COL_PRICE_USD]) *
df[COL_AMOUNT])
```

> **Perspectives on a portfolio**
>
> We can analyze changes in various ways. Assume Jeff purchased 10 shares of Company A for $100 each ($1,000) and 100 shares of Company B for $5 each ($500). Now, let's consider the current prices of both shares. Company A is priced at $130, while Company B is at $7.50. Jeff's value has increased significantly, showing a gain of $300 with Company A and $250 with Company B. Strictly speaking, he achieved a 30% gain with Company A and a 50% gain with Company B. If he had invested $1,000 in Company B and $500 in Company A, his return would have been $650 instead of $550.
>
> One approach to investing wisely might be to gain multiple perspectives on assets. If you want to feel great, observing a successful bullish day on the stock exchange and the overall increase in your portfolio's value can provide the emotional boost you desire. Having $5,000 more than the previous day feels more substantial than a 3% increase. However, when assessing stock performance, the key is to focus on percentage changes. This method allows for better stock comparisons.
>
> Remember to look at different time frames. Sometimes, the short-term performance of a stock looks far gloomier than if you look at the stock's performance in the long run. Whatever you want to analyze, all the data is available. All you need to do is decide what to focus on.

Because we have all the data we need, it's time to export it to a Google Sheets document. We'll use the gspread library for this purpose. It's essential to establish the necessary permissions to write to that document. Numerous guides online explain how to set up access to Google Sheets for applications. Ultimately, you'll obtain a JSON file containing the key required for authentication.

Additionally, safeguard your access key. Although someone accessing a spreadsheet with your investments might not lead to financial loss, it's still concerning to think that unauthorized individuals could gain insight into your investment portfolios.

Once the security is properly set up, we export all data to a worksheet called *stock*. The code provided here includes two methods. The first method accepts the worksheet name and the data from the worksheet, and the second method then exports that data:

```
def export_df_to_sheet(worksheet_name, df):
    worksheet = get_spreadsheet().worksheet(worksheet_name)
    worksheet.update([df.columns.values.tolist()] + df.values.tolist())
```

Extracting a DataFrame into a Google sheet is simple, but listing 6.8 shows how to add live data. In this method, we assemble a cell function for a cell in Google Sheets that collects data live from Google Finance using the ticker as an identifier. First, we need to find a column character position based on the position in the table. So, if, for instance, the "total value" is in the fourth position, we would get the character D. Then, we parse through all the tickers, create the cell function, and export it to the dedicated cell identified by the column position and the iteration counter through the ticker array.

Listing 6.8 Adding live data

```
col_amount_character = (get_char_by_col_pos
                        (pos_col_amount))              ◁─┐
col_tot_val_character = (get_char_by_col_pos             │
                        (pos_col_tot_val))             ◁─┤  Gets column
col_live_character = (get_char_by_col_pos                │  positions
                        (pos_col_live))                ◁─┤
col_update_character = (get_char_by_col_pos              │
                        (pos_col_live+1))              ◁─┘

update_cols = []
counter = 0
for ticker in tickers:
    update_cols.append(f'=GOOGLEFINANCE("{ticker}")*'     Assembles cell
                       f'{col_amount_character}'          function for
                       f'{counter+2}')              ◁──   export
    counter += 1
worksheet.update([update_cols],
                 col_live_character + "2",
                 raw=False,                               Updates
                 major_dimension = "COLUMNS" )  ◁──       worksheets
```

Exporting stocks to the worksheet gives us a solid foundation to export additional assets. We can reuse some of the code developed for stocks. Let's explore how to process ETFs, bonds, and cryptocurrency positions and export them to your spreadsheet.

### 6.5.2 *Exchange-traded funds*

Exchange-traded funds (ETFs) are identified by a symbol or ticker, such as VOO for the Vanguard S&P 500 or SPY for the SPDR S&P 500 Trust. Price updates occur during the exchange's opening hours. ETFs also sometimes pay dividends to shareholders.

You can collect ETF data with yfinance using the same interface as stocks. The ratios provided by the interface are slightly different. A yfinance ticker object for stocks (a single company) provides results different from pooled investments (many assets). The price-to-earnings (P/E) ratio returned by the methods of the object that has loaded MSFT reflects data from Microsoft. If we load Vanguard S&P 500 data identified by VOO into a ticker object, the P/E ratio will represent the weighted average of all P/E ratios of the assets pooled in that ETF.

136    CHAPTER 6  *Building an asset monitor*

Let's collect and export all ETFs to a new worksheet in the spreadsheet. We can reuse the `merge_value_into_df` function to enrich the data we collected from the brokers with yfinance data. The ratio `navPrice` represents the current market value of an ETF, and yield refers to the passive income that is paid out:

```
all_etfs_held = all_ positions[all_positions['asset_type'].isin(["ETF"])]
full_etf_data = all_etf["yahoo"].unique().tolist()
essential_etf_data = merge_values_into_df(all_etfs_held,
                                          full_etf_data,
                                          ["navPrice", "yield"])
```

> **Observe the fine-grained differences**
>
> Those with an eye for detail may be wondering why the metrics used in listing 6.4 (current prices and dividend rate) differ from those used for ETFs. On an abstract level, they return the same information: What is the asset's price now? What does an investor get as passive income?
>
> These small details may help us create a greater awareness of the nature of an asset through the programmer's lens, shaped by modeling the world through object-oriented programming. An ETF is a pooled investment containing various asset types, such as stocks, bonds, or other ETFs. A programmer might refer to it as an array containing objects of different asset types. Each asset in the ETF can generate passive income. While dividends (from stocks) and coupon payments (from bonds) yield the same outcome for investors (in the most abstract sense, the asset returns money), they differ significantly in detail. A *dividend* is a voluntary payment made by a company, which can influence the share price when paid out. Many investors expect companies to continue paying dividends, but a company may choose not to pay them.
>
> In contrast, a *coupon payment* is a mandatory disbursement that a borrower must make to bondholders. Thus, yield is the abstraction of dividends and interest payments. The same principle applies to net asset value (NAV) and the current price, as the NAV reflects the average of an asset when aggregating the current prices of the assets.
>
> In the spreadsheet, however, we call all returns *yield* at the abstracted level; the focus is on determining how much passive income we'll likely make. As we also call staking rewards from crypto yields, we must know that this value can fluctuate wildly if we have a cryptocurrency with strong price fluctuations.

After collecting all ETFs, we can convert the currency to a valuation by a single currency. It works the same way with stocks, as shown earlier in listing 6.6. In addition, aggregating and exporting work similarly. As we've encapsulated the code into a function (see listing 6.9), the code to process ETFs is reduced to a few lines.

**Listing 6.9  Exporting ETFs**

```
all_etfs_held = all_positions[all_positions['asset_type'].isin(["ETF"])]
yfin_data_etf = collect_fin_data(all_etfs_held[COL_YAHOO].unique().tolist())
```

```
etf_info = merge_fin_data(all_etfs_held, yfin_data_etf, ["navPrice", "yield"])
etf_info = calculating_price_data(etf_info, "navPrice", "yield")
export_etf_columns = [COL_TICKER, COL_PORTFOLIO,
                      COL_TOT_VALUE, COL_TOT_YIELD,
                      COL_AMOUNT, COL_TOT_INIT_VALUE]
export_df_to_sheet(COL_WORKSHEET_ETF, etf_info[export_etf_columns])
add_live_data(COL_WORKSHEET_ETF,
              etf_info[COL_GOOGLE].tolist(),
              export_etf_columns)
```

One of the beautiful aspects of using libraries such as yfinance is that, ultimately, you can encapsulate a lot of functionality and easily add new assets if they share the same interface. We need to recognize that we should view ETFs differently than stocks, as specific metrics that apply to a single stock can't be easily aggregated for pooled investments.

Figure 6.5 outlines the worksheet for ETFs with sample data. Be aware that some data, such as projected target price, is missing because it can't be obtained through yfinance.

| ticker | portfolio | value | Yield | amount | init_val | live | chg_since_last_update |
|---|---|---|---|---|---|---|---|
| SPY | Index | $6.208,08 | 75,117768 | 10,21 | $4.336,90 | $6.055,04 | -$153,04 |
| VOO | Index | $6.200,53 | 76,886572 | 11,09 | $4.159,64 | $6.045,05 | -$155,48 |

**Figure 6.5** In the ETF Worksheet, we don't have a column for the projected gains as it's difficult to forecast price development accurately over multiple assets.

### 6.5.3 Bonds

If you buy stocks, you'll recognize companies by their ticker symbols. So, after some experience, you might refer to holdings as MSFT, AAPL, or NVDA instead of Microsoft, Apple, and NVIDIA. The same thing can apply to ETFs. Although they might refer to a collection of assets, many investors understand symbols such as VOO or SPY as Vanguard S&P 500 ETF or SPDR S&P 500 ETF Trust.

Bonds are often more challenging to identify in data collected from a broker than stocks. Bonds are different because they are emitted at regular intervals, and each emission gets a different identifier. You can't use the jargon to say you buy more VOO or NVDA. You lend money to an entity under given conditions, which includes coupon payment rates and maturity dates. If you decide to lend more money to a bond issuer on a later stage, you subscribe to a new emission with different conditions. You can still identify each bond through a unique identifier, such as an International Securities Identification Number (ISIN) such as US9128CLA70 on financial platforms.

So, instead of enriching data with yfinance, we can go a different route with bonds. The following code example shows how to migrate yield information that we store in the SQLite table offline_asset into the calculations. The yields of bonds are stored in the database, and we merge them into the DataFrame:

```
bond_rates = all_offline_assets[
    all_offline_assets[COL_ASSET_TYPE].isin(['BOND'])
][["yield"]]
bond_df_merged_rates = all_bonds_held.merge(bond_rates, on=COL_TICKER)
bond_df_merged_rates[COL_TOT_YIELD] = (
    bond_df_merged_rates[COL_TOT_VALUE]
* bond_df_merged_rates[COL_YIELD]
/ 100)
```

We could examine bond capital appreciation and, of course, extend this code to add risk ratings. However, these values rarely change if you invest cautiously in bonds, so we keep it simple. Figure 6.6 shows a bond worksheet with reference data.

Figure 6.6 In the bond worksheet, the value represents the par value (the value we'll get returned at maturity), and we also get the annual yield, besides the number of bonds we hold.

### 6.5.4 Cryptocurrencies

In this example, we showcase how to retrieve information about assets from a crypto exchange. Listing 6.10 illustrates the functionality, using Binance as a reference example. We use the python_binance API. To gather the data, we employ the get_simple_earn_locked_product_position and get_simple_earn_flexible_product_position functions. These methods return our holdings on Binance, depending on their status. We can lock them temporarily, which means we get higher staking returns, or have them available to sell at any time, reducing staking returns. The method returns all of our positions in the same data structure.

#### Listing 6.10 Loading data from Binance

```
from binance.client import Client
binance_client = Client(os.getenv("exchange.binance.api"),
                        os.getenv("exchange.binance.secret"))
```

## 6.5 Processing assets

```
locked_assets = pd.DataFrame(              ◄─┐
    [                                        │  Loads cryptos in a
        (pos["asset"], pos["amount"], pos["apy"])   simple earn locked
        for pos in binance_client              │  position
        .get_simple_earn_locked_product_position()['rows']
    ],
columns=[COL_TICKER, COL_AMOUNT, COL_YIELD])  ◄─┘

flexible_assets = pd.DataFrame(            ◄─┐
    [(pos["asset"], pos["totalAmount"],      │
      pos["latestAnnualPercentageRate"])     │  Loads cryptos in a
      for pos in binance_client              │  simple earn flexible
      .get_simple_earn_flexible_product_position()['rows']],  position
      columns=[COL_TICKER, COL_AMOUNT, COL_YIELD])  ◄─┘

assets = pd.concat([locked_assets,
                    flexible_assets])      ─┐
assets = assets.astype({COL_AMOUNT: 'float',│  Merges and unifies
                        COL_YIELD: 'float', │  the structure
                        COL_TICKER: 'string'})
assets.set_index(COL_TICKER, inplace=True) ─┘
```

As we've now collected the positions from Binance, we can also load our offline assets. In this example, we assume we have our cryptocurrency, which is associated with the keys we've stored on a hardware ledger. The amount and current staking rate are stored in the `offline_asset` table:

```
ledger_cryptos = all_offline_assets[
    all_offline_assets[COL_ASSET_TYPE].isin(["CRYPTO"])]
```

As we now have all our cryptocurrency in a DataFrame, we only need to add the prices. We load the current prices from CoinMarketCap. The code in listing 6.11 shows how to do that. We first create a session object and then request the data based on the cryptocurrencies provided in a list and US dollars as the target currency. Lastly, we extract the price as a value to merge this into the DataFrame with our holdings. Be aware that you again need to register and get a secret to access CoinMarketCap.

**Listing 6.11 Loading price data from CoinMarketCap**

```
session = Session()
session.headers.update({
    'Accepts': 'application/json',
    'X-CMC_PRO_API_KEY': os.getenv("broker.coinmarketcap.com")
})
res = session.get(
    'https://pro-api.coinmarketcap.com/v2/'
    'cryptocurrency/quotes/latest',
    params={
        'symbol': ','.join(df.index.unique()),
        'convert': 'USD'
    }                              ─┐  Loads data from
)                                   └─ CoinMarketCap
```

```
if res.status_code != 200:
    print(f"API Error: {res.status_code} - {res.text}")
    return df

data = res.json().get("data", {})
prices = {
    coin: data[coin][0]['quote']['USD']['price']
    for coin in data
    if 'USD' in data[coin][0]['quote']
}
df[COL_PRICE] = df.index.map(prices)
```

*Extracts data from returns*

There's one small detail to watch out for when exporting data. Google Finance doesn't provide data on many cryptocurrencies on its platform. So, instead of Google Finance, we need to load data from a different provider. The code for assembling is outlined here:

```
update_cols.append(
    f'=IFERROR(REGEXREPLACE('
    f'IMPORTDATA("https://cryptoprices.cc/{ticker}");'
    f'"[.]";","'
    f')*{col_amount_character}{counter+2};'
    f'{col_tot_val_character}{counter+2})'
)
```

We load the data from the Crypto Prices site (https://cryptoprices.cc). Because some errors may be returned, depending on the access frequency, we fill the cell with the value from the last export if we can't obtain a proper value. Figure 6.7 shows an export of crypto assets into the crypto spreadsheet of the worksheet.

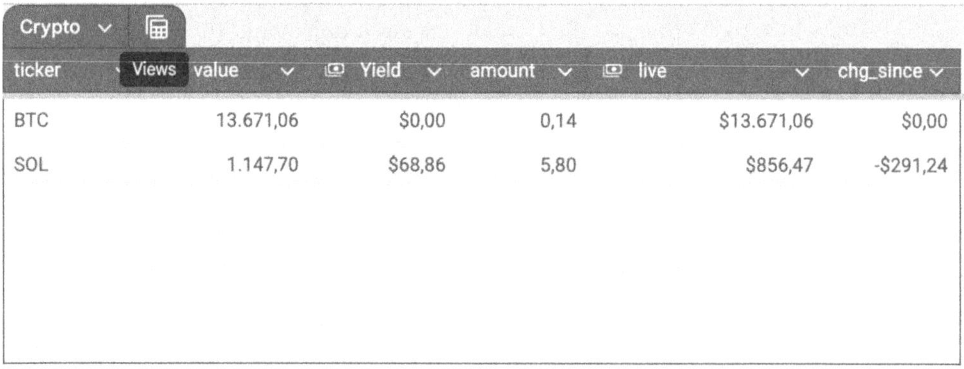

| ticker | value | Yield | amount | live | chg_since |
|---|---|---|---|---|---|
| BTC | 13.671,06 | $0,00 | 0,14 | $13.671,06 | $0,00 |
| SOL | 1.147,70 | $68,86 | 5,80 | $856,47 | -$291,24 |

Figure 6.7  The crypto worksheet returns the total value, the staking yield, the amount we own, and the live data.

## 6.6 Outlook

The Jupyter Notebook we developed throughout the chapter can be a template for creating your personal asset monitor. Within this framework, we establish a dedicated worksheet for each asset type, emphasizing a key concept. Although all assets have the potential for capital appreciation and passive income, their specific characteristics and behaviors vary significantly.

No book can provide a foolproof, step-by-step guide to getting rich overnight. If someone claims otherwise, it's likely a scam. Think about it—if someone had a sure-fire way to create wealth from nothing, the odds of them sharing it with you are slim; they'd probably be sailing the world on a yacht or living among the ultra-rich.

A book like this *can* equip you with the tools to focus on the details necessary to make something solid. This asset monitor is a starting point. What aspects do you want to analyze in more detail? Perhaps you're focused on a single asset class but want more profound insights. Why not create custom worksheets tailored to your interests—whether it's risk analysis, environmental, social, and governance (ESG) factors, or valuation metrics? You decide what matters most.

Being able to track assets is a precondition for monitoring stock performance. If we can explore performance, we also have a good foundation for tracking risks. Let's move on to chapter 7 for more details on that.

## *Summary*

- An asset monitor helps you collect information about all of your assets in one place.
- Using Python, we can access brokers such as Alpaca or Interactive Brokers, extract data, and merge it into a single dataset.
- We can enrich this dataset with data from financial platforms such as Yahoo Finance, giving us all the details we need about our holdings.
- You can use Google Sheets as an asset monitor and write into worksheets using Python and the gspread library.
- Unifying the view on your assets helps convert all shares into the same currency if you hold assets in different currencies.
- Sometimes, tickers collected from brokers differ from those used by financial platforms. We can solve this using lookup tables.
- Occasionally, we can't retrieve data for certain assets. However, we can duplicate the information about these assets in a database and still process the data for financial analysis.
- Stocks and ETFs share a similar interface. We can collect them through the same commands, but not all methods available for one type of asset are available for the other.

- Although they differ in detail, we can sum up dividend payments from stocks, coupon rates from bonds, and staking rewards from crypto as "yield" to have a common terminology for passive income.
- When collecting data from Binance, we can load actual price data from CoinMarketCap.
- Traditional finance platforms have limited support for cryptocurrency, but we can use a different provider, such as Crypto Prices (https://cryptoprices.cc) and CoinMarketCap, to get live data in cells.

# Risk management

**This chapter covers**
- Classifying risks
- Mitigating risks
- Hedging strategies
- Optimizing your portfolio using the Markowitz model
- Assessing nonfinancial risks

Exploring assets that can multiply their original value many times is thrilling. However, if you stake your life savings on extraordinary profits, you might find yourself sleepless at night, questioning whether you abandoned your common sense the moment you made that investment.

In our minds, we can picture the stereotype of a gambler who seeks the thrill. However, we can also envision a stereotype of a risk-averse investor: a dry person who lectures us on efficient market theory and continually advocates for putting all of our money into diversified ETFs. They occasionally insist that investing in single stocks with low-risk ratings is too risky. Encountering them when you dream about living in a big mansion with the potential returns can feel like a slap in the face. No matter how enthusiastic we are, they always have an explanation for why things won't unfold as we hope. Whether it's human bias, statistics about fund managers and their historical returns, or something else, the recommendation remains the same: you can't beat the market, so invest in it by buying shares in index funds.

The debates about risks versus returns are endless. One side argues that investors like Warren Buffett, Jim Simons, and Peter Lynch have consistently outperformed the market, suggesting that anyone can do the same. Energy goes where attention flows; if you're patient and self-reflective, you'll become wealthy if you focus on the right topics. The other side keeps reasoning about the academic insights of giants such as Eugene Fama or Burton Malkiel, including the efficient market theory and random walks. It often seems that each side has its statistics: one shows that actively managed hedge funds by a strong fund manager beat passive funds, and the other claims that studies show that blindfolded monkeys throwing darts can pick a portfolio that beats those of seasoned investors, as the market is unpredictable.

This chapter can be seen as an antithesis to chapter 4, in which we focused on what we could gain if we analyzed the growth potential of stocks. Here, we explore what we can lose if things go wrong, arriving at the synthesis: we need to study both risk and returns and decide how much risk we can accept in a nondeterministic environment.

In this chapter, we first classify risks. After learning about risks, we examine ways to measure them and, finally, how to mitigate them.

## 7.1 *Ukemi*

In martial arts, the first lesson isn't how to jump or kick—it's how to fall safely. The Japanese call this *ukemi*. The same principle applies to systems: safeguard first, then scale.

Developers already understand this concept through test-driven development (TDD), where unit tests are written before the code. Experienced developers have likely encountered projects lacking clean code and TDD practices—they often turn into black boxes where small changes lead to unpredictable results. Returning to chaos is unthinkable once you've worked in a clean, structured environment. While clean development may seem slower due to peer reviews and careful implementation, it reduces costly bug fixes.

Risk management in investing follows a similar logic. By implementing best practices early, you prevent problems before they arise, protecting both your portfolio and peace of mind.

### 7.1.1 *Stop-loss*

A crucial *ukemi* in investing is the stop-loss order. Think of it as a safety net: a predefined price at which your broker automatically sells a position to limit losses. If there's one thing you can do to reduce stress, it's setting a stop-loss for every position. Without it, investing is like performing acrobatics without a net—why risk unnecessary losses when they can be prevented?

Stop-losses can also be adjusted as share prices rise. Suppose you buy a stock at $8, which surges to $25. Believing in further growth, you initially set a stop-loss at $7.

Instead of selling at $25, you raise the stop-loss to $22 after the surge. This resolves a common dilemma: if the stock climbs higher, you stay in the game, but if it falls, you still lock in gains at $22. Without a stop-loss, you might regret not securing your profits if the stock drops back to $8. Figure 7.1 illustrates a stop-loss order.

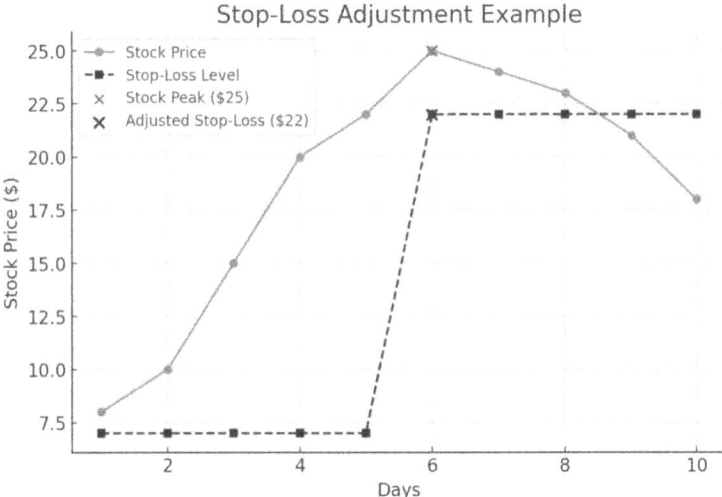

Figure 7.1  In this reference for a stop-loss order, the stop loss is adjusted to $22 on day 6 after the share price rises. When the stock goes below $22, the stop loss will be triggered, and the investor will sell at a market price on day 9.

In chapter 11, we'll cover how to set stop-loss orders effectively through an API. However, you can put one through your broker if you hold assets. Select Good Till Canceled for your order to keep your safety net in place.

> **Stop-loss in practice**
> The example in figure 7.1 shows that if I set a stop loss at $22 and the share price falls below $22, the shares will be sold. Would it not be wise to place a stop loss on all positions? Let's consider three aspects:
> - *Taxes*—If you sell a stock at $22 that you bought at $8, you've made a profit. Depending on local tax regulations, this profit may fall under capital gains tax. Sometimes, you don't want to pay taxes immediately, especially if you could write off gains in positions to cover losses in others at a different time.
> - *Transaction costs*—If you sell, you must pay a small fee for the transaction. If you want to buy again immediately, remember the spread between the ask and bid price: If you sell all of your shares and immediately repurchase the same number, you would likely lose money. Sometimes, you want to hold stocks long-term, and rebuying them at a similar price might be costly.

> *(continued)*
> - *Fluctuations*—Assume the share price is below $22. You sell, but right after, the price goes up again, far above $22. You can rebuy the shares at a higher price, but you would have made a loss. What if you could buy the right to sell at a fixed price and the right to buy at a certain price? This would be the next complexity to manage risks after stop loss: welcome to the world of options.

### 7.1.2 Risk classification

As a developer, you thrive on creative momentum when implementing new features. The excitement of exploring ideas can feel intoxicating, and overthinking potential failures may slow progress.

The software needs to be deployed at some point, and the threat of real users complaining about bugs might keep developers and their managers awake at night. Suddenly, Murphy's Law takes over—what can go wrong will go wrong, and your perspective shifts. Site reliability engineers (SREs) embody this mindset, ensuring flawless execution. While early-stage development is driven by creativity, SREs must think destructively, anticipating failure at every step. A good SRE always classifies and prioritizes risks.

Engineers recognize that a complete system outage is worse than a partial slow response time. Likewise, owning a stock experiencing daily share price fluctuations is preferable to holding assets in a company that goes bankrupt. Of course, the first scenario might lead to the second and can be a warning sign, and, at the same time, fluctuations are part of the market. To manage risk effectively, we must be able to measure risks and classify them by their possible effect.

> **Bikeshedding**
>
> "Bikeshedding," or Parkinson's Law of Triviality, describes the tendency to focus excessively on minor, easy-to-understand details while overlooking more complex and critical issues. The term originates from an example where a committee debates the color of a bike shed for hours but barely discusses a nuclear power plant proposal.
>
> Bikeshedding is a common problem in all fields, including investing. You might fixate on a temporary 5% dip in one stock while ignoring a far more serious risk—another company in your portfolio teetering on the edge of default. Staying focused on what truly matters is key to sound decision-making.

To understand systemic risk, we can create a mental model of the market and identify events that could destabilize the entire system. *Systemic risk* refers to disruptions that threaten the financial system. A classic example is the 2008 financial crisis, where the collapse of major institutions nearly triggered an economic meltdown.

While doomsday scenarios such as nuclear war technically qualify as systemic risks, they are beyond the scope of financial planning. Building a bunker is more practical than safeguarding your portfolio if you're worried about such events.

Excluding extreme catastrophes, we can still categorize financial risks systematically, helping investors prepare for market-wide threats and mitigate potential damage. Let's see what can go wrong to understand how we can prepare ourselves:

- *Market risk*—Stock prices are significantly affected by overall market trends. Economic downturns, geopolitical events, or shifts in market sentiment can lead to widespread declines, even when individual companies perform well.
- *Sector risk*—Investing in stocks concentrated in a specific sector (e.g., technology, energy) exposes investors to risks that may affect that entire sector, such as regulatory changes, demand shifts, or technological disruption.
- *Asset-specific risk*—Individual stocks carry the risk of poor performance due to company-specific issues such as mismanagement, declining sales, product failures, or scandals. This is also known as *unsystematic risk*.

---

**The power of compounding vs. high-risk investing**

Imagine two investors: Ivan is an aggressive investor willing to take significant risks, while Alicia takes calculated risks, only as much as necessary.

Both start with $100,000 and invest for 10 years.

- *Ivan's approach*—He wins big sometimes and loses big at other times, ultimately breaking even at $100,000 by year 10. However, at that point, he makes an exceptional investment that doubles his money overnight, bringing his total to $200,000.
- *Alicia's approach*—She achieves a steady 10% return per year. If she withdraws her profits each year, she also ends up with $200,000, the same as Ivan.

    But if she reinvests her gains, the formula for compound interest applies:

$$P(1 + i)^n$$

where
  P = 100,000 (initial capital)
  i = 0.10 (10% return)
  n = 10 (years)
These numbers result in the following:

$$100{,}000(1.1)^{10} = 259{,}374$$

By reinvesting her returns, Alicia ended up with $259,374, outperforming Ivan's final amount. In the long run, consistent compounding often beats sporadic windfalls.

Every investor hears this phrase at some point in their career: "Past performance is no guarantee of future results." Relying too heavily on history repeating itself can lead to costly mistakes. Yet completely ignoring historical patterns is just as dangerous. Because we can classify risk, we must consider how to measure it based on past evidence.

### 7.1.3 Risk measurement

The economy is a complex, interconnected system that moves in cycles—bubbles, crashes, and recoveries. While no event unfolds identically, recurring patterns emerge. The challenge is distinguishing between genuine trends and coincidences. This perspective helps macroeconomists predict the ripple effects of disruptions. Take the war in Ukraine: concerns over the Ukrainian grain harvest signaled potential famine risks, leading to fears of unrest in emerging markets that are rich in raw materials. Such unrest could disrupt mining, affecting companies reliant on gold, cobalt, and nickel. Similarly, sanctions on Russian gas drove up European energy prices, fueling inflation.

Figure 7.2 illustrates risk factors for a hypothetical US-based AI company. What if an emerging AI platform such as DeepSeek disrupts the market in 2025? Or what if a societal countermovement against AI gains traction, which can be seen as a market risk, making it harder to sell AI services? AI developers in some countries experience more challenging regulatory environments than their peers from different regions. Those who worked in environments with more strict regulations can attest that new regulatory frameworks might become a problem for companies unprepared for this change.

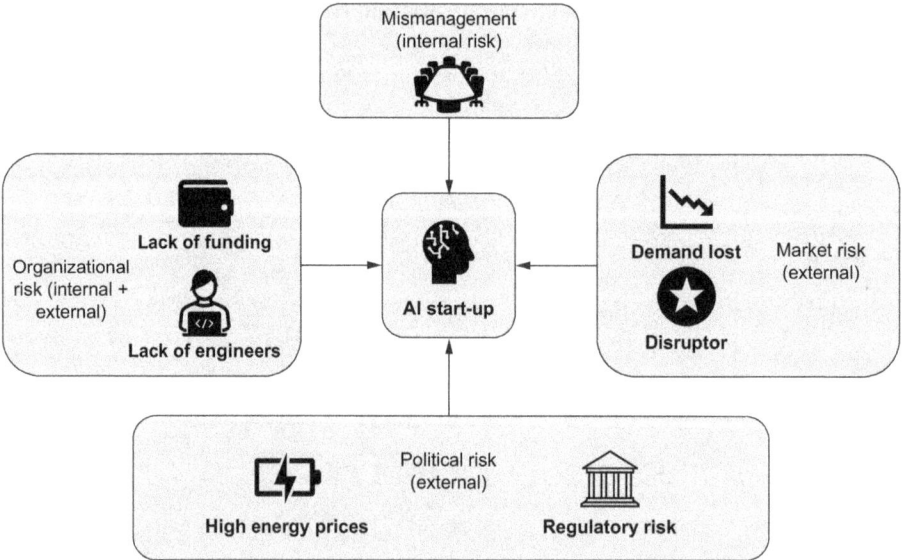

Figure 7.2 A high-level risk model containing some of the challenges an AI startup faces

These are just a few potential risks, reinforcing the "Understand the businesses you invest in" principle. Before investing, ask yourself these questions:

- Do you know what could go wrong in a company?
- Do you understand its most significant risks and threats?

If not, reconsider your investment. Otherwise, you would have to learn how catalysts, which you're unaware of, play a role in driving share prices up and down.

Figure 7.3 presents a risk matrix to classify threats. Take the risk of an anti-AI movement: unlikely, but potentially catastrophic if it gains momentum and demands AI bans. Another risk—rising energy prices—could slow AI expansion if power plants can't scale fast enough to control costs.

| Likelihood | Harm severity | | | |
|---|---|---|---|---|
| | Minor | Marginal | Critical | Catastrophic |
| Certain | High | High | Very high | Very high |
| Likely | Medium | High | High | Very high |
| Possible | Low | Medium | High | Very high |
| Unlikely | Low | Medium | Medium | High |
| Rare | Low | Low | Medium | Medium |
| Eliminated | Eliminated | | | |

Figure 7.3 How to map risk in a matrix based on severity and likelihood. We commonly create strategies to meet risks with higher harm severity first to mitigate the effect once the consequences become unavoidable.

To use risk matrices efficiently, you can review your positions and assess risks to define actions. Let's go through an example. Let's assume you hold Coca-Cola, Apple, and Pfizer stock. You can research possible risk scenarios, such as the following: "What if there is another pandemic?" or "What if there are new trade wars?" Let's assume further that we conclude through a small assessment of the current political situation that, based on a personal evaluation, we consider an escalation of a trade war between the United States and China as possible. Then, we can go through all positions in the portfolio. Quick research and personal assessments indicate that potential harm from Coca-Cola and Pfizer is marginal. Still, we may conclude that an escalation of a trade war would be critical for Apple, leading to a high-risk rating based on the matrix.

Investor Ray Dalio recommends acting on principles when investing. Some investors may decide to get active in times of high risk. Others might be more relaxed and act only when the risk rating reaches "very high." One key principle of managing risks is to define what to do if catastrophes happen. Defining concrete actions when events occur and following these actions no matter what ensures efficiency.

So, let's assume you decide your principle is to sell all shares when they reach the highest risk level, and let's imagine an event that makes a trade war certain. Following your principle, you would immediately sell all the shares of high-risk companies. Yes, this may sound bureaucratic, but you can never forget a quote attributed to Mike Tyson: "Everybody has a plan until they get punched in the face." When filled with emotions, you might still do the right things, if you have clear guidance on what to do. Without guidance, and when panic takes over, it can become more difficult to make rational and correct decisions.

Assessing risks also means understanding *beta*, a measure of an asset's sensitivity to market fluctuations:

- *Beta = 1*—Moves with the market
- *Beta > 1*—More volatile than the market
- *Beta < 1*—More stable than the market

Think of beta like a system's performance under load. High-beta assets spike under stress, while low-beta assets remain stable.

Beta often aligns with common sense. In a bear market, unemployment rises, consumers prioritize essentials (supermarkets benefit), and discretionary spending declines (car dealers suffer). However, company-specific risks can be independent of market trends—mismanagement alone can drive a company into distress. In the next section, we'll explore how to measure risk effectively.

## 7.2 Generating risk profiles for individual stocks

Historical data about a company helps us assess performance by examining fundamental factors (e.g., debt trends). In addition, we can study chart movements, often referred to as *technical analysis*, to explore the potential risks of a decline in share prices. The approach varies based on a company's stage and size.

As a programmer, you've likely encountered applications with inconsistent response times—high variability erodes user trust. The same principle applies to stock prices. If an asset's price has fluctuated significantly in the past, it signals risk. And sometimes, what goes down doesn't always come back up. Let's take a deeper look at past price movements.

### 7.2.1 Value at risk (VaR)

*Value at risk (VaR)* is a tool for measuring the potential loss of an investment or portfolio over a specified period, under normal market conditions, at a given confidence level. It answers the question, "What's the worst loss I could face, and how likely is it?"

As a programmer, you can think of VaR as setting a threshold for system downtime: "What's the maximum downtime we might experience within a week, 95% of the

## 7.2 Generating risk profiles for individual stocks

time?" Now, replace "downtime" with "loss," and that's essentially what VaR is. Let's break it down:

- You monitor a portfolio (a collection of assets).
- You need a time frame (e.g., days, months) and a confidence level.
- These can be used to determine risk, such as the following: "We're 95% confident that the portfolio won't lose more than $30,000 in one day."

Here's a practical example: your portfolio is worth $1,000,000. Analysts estimate a one-day VaR at 95% confidence of $30,000. This means there's only a 5% chance your portfolio will lose more than $30,000 on any given day. So, 95% of the time, your loss will be $30,000 or less.

To calculate VaR, we simulate the potential future risks based on historical data. There are two common approaches:

- *Variance-coeffect method*—This approach assumes that returns follow a normal distribution. It's similar to predicting load times using standard deviation.
- *Monte Carlo simulation*—This method simulates numerous potential outcomes, like stress-testing code under various edge cases.

Using these methods, we can estimate the potential risk to our portfolio, just like you'd analyze system performance under different scenarios.

A *Monte Carlo simulation* is a computational technique for modeling the probability of different outcomes in a process with inherent uncertainty. It relies on repeated random sampling to obtain numerical results, making it useful for scenarios where traditional analytical methods are infeasible. In listing 7.1, we outline an example of a Monte Carlo simulation using Apple share prices. We need parameters such as confidence level. Then, we load the stock data to collect returns and calculate the means and standard deviation. This is the basis for running a Monte Carlo simulation, meaning we simulate future returns based on past returns. We plot and print the results.

### Listing 7.1 Monte Carlo simulation for VaR on Apple

```
import numpy as np
import yfinance as yf
import matplotlib.pyplot as plt

ticker = "AAPL"
confidence_level = 0.95          Sets up the
num_simulations = 10000          parameters
time_horizon = 1

stock = yf.Ticker(ticker)                              Fetches historical stock
hist = stock.history(period="1y")                      data and calculates
returns = hist['Close'].pct_change().dropna()          historical returns

mu = returns.mean()              Estimates the mean and
sigma = returns.std()            standard deviation of returns
```

```
last_price = hist['Close'].iloc[-1]         ⎫  Monte Carlo
sim_returns = np.random.normal(mu,          ⎬  simulation of
                               sigma,       ⎪  stock price paths
                               num_simulations)
sim_prices = last_price * (1 + sim_returns)
                                                ⎫  Calculates VaR at
threshold = np.percentile(sim_prices - last_price,  ⎬  given confidence
                          (1 - confidence_level) * 100)  ⎭  level

plt.hist(simulated_prices - last_price, bins=50,
         alpha=0.75, color="blue", edgecolor="black")
plt.axvline(threshold, color="red",
            linestyle="dashed", linewidth=2)
plt.title(f"Monte Carlo Simulated "
          f"P&L Distribution for {ticker}")         ⎬  Puts out
plt.xlabel("Profit/Loss")                               the result
plt.ylabel("Frequency")
plt.show()

print(f"{confidence_level * 100}% Monte Carlo "
      f"VaR for {ticker}: ${-var_threshold:.2f}")
```

Figure 7.4 shows the result of a Monte Carlo simulation as a plot, outlining that this stock is relatively stable. The results indicate that there is a 95% chance the loss won't exceed $5.50 per share.

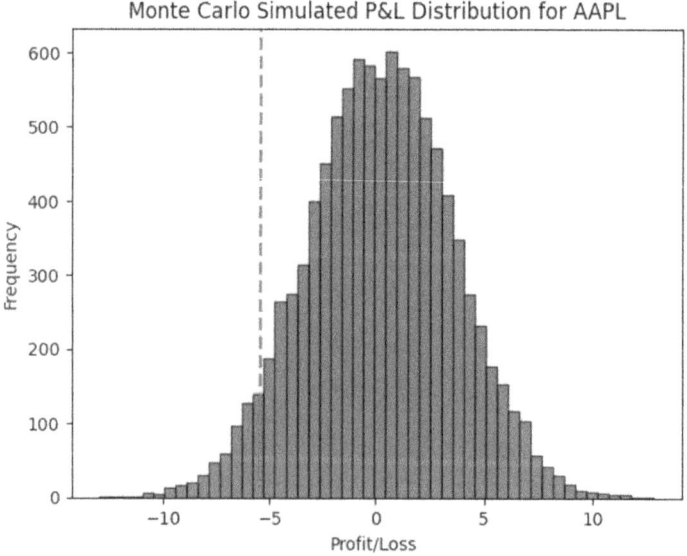

Figure 7.4  The result of a Monte Carlo simulation concludes that based on the historical data, only 5% of the time were the losses of Apple share prices higher than $5.50 a day.

For this, we calculated an example based on Apple. We can run a Monte Carlo simulation on all portfolio stocks and aggregate these results to the total VaR of the whole portfolio.

Please remember that Black Swan events are unpredictable events beyond what is normally expected. Excluding these outliers, VaRs can be seen as worst-case scenarios based on historical data under normal circumstances. Investors can calculate the VaRs of all their holdings and match them with their risk appetite. In some cases, investors may decide to decrease (or also increase) the risks.

### 7.2.2 Correlation

*Correlation* measures how assets move relative to one another. Positively correlated assets move in the same direction; negatively correlated ones move oppositely. It's like service dependencies—when one microservice fails, does it take down others?

In chapter 3, we already logged returns and simple returns. Using the code we used in previous chapters, let's load the data for three companies:

```
def collect_prices_returns(tickers: list):
    close_prices = pd.DataFrame()
    log_returns = pd.DataFrame()

    for ticker in tickers:
        close_prices[ticker] = yf.Ticker(ticker).history(
            start='2024-01-01',
            end='2024-12-31',
            interval="1d")['Close']
        log_returns[ticker] = np.log(close_prices[ticker]
                                    / close_prices[ticker].shift(1))
    return close_prices, log_returns
tickers = ["MSFT", "AMZN", "GOOGL"]
close_prices, log_returns  = collect_prices_returns(tickers)
```

Now that we have the log returns and the closing prices in memory, we can run a fundamental statistical analysis. The following code shows how to run the mean, standard deviation, and variance aggregations on the stock prices:

```
price_stats = (
    close_prices[tickers]
    .agg(['mean', 'std', 'var'])
    .T.reset_index()
    .rename(columns={'index': 'ticker'})
)
```

The closing prices of the stocks fluctuate, as shown in table 7.1, over the year.

Let's investigate standard deviation (`std`) and variance (`var`). *Variance* measures the average squared deviation from the mean. It tells you how much the values in a dataset spread out from the mean. Variance is in squared units, making it less interpretable for practical use.

Table 7.1  Mean, standard deviation, and variance on share prices of Microsoft, Amazon, and Alphabet

| Company | mean | std | var |
|---|---|---|---|
| Microsoft (MSFT) | 418.73445 | 18.19813 | 331.17207 |
| Amazon (AMZN) | 184.49020 | 17.32285 | 300.08126 |
| Alphabet (GOOGL) | 163.31029 | 15.40605 | 237.34623 |

Standard deviation is simply the square root of variance. It measures the same dispersion but in the same units as the original data, making it more interpretable. Variance (`var`) is helpful in theoretical statistics and when comparing relative dispersion across datasets. standard deviation (`std`) is used in most practical applications because it retains the original unit of measurement.

> **TIP** As some analysts may use variance, it's still essential to understand how variance can be used in financial analysis. Otherwise, you can focus on standard deviation in your analyses.

Previous chapters show that the overall share price is just one part of a company's capitalization; for example, 418 (the mean of Microsoft) doesn't mean we're doing better than 163 (the mean of Google). A company's share price is just a number that doesn't relate to any other share price. If Microsoft decided to split the shares 1:10, the mean would be 41.8, with 10 times more shares than before.

The absolute price of a share in a given currency is not a reliable measure for comparing the performance of different stocks. For meaningful comparisons, we should use percentage changes in value, with log returns offering an even better basis for analysis:

```
rets = (
    log_returns[tickers]
    .agg(['mean', 'std', 'var'])
    .T * [TRADING_DAYS, TRADING_DAYS**0.5, TRADING_DAYS]
)
rets = rets.reset_index().rename(columns={'index': 'ticker'})
rets
```

The results of this script, shown in table 7.2, help us compare the companies. Microsoft was more stable during the test period than Amazon and Alphabet. Keep in mind that these patterns might be different in other years.

Table 7.2  Mean, standard deviation, and variance on log returns of Microsoft, Amazon, and Alphabet

| Company | mean | std | var |
|---|---|---|---|
| Microsoft | 0.14443 | 0.20078 | 0.04031 |
| Amazon | 0.39247 | 0.28154 | 0.07926 |
| Alphabet | 0.33129 | 0.28045 | 0.07865 |

## 7.2 Generating risk profiles for individual stocks

Let's put stocks in correlation: when calculating the *covariance* between stocks, you measure how their returns move relative to each other. Covariance helps you understand the relationship between different assets in a portfolio. If we call the `cov()` method on the DataFrame with the log returns and multiply it with the number of trading days, we get the covariance matrix:

```
cov_matrix = log_returns.cov() * TRADING_DAYS
cov_matrix
```

Let's look at the results. Covariance tells us if the variables move together, but not how much. If the covariance value is larger than 0, the assets tend to move in the same direction, and if the value is lower than 0, they tend to move in opposite directions. The numbers in table 7.3 indicate that there might be some dependencies among the price movements of these three stocks.

Table 7.3  Covariance of Microsoft, Amazon, and Alphabet

| Company | MSFT | AMZN | GOOGL |
|---|---|---|---|
| Microsoft | 0.04031 | 0.03887 | 0.03239 |
| Amazon | 0.03887 | 0.07926 | 0.04290 |
| Alphabet | 0.03239 | 0.04290 | 0.07865 |

We need the correlation to understand how much these variables move with each other. This tells us both the strength and the direction of the relationship. Correlation standardizes covariance by dividing by the standard deviation, resulting in a bounded value between −1 and 1. We get results such as the following:

- +1: Perfect positive correlation (move exactly together)
- 0: No relationship
- −1: Perfect negative correlation (move exactly opposite)

To calculate the correction, we need to run the `corr()` method on the DataFrame with the log returns. Note that as the correlation is independent of dimensions, we don't need to multiply by trading days as we had to with the covariance:

```
corr_matrix = log_returns.corr()
corr_matrix
```

Like variance and standard deviation, we might prefer one method (correlation) over the other (covariance). As covariance might be used in some analyses, it's still helpful to know that this method exists.

Looking at the results in table 7.4, we get deeper insights. These three companies correlate a lot, which is logical. They all focus on cloud computing and AI, and they provide similar solutions to clients.

**Table 7.4 Correlation of Microsoft, Amazon, and Alphabet**

| Company | MSFT | AMZN | GOOGL |
|---|---|---|---|
| Microsoft | 1.00000 | 0.68765 | 0.57522 |
| Amazon | 0.68765 | 1.00000 | 0.54331 |
| Alphabet | 0.57522 | 0.54331 | 1.00000 |

This leads to a hypothesis: if the market believes there is no more room to grow in the cloud business or the AI hype is over, all three positions might lose heavily. Let's look at another example by comparing NVIDIA with Walmart:

```
close_price, log_returns = collect_prices_returns(["WMT", "NVDA"])
corr_matrix = log_returns.corr()
print(corr_matrix)
```

Looking at table 7.5, we observe an intuitively correct result. NVDA is a technology stock. If things go well, investors will believe in AI growth and purchase stocks like NVIDIA's. However, they might want to move to more defensive stocks, such as Walmart, if they start doubting AI.

Conclusively, one possible strategy is to pick stocks with a negative correlation. Based on historical data, if NVIDIA goes down, Walmart goes up. This might reduce possible gains in a sunny-day scenario, but also mitigate losses in a rainy-day scenario.

**Table 7.5 Correlation between Walmart and NVIDIA**

| Company | WMT | NVDA |
|---|---|---|
| Walmart | 1.00000 | -0.00532 |
| NVIDIA | -0.00532 | 1.00000 |

This means we can use algorithms to assess risks. Before applying concrete hedging techniques to mitigate risks, let's explore risk on a more generic level.

## 7.3 The human factor

Many engineers have encountered this scenario: the company brings in a new, ultra-strict chief security officer (CSO). Suddenly, after enjoying freedom in previous roles, you now need approvals for everything. Simple tasks become bureaucratic nightmares, requiring endless workarounds.

Yet, despite the fortress-like security policies, you stumble upon something absurd—an outsider with unrestricted access to server rooms for maintenance work or hidden "super users" with god-mode permissions.

Investing works the same way. Strict risk controls can give a false sense of security, while hidden vulnerabilities can expose you to unexpected threats. Let's explore this further and how this connects with investment.

### 7.3.1 Negligence

Ask any cybersecurity engineer about the most significant threat, and the answer is likely *human negligence*. Technical security is deterministic—you can model interactions, strengthen encryption, and enforce multifactor authentication. But you can't stop someone from writing their password on a sticky note beside an unlocked phone.

The same applies to investing. Your most considerable risk isn't just market volatility or scams—it's *your own psychology*. Engineers who understand blockchain may avoid crypto scams but still fall victim to greed, fear, and impulsive decisions. Technology can help: you can set trading limits, restrict access, or execute orders at fixed intervals—but when emotions take over, those safeguards can be overridden.

No security manual can eliminate user mistakes, and no investing book can erase emotional biases. However, awareness is the first step. Fear of Missing Out (FOMO) causes investors to chase unsustainable gains, but recognizing this bias helps mitigate its effect.

Engineers working in teams use methodologies such as *Scrum* to improve processes through retrospectives. Investing benefits from a similar approach—analyzing past decisions with hard data and peer reviews. By tracking your portfolio (chapter 6), you gain insights into what worked and what didn't.

If you know your psychology is a weak point, take action. *Self-reflection*—understanding your deeper motivations—extends beyond trading into personal growth. Brokers offer risk management tools, such as these:

- *Risk profiles*—Restricts high-risk trades
- *Cool-off periods*—Delays access to risky features

Sometimes, that extra waiting period is the difference between a reckless gamble and a rational decision after a night's rest. Like cybersecurity, investing isn't just about technical expertise—it's about controlling human behavior, including your own.

### 7.3.2 Risk avoidance

Financial advisors and brokers often begin assessing your risk appetite during the Know Your Customer (KYC) process. Despite what some die-hard advocates may claim, there's no single best investment strategy—only strategies that align with your risk tolerance.

The simplest way to mitigate risk is to choose safe investments. Index funds, for example, are widely considered low-risk. While individual companies can fail, index funds would only collapse if the entire economy did—at which point, our portfolio performance would be the least of our concerns.

Many investors view index funds as the holy grail of investing. After all, if the odds of beating the market are low, why take unnecessary risks trying? Many people also worry about the "perfect" time to invest. After making a purchase, they often panic if the market dips, leading to short-term mistakes. To mitigate this, you can use *dollar-cost averaging (DCA)*—investing a fixed amount at regular intervals, regardless of market conditions. While not perfect timing, DCA reduces the risk of buying at a peak and smooths out market volatility over time.

A balanced approach works well if you still want to invest actively. You can allocate a fixed amount to index funds and a smaller portion to individual investments. And if you beat the performance of index funds multiple years in a row, you can still adjust the ratio of actively and passively managed investments as much as you like.

The most obvious risk-reduction strategy is investing in businesses you understand. Familiarity allows you to assess risks more accurately and identify opportunities others might overlook. This aligns with value investing, which focuses on buying undervalued companies based on fundamental analysis.

One core principle of value investing is the *margin of safety*—buying assets priced below their intrinsic value to provide a cushion against potential losses. To use an engineering analogy, imagine a client requests an application that must handle 100 peak-load requests. If you build it to handle exactly 100, there's no margin for unexpected surges. The same applies to investing—without a margin of safety, even a slight miscalculation can lead to failure.

### Time horizon and risk

Investment strategies differ. Long-term investors often buy securities and hold them for long periods. Some investors even like the idea of keeping value stocks forever. Short-term trading is usually seen as a strategy closer to gambling. Traders look for chart patterns and buy and sell shares often during the day when they believe they have identified short-term trends. High-frequency trading (HFT) is another strategy focused on buying and selling within milliseconds and seconds, for which traders would need the infrastructure to be faster than other high-frequency traders. The idea is to exploit very short-term price differences for arbitrage.

Trading and long-term investing require different approaches to risk. If you believe your investments will grow by 10% annually over the next decade, a single bad trading day is unlikely to concern you. However, in HFT, the risk is significantly higher. Imagine an investor buys shares of ACME at $100, expecting to sell at $120. If the price drops to $80 instead, they face immediate losses. When using leverage, the longer they hold the position, the more they pay in interest, adding to their risk.

Short selling carries even more significant risks. As explained earlier in this book, shorting means borrowing stocks to sell them, hoping to repurchase them later at a lower price. Suppose an investor short sells 10 shares of ACME at $100, expecting the price to drop. If the stock instead rises to $120, they must repurchase at a loss. Unlike leveraged trading, short sellers also incur borrowing fees and dividend payments, making waiting out an unfavorable market move costly.

Contrast this with long-term investing. Suppose you invest in ACME because you believe in steady demand for its products. You hold the stock for years, confident in its future. But what if the company loses a key business deal or a highly anticipated product becomes a flop? The warning signs may not be immediate—some investors may quietly sell, while others remain unaware. Then, during ACME's next earnings

> call, a disappointing report triggers a sudden 30% crash. You research the stock, read analyst reports, and realize ACME may never recover to your purchase price.
>
> But then again, in many long positions, drops after earnings calls are temporary. Investors may have feared that a company's winning streak had reached its end, only to be corrected by the market. Netflix and Meta experienced downtime in 2022 but have since recovered. Others, such as Kodak or Peloton, have not. Risks for long-term investors are different than those for traders. They can sit out temporary down periods, but if they overlook that the product they had bet on years ago has become obsolete with time, they can lose a lot of money too. Some investors might even see the decline of their assets, but avoid selling due to loss aversion.
>
> Understanding these different risk dynamics is crucial when selecting an investment strategy. Whether trading actively or investing for the long term, managing downside risk is essential to avoiding costly mistakes.

The risk-return tradeoff is like scaling a system—you can choose a safe, low-performance setup or an aggressive, high-performance architecture with potential failure risks. If your portfolio feels too risky, you can shift future investments toward safer assets. But the key is always risk awareness. Some strategies carry exceptionally high risks:

- *Leverage*—Borrowing money to invest. While it amplifies gains, excessive leverage can lead to disastrous losses.
- *Short selling*—Betting against a stock. Losses are theoretically unlimited if the price rises instead.
- *Derivatives*—Complex financial instruments that can magnify both gains and risks.

Understanding risk appetite versus risk capacity is crucial. *Risk appetite* is your willingness to take risks, while *risk capacity* is your ability to withstand losses. Think of it like coding for edge cases—you might be comfortable experimenting in a development environment (appetite), but you wouldn't push risky, untested changes to production (capacity).

### 7.3.3 Resilience

Imagine you buy two stocks at the same price. After a year, Company A dropped to 20% of its initial value, while Company B rose to 150%. You decide to sell one. Which one? Most investors instinctively sell Company B, locking in gains while hoping Company A recovers. But what if Company B keeps rising and Company A continues its decline?

Athletes, especially tennis players, often lose momentum after a mistake. The best ones recover quickly. Successful investors do the same—they accept losses, adapt, and move forward. Every investor loses money at some point. The key is handling it wisely.

Loss aversion—the tendency to avoid realizing losses—traps many investors. You may hesitate to sell a losing stock, thinking it might rebound or that you'll only lose if you sell. However, ignoring loss aversion can lead to even bigger losses. Instead, step back and remove emotions from the equation.

Imagine evaluating your portfolio from scratch. If you didn't own Company A, would you buy it today? Is it truly undervalued, or is it in a downward spiral with no recovery? If the latter, sell it and reallocate the funds elsewhere.

Conversely, if new information suggests Company A is a great buy, you might invest more. But be brutally honest—don't let sunk costs cloud your judgment.

This book teaches you how to analyze markets with algorithms, not what to invest in. If you struggle with tough decisions, recognize that your emotions and biases can distort judgment.

A trusted peer review, such as Warren Buffett's with Charlie Munger, can help. But choose your advisors wisely:

- The loudmouth at the bar bragging about stock market wins? Not reliable.
- A licensed financial advisor, vetted by a reputable institution? Possibly worth it.

Ultimately, the smartest investors cut losses, reassess facts, and stay disciplined—even when it's uncomfortable. The ability to face discomfort with a rational mind and be ready to follow thought-through principles may be one of the most significant successful factors in investing.

## 7.4 Hedging

Most of us have encountered Murphy's law: *What can go wrong, will go wrong*. Developers embrace this mindset, building metrics to assess code quality and unit tests to catch potential failures. This habit of assuming the worst and preparing for it is invaluable in investing.

Hedging is a risk management strategy that reduces or offsets potential losses, like insurance. You sacrifice some potential gains to protect against severe downturns by taking an opposing position in a related asset. While it won't eliminate risk entirely, it helps you sleep at night, knowing you're shielded from extreme scenarios. Next, let's explore some practical ways to mitigate risk.

### 7.4.1 Derivatives

Derivatives are arrangements whose value derives from an underlying asset, such as a commodity, currency, or security. They can be categorized this way:

- *Options*—Buying a put option on your stock protects against price drops.
- *Futures*—A farmer selling wheat futures locks in a price, avoiding losses if prices fall.
- *Swaps*—Interest rate swaps help companies hedge against rate fluctuations.

Let's illustrate these concepts with examples:

- *Options example*—Pedro owns ACME stock, purchased at $100 per share. He knows the stock could move in either direction with an earnings call approaching. To hedge his risk after the earnings call, he buys a put option to sell ACME at $95. If the stock stays above $95, it's like paying an insurance premium without needing to file a claim. But if ACME drops below $95, he can sell at that price, minimizing losses.

- *Futures example*—Farmer Yumi expects a plentiful harvest this year. However, she also knows grain prices will likely drop if all farmers have high yields. To protect against this risk, she buys futures, locking in a pre-agreed selling price. If market prices fall due to oversupply, she can still sell at the higher, predetermined price.
- *Swap example*—A swap can be a complex agreement between companies or countries to exchange assets with cash flow for some time. Imagine two companies—one based in the United States and another in Europe. The US company needs euros to expand its business in Europe, while the European company needs US dollars to enter the American market. Instead of each company borrowing in a foreign currency and facing exchange rate risks, they enter a swap agreement:
  - The US company borrows dollars at a favorable interest rate and exchanges them for euros with the European company.
  - The European company borrows euros at a favorable rate and gives them to the US company in exchange for dollars.
  - Over time, both companies pay each other back in their local currencies, reducing transaction costs and currency risks.

This structured agreement ensures both parties benefit by securing better loan terms and minimizing exchange rate fluctuations.

> **Advanced derivatives trading: All about options**
> Derivatives are far more complex and can't be reduced to insurance. Option traders use advanced trading strategies for income generation. Experienced traders can choose from a compendium of option strategies. Note that there are many strategies on the market. Although we can't cover them all, let's look at a couple of them:
>
> - *Covered call*—Let's say you own 100 shares of a stock at a share price of $100. You believe this stock will continue to pay reliable dividends, but will hardly ever be over $110. So, you sell a call option at $110. You gain money for the premium you just sold. If the stock stays below the strike price, you make some extra money and don't have to sell the stock. If the stock is on a rally and increases to $120, you would have to sell it for $110, which leads to a loss, as the difference is higher than the premium you earned.
>
>   Every option has an expiration date. If the expiration date has passed, the option expires. There are also different types of options. European-style options can be exercised only at expiration, and American-style options can be exercised at any time before expiration.

*(continued)*

- *Cash-secured put*—Let's say there is a stock with very volatile share prices. You believe that the stock will gain a lot of value in the long run, but you don't want to buy it at a high price. You can sell a put option at a lower strike price. If the share price drops and the buyer of your option exercises it, you buy this stock at a lower cost. If your strategy works out, you'll have gained twice. You've earned money by selling a premium, and you've bought a stock with a bright future that gains in the long run.

  If you miscalculate and, let's say, that specific company runs into a crisis causing the share price to plummet, you might lose a lot of money. Imagine investing in Enron before its collapse, only to have to buy shares from other stockholders at a high price as the company's value approaches zero.

- *Iron condor*—This is a more advanced option strategy that is commonly used to profit from low volatility in the market.

  To recap, selling an option means you receive a premium in exchange for taking on the obligation to buy or sell an asset at a specified strike price if the buyer chooses to exercise. Conversely, when you purchase an option, you acquire the right to buy or sell the asset under specific terms.

  An option is said to be out of the money (OTM) when it has no intrinsic value—for example, a call option whose strike price is above the current market price, or a put option whose strike price is below it. If the asset price never crosses the strike, the option expires as worthless. If it does cross, the option becomes in the money (ITM).

  In an iron condor strategy, you sell an OTM call and an OTM put, expecting the underlying asset's price to remain within a defined range. If the price stays between the strike prices at expiration, both options expire worthless, and you keep the entire premium collected. This is the ideal scenario, and it reflects a bet on price stability.

  However, the risk grows if the asset moves sharply up or down. To hedge against significant losses, you also purchase an OTM call and an OTM put. These long options cap your maximum loss, converting the strategy into a credit spread on both sides.

Let's walk through an example: imagine ACME stock is trading at $100. You construct a European-style iron condor with six months until expiration:

- Sell a call option with a strike price of $120.
- Sell a put option with a strike price of $80.
- Buy a call option with a strike price of $130.
- Buy a put option with a strike price of $70.

In this setup, you collect premiums from the short call and put, and you pay smaller premiums for the protective long options. The net result is a net credit, your maximum potential profit, if ACME stays between $80 and $120.

Suppose an unexpected lawsuit from a disgruntled customer, Wile E. Coyote, sends ACME's stock tumbling. At expiration, the price is $20. The buyer of the $80 put

> option exercises their option, and you're assigned—you must buy shares at $80, even though they're only worth $20. That's a $60 per share loss.
>
> But because you bought the $70 put as protection, you can now sell those shares at $70, limiting your loss to $10 per share (the difference between the short and long put strikes), minus the net credit you originally received.
>
> This structure—collecting premium while using long options to cap risk—makes the iron condor a defined-risk, nondirectional strategy. The protective aspect of buying cheaper options to hedge against your sold options is called a *credit spread*.

### 7.4.2 Diversification

Ongoing discussions debate whether randomly picking stocks—akin to throwing darts—can yield better results than actively managed funds, a question raised by Burton Malkiel in *A Random Walk Down Wall Street*. While opinions vary, nearly everyone agrees that putting all your eggs in one basket is risky. Significant risks remain even if you invest in a company with the highest market capitalization, such as one of the *Magnificent Seven* (Alphabet, Amazon, Apple, Meta, Microsoft, NVIDIA, and Tesla). The company might not face bankruptcy in your lifetime, but stock prices reflect market sentiment. You could buy at a peak, only to see years of stagnation or decline.

A common risk-management strategy is diversification—avoiding a single point of failure. Programmers can relate: relying on a single server invites disaster if it crashes. But does spreading investments across all Magnificent Seven stocks provide proper diversification? As we've learned, fluctuations in stock prices are often correlated. These companies share the same sector, so events affecting one could affect them all. While your eggs may be in seven baskets, they're still in the same AI truck heading down the road of capital appreciation—if that truck veers off course, all of your eggs are at risk.

Proper diversification means reducing exposure to a single market. This could involve holding stocks across different sectors or investing in a mix of assets such as bonds and real estate.

### 7.4.3 Pair trading

*Pair trading* is a market-neutral strategy where an investor goes long on one asset and short on another, typically within the same industry or among correlated assets. The goal is to profit from relative price movements rather than overall market direction, reducing exposure to market fluctuations.

Let's consider a practical example. Suppose you analyze two AI sector companies:

- Company A has strong growth potential.
- Company B is slowing down, with limited upside.

You short $100 of Company B's stock and use the proceeds to buy Company A's stock. If the AI boom continues, Company A will grow significantly while Company B will rise only slightly. Your trade is profitable, provided interest costs on your short position don't erode gains.

Now, let's explore a different scenario. Suppose the AI market crashes due to competition from a Chinese AI firm or overvaluation concerns. If both stocks decline, you lose on your long position but gain on your short position, potentially offsetting losses.

However, risks remain. Short selling incurs interest costs, and if your prediction is wrong—Company A declines while Company B unexpectedly rises—you could face amplified losses. Proper risk management is essential. Figure 7.5 outlines this principle, marking Company A as a rising star and Company B as a poor dog, which are the Boston Consulting Group (BCG) Growth-Share Matrix classifications.

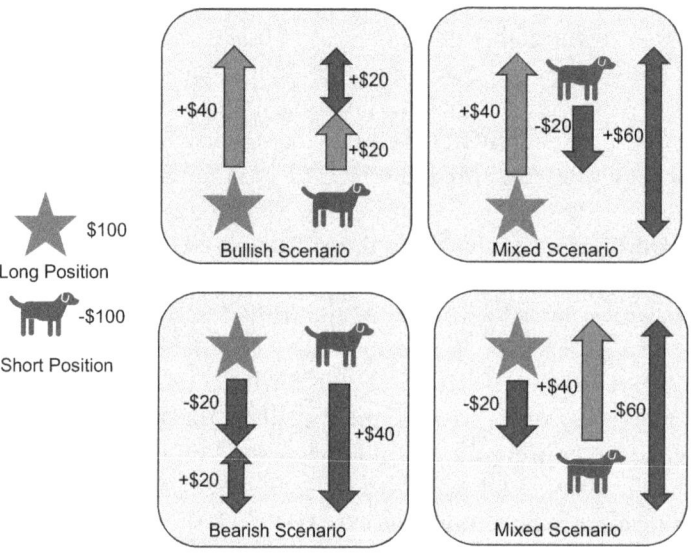

Figure 7.5 The investors are long on A and short on B. In the bull case, the long position increases more than the short position, and the long gain minus the short loss is the profit. In a bear case, the short position loses more than the long position. The profit is the gain from the short position minus the loss in the long position.

### 7.4.4 Risk pairing

Passion for innovation can drive investment decisions. Some see Small Modular Reactors (SMRs) as the future of energy, while others envision carbon capture technologies such as direct-air capture becoming financial gold mines. However, investing in emerging technologies is inherently risky.

Yes, data centers require constant energy, and nuclear power is promising, but what if SMRs fail to meet expectations or public sentiment stalls their adoption? Similarly, direct-air capture aims to remove $CO_2$ from the atmosphere, but its success hinges on reducing operational costs. What if that never happens?

Balancing speculative bets with stable investments is a smart way to manage this risk. The key is understanding your risk tolerance. For instance, if 80% of your portfolio is in index funds and 20% in high-risk assets, even a total loss in the speculative portion wouldn't threaten your financial foundation. Over time, the growth of stable investments can help absorb those losses, making risk more manageable. In addition, you can use staged investing. Assuming that, as a developer, you have streaks of high income, you can keep investing smaller portions into emerging technologies while maintaining the 20% to 80% risk ratio.

> **Catalysts and events**
> Hedging isn't just about *how*—it's about *when*. Earnings calls are critical moments for long-term investors. Brokers notify you in advance and provide analysts' forecasts on potential price movements. Earnings calls can be make-or-break. Reviewing transcripts—something GenAI can summarize—helps, but summaries alone may not be enough.
>
> Bad earnings? The stock drops. But is it a buying opportunity? That's the real question. So, as an investor, you want to always be on the lookout for special events that might shift share prices more heavily in one or another direction.

## 7.5 Nonfinancial risk

Some risks aren't reflected in a company's financial statement and can be summed up as nonfinancial risks. The subcategories are broad and may differ by industry. The overall global economic situation, for instance, affects all companies. Economic downturns harm companies unless a business model is targeted to perform well during crises.

The 2020s are likely to be a decade that leads to more global challenges than many other decades before. COVID-19 and geopolitical conflicts have created challenges in many parts of the world. With the unfolding of social media and AI, we also witness more extreme views. Many people speak about a very heated and aggressive situation in many countries. They are afraid that a straw will break the camel's back at some point, and we'll end up with big riots and unrest in which religious and political extremists fight each other.

Optimists might disagree with this view and assert that everything will be all right. As an investor, you can remain impartial. Will there be unrest in country X? The correct answer might be "I don't know!" Instead, we're interested in the probability of unrest. We need to find ways to quantify risks in numbers. Let's explore potential methods to measure nonfinancial risks, encompassing all risks not addressed by financial risk management.

## 7.5.1 Markets

Market trends are commonly symbolized by two animals: the bull and the bear. These aren't just arbitrary animals; they symbolize specific movements in the market:

- *Bull market*—The bull charges upward with its horns, symbolizing a rising market. Stock prices are climbing, optimism is in the air, and investors feel confident.
- *Bear market*—The bear swipes downward with its paws, symbolizing a declining market. Stock prices are dropping, uncertainty looms, and fear takes over.

Some investors get overexcited during bull markets. They take too many risks to replace good gains with exceptional gains. However, ignoring risks by picking random securities that promise huge gains without looking into the details of those assets can lead to a disaster.

Some investors might tell you to ignore Mr. Market. If you've invested in solid companies with a bright future, their share price may decrease during a bear market, but the future looks bright in the long run. At the same time, you can't ignore that sometimes companies might get into serious trouble during a market crisis, from which they can't recover. Selling them as soon as possible is often the only alternative to minimize permanent losses. Making the right decisions is hard. You don't have all the information you need, and psychological factors might affect you. Looking at a position when it's 20% below the purchase price still gives you the idea that there can be a turnaround. But selling that position at 20% below the purchase price is like acknowledging a loss. For many of us, this leads to negative emotions. It's human to push these feelings away and to keep the illusion that everything will be good again at some point, even if some facts tell us that it would be better to walk away with a slight loss.

As a risk-taker, you might see a bear market as an opportunity to short sell assets. This means you borrow shares from someone to sell them and repurchase them at a lower price later. While famous investors, such as Michael Burry, became wealthy by predicting the housing bubble crash in 2008, other investors had been wrong with their predictions.

Managing emotions and sticking to discipline and fact-based decision-making may be key to being a good investor. Anyone who feels that they might not have the nerve to stay disciplined during difficult times or knows they won't be able to sleep when the market is in turmoil should consider adjusting their strategy to their risk profile.

Some investors try to sell growth stocks at the end of a bull run to stock up on defensive stocks. Once the next bear market is over, you can repurchase growth stocks at a lower price. This leads to one big question: Can we predict a bear or bull market?

## 7.5.2 Economic data

Some analysts try to look at economic data to predict a recession. One of these metrics is the "10-Year Treasury Constant Maturity Minus 2-Year Treasury Constant Maturity." Some investors see the spread between the yields on 10-year and 2-year US Treasury bonds as a yield curve proxy indicator of a recession. Figure 7.6 shows a graph that outlines these numbers.

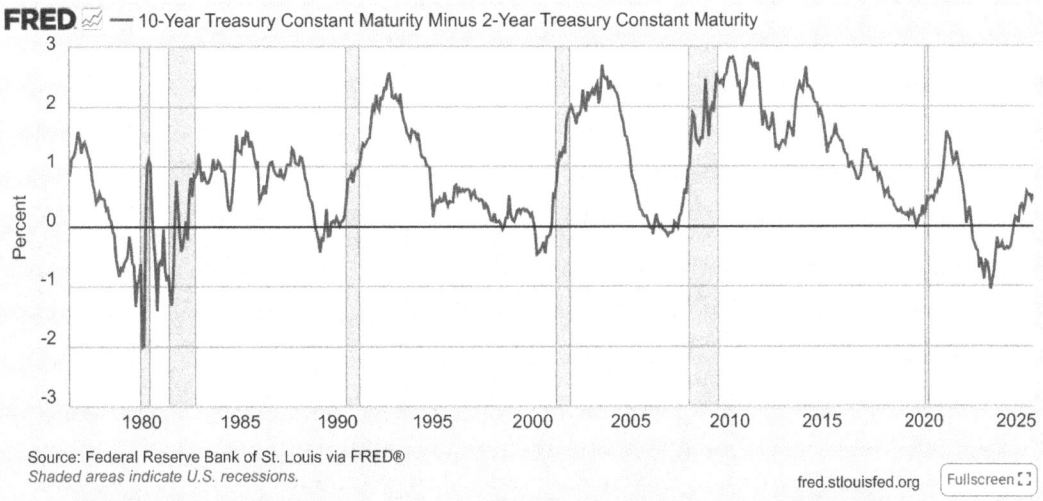

Figure 7.6 The 10-Year Treasury Constant Maturity Minus 2-Year Treasury Constant Maturity

Another indicator is the unemployment rate, which we can collect through the Federal Reserve Economic Data (FRED), as shown in figure 7.7. The more people are employed, the greater the risk we face. We might exclude 2020, as the COVID-19 crisis resulted from unforeseeable events.

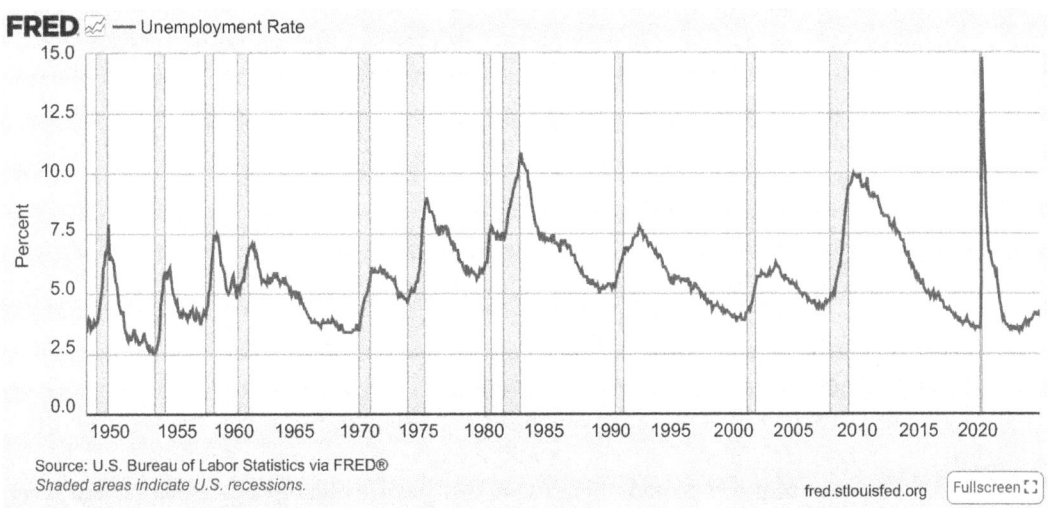

Figure 7.7 Unemployment rate over the years

The graph shows that unemployment gradually increased before most recessions. Then, when the recession was here, it went up enormously.

Reading charts can only give you indications. Whoever listens to podcasts and interviews with experts will detect contradicting views. While some predict imminent crises, others predict colossal growth.

### 7.5.3 *Assessing nonfinancial risk*

Public companies must report their numbers using predefined standards and would be in trouble if they violated the regulations. Some accountants might try to disguise some unpleasant details with tricks in their reporting, but experienced financial data analysts have a framework in which they can interpret the numbers and decide if something is off.

We'll investigate nonfinancial data in chapter 11 in more detail to explore how we can integrate insights outside of financial statements into more advanced analyses. For now, let's start with the awareness that nonfinancial risks are defined by what they are not. We might look for social media sentiments, weather data, and other sources. Still, unlike financial data, no central data repository is available to host all possible data to analyze nonfinancial risks. It wouldn't even be clear what we would need to store.

Let's reference the fictitious case study for ACME that we used to discuss options trading. Let's assume a disgruntled customer, Mr. Coyote, sues ACME Corporation because their products don't live up to the promises in the sales material. Let's also assume that his case gets some media coverage. How can we rate the reputation risk for ACME? Experienced analysts may take similar cases from the past as a reference and assess the reputation risk for ACME; others might analyze the sentiments on social media posts related to the case. However, different analysts may come to different conclusions.

The ACME case study is most likely only relevant to one company. Let's also look at a systemic risk. Let's assume a country gets a new political leader. We can analyze transcripts of speeches and create sentiment analyses based on keywords. This way, we might also detect hidden messages between the lines. We might also investigate the election campaigns to determine who donated how much to this new leader to understand his priorities further.

Let's assume this new leader is erratic, contradicts his predecessors, and does many things differently. Some investors might view a country's political leader as a risk to the economy, while others may assume that he will stir up stagnation and do good things. Maybe some companies will benefit while others suffer. It's challenging to translate behavior into risk. While many believe that a politician who is rude, aggressive, and with plenty of evidence of narcissistic behavior must be a risk for every country, we might lack proof for what we might call common sense. Predicting the future based on data requires enough historical data. As every leader of the past is a different person who ruled under other circumstances, it's hard to create an accurate model to compare current performance with past performance. Therefore, analyses based on nonfinancial risks, especially politics-related ones, can be speculative: It's likely harder to predict the possible effect of a legal case or elections on a corporation's share price than assessing the financial risk of a company going bankrupt.

One additional question is whether we'll group nonfinancial risks into subgroups. The following is one attempt:

- *Operational risks*—System downtime, security breaches
- *Regulatory risks*—Lawsuits, compliance fines
- *ESG risks*—Environmental, social, and governance factors
- *Tech obsolescence*—R&D spending, patent filings
- *Political risk*—Country stability, trade restrictions
- *Reputation risk*—Social media sentiment, brand issues
- *Management risk*—CEO turnover, employee satisfaction

Professional investors and organizations, such as central banks, have more refined risk taxonomies, which may be overkill for a private investor to study. We can also dive deeper into specific risks. The current decade has experienced a pandemic, geopolitical conflicts, political paradigm shifts, and the effect of climate change through wildfires and hurricanes. Instead of asking on a generic level, such as what ESG risks a company might face, we can also ask more concrete questions: How will climate change affect that company's business?

We may consider two approaches to addressing the topic. We can develop individual scoring systems that collect data from various sources and build algorithms. If we take our work seriously, we could write books about each risk type and company, as we might consider building digital twins and simulating the effect of various catastrophes.

As this is a lot of effort, we may use an alternative approach. In chapters 8 and 9, we examine large language models (LLMs) in more detail. But if we agree that risk assessments always contain room for error because there are unknowns, we can also use LLMs for basic risk assessments, knowing that they might hallucinate. Even if we need to review an LLM's response, we might still discover patterns that are helpful in our risk strategy. In chapter 8, we'll also provide an example of how to assess nonfinancial risks.

## 7.6 Portfolio optimization

Let's explore how to optimize our portfolios. We can collect data and then define the riskiness of individual positions. We can also use these techniques to create portfolios that optimize risk and return rates. Let's start by exploring the Markowitz-efficient portfolio in detail.

### 7.6.1 Markowitz-efficient portfolio

A Markowitz-efficient portfolio is any portfolio that lies on the efficient frontier, as defined by modern portfolio theory (MPT), introduced by Harry Markowitz in 1952.

The *efficient frontier* represents the set of optimal portfolios that offer the highest expected return for a given level of risk (standard deviation). A portfolio is Markowitz-efficient if there's no other portfolio with a higher return for the same risk or a lower risk for the same return. These portfolios are obtained by diversifying assets to minimize variance while maintaining an optimal return. We do this by loading data in memory, comparing past share price volatility and returns, and constructing a portfolio that optimally balances risks and returns.

Let's see how to create an efficient portfolio. In listing 7.2, we start by loading stock data. For this example, we take Apple (AAPL), Walmart (WMT), Alphabet (GOOGL), Coca-Cola (KO), Pfizer (PFE), Berkshire Hathaway (BRK-B), and NVIDIA (NVDA). In the code, we collect data for three years.

> Listing 7.2   Collecting data for the Markowitz-efficient portfolio

```
import numpy as np
import pandas as pd
import matplotlib.pyplot as plt
import yfinance as yf
from datetime import datetime, timedelta

def load_stocks(tickers, year_backs):
    start_date = datetime.today() - timedelta(days=365*year_backs)
    end_date = datetime.today()
    stock_data = yf.download(tickers, start=start_date,
      end=end_date)['Close']
    return stock_data.pct_change().dropna()

tickers = ["AAPL", "WMT", "GOOGL", "KO", "PFE", "BRK-B", "NVDA"]
year_backs = 3
returns = load_stocks(tickers, year_backs)
```

After loading the data with the returns, we set up the parameters for calculating the efficient frontier in listing 7.3. The number of trading days doesn't equal the number of yearly days, as we must factor in weekends and public holidays.

> Listing 7.3   Setting up variables

```
TRADING_DAYS = 252

mean_returns = returns.mean() * TRADING_DAYS          Annualized mean returns
cov_matrix = returns.cov() * TRADING_DAYS             and covariance matrices

num_portfolios = 10000                                Number of portfolios
num_assets = len(tickers)                             to simulate

port_returns = np.zeros(num_portfolios)
port_volatility = np.zeros(num_portfolios)
sharpe_ratios = np.zeros(num_portfolios)
all_weights = np.zeros((num_portfolios, num_assets))
```

It's time to talk about the risk-free rate and the Sharpe ratio. The Sharpe ratio, developed by William F. Sharpe, is a performance measure used to evaluate the risk-adjusted return of a portfolio. A higher Sharpe ratio means the portfolio has a better return per unit of risk. A Markowitz-efficient portfolio doesn't necessarily have the highest Sharpe ratio. The tangency portfolio on the efficient frontier, which maximizes the Sharpe ratio, is often the best portfolio when risk-free borrowing/lending is allowed.

Think of the Sharpe ratio as a return-to-risk efficiency metric, which measures how much helpful work a function does per unit of computational cost. In investing, it tells you how much extra return you get per unit of risk taken.

Some investments are de facto risk-free, ignoring black swan events; the assets can't go broke. The risk-free rate is the baseline where the lowest return can be found with the least risk. If you have assets for which you expect lower returns but are at a higher risk, these would be the first to be removed from a portfolio. So, every asset with a risk must provide higher returns than an asset without risk. But what is a risk-free rate?

A possible but wrong way to think of a risk-free rate is to consider the stock market's average, as shown in figure 7.8. Taking the returns since 1950, we get average returns of approximately 9.21%. Even if we factor in a 3% inflation rate, we still get solid returns.

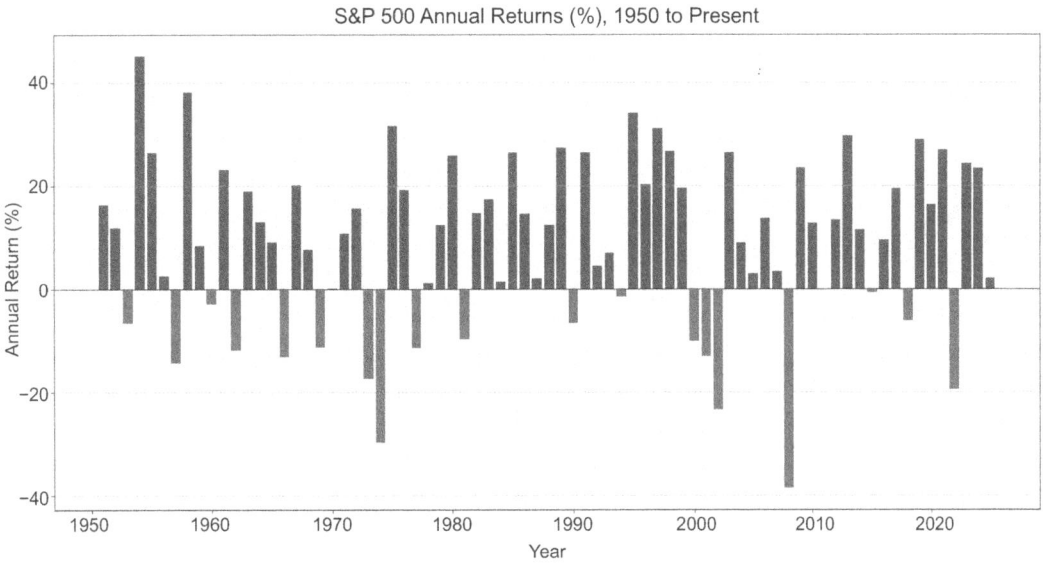

Figure 7.8 Market returns from 1950 until the present day

A risk-free rate means I can trust that I'll get x amount of money at a specific time. Average returns on stock markets don't help here. Instead, T-bills are assumed to have zero default risk as the US government backs them. At the time of writing this book, the treasury bill rate was 4.22%. So, this is what we need to beat. The value fluctuates significantly, so if you run these examples on your own, be sure to update the information with the latest data.

**NOTE** In chapter 5, we show how to collect historical data for bonds.

Listing 7.4 creates a Markowitz-efficient portfolio. The first step is to set the risk-free rate to 0.0422. We then run a Monte Carlo simulation for random portfolios to find a good match. We store portfolios with all the assets and assign them random weights. Then, we calculate the returns and volatilities based on these random portfolios. To calculate the Sharpe ratio, we must subtract the risk-free rate from the returns and then divide by volatility. In the final step, we get the optimal weights.

### Listing 7.4 Creating a Markowitz efficient portfolio

```
risk_free_rate = 0.0422

for i in range(num_portfolios):                          ◁── Monte Carlo simulation
    weights = np.random.dirichlet(np.ones(num_assets), size=1).flatten()
    all_weights[i, :] = weights
    port_returns[i] = np.dot(weights, mean_returns)
    port_volatility[i] = np.sqrt(np.dot(weights.T,
                                 np.dot(cov_matrix, weights)))
    sharpe_ratios[i] = (port_returns[i] - risk_free_rate) /
     port_volatility[i]
#
max_sharpe_idx = np.argmax(sharpe_ratios)                ◁── Finds the optimal
optimal_weights = all_weights[max_sharpe_idx, :]             Sharpe ratio portfolio
```

After calculating the optimal portfolio with the best Sharpe ratio, let's look at the code to plot the results in listing 7.5. We set the labels and highlight the best portfolio with the highest maximum Sharpe ratio. We plot the results as a scatter plot.

### Listing 7.5 Plotting the efficient frontier

```
plt.figure(figsize=(10, 6))
plt.scatter(port_volatility, port_returns, c=sharpe_ratios,     ◁── Sets plotting
            cmap='viridis', marker='o')                             parameters
plt.colorbar(label='Sharpe Ratio')
plt.xlabel('Volatility (Risk)')
plt.ylabel('Expected Return')
plt.title('Efficient Frontier with Actual Stock Data')

plt.scatter(port_volatility[max_sharpe_idx],
            port_returns[max_sharpe_idx],
            c='red', marker='*', s=200,
            label='Max Sharpe Portfolio')
plt.legend()                                                    ◁── Plots a
plt.show()                                                          scatter plot
```

## 7.6 Portfolio optimization

Let's look at the plot we created in figure 7.9. We see the random portfolios plotted. Some portfolios would bring higher returns at a higher risk, but we're interested in the portfolio with the best risk-return ratio.

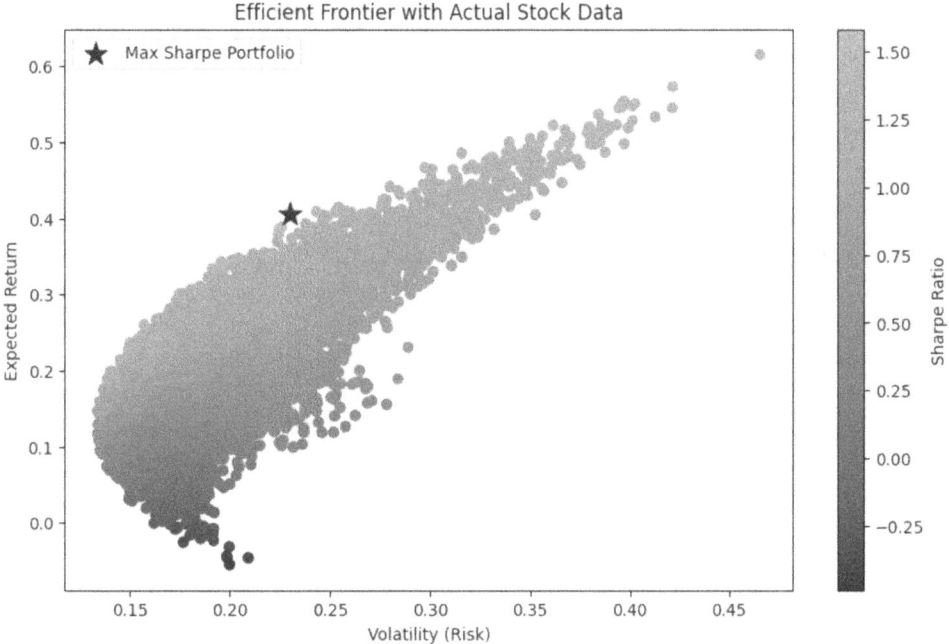

**Figure 7.9** Showing the efficient frontier with the portfolio with the best Sharpe ratio

To get the portfolio with its weights, we need only to get the results in a DataFrame and display them:

```
optimal_portfolio_df = pd.DataFrame({
    'Stock': tickers,
    'Optimal Weight': optimal_weights
})
print(optimal_portfolio_df)
```

Let's look at the results, which, based on historical data, give us some insights about the most efficient portfolio, as shown in table 7.6.

**Table 7.6** Results of a Markowitz portfolio calculation

| Stock | Optimal weight |
|---|---|
| AAPL | 0.045226 |
| WMT | 0.015196 |

Table 7.6 Results of a Markowitz portfolio calculation *(continued)*

| Stock | Optimal weight |
|---|---|
| GOOGL | 0.005023 |
| KO | 0.004842 |
| PFE | 0.293244 |
| BRK-B | 0.000245 |
| NVDA | 0.636224 |

NVIDIA was a star performer over the past few years. And nobody would have expected a portfolio with data from recent years in which NVIDIA wasn't dominant. We also see Pfizer as quite dominant, which might be logical considering COVID-19, in which Pfizer had huge earnings through vaccine sales. We would have to buy and sell positions in our existing portfolio to use the insights until we have the weights as proposed in table 7.6.

We get different results if we change the risk-free rate and time horizon parameters. Past performance may indicate possible future results, but the future remains uncertain. Especially at the beginning of this decade, the world economy was enormously affected by the pandemic and other global crises. Many investment firms that estimate target prices of stocks are getting predictions wrong more often than before, which underlines that we can't eliminate uncertainty.

Statistical methods can't eliminate risks, but can help us manage them better. Following the best practices created by researchers such as Harry Markowitz enables us to calculate likely gains and risks. Many may start their investment approach by looking at single assets. They analyze single companies and pick likely performers based on their expected earnings and other ratios. Investors who learn to analyze portfolios can extend their approach. They still look for valuable companies and validate how new assets fit into their portfolios. Sometimes, they might decide not to buy shares because they don't fit into what they already own.

### 7.6.2 *Shiller P/E ratio*

The Shiller P/E ratio (often also referred to as the CAPE ratio [cyclically adjusted price-to-earnings ratio]) is a stock market valuation metric that smooths out earnings fluctuations and gives a clearer picture of long-term market valuation. It helps gauge stock market valuation. Using this method, you take the current price of a stock or index, such as the S&P 500, as the numerator. You use the average real (inflation-adjusted) earnings over the past 10 years for the denominator. The purpose of this 10-year smoothing is to eliminate short-term noise from economic or market disruptions.

## 7.6 Portfolio optimization

High CAPE ratios suggest overvaluation, while low ratios suggest undervaluation. We can track and monitor the CAPE ratio for broad indices (e.g., S&P 500). Then, we can decide what to do next. We can adjust equity allocation based on CAPE:

- *High CAPE (overvalued market)*—Reduce equity exposure and shift to bonds, gold, or alternatives.
- *Low CAPE (undervalued market)*—Increase equity exposure.

Let's look at an example. The historical average CAPE ratio for the S&P 500 is around 16–18. The market may be overheated if the CAPE exceeds this range (e.g., > 30). A low CAPE (e.g., < 10) may suggest buying opportunities.

We must still be aware that a CAPE ratio is an indication, but not a definitive prediction. A high CAPE ratio doesn't mean a crash is imminent, and a low CAPE doesn't guarantee immediate gains.

We must also be aware of limitations. Economic changes, such as structural shifts (e.g., lower interest rates or changing tax laws), can influence what a "fair" CAPE might be today compared to historical norms. Sector composition is also a topic. The composition of indices changes over time (e.g., tech-heavy markets today versus industrial-heavy in the past), which can skew CAPE comparisons.

For long-term investors, CAPE is a tool for assessing potential future returns over a decade or more, not short-term trades. It also helps them stay grounded during periods of market exuberance or pessimism. In short, the CAPE ratio provides a historical perspective on market valuation, assisting investors in making informed decisions about risk and reward. We can collect the ratio for stock exchanges from web pages, as shown in figure 7.10.

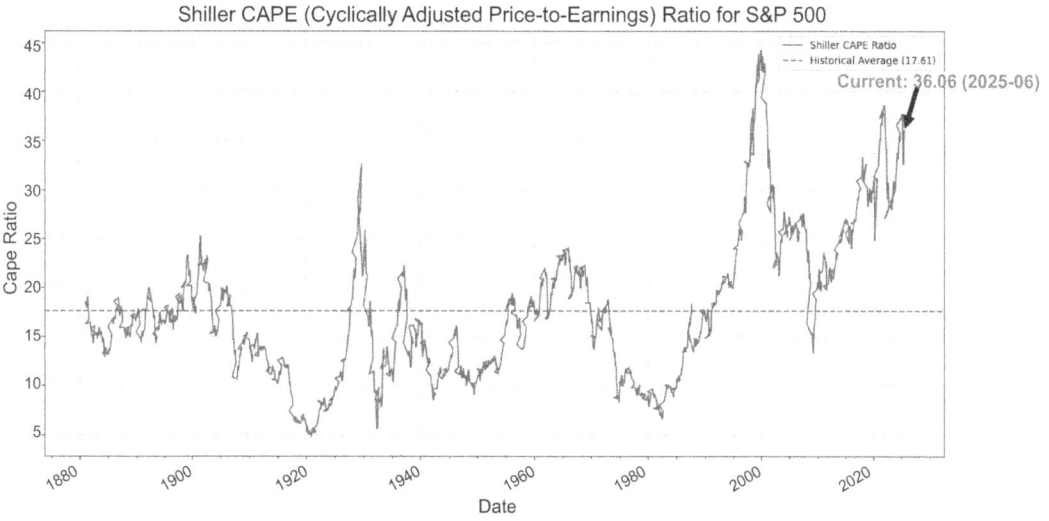

**Figure 7.10 Shiller CAPE ratio per month**

The Shiller CAPE ratio is high on this chart, which could indicate that the market is overvalued. Someone with strong views on the validity of this indicator would tell us to get out of equities. But this is just one interpretation out of many. Others may see more room to grow. Some might see an upcoming market correction, but until then, you can still gain a lot. The hard truth is that financial experts often contradict themselves; after all, it's up to you to decide whom you want to believe.

Some investors combine Markowitz-efficient portfolios with the CAPE ratio. They use the CAPE ratio for macro allocation and adjust the stock/bond allocation based on CAPE. When CAPE is high, they reduce the stock exposure to lower drawdown risk. When balancing the portfolios, they use the Sharpe ratio for micro-optimization. Here's an example:

- If CAPE is low (e.g., < 20), allocate 80% to equities and 20% to bonds.
- If CAPE is high (e.g., > 30), allocate 50% to equities, 30% to bonds, and 20% to gold.

Within the equity portion, they optimize weights using the Sharpe ratio. As with every strategy, there are exceptions and risks.

### 7.6.3 Rebalancing

*Rebalancing* is the process of adjusting the weights of assets in a portfolio to maintain the desired asset allocation over time. It helps control risk, optimize returns, and prevent drift from the original investment strategy.

Rebalancing is important. Market movements cause asset weights to shift away from the target allocation. We also want to manage risks to prevent overexposure to certain well-performing assets (reducing concentration risk) and optimize returns to ensure that gains are captured and reinvested according to the original strategy. There are three main strategies for rebalancing:

- *Periodic rebalancing (time-based)*—Rebalance on predefined intervals.
- *Threshold-based rebalancing (percentage-based)*—Rebalance only when an asset deviates by a certain percentage from the target allocation (e.g., ±5% drift).
- *Hybrid approach (time + threshold)*—Combine both methods.

A hybrid approach often works best. We must remember that too-frequent rebalances cost money. Each sell and buy order leads to transaction costs and maybe tax consequences.

In addition, we can consider different methods of rebalancing. One way is to buy and sell from positions within a portfolio to return to optimal weight. In that case, we calculate the efficient portfolio at a specific time. Let's say we rebalance quarterly. Then, we run our algorithms, sell those underperforming assets, and buy more of those that performed well.

> **Selling underperformers and buying overperformers**
>
> If we rebalance, we must define rules for what to sell and buy. One of the best investment practices is buying more high-performers and selling low-performers, which might contradict our instinct to hold on to stocks that have lost value in the hope that they will rebound.
>
> At the same time, we need to be aware of not tuning our algorithms in a way that risks de-diversifying. Imagine you have one superstar in your portfolio that grows far more than any other stock. Some algorithms might conclude that selling the rest and buying only the superstar would be best.

Investors with a strong cash flow, such as programmers who make a lot of money by working on projects, can also decide to balance by making optimal buy decisions. They deposit new cash into their brokerage account and run the algorithms, but instead of selling weak positions, they buy recommended stocks with the new money.

Let's look at some code. We take the basis allocation from the results we collected from the efficient portfolio:

```
target_allocation = {
"AAPL":         0.016804,
"WMT":          0.007427,
"GOOGL":        0.015956,
"KO":           0.142700,
"PFE":          0.193730,
"BRK-B":        0.009315,
"NVDA":         0.614068
}
```

In this model, we assume we've invested in all stocks equally in dollars (although this is unlikely, but we need to start somewhere). As you've learned how to collect data from your brokers in chapter 6, feel free to load it and use these positions as a base:

```
import pandas as pd
current_portfolio = {
"AAPL":         10000,
"WMT":          10000,
"GOOGL":        10000,
"KO":           10000,
"PFE":          10000,
"BRK-B":        10000,
"NVDA":         10000,
}
```

Before we go into more detail, let's set up some parameters. We need to map our current portfolio to the weights in listing 7.6. We set a threshold of 0.05 and sum up all values. Then, we review each position and set the current allocation based on weights.

**Listing 7.6 Rebalancing preparation**

```
threshold = 0.05
total_value = sum(current_portfolio.values())

current_allocation = {stock: value / total_value
                      for stock, value
                      in current_portfolio.items()}
```

- `threshold = 0.05` — Defines the rebalancing threshold (e.g., 5% deviation from target)
- `current_allocation` — Computes current allocations based on the weights

Now, we can calculate the deviations in listing 7.7 from our target allocation and identify the rebalancing actions. We review all stocks with a higher deviation than the threshold defined before and calculate the required adjustments.

**Listing 7.7 Calculate required adjustments**

```
dev = {
    stock: current_allocation[stock]
    - target_allocation[stock]
    for stock in target_allocation
}

rebalance_needed = {
    stock: value
    for stock, value in dev.items()
    if abs(value) > threshold
}

adjustments = {}
for stock in rebalance_needed:
    target_value = target_allocation[stock] * total_value
    current_value = current_portfolio[stock]
    adjustments[stock] = target_value - current_value
```

- Finds rebalancing
- Defines sell and buy actions

In the last step, we must put everything in a DataFrame and analyze the results to create a DataFrame that holds buy and sell recommendations:

```
rebalance_df = pd.DataFrame({
    "Stock": list(adjustments.keys()),
    "Current Value ($)": [
        current_portfolio[stock]
        for stock in adjustments
    ],
    "Target Value ($)": [
        target_allocation[stock] * total_value
        for stock in adjustments
    ],
    "Adjustment ($)": [
        adjustments[stock]
        for stock in adjustments
    ],
    "Action": [
        "Buy" if adj > 0 else "Sell"
```

```
        for adj in adjustments.values()
    ]
})
```

With that, we get some results, as shown in table 7.7. We must create four sell and two buy orders to balance our portfolio. Keep in mind that most portfolios can't be ideally matched. This is especially true if you own high-priced shares in a company and your broker doesn't allow you to sell fractions of a share (at the time of writing this chapter, a few brokers still don't support it). If one share is around $1000, such as BlackRock, selling half a share is often impossible.

Table 7.7  Rebalancing actions

| Stock | Current value | Target value | Adjustment | Action |
|---|---|---|---|---|
| AAPL | 10,000 | 1,176.28 | −8,823.72 | Sell |
| WMT | 10,000 | 519.89 | −9,480.11 | Sell |
| GOOGL | 10,000 | 1,116.92 | −8,883.08 | Sell |
| PFE | 10,000 | 13,561.1 | 3,561.10 | Buy |
| BRK-B | 10,000 | 652.05 | −9,347.95 | Sell |
| NVDA | 10,000 | 42,984.76 | 32,984.76 | Buy |

## Summary

- *Ukemi* is a term borrowed from martial arts. In this chapter, we use it to raise awareness of the importance of learning to deal with possible setbacks before taking risks.
- Stop-loss orders can be the most efficient loss protection tool. You instruct your broker to sell the position once it reaches a specific price.
- "Bikeshedding," or Parkinson's Law of Triviality, tells you about the risk of overlooking the most significant threats as you get distracted by trivial topics.
- Bull markets represent growth markets, and bear markets are markets of decline. Often, the challenge is less to create a well-performing portfolio during good times, but to minimize losses during bad times. Value at Risk (VaR) calculates how much you can likely lose in extreme cases in a period. We can use Monte Carlo simulations to measure the VaR of stocks.
- Correlation in the context of two share prices means their price movements are often interlinked. If stock A goes up, so does stock B, in most cases.
- We can use past returns and variances to determine risks. Then, we can select a portfolio of many stocks to produce the desired mix of expected risk-adjusted returns.
- We can use Monte Carlo simulations to calculate efficient portfolios.
- Human psychology is a significant risk factor when investing.

- Hedging describes practices to protect oneself against risk using techniques and assets such as derivatives, diversification, pair trading, or risk pairing.
- Derivatives are like insurance against changing prices. Some derivative traders also use them to create additional income.
- Diversification is essential but requires a deep understanding of the assets within one portfolio that might correlate.
- Pair trading is the idea of offsetting risk by going long in one position and short in another.
- Risk pairing means pairing risky investments with less risky assets.
- Nonfinancial risks comprise all risks without a direct link to finance. This broad category includes issues caused by geopolitical changes or overall market movements.
- You might be unable to protect yourself against all nonfinancial risks, as this category is vast, but you can identify the most concerning risks through a risk matrix.
- One way to protect a business against nonfinancial risks is by keeping a margin of safety and preparing for risks by anticipating worst-case scenarios.
- Some companies are more resilient against market movements than others. The beta ratio measures a stock's volatility relative to the overall market. The lower a stock's beta, the more resilient it is against market movements.
- Some investors see macroeconomic data, such as unemployment rates and the 10-Year Treasury Constant Maturity Minus the 2-Year Treasury Constant Maturity, as indicators of possible recessions.
- Past performance indicates a possible future performance, but doesn't guarantee it.
- Having multiple assets in a portfolio, with past returns for possible gains and past share price volatility as risk, allows us to create strategies.
- The Markowitz efficient portfolio recommends optimal weights in your portfolio based on historical data. These weights—in a closer sense, the distribution of shares within a portfolio—can be calculated through Monte Carlo simulation and reflect the optimal risk and return rate.
- The Shiller P/E ratio, also known as the CAPE ratio, is a valuation measure that uses real earnings per share over 10 years to smooth out fluctuations in corporate profits. It's often used to assess if a market, such as the S&P 500, is overvalued.
- Portfolios often become skewed with time. To overcome this, they need to be rebalanced. However, rebalancing too frequently can accumulate substantial transaction costs.

# AI for financial research

**This chapter covers**
- The challenges of using machine learning to predict stock prices
- Research investments with large language models
- Submitting prompts to large language models with Python
- Using prompt engineering to improve our queries

Let's start this chapter with a radical idea: What if we stopped using code for financial research and relied on generative AI (GenAI) chatbots for investment advice? We can ask a large language model (LLM) questions such as "I am a risk-averse investor, and I want to invest in stocks in the Information Technology sector. What are three stocks with maximized returns and minimized risks?" Would you buy the three recommended stocks without additional due diligence?

This chapter examines the discriminative applications of machine learning (ML) in finance in the first part. We'll highlight the limitations of linear regression and similar algorithms in chaotic systems, such as stock prices, which often lack patterns and are typically characterized by "random walks." We'll also outline how these algorithms can be used meaningfully in more isolated scenarios.

When introducing LLMs later in the chapter, we'll emphasize that mindlessly following an LLM's investment advice is risky due to the potential for hallucinations and outdated information. We will, however, highlight the usefulness of GenAI in financial research, particularly when seeking to gain a deeper understanding of a company that presents an investment opportunity. In simplified terms, instead of getting particular investment advice based on a generic question, such as "Recommend me three stocks," we can pass more detailed inquiries such as, "Tell me about the management style of the management board of company X." With answers to a lot of company details, we can build an individual scorecard about a company to make an investment decision.

We'll demonstrate how to integrate LLMs from organizations such as Google (Gemini) and OpenAI (GPT), as well as open source models from Hugging Face, and how to configure specific parameters for these models. While the book has been programming-oriented to this point, we'll now find out how to automate insight generation.

## 8.1 From code to machine learning

In the past chapters, we've demonstrated how to analyze companies to hypothesize which ones are better suited for investment. Regardless of our algorithms and strategies, we can justify our actions if our approach is grounded in evidence-based decision-making.

> **NOTE** Using terms such as *hypothesize* instead of stronger words, such as *judge*, can serve as a reminder to stay aware of the room for error. Even the most successful investors have misjudged investment opportunities in the past, and it's helpful to remember that we often follow assumptions when investing in volatile assets. Overconfidence in your ability to predict the future is a form of self-deception that can lead to unexpected losses and painful lessons.

Using computer-generated models trained on vast historical data, we delegate decision-making processes to algorithms at an advanced stage of automation. Humans might not even understand why the model decided to buy or sell, as they are black boxes. Investors will appreciate sophisticated trading algorithms that automate profits, but a trading bot that incurs losses after market changes is a trader's nightmare. Let's delve into the details of traditional ML to gain a deeper understanding.

> **Behavioral finance**
>
> The works of Robert F. Shiller, Daniel Kahneman, Amos Tversky, and others have shown that investors often act irrationally. Reading up on biases and deeply ingrained behavioral patterns, such as loss aversion, makes us wonder if our emotions and unconscious behavior might be our biggest obstacle to financial freedom.
>
> We can compare this situation to information security. If the human factor is the biggest challenge, solving the human factor is the solution. This brings us to an interesting

> question: Do we save ourselves from our biases if we let computers do the trading? We'll show that eliminating the human risk factor by reducing investment decisions to ML algorithms also faces some challenges.

ML involves statistical algorithms that learn from data and perform tasks without requiring explicit instructions. These algorithms can be categorized into trained models that use *supervised* and *unsupervised learning*.

Supervised ML models are trained with labeled data. Imagine a dataset that contains quantifiable financial data about a company in columns, which are called *features*, tagged with an indication of whether the stock price is higher or lower one year later—the *label*. With a supervised learning algorithm, we can train a model that predicts whether a stock will increase or decrease in value when the model is fed unlabeled data. Depending on the direction of the stock price, we can label the stock as "buy," "sell," or "hold." We can also classify stocks as strong buy or strong sell if an analysis concludes that the stock might move above average when we compare the expected performance with other stocks. This example represents a *classification* approach. Another similar approach is *regression*; instead of classifying as buy or sell, we estimate the stock price changes in percentage terms (returns) over one year.

> **NOTE** In investment theory, the term *factor* is used for parameters that can affect trade decisions, such as value, size, momentum, quality, or volatility. Factors are typical candidates for features in analytical datasets for data models.

To train a model, we need labeled data, but what if the data isn't labeled? Unsupervised learning is about finding structure in data, and we're successful if we can find ways to label the data meaningfully. Shares of companies are a perfect textbook example to illustrate the applications of unsupervised learning, as we can extract two key values from the time series data on share prices: returns and volatility. We'll illustrate in the upcoming example how to plot this data and create labels by clustering the data on the plot.

Identifying *outliers*—assets with distinct values from others—can bring value to investors with a higher risk appetite. We've found an asset that might behave differently from other assets on the market. If we strongly believe in the stock's growth or decline hypothesis, we might buy or short sell it.

Investment firms use ML to analyze stocks. They collect historical data and forecast earnings, revenue growth, and, of course, stock prices. Financial data providers often provide investors with an average of the forecasts of different companies. Figure 8.1 shows the NVIDIA price forecast based on data collected via yfinance.

In this figure, we collected someone else's forecasts and plotted them. As past performance doesn't guarantee future results, forecasts can be wrong. To improve the likelihood of success when deciding based on analyst forecasts, details on historical performance facilitate decision-making. The more successful selected analysts have been in the past, the more likely it is that their next forecast is solid too. Sharing the

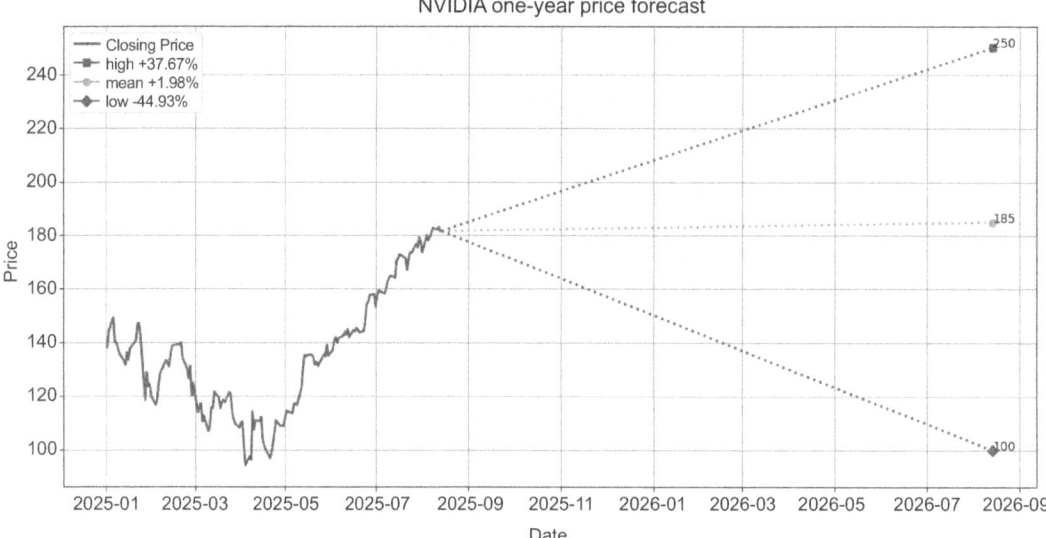

Figure 8.1  One-year price forecasts for NVIDIA based on data collected via yfinance, divided into high, low, and mean

historical performance of investment analysts who shared their insights is one of the key features of paid pro subscription services of financial analyst platforms.

We also want to understand how to create models ourselves to predict prices. Before investigating that, let's explore how to use unsupervised learning.

### 8.1.1 Unsupervised learning example

Stock market indices are often used as an entry point to analyze individual stocks, as they already list a preselection of promising stocks. The S&P 500, for example, tracks the stock performance of 500 of the largest companies listed on US stock exchanges. It would be inefficient to examine each stock in the index manually. Let's see if we can improve our results using Python code.

What if we clustered stocks by performance and picked more interesting ones for us? We focus on stocks with excellent past returns and explore them first. Let's load the S&P data to visualize stocks based on their performance using code. The following code retrieves the tickers of S&P 500 constituents from Wikipedia using Pandas to parse HTML pages:

```
sp500_url = 'https://en.wikipedia.org/wiki/List_of_S%26P_500_companies'

data_table = pd.read_html(sp500_url)
tickers = data_table[0]['Symbol'].values.tolist()
tickers = [s.replace('\n', '') for s in tickers]
tickers = [s.replace('.', '-') for s in tickers]
tickers = [s.replace(' ', '') for s in tickers]
```

In the second step, we load all constituent performances from the current year. We iterate through the tickers and load stock price data in listing 8.1. For each stock, we load one year of data.

**Listing 8.1 Calculating returns and volatility**

```
prices_list = []
start_date = datetime.now() - timedelta(days=365)

for ticker in tickers:
    prices = yf.download(ticker,
                         start=start_date,
                         interval="1d")['Close']       ◁─┐ Loads historical
    prices = pd.DataFrame(prices)                        │ price data
    prices.columns = [ticker]                            │
    prices_list.append(prices)

prices_df = pd.concat(prices_list,axis=1)
prices_df.sort_index(inplace=True)

returns = pd.DataFrame()
returns['Returns'] = prices_df.pct_change().mean() * 252    ◁─┐ Calculates returns
returns['Volatility'] = (prices_df.pct_change().std()         │ and volatility
                         * sqrt(252))                       ◁─┘
```

> **NOTE** In the code here, 252 represents the trading days per year. Stock exchanges are closed on weekends and public holidays. Therefore, the number of trading days is lower than the total number of days per year.

Using this code so far, we have a data structure that contains the returns and the volatility aggregated by a year. While the purpose of the returns is clear (we want to maximize our gains), volatility represents risks. The greater the fluctuation in a stock's value, the higher the risk.

> **NOTE** Is high volatility also a risk, if an ongoing upward momentum causes substantial price changes? We need to verify that your soaring stock isn't part of a bubble and check ratios to see if a high valuation after a rally remains justified.

K-means clustering is a vector quantization method to partition data into clusters. By grouping data by values, we can create labels. A central parameter for this algorithm is the number of clusters we want to make. An elbow curve, as shown in the following code, helps us determine the optimal number of clusters. Listing 8.2 illustrates how to do this, and the results are presented in figure 8.2.

**Listing 8.2 Calculating elbow curve**

```
data = np.asarray([np.asarray(returns['Returns']),
                   np.asarray(returns['Volatility'])]).T
distortions = []
for k in range(2, 20):
    k_means = KMeans(n_clusters=k)
```

```
        k_means.fit(data)
        distortions.append(k_means.inertia_)

fig = plt.figure(figsize=(15, 5))
plt.plot(range(2, 20), distortions)
plt.grid(True)
plt.title('Elbow curve')
```

Figure 8.2 illustrates the outcome of the elbow curve. Here, we also see a dent in the chart that gives the curve its name.

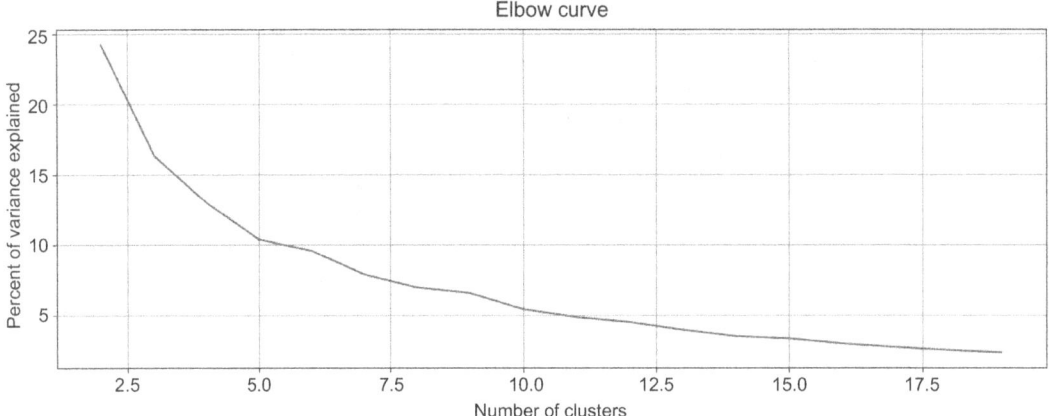

Figure 8.2  Elbow curve indicating the number of clusters for one year of data until May 13, 2025

Based on that graph, we pick a number close to the elbow of the curve, which is a point where the curve visibly bends. The elbow represents a cutoff point, indicating that the diminishing returns aren't worth the additional costs. It's therefore an optimal parameter. In the following example, we use 5. Let's create the data for this cluster using the source code in listing 8.3, which uses the K-means algorithm.

### Listing 8.3  Creating clusters

```
centroids,_ = kmeans(data, 5)

idx,_ = vq(data,centroids)
details = [(name,cluster) for name, cluster in zip(returns.index,idx)]
details_df = pd.DataFrame(details)
details_df.columns = ['Ticker','Cluster']

clusters_df = returns.reset_index()
clusters_df['Cluster'] = details_df['Cluster']
clusters_df.columns = ['Ticker', 'Returns', 'Volatility', 'Cluster']
```

Listing 8.4 shows how to plot the data. Stock tickers can be seen if we hover the mouse over the dots on the plot visualized in figure 8.3. It's possible to add the labels for each stock, but with 500 constituents, the diagram would be too crowded with small text labels.

Listing 8.4 Plotting

```
fig = px.scatter(clusters_df, x="Returns",
                 y="Volatility", color="Cluster", hover_data=["Ticker"])
fig.update(layout_coloraxis_showscale=False)
fig.update_traces(
    marker=dict(size=8, symbol="diamond",
                line=dict(width=2, color="DarkSlateGrey"))
)
fig.show()
```

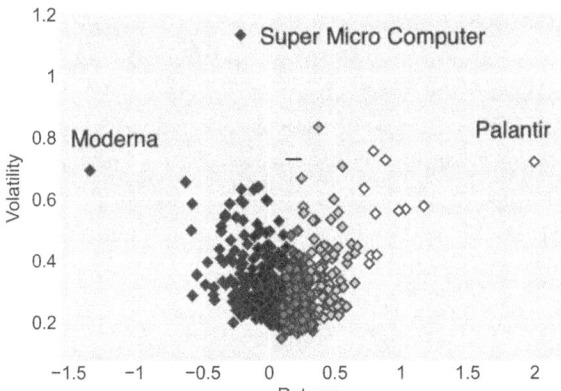

Figure 8.3 A plot with four clusters. Hovering with the mouse over the single dots reveals each ticker.

This example demonstrates the application of unsupervised learning to categorize stocks into clusters based on shared characteristics. If we interactively examine this scatterplot, we can draw conclusions by exploring each dot. We can explore each asset and decide which one to investigate further. We can, for example, review the three outliers. The dot on the left (Moderna) could be an interesting option if we look for companies that can undergo a turnaround. We may also choose high-performing assets to pick winners that can grow further and explore the dot on the right, such as Palantir. We're also interested in the stock with the highest volatility, which in the scatterplot is Super Micro Computer. Regardless of the strategy we use, being able to hover over each dot provides a more straightforward overview of the differences in the assets available to us.

Unsupervised learning helps us better understand assets. Let's examine supervised learning to determine whether it can predict stock future performance.

### 8.1.2 Supervised learning example

Unsupervised learning helps us bring meaning to chaos by structuring vast data. Once labeled data is available, it's time to think about the next steps, which leads us to supervised learning. Let's build an analytical dataset using these labels and learn how to predict which companies are likely to become winners.

**BUILDING AN ANALYTICAL DATASET**

Based on the previous scatterplot, we can create labeled datasets. Each stock, represented by the ticker, is part of a cluster. The cluster with the highest returns in the exploration before contains the tickers PLTR (Palantir), GEV (GE Vernova), AXON (Axon Enterprise), TPL (Texas Pacific Land Corporation), TSLA (Tesla), VST (Vistra Corp), NRG (NRG Energy), TPR (Tapestry Inc), AVGO (Broadcom), PODD (Insulet Corporation), and HWM (Howmet Aerospace). We can use this grouping as a label for all tickers in the dataset.

We have identifiers (tickers) and labels (clusters); now we need to identify the features associated with these identifiers. In this use case, we must create a 2D analytical dataset to run a supervised ML algorithm on data, such as linear regression. Think of a traditional database table with columns representing the *features* we want to investigate. One additional column represents the *label* or the outcome; in this case, it's the cluster. Here, the ticker serves as the unique primary key. We want to use supervised ML algorithms to find correlations between the values of the features and the labels with the help of a significant amount of data. In figure 8.4, we outline using supervised ML to find promising stocks using linear regression. The challenge is to select the best features from a vast list of potential candidates.

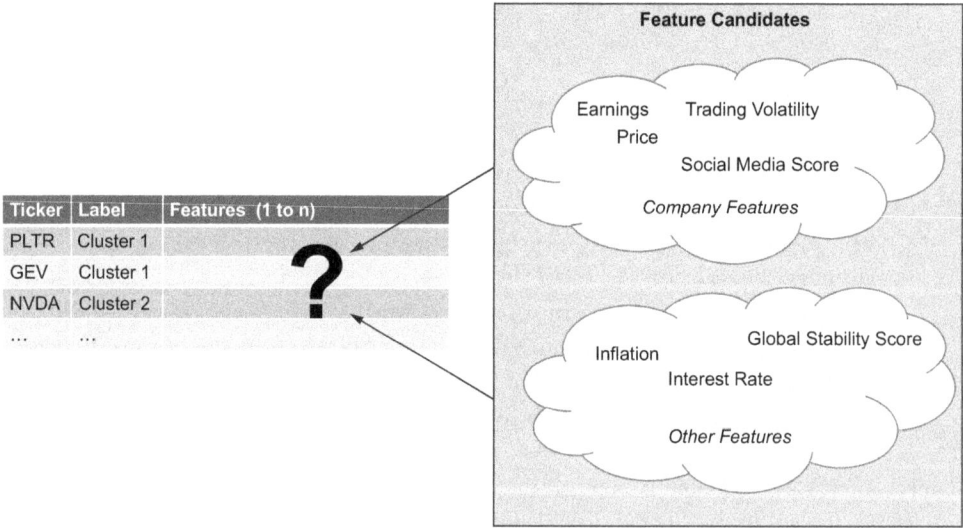

Figure 8.4 A labeled dataset for which we need to select features. Each feature will represent one column.

Every quantifiable aspect that can, at least in theory, affect a share price can become a feature in an analytical dataset. We can pick features based on financial data such as historical share prices, expenses, or earnings. During feature selection, we can go far beyond corporate data, including financial and nonfinancial data. We can include macroeconomic data such as the unemployment rate, inflation, or economic growth as features. Some features can also be specific to ML models for certain sectors, such as weather data for companies whose success depends on it, like those in the agricultural industry.

> **NOTE** The more specific attributes we use, the narrower our scope needs to be. If we use weather as a feature, we must incorporate only companies that rely on weather data, such as those in the agricultural industry. Otherwise, if most companies are unaffected by weather data, we exacerbate the signal-to-noise problem.

Choosing the label—the intended outcome—is easier than selecting features, as we aim to identify company stocks with rising share prices. Once we've chosen the desired features, we construct a time series dataset using these features. We also need to determine a suitable time interval for assessing price movements. Stock markets are highly volatile, so using ML to predict movements in short time frames, such as days or a few weeks, isn't advisable. At the same time, for some industries, having a time interval that is too large can also be troublesome, as some changes within the time interval may render certain features obsolete (consider how the emergence of AI reshuffled the cards for some companies). Candidates for time intervals could be quarters, semiannual periods, or annual periods.

The next step is to collect and aggregate historical data. Suppose we decided on a one-year time frame. We then collect data from all the companies in our analysis from one year ago. Once we have this dataset, we run supervised ML algorithms.

When we have enough data, we split the data sample into two groups: training data and test data. We use a ML algorithm, specifically a linear regression algorithm, to train the model using the training data. In simplified terms, the algorithm processes the data and identifies correlations between the features and the label.

After the training, we can use this model for inference. We feed an unlabeled dataset to the model, and the model returns a likely outcome. As we've kept the test data aside, we can now test our model. The more the model's inference matches the labels, the more accurate our model is.

Many hedge funds base their stock selection on this approach. However, practical wisdom also suggests that if a few features were sufficient to predict prices and success were easy, every book exploring financial investment would begin with a chapter on ML. Succeeding using ML can lead to vast profits, but it's also hard. Let's look at some details on why being successful in this field goes beyond a showcase.

The cluster we created contains one year of data up to May 13, 2025. This portfolio shows a diverse range of businesses across stable sectors, including industrials and consumer discretionary, in clusters containing shares whose prices have grown. If we created a cluster with one year of data up to January 1, the cluster containing profitable shares would likely include a far greater number of stocks in the technology sector.

> **NOTE** The code in the download section of this book allows you to use different end dates to create clusters.

So, what happened? A new US president with new policies shook up the stock market. When the tariff policies were announced, the share prices of technology stocks that depend more on other international markets were more affected than those of companies such as Texas Pacific Land Corporation, whose business is less dependent on international trade. Consequently, we must remain flexible and consider training multiple models in parallel.

Another challenge is the volume of data and the associated data preparation. In this example, we used the S&P 500, which is a collection of successful companies. The business model of hedge funds is to generate substantial returns for clients, providing a solid foundation for the fund manager to enrich themselves through fees. The smaller the company, the greater the chance of profits. Therefore, we need to investigate companies beyond the S&P 500. Collecting and aggregating data is a significant topic in big data. Depending on the number of features you want to support, you must build data pipelines to load data from various sources, including social media, financial documents, and many more. Having a vast amount of data also requires many resources to process it. Lastly, overfitting is one of the challenges of supervised learning and ML. ML models still face the challenge of distinguishing the signal from the noise.

If you come up with great ideas and possess the skills in ML, there's still considerable room to create ML models that perform well. However, let's consider a simpler scenario for a showcase instead.

#### STOCK PRICE PREDICTION

We'll outline this approach with a reference example that uses a random forest algorithm in listing 8.5. In the preceding example, we outlined the use of several fundamentals to predict the outcome. This was great to explain the power of supervised learning, but we want to use a more straightforward and reproducible scenario for a practical approach using historical pricing data. We load data through yfinance, as we've done before. The interesting aspect is to define a label by setting the column target with the next day's price. This way, we create a training dataset.

Listing 8.5  Loading data for the random forest

```
import yfinance as yf
import pandas as pd
import numpy as np
from sklearn.ensemble import RandomForestRegressor
from sklearn.model_selection import train_test_split
from sklearn.metrics import mean_squared_error
from statsmodels.tsa.arima.model import ARIMA
import matplotlib.pyplot as plt

start_date = "2018-01-01"
end_date = "2023-01-01"
```

```
ticker ="AAPL"
df = yf.Ticker(ticker).history(start=start_date, end=end_date)
df = df[["Open", "High", "Low", "Close", "Volume"]]

df["Target"] = df["Close"].shift(-1)
df.dropna(inplace=True)
```

Now, it's time to split our data into training data and test data. In listing 8.6, we first define the datasets x and the labels y. We use 80% of the training data, leaving 20% for testing to validate the model. We collect the output. The variable rf_rmse contains the root mean-squared error, which indicates the model's accuracy based on validation using the test data.

Listing 8.6 Training data for the random forest

```
X = df.drop(columns=["Target"])
y = df["Target"]
X_train, X_test, y_train, y_test = train_test_split(X, y, shuffle=False,
                                                    test_size=0.2)
rf_model = RandomForestRegressor(n_estimators=100, random_state=42)
rf_model.fit(X_train, y_train)
rf_preds = rf_model.predict(X_test)
rf_rmse = np.sqrt(mean_squared_error(y_test, rf_preds))
results = pd.DataFrame({
    "Date": df.index[-len(y_test):],
    "Actual": y_test.values,
    "RandomForest": rf_preds,
}).set_index("Date")
```

Listing 8.7 lets us plot the results. The x-axis represents the data, and the y-axis represents the price.

Listing 8.7 Plotting the results

```
plt.figure(figsize=(12, 6))
plt.plot(results.index, results["Actual"], label="Actual", linewidth=2)
plt.plot(results.index, results["RandomForest"], label="Random Forest",
alpha=0.7, linestyle="dashed")
plt.title("Stock Price Prediction: Random Forest")
plt.xlabel("Date")
plt.ylabel("Price")
plt.legend()
plt.grid(True)
plt.tight_layout()
plt.show()
```

Figure 8.5 shows the differences between the forecast and the actual values, which underline that inaccuracies sometimes occur and are sometimes more pronounced than others. If you experiment with data, you may often run into scenarios where predictions are inaccurate. Sometimes, the solution is to use more data. You can also try other ML algorithms, such as AutoRegressive Integrated Moving Average (ARIMA), which may yield more accurate results on several occasions.

Figure 8.5  This difference between actual and forecasted prices shows that, in some cases, the predictions are more accurate than others.

We can compare a reliable model for forecasting stock prices with the Midas Touch, an allegory for the ability to make people extremely rich quickly. Although a few entities, such as RenTech (we'll fill you in on this company a bit later), are said to have this capability, building efficient stock forecasting algorithms is tough. Let's look at the challenges.

## 8.1.3 Market challenges

The financial market provides advantages and disadvantages for ML use cases. One advantage is the quality of data and access to audited data. Those who want to showcase ML can use financial data more easily than any other data source for simple demonstrations.

The financial market also presents challenges for ML use cases. Let's start with the efficient market theory and explore other aspects that make forecasting prices more difficult.

#### EFFICIENT MARKET THEORY

The *efficient market theory* posits that the price of an asset accurately reflects its intrinsic value, given that investors have access to all relevant information. This leads to one of the most debated and controversial theories in finance: nobody can beat the market in the long run by purchasing undervalued stocks. Warren Buffett and other investors who outperformed the stock indices disagree.

Suppose we agree that we may not find any undervalued stocks of well-established companies. In that case, we can only outperform the market if we identify newcomers that will surpass others through a hidden advantage that we can reveal through new analytical approaches. In his "Do Stocks Outperform Treasury Bills?" paper (https://mng.bz/KwrZ), Hendrik Bessembinder showed that most stocks of the historical stock market had negative cumulative returns. A few companies that create exceptional returns enable the stock market to outperform the average returns of other assets, such as bonds. Many investors have searched for decades for companies with "a secret sauce." However, if we sought features in a ML model that would reveal hidden qualities in a company, ML models based on past performance numbers would likely only provide limited assistance.

### RANDOM WALK

A *random walk* describes how the stock market often doesn't follow deterministic rules but does exhibit chaotic behavior. Benjamin Graham, Warren Buffett's mentor, created the allegory of Mr. Market, in which he compares the stock market to a person with manic-depressive traits. Changes in single markets, such as the US market, the world's largest, can impact other markets worldwide. This makes prediction even more complex. Because stock prices depend significantly on mass psychology, attempting to predict human emotions on a global scale through ML ultimately leads to speculative approaches, akin to consulting the stars.

The phrase "irrational exuberance," coined by Alan Greenspan and often used by Yale professor Robert Shiller, outlines that investors frequently don't act rationally. It seems to be a universal rule of investment that, investors repeatedly become greedy and put their hope in one new trend that will make them immensely rich; the famous tulip mania of the 17th century in the Dutch Republic is often quoted as a reference to a bubble.

Some investors attempt to counteract irrational exuberance by investing for the long term. They examine business models and other factors, such as a company's economic moat, and select only companies that meet sufficient quality criteria to withstand all market fluctuations. However, the integration opportunities of ML algorithms based on time series data for such specific decision-making scenarios are often limited or require more effort than usual to be successful. For this reason, many strategies based on randomness, such as Monte Carlo simulation, are helpful when examining stocks.

### SOCIETAL AND TECHNOLOGICAL CHANGES OVER TIME

Some data sources, such as social media sentiments, weren't available in the more distant past, and we would hardly be able to collect information on what the masses thought about Coca-Cola or other stocks in the 1980s at specific times.

Companies in the past had vastly different environments regarding available technology, regulations, and taxes. Integrating computers, the internet, and AI has impacted how companies operate. Successful ML models from the past must be retrained and improved to stay competitive.

Decades ago, only a few companies would have considered writing an environmental, social, and governance (ESG) report to outline that they weren't purely profit-oriented. Not being concerned about maximizing profits could have been seen as a weakness during more competitive periods. Today, analysts and ML models weigh in on ESG factors, and at some point, ESG performance may impact a company's stock price similarly to its earnings results.

> **NOTE** Some analysts consider ESG factors to be political. Companies adjust their diversification and environmental policies in response to a country's governmental trends. Purely profit-oriented investors will also include ESG ratings in decision-making if share prices are affected by companies' unethical behavior.

**SEASONALITY AND ECONOMIC TRENDS**

In chapter 3, we stated that some quarters of the year create different economic outputs. For industries such as retail, the Christmas season has a different impact than the summer holidays. Some companies can face severe problems if a new product flops near the end of the year, even if the numbers in the preceding months had been impressive.

Assuming we create models that predict the stock price annually to bypass seasonality, we still face economic cycles. A stock price forecasting model trained during a recession might deliver different outputs than models trained in a bull market. Companies focusing on automated trading, such as Renaissance Technologies (RenTech) mentioned earlier, have faced challenges due to changing market trends. Models that had previously produced profits suddenly started to incur losses overnight.

**ACCOUNTING PRACTICES AND LEADERSHIP CHANGES**

Although we learned in chapter 3 that companies must follow accounting standards, companies still have some flexibility in presenting numbers within these standards. Companies regularly reassess their strategies, and new executives may adopt new approaches to achieve greater success than their predecessors. Those responsible for achieving the goals will also strive to ensure that their efforts to fulfill this strategy are reflected in the numbers, thereby pleasing shareholders. These different accounting strategies are a challenge for ML algorithms.

If we examine companies that have existed for decades, such as IBM or General Electric, we also observe that their focus shifts over time. Can we use the past as a reference if the overall strategy within a company changes? Likely not.

**MARKET BUBBLES**

Historically, we know there have been numerous manias and bubbles, in which investors no longer acted rationally. Let's look at Cisco as a reference for a company that existed during the dot-com bubble. At its peak in 2000, the stock price was above $77, and this price has never been reached again. We need to detect these phases of irrational exuberance and ensure that a model can detect trends that might not be sustainable in the long run.

### 8.1.4 Technical challenges

Although we have numerous success stories of a few champions who used ML to achieve outstanding performance, we also have reference stories of companies that exclude ML due to technical challenges in forecasting prices. Let's look at some of them.

#### VOLATILITY

Figure 8.6 shows the price of an asset over time. At the beginning and end, the asset's price is close to where it started. Without knowing what happened in between, we could also assume that the price of this asset is stable; however, we wouldn't be aware that the price has moved significantly.

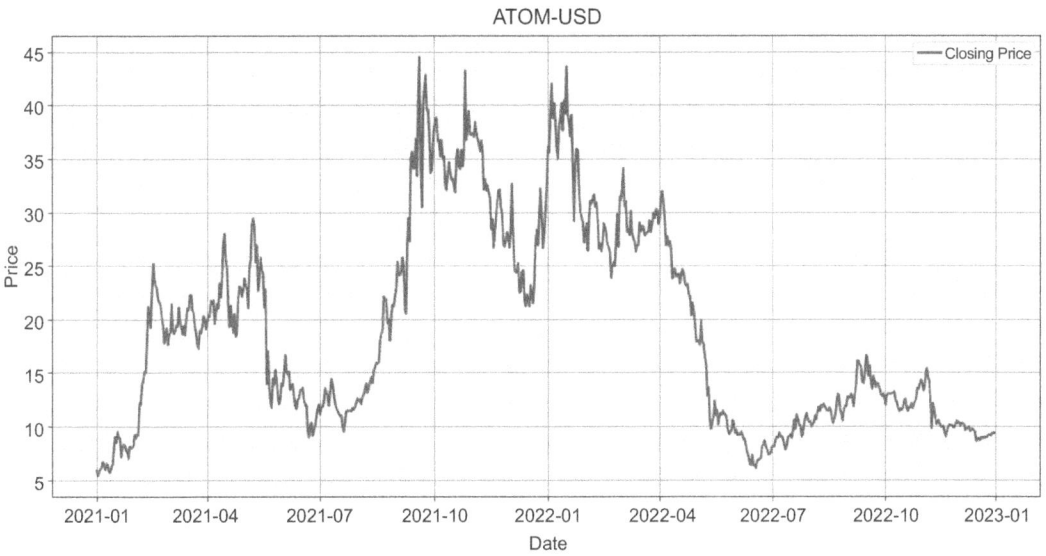

Figure 8.6   Price development of Cosmos (ATOM) between 2021 and 2023

Of course, we can always investigate volatility by collecting daily returns over time, conducting statistical analysis, and incorporating this aspect as a decision factor. Still, stock volatility makes it more challenging for ML algorithms to identify strong assets.

#### OVERFITTING AND UNDERFITTING

Chapter 3 highlighted the many ratios that could be explored to assess a company's performance. All of these ratios are potential candidates for ML features. Besides the fundamentals and technical data, such as the stock price, numerous external factors, including the country's overall economic situation, social media sentiments, news, weather, insider trades, and more, can also influence the stock price.

If we select a minimal number of features, we risk underfitting, which occurs when a ML algorithm fails to identify strong correlations between the features and the label. Considering the vast number of possible features, we also risk failing due to the opposite by overfitting the models if we add too many features. Some statisticians often speak of the signal and the noise. Features that aren't interesting—the noise—frequently prevent us from seeing the factors we would need to see to predict an outcome, the signal.

**EFFORT**

If we train and update multiple models regularly, we must find efficient practices to manage them well. Models need to be versioned, and it must be possible to redeploy every historical model if necessary. Changes in models also need to be transparent so that we can better understand how they have evolved in retrospect.

In addition, companies in various industries and sectors exhibit significant differences, as illustrated in chapter 3. A model that works for one industry may not be effective in another. So, we would have to create specific models for separate industries and sectors, making the process even more complicated, as we need to maintain many models in parallel.

Figure 8.7 shows the MLDevOps Cycle. This picture illustrates the entire lifecycle of model generation, encompassing data exploration and deployment options. We collect and prepare data, and then build and validate ML models. Once validated, the model is versioned, packaged, and deployed to a production environment. New results are continuously collected in this operational setting, enabling us to refine our understanding of model performance. New data sources are identified and integrated as the process evolves, feeding the next model development cycle.

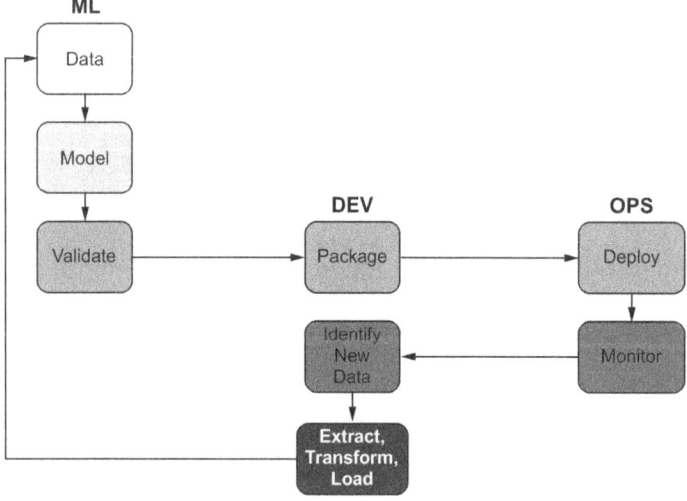

Figure 8.7 The MLDevOps Cycle, including preparation and deployment

In larger organizations, the efforts required to maintain models can become immense, slowing down overall progress within the company. It's one task to create models, but another to maintain them to avoid chaos.

### 8.1.5 Narrowing the scope

A ML model that accurately forecasts *all* stock prices would be like the golden goose from the fairy tale, and the universal money-making formula, of course, doesn't exist. Many companies successfully use ML use cases for more isolated scenarios. If you apply your skills wisely and focus on the right goals, there are plenty of chances to predict future gains better than others. Let's look at a narrowed use case.

A business model describes how a company generates revenue and achieves economic success. For example, Netflix and Spotify have subscription-based and advertisement-based revenue models. The goal is to maximize the number of users who pay a monthly subscription fee.

We can develop specific ML models to measure success, incorporating generic economic data, sentiments, and other data sources to predict industry outcomes. Such a model can't eliminate all risks, such as mismanagement or geopolitical changes, but it can help assess possible results for a market niche.

ML is part of discriminative models. We expect them to return quantitative results, such as a binary classification (e.g., "yes", "no", "up", or "down") or a number based on a regression algorithm, which forecasts the likely future share price of an asset. Suppose a ML model recommends we sell company shares of a company that we believe has the brightest future imaginable. The output format will always be the same; the results won't contain any creative analysis but will indicate buy, sell, or hold. Traditional ML won't explain its reasoning. The adage "Every use case has its best-suited tool, but not every tool is suitable for every use case" applies. Discriminative ML frameworks can be beneficial for use cases where no creativity is required. If you, for instance, plan to build a robo trader to automate transactions to trigger orders based on the data on the market, traditional ML use cases will provide the value you need. Now, it's time to investigate a different form of AI that generates new results, which we could also call creative in some cases, addressing different use cases.

> **RenTech and automated trading**
>
> If you're interested in quantitative trading, study RenTech's history and learn how this company became one of the most successful hedge fund management firms. One special lesson, which can't be fully captured in depth in a book focused on teaching programmers the basics of investment, is the challenges Jim Simons and his colleagues had to overcome to succeed.
>
> It's easy to imagine yourself looking at a screen and cheering that your model trades better than the market. But you also must see the periods in which a model that just

> *(continued)*
> made profits the weeks before suddenly makes losses. Everyone around you asks the same question: Why? And, as can often be the case with ML, you may not have an immediate answer.

## 8.2 From machine learning to generative AI

ML has a specific use case. Models trained for forecasting stock prices, as a representative of discriminative AI, can't be used in other scenarios. In contrast to the discriminative models we've seen, GenAI targets universal applications. It's self-evident that an ML model trained for different use cases, such as medical applications, can't predict stock prices. However, if we asked a public LLM, such as OpenAI GPT or Google Gemini, any question, whether it's about finance or other topics, in most cases, we get results that at least sound right.

So, what makes GenAI so different? The obvious answer is that, when examining chat use cases, using an LLM to generate answers is an advanced natural language processing (NLP) use case, and its purpose, techniques, and applications fundamentally differ from those of a linear regression use case, which aims to predict trends in a stock price. Traditional NLP applications can be compared with house cats, whereas LLMs could be seen as big cats. But in that context, comparing GenAI using LLMs and ML is like comparing cats with mice. Both are mammals; they share a commonality, just as LLMs and ML are part of analytics, but they are still distinct species.

Conversely, we still explored the possible limitations of computer-generated models in a chaotic domain, which gives an excellent idea of what to look for when researching a different analytical domain. GenAI, although "a different species," is another form of computer-generated model, and it makes sense to examine whether the same limitations apply.

We won't go into the details in this book, but here's two books that describe how the transformer model and attention algorithms have become game changers: *Generative AI in Action* by Amit Bahree (Manning, 2024; www.manning.com/books/generative-ai-in-action) and *Introduction to Generative AI* by Numa Dhamani and Maggie Engler (Manning, 2024; www.manning.com/books/introduction-to-generative-ai). To summarize the evolution, a paper called "Attention Is All You Need" (https://mng.bz/Pw55) suggested an improvement when building text-based models. Instead of exploring the relationship between every word in a sentence, the idea is to focus on the relationship between the essential words in sentences. This led to the transformer model. This new approach allowed us to collect vast amounts of data and provides the basis for LLMs, which are trained by millions of parameters.

### 8.2.1 Comparing LLMs

Let's start with an experiment. We'll ask GPT-4o, Gemini, and Finance Chat about investment strategies. We'll provide the following three prompts related to investment and compare the differences in the answers provided by the LLMs:

- What is the current trend in the stock market?
- Provide me with three reference examples that Warren Buffett would invest in based on his strategy that aren't currently in his portfolio.
- Provide me with three reference examples of investments that Peter Lynch would make based on his strategy that aren't currently in his portfolio.

This chapter summarizes the results, highlighting that LLMs aren't infallible. This test run was executed in June 2024, before the market experienced some losses in August 2024, from which it largely recovered. Note that one challenge using LLMs is nondeterminism. Different users may receive different answers depending on the LLM they use and the parameters they specify.

#### SUMMARIZING THE ANSWERS

Although Gemini and GPT also raised concerns, all LLMs painted a positive picture of the market. They advertised to investors to diversify their portfolios, which is standard advice most financial advisors give. No LLM provided a strategy that would have prevented us from experiencing the hiccups in August 2024. There are some investment recommendations, such as using passive investment methods, but this advice is one of the most common recommendations investment experts give to new investors.

The answers to specific questions about Warren Buffett's and Peter Lynch's investment strategies are more conclusive. Both are investors who follow a particular approach. Peter Lynch was a growth investor until he retired, and Warren Buffett is known for his value investment style. Table 8.1 shows the results.

Table 8.1 Results of prompts related to stocks

| Investor | GPT-4o | Gemini | Finance Chat |
|---|---|---|---|
| Buffett | Microsoft, Costco, Visa | Costco, Microsoft, Procter & Gamble | Allegion, Danaher, Coca-Cola |
| Lynch | Etsy, Zoom, Square | Trade Desk, Etsy, Shopify | Tesla, Allegion, DCP |

#### INTERPRETATION OF RESULTS

Some magazines, such as *The Economist*, warned investors about a possible stock market overvaluation in July 2024. Although we can acknowledge that LLMs can generally detect volatility, they aren't yet capable of providing a conclusive or detailed view of the stock market, as a reader might expect when reading articles in the *Financial Times, Wall Street Journal*, or any other newspaper, making it more sensible to consult a professional rather than an LLM.

Regarding the investor's comparison, GPT-4o and Finance Chat returned stocks already in the Berkshire Hathaway portfolio (www.cnbc.com/berkshire-hathaway-portfolio/): Visa and Coca-Cola. GPT-4o and Gemini came up with the same picks for Warren Buffett (Microsoft, Costco) twice, and had one match with Peter Lynch (Etsy). GPT-4o picked a company, Square, that was renamed in 2021. Additionally, it chose a company (Zoom) strongly associated with the COVID-19 pandemic. Finance Chat picked a company called Allegion twice.

These tests highlight the risks associated with seeking investment advice. Did GPT-4o and Gemini choose the same stock because they use the same data sources? How old are the data sources? Why did Finance Chat pick an Irish company (Allegion) twice? On which data were all three models trained?

### 8.2.2 Complementing ML with GenAI

It's challenging to compare GenAI with traditional ML as, to some extent, they fulfill different purposes. ML is more concise, whereas GenAI can be seen as a Swiss army knife for creative problem-solving tasks. One way they can be used together is by using GenAI as a research tool for ML models. The idea behind ML is to train a model that receives data, examines specific parameters, and predicts an outcome based on historical data. One challenge is selecting the proper parameter to maintain the model.

GenAI, a tool that provides more generic answers, can help accelerate the research process to identify suitable features for an ML model. In short, don't think of old-school ML or GenAI; instead, consider using both in tandem in your explorations.

### 8.2.3 Challenges

Based on our small experiment and existing knowledge, we can identify the challenges we face when using LLMs for investment advice. Some are crucial to make informed investment decisions, determining whether we achieve gains or losses. Hardly anyone wants to lose money because of some risky speculation that an LLM might be right.

#### DATED INFORMATION

Imagine you're seeking investment advice, and the model was trained on outdated data. You'll find a recent article on the internet about potential risks uncovered about a specific asset. The LLM might not have learned about it yet.

#### HALLUCINATIONS

Ultimately, an LLM is a model with billions of parameters. The maintainers of LLMs generate them by training these models on vast amounts of data sources, primarily from the internet. While LLMs might return astute advice that could help you make decent returns, they could also return questionable answers.

### 8.2.4 Final judgement on ML and GenAI

Traditional ML is also referred to as discriminative AI. *Discriminative* means distinguishing or separating from others, whereas *generative* aims for creative output. ML focuses more on specific use cases to extract results from data, whereas GenAI's applications are broader and lead to unexpected outcomes. The approach of both methods may differ, but the outcome is the same if the scope of an investment analysis is too broad. Trusting forecasts in a highly volatile environment is a risk. Remember, past performance isn't indicative of future results.

As we've demonstrated, both methods offer value within a narrow scope; therefore, let's explore how we can use GenAI in our financial research. We'll indicate that GenAI can provide value in economic research when applied correctly.

## 8.3 Practical use of GenAI

GenAI offers various methods for searching for assets with high returns. In this section, we list some of them. Be aware that GenAI is an evolving technology; we continue to see unexpected innovations that introduce new possibilities for investors. Continue to explore new ways to optimize results using LLMs. We'll introduce some advanced use cases in chapter 9.

### 8.3.1 Using LLMs as research assistants

LLMs reduce the time required to perform time-intensive tasks, particularly research-related work that necessitates exploring numerous resources to achieve results. Instead of asking in general what the best stocks are to invest in, we can ask questions that require an LLM to look for explicit details. One exemplary detail for a decision-making scorecard for a purchase decision is the management performance of a company's executive board. Using LLMs, we can generate an initial summary of a company's leaders more quickly than if we queried each manager on LinkedIn. The same applies to pending lawsuits, insider trades, business models, or customer segmentation. What could have taken hours to research by traditional web research, an LLM can often provide within a few seconds. Let's dive deeper into two use cases.

**SUMMARIZING DOCUMENTS**

Investing requires extensive research and thinking. Many professional investors, such as Warren Buffett, devote significant time to reading and gathering information about a company. Many companies publish lengthy documents, and we can obtain transcripts of various calls and presentations. Reading all of them from start to finish takes a lot of time.

One specific use case of LLMs is passing these documents to an LLM and asking it to summarize them, focusing on the topics that are specifically interesting to you. For example, a 60-page document can be summarized into a one-pager with the most essential facts.

**CODE GENERATION**

This book presents a substantial amount of code for analyzing stocks. At the same time, every interested programmer can get a lot of algorithms themselves from an LLM. An LLM can generate substantial, meaningful code that makes programming easier and faster, from collecting data to calculating ratios or using ML.

## HIGH-LEVEL ANALYSES OF NONFINANCIAL RISKS

In chapter 7, we highlighted that using algorithms to assess multiple nonfinancial risks can lead to significant efforts, as the term *nonfinancial risk* can encompass a broad range of factors that aren't financial and therefore lack a clear definition. We can use data to predict the impact of pandemics, wars, and natural catastrophes on individual companies, and we'll learn that some might be affected by others. However, detailed assessments can lead to significant efforts. Let's ask ourselves how accurate our analysis must be. Perhaps for a private investor, a high-level overall evaluation is sufficient, allowing us to validate the output of LLMs.

You can submit a prompt such as "Assuming that risks can have a rating from 10 (maximum) to 0 (minimum), I would like to assess the risk of pandemics, global trade wars, and climate change to each asset in my portfolio. Provide at least one sentence why. If there is no way to associate the risk, a statement that you don't have enough data is also fine."

Table 8.2 is a reference result provided by GPT-4o to the author. It was transcribed to this table; you can offer a similar portfolio analysis with a similar prompt.

Table 8.2  A reference risk assessment provided by GPT-4o (0 minimum, 10 maximum)

| Company | Pandemic | Reason | Trade war | Reason | Climate change | Reason |
|---|---|---|---|---|---|---|
| Google | 2 | Digital services thrive in pandemics. | 6 | Global ad spend is exposed to geopolitical frictions. | 3 | Low direct climate exposure |
| Pfizer | 4 | High initial benefit from COVID, less future upside | 3 | Limited export vulnerability | 2 | Low environmental risk overall |
| Ali Baba | 5 | Chinese consumption dropped in early pandemics. | 9 | Central figure in US-China tech decoupling | 6 | Some exposure to carbon-intensive logistics |
| Orsted | 1 | Renewable energy demand steady or rising | 2 | Localized wind/green projects limit exposure. | 9 | Renewable energy play depends on climate policy. |
| CCJ | 1 | Uranium demand steady | 4 | Export-oriented but essential material | 6 | Positive exposure as nuclear gains from climate urgency |
| Lyft | 8 | Transportation demand falls in lockdowns. | 3 | Mainly domestic US service | 4 | Some regulatory risk for emissions |
| MNMD | 3 | Biotech trials delayed during pandemics. | 1 | Low global export relevance | 2 | No meaningful climate exposure |

Table 8.2  A reference risk assessment provided by GPT-4o (0 minimum, 10 maximum) *(continued)*

| Company | Pandemic | Reason | Trade war | Reason | Climate change | Reason |
|---|---|---|---|---|---|---|
| Uber | 6 | Rides fell and Eats rose in pandemic. | 5 | Operates globally, exposed to trade/friction | 4 | Transition risks from electrification targets |
| TSM | 3 | Demand dropped in the first wave but rebounded fast. | 10 | Key battleground in US-China chip conflict | 5 | Some energy/water footprint issues |

Professional risk analysts will highlight that these assessments are vague and that organizations focusing on risk will likely achieve better results that have also been peer-reviewed. Still, an assessment of an LLM may provide enough information for a private investor to review their strategy. In the previous evaluation, we've allocated 33 points to the pandemic, 43 to the trade war, and 41 to climate change. Although these ratings estimate an LLM, investors can discover that they may be exposed to specific risks and act accordingly. For instance, knowing that one's portfolio is more exposed to, let's say, the risks of a pandemic might lead to more cautious behavior when there are reports that a new pandemic might come.

### 8.3.2 Integrating LLMs into code

LLM providers compete in the market to gain more user visibility. Some LLMs are available in different product versions, with more limited or powerful features. Even if the latest version of an LLM might be more dominant than others for a while, providers regularly release new versions with new features, so any dominance is broken soon.

Public LLMs, such as OpenAI (GPT), Google (Gemini), or Meta (Llama), allow prompting through an API, and we can integrate API calls to them into Python code. We can submit a prompt and receive an answer that we can then further process. We'll also demonstrate how models from Hugging Face differ when downloaded to a local machine for execution.

#### OpenAI

As programmers, we want to submit a prompt to an engine through an API and retrieve the results into variables, rather than pasting requests into a chat box. Listing 8.8 is a sample code that allows us to do that for OpenAI GPT models. You need an OpenAI account and an API key to run this source code. The variable `system_content` is a generic parameter of how you want GPT to answer; you can fill out here that GPT should be concise or instruct the LLM otherwise on how to behave. Using this simple code, we submit a prompt and evaluate the response that the LLM returns.

### Listing 8.8 Submit a prompt via the OpenAI API

```
from openai import OpenAI

client = OpenAI(
  api_key=api_key
)

completion = client.chat.completions.create(
  model="gpt-4o",
  messages=[
    {"role": "system", "content": system_content},
    {"role": "user", "content": question}
  ]
)
```

Generally, the latest models yield the best results. However, in some cases, it's more effective to use a smaller model that generates less latency and incurs lower costs per token. We could, therefore, use GPT-4o mini instead of GPT-4o if costs or latency are essential for us.

The method for the chat completions has multiple parameters (https://mng.bz/rZDj). As the API is being extended, exploring whether new options are available makes sense.

One parameter to try out is the temperature parameter, which defines how much less likely tokens the answer should include. The higher the temperature, the more random the output. We can use temperature as a measure of risk and stick to 0 if we're risk-averse and don't want GPT to speculate.

Having an interface with OpenAI means we can now use Jupyter Notebooks to ask a wide range of questions. However, as with human advisors, it often helps to seek advice from different experts and compare their recommendations. Therefore, let's look at integrating Google Gemini into Python code.

#### GEMINI

Integrating basic Gemini API calls into Python code is relatively easier than integrating with GPT. The snippet in listing 8.9 shows how to prompt using Gemini. Again, we can pick different model versions; we only need to send a question and evaluate the results.

### Listing 8.9 Submit a prompt via the Gemini API

```
model = genai.GenerativeModel('gemini-1.5-pro-latest')
response = model.generate_content("Perform Porter 5 Forces Framework "
                                  "analysis on NVIDIA")
print(response.candidates[0].content.parts[0])
```

In the code sample, we used gemini-1.5-pro-latest. Ranked by their complexity, there are also the Ultra, Pro, Flash, and Nano models. Nano models are designed to be executed in environments with low computing power, such as mobile devices. When writing this book, only a 1.5 version of Pro and Flash is available, making the Pro model the strongest model until a new ultra version is released.

We can also add configuration options. In listing 8.10, we limit the token of our response and add a configuration option for temperature that defines how creative the LLM can be.

**Listing 8.10  Submitting prompts via Gemini with parameters**

```
response = model_flash.generate_content(f"Perform Porter 5 Forces"
                                        "Framework analysis on NVIDIA",
                                        generation_config =
    genai.GenerationConfig(
                                        max_output_tokens=max_token,
                                        temperature=temperature,
                                    ))
```

Integrating GPT and Gemini is easy. We can explore whether integrating other LLMs is comparable and easy. Let's look at two more models before we explore open source models as alternatives.

#### OTHER LLMS

Listing 8.11 shows the API for Claude, which hosts a series of LLMs provided by Anthropic. In this snippet, the parameters `max_tokens` and `temperature` have already been integrated. A Python programmer can incorporate and run the code into any Python script, provided they also have a valid API Key. Observe that the parameters are similar to those of other APIs.

**Listing 8.11  Submitting prompts via the Anthropic API**

```
client = anthropic.Anthropic(api_key=key)
message = client.messages.create(
    model="claude-3-opus-20240229",
    max_tokens=1000,
    temperature=0,
    system="You are Claude, an AI assistant.",
    messages=[
        {"role": "user", "content": question}
    ]
 print("Claude's response:", answer.content)
```

As shown in listing 8.12, the integration of Mistral, another LLM created by a French company, demonstrates that integrating API calls is straightforward. It seems trivial to integrate the code. There might be some minor differences in how the methods are named, but essentially, for all LLMs, it's all about selecting a model, configuring some parameters, and sending a query with a question to the LLM

### Listing 8.12 Submitting prompts via Mistral API

```
model = "mistral-large-latest"
client = Mistral(api_key=api_key)
chat_response = client.chat.complete(
  model = model,
  messages = [
    {
      "role": "user",
      "content": question,
    },
  ]
)
print(chat_response.choices[0].message.content)
```

But all of these LLMs, even if we just provided simple snippets, have one thing in common: a developer needs to get an API key to work with it. The companies behind these LLMs use their models to generate revenue. This means some of these LLMs are only accessible if the entity that provides the API key pays a subscription fee.

Additionally, all of these LLMs are hosted within the company's infrastructure. Suppose someone aims to create a fintech start-up that develops sophisticated investment strategies. In that case, the programmers might not like the idea that a separate company might investigate requests on their LLMs. They would prefer to host their LLMs in-house.

We've seen that all of these providers have their API. Programmers will want one API and use models as parameters instead. In chapter 9, we'll explore the use of LangChain, which provides this feature to us.

#### FINANCE CHAT

After demonstrating how to integrate proprietary LLMs into code, we'll now explore how to incorporate open source LLMs trained on finance-related use cases. Hugging Face has become the go-to platform for hosting open source LLMs.

> **NOTE** For engineers who have experienced the late 1990s and the battle between open source and closed source products, the current discussion on open source and AI often feels like a continuation of the past. Some names have changed. It's no longer Windows versus Linux or Bill Gates versus Linus Torvalds. The battle is between commercial products and Hugging Face, or Sam Altman and a group of engineers who wanted to remove him when his authority within OpenAI was questioned.

Open source LLMs face the same opportunities and challenges as open source software systems. While they might have less revenue than companies that license software, they often have the support of the academic world. Advocates of open source also claim that their ethical approach is favorable. The source code and the architecture are publicly accessible, and providers of open source LLMs offer more insights into the training process.

> **Finance-related LLMs**
>
> Some LLMs are explicitly trained for specific domains. Bloomberg GPT is a known reference for an LLM trained with finance data. As Bloomberg GPT is a commercial LLM, it's not included in this investigation.
>
> Another option to enhance financial knowledge in data is fine-tuning pretrained models using financial data. For example, a ML engineer could collect transcripts of earnings calls, where executives discuss a company's financial results and train existing LLMs with them. As a result, the model would keep what it already knows and add new knowledge. We'll explore that in chapter 9.

From a programmer's point of view, the most significant difference in using open source models is that we, in the standard case, load a model onto our infrastructure and execute inference there instead of calling an LLM hosted on a remote server. In listing 8.13, we use the AdaptLLM/finance-chat model, which is available on Hugging Face (https://huggingface.co/AdaptLLM/finance-chat). Running the source code given here will trigger the model download onto the computer if it's not already present and then execute inference on the model locally. If you try out this code, be aware that it might take some time to download the model when you call this code for the first time.

### Listing 8.13 Executing prompt with open source models

```
from transformers import AutoTokenizer, AutoModelForSeq2SeqLM

def ask_huggingface(model_name, query):
    model = AutoModelForCausalLM.from_pretrained(model_name)
    tokenizer = AutoTokenizer.from_pretrained(model_name)

    our_system_prompt = """\nYou are a helpful, respectful and honest assistant. Always answer as helpfully as possible, while being safe.  Your answers should not include any harmful, unethical, racist, sexist, toxic, dangerous, or illegal content. Please ensure that your responses are socially unbiased and positive in nature.\n\nIf a question does not make any sense, or is not factually coherent, explain why instead of answering something not correct. If you don't know the answer to a question, please don't share false information.\n"""
    prompt = f"<s>[INST] <<SYS>>{our_system_prompt}<</SYS>>"
            f"\n\n{query} [/INST]"

    inputs = tokenizer(prompt, return_tensors="pt",
                       add_special_tokens=False).input_ids.to(model.device)
    outputs = model.generate(input_ids=inputs, max_length=4096)[0]

    answer_start = int(inputs.shape[-1])
    pred = tokenizer.decode(outputs[answer_start:], skip_special_tokens=True)
    return pred
```

```
question = "What is the current trend in the stock market?"
model = "AdaptLLM/finance-chat"
response = ask_huggingface(model, question)
```

Using Hugging Face, we can avoid the cost of commercial LLMs. But there is a downside to this. If we run a model locally, we first need the necessary hardware to support it. This includes the required disk space and the processors to execute the model.

Inference may take some time, depending on the local machine's hardware. Expect a few minutes, depending on the number of GPUs you provide to the model. Remember that you may need to allocate time to install additional Python libraries.

## 8.4 Prompt engineering

Many YouTube videos teach interested followers how to optimize prompts. What sounds like a complex discipline, especially the term *engineering*, may make it sound sophisticated. Still, it has a simple problem statement: don't just ponder what to ask, but also how. The better you can explain what you want and the more context you can provide, the better answers you'll get. Nobody needs an engineering degree to apply prompt engineering, but it's perhaps one of the biggest low-hanging fruits for achieving better results using AI. Let's kick off prompts by defining an investor's profile.

### 8.4.1 An investor's profile

Imagine a random person approaches a human financial advisor with a generic question, such as "Please provide me with a good portfolio." A professional investment expert wouldn't recommend anything without knowing more about their client. Using well-prepared questions, good advisors guide their clients to share more about their risk tolerance or investment goals.

Like a human financial advisor, an LLM will provide more sophisticated answers if given more context. The following question is a first improvement of the previous reference question:

> I am a risk-averse investor who wants to invest in stocks. I currently have $100,000 available for investment. My goal is to maximize my passive income. I want to invest exclusively in companies in the Information Technology sector. Can you provide me with a reference portfolio with maximized returns and minimized risks?

Once the input is sent to an LLM, it will be tokenized. The LLM will identify specific tokens as keywords. In our example, these terms will include *risk-averse investor, stocks, the information technology sector, maximizing returns,* and *minimizing risks.* The more we integrate domain-specific language, the better answers we might receive, as the high-quality sources of an LLM upon which it was trained were provided by domain experts who used their domain-specific language.

> **TIP** Reading the investment sections of newspapers, such as *The Financial Times* or *The Wall Street Journal,* and learning the meaning of specific terms can

be a simple yet powerful way to improve query results. The next time, don't wonder why the stock market went down or up; ask why it "plummeted" or "soared."

If you start investing, you'll have many research questions about companies or investment opportunities. Likely, you don't want to repeat yourself by adding all the context to each question you have.

A good human advisor will collect notes about you. However, as time passes, they may forget the details. One day, they become excited about a fantastic high-growth start-up, only to realize too late that this opportunity doesn't align with a client's risk profile. Another time, they suggest an international exchange-traded fund (ETF), forgetting it triggers withholding tax issues based on the client's residency. Mistakes like these can cost you money.

This is where LLMs have a clear edge: they don't forget. Once you provide a context, it remains consistent across all interactions—unless you explicitly remove or modify it. Unlike human advisors, who might overlook details, an AI will continuously apply your parameters, ensuring that every recommendation strictly adheres to your preferences.

Establishing context is the first and most crucial step in using AI for financial guidance. This context defines the rules your AI assistant will follow when analyzing investments. Let's examine some parameters and explore how we can adjust our conversation. The following can be viewed as a template, combined into a large chunk of text, and provided to an LLM as general knowledge about you.

#### GOALS

Provide goals that are as precise as possible. What are you in for? Most likely, it's not just because a friend told you to explore stocks. Do you aim to become a brilliant outlier in the investment world—the one person who is smarter than everyone else and who will beat the market? Or, do you have a more modest goal to grow patiently and earn enough money to live off a reasonable passive income each year?

Many financial advisors argue that you should quantify your goals. How much money do you aim for? Do you have a number in your head? This brings us to our next question: What are you willing to risk to fulfill your goals?

#### RISK PREFERENCE

Imagine you've made a risky deal. If all goes well, you might be up 30%. If all goes bad, you might lose a lot of money. Some people go to bed and sleep like babies. Others toss and turn, worrying about possible losses.

You don't gain anything by claiming to be bolder than you are. After all, many investors in the past were successful because they were cautious.

Knowing your risk preference requires a lot of self-awareness. The more you understand yourself, the more precise you can be in your persona.

### EXPERIENCE

Warren Buffett mentioned one golden rule: invest only in what you understand—adding details about what you know can be low-hanging fruit in your investment portfolio. Sentences such as "I am a programmer, and I work in the financial services industry" can help. You can even mention your former and current employers or clients with whom you have a strong relationship.

Additionally, specify which assets you have experience with. You can also exclude certain assets if you prefer. Cryptocurrency is a good example of a polarizing asset. If you want or don't want crypto in your portfolio, mention it.

### TAX CONSIDERATIONS

If you tell an LLM your citizenship and residency, it can provide advice on details that tax consultants typically charge for. Don't hesitate to add a sentence like this: "I am a citizen of Country X, and my tax residency is in Country Y, so I need a portfolio that minimizes tax-related expenses." Remember that LLMs can hallucinate, and cross-checking tax advice from an LLM with a human advisor is always a good idea.

### ETHICAL OR PERSONAL PREFERENCES

Some investors keep their religious, ethical, and political views out of investing. For others, it might be one of the most critical aspects in their strategy. Would you feel uncomfortable investing in companies that don't align with your values? No matter what you care for—climate change, politics, abortion laws, animal rights, or something else—mention it; after all, it's your money.

You can also engineer your prompts to adjust the style of the answer. Some prefer a detailed explanation, while others appreciate a concise yet direct response. Let's craft a reference persona:

```
"I have a computer science background. I have
worked on various digital transformation projects
for multiple companies. I understand well how AI
can change companies' businesses. I am looking
for companies' stocks that might be transformed
through AI but have not yet been overrun by
investors.

I aim to achieve financial independence within the
next five years. I have approximately 500,000 USD
available for investment. I want to be able to
calculate the money I make passively, considering
the average yield of my assets (interest, staking
rewards, and dividends).

I mainly hold stocks and ETFs. I also have bonds
and crypto. I want to keep some amount in index
funds.

I am interested in the future of autonomous
driving and the monetization of climate change
```

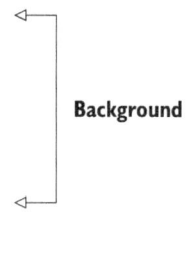

Background

Experience

mitigation. I also believe in the increasing demand
for reliable, nonvolatile energy sources, such as
nuclear energy, driven by the growing need for
sustainable energy solutions. I am also open to
alternative sources of energy, including atomic
energy.

I use Interactive Broker and Alpaca as brokers.
I use cold wallets to store cryptocurrency.

I have uploaded a text file with all the stocks
I hold. It is called stocks.txt and shall be
included in the research if needed.

⟵ **Experience**

I can take risks if decisions have been thoroughly
researched. If the valuation of the asset is
temporarily lower, I have no problem as long as
I see long-term potential. I am okay with shorting
some positions, but I prefer long-term quality
investing. I do not do day trading.

I want to diversify. Diversification also includes
assets worldwide, as I see political risks in the US.
Otherwise, I am fine with holding most assets in the
US market.

⟵ **Risk**

I am a US American citizen. My tax residency is in
the UK. I want to minimize the taxes I have to pay.  ⟵ **Taxes**

I do not like to invest in the tobacco industry
and companies that ignore animal rights.  ⟵ **Ethics**

### 8.4.2 Using prompts to find companies to invest in

Growth investors often seek small-cap companies with a high probability of experiencing a substantial revenue increase over the years. So, can we find these companies using prompts to an LLM? We need to define in detail what we're looking for. Let's do this with a reference example. Netflix's business model is quite simple, as shown in Figure 8.8: the more viewers subscribe to Netflix monthly, the more earnings the company will make. If we predict that the revenues from subscriptions will exceed their expenses, Netflix will be profitable. If these profits continue to increase, the share price will likely rise.

Predicting Netflix's costs will likely be challenging, as it requires a deep understanding of internal filming projects and licensing negotiations, to which we don't have access (unless we work for Netflix). However, we can estimate subscriber growth using LLMs.

What can influence subscriber numbers? We must determine what attracts customers to Netflix and keeps them engaged. For instance, customers sometimes feel locked in. Many shows in the program are on a customer's to-do list, or the kids in the family account become so accustomed to this service that a parent can't simply cancel the

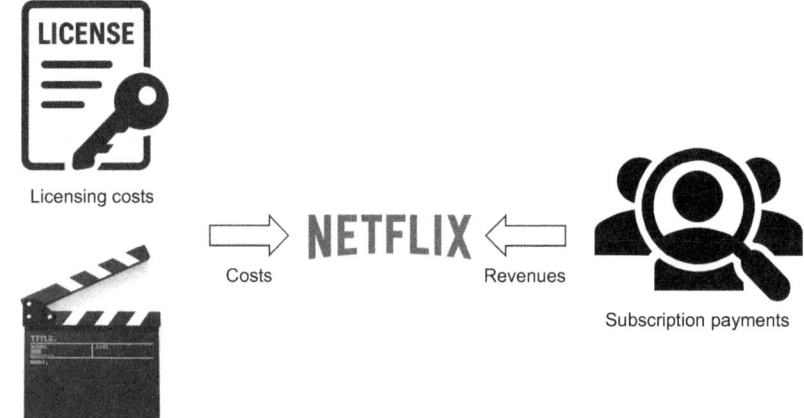

Figure 8.8 A highly simplified model reduced to the most central figures that Netflix is profitable if revenues from paying subscribers exceed production and licensing costs. While, of course, many more numbers exist that influence accounting sheets, such illustrations help us to extract these numbers that can be most decisive about a specific company's long-term success.

subscription without risking a family crisis. And often, because you get a report on what your kid watches, some parents don't want to miss unique features to monitor their kids' TV habits. Such a business with a constant growth scenario and a vendor lock, or economic moat to use a term more frequently used among investments, sounds like a paradise for investors. Examining the development of stock prices, particularly after the transition from mailing DVDs to streaming services, is compelling.

> **Python or chatbots**
>
> Some users experimenting with LLM chatbots may notice they are invaluable when investigating assets. Some chatbots offer additional research options after users submit prompts. It's fair to ask if we still need Python to get results. Chapter 9 will provide more details on this topic. For now, let's sum up what standalone chatbots don't resolve.
>
> In most cases, the chatbot provider won't provide Retrieval-Augmented Generations (RAGs) with vectorized data specific to finance use cases. Additionally, as LLMs may overlook data from smaller and less well-known companies, they may occasionally miss crucial details. Lastly, regardless of which provider you choose, the results will always be stored on the provider's side, and you'll face challenges in keeping track of resources across different platforms.
>
> Therefore, using chatbots can help us answer questions. If we want to work with more LLMs and add specific additional data, though, we might still need to use some code to accomplish this. In chapter 9, we'll demonstrate how to use AI agents.

Although the business model may be compelling, Netflix may no longer be in a significant growth phase. But what if we described what made Netflix successful in a prompt and see if we could find a similar company?

The more context and details we provide about how we want an LLM to answer, the more specific responses we can get. Let's review a checklist to see if our prompt can be improved.

- *Are we specific enough?* We can define what we want in detail. We can also ask about register in answers (from more formal to less formal). Have we listed the details that matter to us?
- *Do we express ourselves succinctly?* Imprecise and unnecessarily long phrases might reduce efficiency.
- *Can we supply examples in the input?* One way to improve answers is by providing examples of what we seek. We might look for companies like ones we know well and where we believe they will be successful.

Let's formulate a prompt to find companies like Netflix. We can invoke different LLMs to compare results:

> I want to find companies with a similar outlook to Netflix's in the early years. I want to buy low and sell at a high price in some years. These companies will be able to scale globally, offer a B2C subscription model, and possess a strong economic moat. These companies will have room to grow and already be listed on the stock exchange. Please give me three examples and the reasons why you chose them.

ChatGPT returned Duolingo and Bumble as results, which some investors on Seeking Alpha saw as a risky investment. Be aware that an LLM's recommendations are just an entry point for further research. Investing in them without your due diligence is risky. You must determine whether the answers provided by the LLMs are sensible.

## *Summary*

- We can integrate ML algorithms as code snippets into web notebooks to aid us in financial research, such as forecasting stock price developments, including uptrends.
- Unsupervised learning may help us identify outliers, which, in the investment scenario, could be companies that perform differently from the rest and present an investment opportunity.
- We can use unsupervised learning to find potential labels for supervised learning algorithms.
- Supervised learning can help us forecast a company's future success by analyzing its historical data.
- Successfully applying supervised learning algorithms can require a high level of technical expertise, encompassing everything from collecting data from multiple sources to processing algorithms at scale.

- As the market is affected by many factors (fundamental data, technical data, or other data unrelated to a specific company), most models risk being either overfitted or underfitted.
- The efficient market theory suggests that for most assets, the market price accurately reflects the asset's intrinsic value.
- The random market theory and the allegory of Mr. Market suggest that a market is unpredictable. This makes ML models challenging.
- Technological and social changes affect investment strategies. For example, ESG regulations are more important to investors today than they were in the past.
- Seasonal and economic trends impact the performance of stocks and must be considered in ML models.
- Different accounting practices within companies make it more difficult to compare companies.
- To integrate ML, we must invest considerable effort in identifying specific industry patterns and retraining models. Only a fraction of hedge funds run largely successful ML use cases.
- LLMs are game-changers in natural language processing (NLP). They employ a new paradigm called the attention mechanism, which focuses solely on the relationship between keywords. This makes it possible to create models trained on billions of parameters and serve as chatbots for users to address generic topics.
- LLMs can be trained to answer specific questions related to topics, including finance and investment.
- LLMs are also excellent for providing an overview of how specific nonfinancial risks can impact individual companies. Just be aware that you might have to review the output due to possible hallucinations.
- Users can choose from various LLMs, and an API for sending queries to an LLM is easy to integrate into Python code. In most cases, all users require an API key to authenticate against the provider and obtain authorization to process LLM inference on the LLM provider's infrastructure.
- Many LLMs come in versions that differ in complexity. Some may require a paid subscription, while others are designed for environments with fewer computing resources, such as mobile phones.
- We can classify LLMs as open source or proprietary. We can download models of open source LLMs to a compute node or local workstation to run the inference there. Proprietary LLMs are executed on the provider's infrastructure.
- AI ethics professionals are concerned about proprietary LLMs, as providers could misuse the information provided to them through users' questions. Additionally, the transparency of how these providers collect information is a significant ethical concern.

- Whether an LLM is open source or proprietary, it can provide us with investment ideas. Betting on LLM investment advice without further investigation is highly speculative.
- LLMs are great for tasks that require them to act like research assistants. When investors require less time for research, they can devote more attention to decision-making processes.
- The code generation capabilities of LLMs enable programmers to write more efficient code and analyze investments in various scenarios using programming languages such as Python.
- Although we can use LLMs to generate investment ideas, their core asset is helping us with due diligence on existing ideas, specifically when we need to find details on possible investments to create a personal scorecard for informed purchase decisions.
- Although LLMs help us speed up finance research tasks, they occasionally make mistakes and provide false information, often called hallucinations.
- The question isn't whether to use discriminative AI (traditional ML) or GenAI; it's rather how to pragmatically use what's there for specific scenarios and combine the possibilities of each technology.
- Prompt engineering is a discipline that enhances the output of LLMs by enabling users to ask more effective questions. It provides ways to pass more details, reference examples, and additional context for a request to an LLM.
- Prompt engineering can't replace common wisdom, as it depends on us to clarify what we want to know to avoid generic questions in an LLM.
- Creating an investor profile that includes information such as goals, risk tolerance, and tax residency can help an LLM provide more refined answers.
- Be as specific as possible and give as much context as possible when submitting prompts. It helps to provide reference examples.

# AI agents

**This chapter covers**
- Building AI agents for structured research
- Using LangChain to build AI agents
- Reusing strong prompts for comparable research
- Exporting the results of your study to Notion

Chapter 8 concluded that large language models (LLMs) are powerful research assistants who can significantly streamline asset analysis. We learned the fundamentals, including the distinction between discriminative and generative AI (GenAI), as well as how to trigger LLM prompts effectively.

Chapter 9 focuses first on the advanced application of LLMs without frameworks to build AI agents. We'll first show scenarios for integrating LLM into workflows. We'll create a prompt repository and design a first workflow to bring more structure to AI-augmented research. Additionally, we'll demonstrate how to export our findings to Notion, a modern note-taking application that helps organize and structure research efficiently.

In the second part of this chapter, we'll integrate frameworks to build AI agents. We'll show how to use them and how much work can be simplified. We'll introduce what is possible in a no-code framework using the platform n8n. Lastly, we'll focus on LangChain, which allows us to code logic in Python. Let's get started.

## 9.1 Requirements

In chapter 8, we used one-shot prompting to query LLMs. In simplified terms, this is submitting a single prompt to an LLM for a single response. Now, imagine that you get access to a human expert, and you're allowed to ask only one question. This scenario is common; consider a press conference where a politician responds to the press's inquiries. You might not get the desired answers if your question is poorly formulated. Compare a single-question, single-answer scenario to the next stage of communication. Imagine being able to interview that expert and engage in a dialogue. Based on past answers, you can ask more directed questions.

### 9.1.1 Successful communication

We can create parallels to AI. In addition to asking one-shot questions for basic scenarios, we can develop a refined strategy for more complex settings. Before we delve into the details, let's consider what is required for successful communication in this analogy.

#### MEMORY

One difference between conversing with AI and human interaction is the reflection of past communication. If Rajesh and Peter discuss a complex topic and gain new insights from that discussion, both can use what they have learned in upcoming talks. At the current stage of development, LLMs don't gain additional insights from interaction with users.

> **NOTE** In the background, the developers of LLMs will undoubtedly analyze conversations between LLMs and users to use the insights gained in building new models. However, this isn't the same as humans learning from single discussions.

One practical approach is to use Retrieval-Augmented Generation (RAG), which enhances LLMs by incorporating relevant external context into their input. In other words, we create additional memory for an LLM by adding specific information that it can use when crafting answers.

#### LANGUAGE SKILLS

Imagine being locked in the Vatican Library with books that have been kept secret for centuries. These books may contain fascinating historical insights. You're the first layperson to study them, but there's one catch: they are all written in ancient languages that you don't understand. We may need assistance accessing these sources, such as translation apps or expert scholars.

LLMs are trained on massive amounts of data. Data that was out of scope during training is inaccessible to an LLM in the same way that we would never learn to speak a language such as Latin. In both scenarios, the LLM and the human could learn new capabilities, but training new LLM models and learning Latin takes time. As we can use external help, the same thing applies to LLMs. One way to provide LLMs with access to information unavailable during training is to include this information during prompting.

We already mentioned that we can provide access to databases to address the challenge of integrating supplemental data and ensure that LLMs get access to other sources. In addition to the obvious candidate of a plain web search as an external data source, we can also incorporate APIs from various data providers, allowing an AI agent to retrieve mailbox content or chat history from messengers. We can task AI agents with parsing these sources, commonly by using API calls that include access tokens, and providing this information to LLMs.

**STRATEGY**

Imagine gathering many brilliant minds in one room to solve a single complex problem. Sometimes, these high-octane brains speculate about great ideas without strategy or moderation, but fail to deliver a tangible solution. Every coordinated moderate team with a goal will likely outperform a rudderless team of geniuses.

When many creative individuals are involved, we often need a leader who can effectively channel their collective creativity and inspire them to work together. Jim Simons created one of the most successful investment funds. What people admire about him is that he was able to assemble a team of brilliant minds recruited from Ivy League universities. Everyone reading books about him will understand that coordinating the geniuses working with him often seemed more difficult than coming up with the math to harvest significant returns. However, once his sharp thinkers were aligned, the funds created by Renaissance Technologies outperformed the market.

Anyone with experience with academic structures will also understand that every scientific journal will downgrade papers without a peer review. Even the brightest scientists need feedback, and the challenge is often not coming up with an idea but working out the nitty-gritty details in a paper.

What works for humans is also valid for AI. We can employ multiple specialized LLMs and isolate them for specific tasks. One LLM generates an analysis, and the second performs a peer review. We can define all the logic so that AI works like an orchestra, where every LLM plays its part to achieve a unified result.

## 9.1.2 Agentic design patterns

Using agentic design patterns is an approach to structuring AI research. DeepLearning.AI (https://mng.bz/V9Qx) introduced four patterns, which we'll explore in detail:

- Reflection
- Tool use
- Planning
- Multi-agent collaboration

**REFLECTION**

The reflection pattern enables agents to iteratively improve their performance by analyzing past actions and adjusting their strategies based on the feedback received. This pattern encourages self-evaluation: after each task, the agent collects outcome data and measures performance against predefined goals or metrics. Through repeated feedback loops, the agent identifies inefficiencies, uncovers patterns, and refines its decision-making over time.

Consider a trading bot as an example. Throughout the trading day, it follows predefined strategies to execute trades. At market close, the bot aggregates key performance indicators—such as profitability, risk exposure, and execution accuracy—and evaluates which strategies underperformed or missed critical signals. Based on these insights, it revises its approach for the next trading session. It may tighten risk thresholds, deprioritize low-yield strategies, or fine-tune execution timing. This continuous cycle of action, evaluation, and adaptation lies at the heart of the reflection pattern.

**TOOL USE**

The tool use pattern empowers agents by integrating external tools, libraries, or APIs to expand their functional range. Rather than relying solely on internal logic, agents can delegate specific tasks to specialized systems, such as data retrieval, transformation, or advanced computations.

This pattern mirrors how humans use calculators or web services to solve domain-specific problems efficiently. An AI agent may call a stock price API to retrieve real-time data or invoke a sentiment analysis tool to interpret market news. When needed, the agent autonomously identifies which tool to activate, orchestrates the calls, and integrates the results into its broader decision-making process.

By outsourcing complex subtasks to purpose-built tools, agents remain lightweight and modular, enabling them to tackle diverse challenges without reinventing the wheel. Let's explore how to coordinate these subtasks.

**PLANNING**

The planning pattern enables agents to construct and execute multistep strategies to accomplish complex goals. It introduces dynamic adaptability by allowing agents to generate workflows in real time based on current objectives, available resources, and operational constraints.

In this approach, the agent begins by defining the end goal. It then evaluates the current environment, identifying constraints, dependencies, and tools. If a preferred resource is unavailable, the agent seeks alternatives. Based on this assessment, it constructs a sequence of actions that takes dependencies into account and executes the plan step-by-step, continuously monitoring outcomes.

Consider an AI-driven stock advisory system that evaluates hundreds of companies daily. To identify promising investments, it dynamically builds a research workflow that gathers financial data, scans news articles, processes sentiment data, and ranks opportunities. If a company's profile changes due to a significant earnings surprise, the agent adapts its plan, reprioritizing the analysis and sending timely alerts.

The planning pattern emphasizes structure with flexibility, turning reactive agents into proactive strategists. Let's see how multiple agents can coordinate work.

#### MULTI-AGENT PATTERN

The multi-agent pattern coordinates multiple specialized agents to solve complex tasks collaboratively. This design emphasizes parallelism, specialization, and delegated reasoning, where each agent contributes a unique perspective or capability, thereby enhancing overall system performance. An orchestrator or moderator coordinates the overall process, ensuring that agents operate in sync and that their outputs are integrated effectively.

Imagine a stock buy decision modeled as a deliberative process, similar to a courtroom. One agent is the optimist, advocating for the purchase by analyzing growth potential, profitability, and momentum. A second agent acts as the skeptic, focusing on downside risks, macroeconomic headwinds, or signs of overvaluation. A third neutral agent acts as the adjudicator. It reviews the arguments from both sides, weighs their merit, and synthesizes a final investment recommendation. This pattern mirrors expert panels in human decision-making, promoting robustness through diverse perspectives and modular task handling.

#### A REFERENCE WORKFLOW

To illustrate everything we learned so far in one reference case for AI agents, let's create a reference case for investment analysis. Such a workflow is shown in figure 9.1.

In the first stage, a workflow needs to be triggered. Let's consider some possibilities:

- *Scheduled event*—Every Monday morning, a time-based job scheduler triggers a prompt submission querying about events from the last week that could have affected the positions of the user's investment portfolio.
- *User query*—A user would like to reassess the risks of his portfolio and submits a prompt to identify possible assets that would be more affected by a political crisis than others. We can feed AI agents from common messaging apps. You can therefore prompt by typing into WhatsApp, Signal, Telegram, or whatever messenger you prefer.
- *Alert*—A predefined alert triggers a workflow when the market moves vigorously in a direction, prompting specific questions about market activity and its potential effect on the user's portfolio.

An orchestrator starts with a retrieval process. In figure 9.1 we show one workflow. Based on the query, the agent is, of course, not limited to one workflow alone. The first step is the retrieval of information. AI engineers train each LLM model version with data up to a specific moment in time. Once they release the model, they start working on new models, but likely won't touch existing models anymore. RAG provides

## 9.1 Requirements

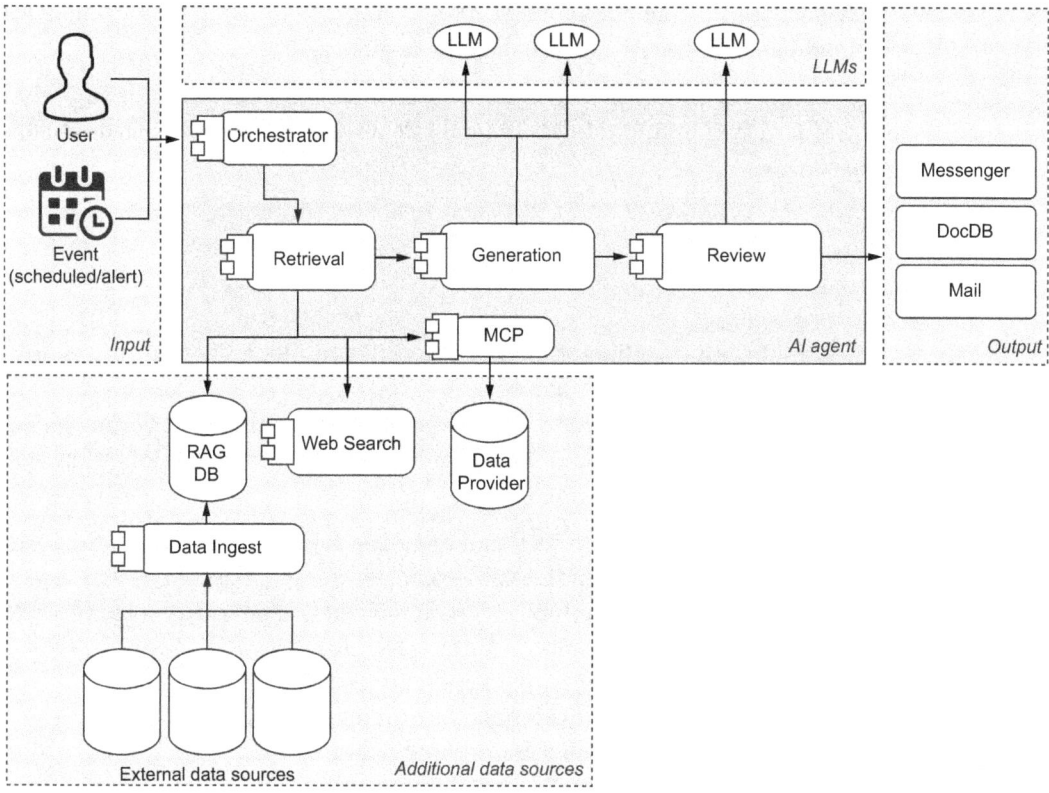

**Figure 9.1** A reference workflow for an AI agent

additional data to LLMs, bridging the gap between the model's release and the prompt's submission. For this use case, we defined three categories:

- *RAG databases*—Additional jobs collect data from different sources and provide this data in a vector database, which allows a workflow to supply this additional data to the generation workflow with LLMs. We need to be aware that we likely have to manage additional components that will require some maintenance. Data ingestion jobs will collect data from different sources to put them into a RAG database.
- *Web searches*—AI agents commonly provide a standardized interface to search engines so that they can use the content provided from search engines for the generation of responses.
- *Model context protocols (MCPs)*—An MCP is a new interface that allows AI agents to connect to data sources and collect data from data sources in a standardized format. We can see them as APIs designed explicitly for LLMs. If we need to get, for instance, the latest share price of a stock for a response, an LLM can query this information while it generates an answer. One significant advantage over

RAG databases is that the more MCPs are available to us, the less we need to maintain jobs that aggregate the data for ourselves.

Once we have the data retrieved, we need to start with the generation of responses. We can consider using multiple LLMs to generate answers. Here, we have the following options:

- *We can provide different LLMs with the same prompts.* As different LLMs have been trained in different ways and with different data, we can ask LLMs the same prompts to find out if LLMs come back with different insights.
- *We can provide different LLMs with different prompts.* We can ask each LLM a specific question. In investment analysis, one LLM can look for bullish scenarios, and the other one for bearish ones.
- *We can, of course, mix approaches.* The more we prompt, the more results we get. One reason to reduce the number of prompts is the cost-effectiveness, as each generation of results incurs a cost.

The standard "RAG only approach" is to augment the sources and collect results with one LLM. However, with multiple LLMs, we can also employ an additional step to review all results generated by multiple LLMs in another stage with a separate LLM. Lastly, we need to output the results. We can store all results in a database, such as Notion, as we've shown in chapter 8, or any other channel we like to use.

We can map all stages to agentic design patterns and reflect on the results we generated. We use various tools to collect additional data for LLMs, plan our execution, and adjust workflows as needed, employing different LLMs.

## 9.2 Agentic workflows without frameworks

Let's show how we can facilitate agentic workflows without specialized frameworks. We use a data science notebook for ad hoc research. We aim to automate and approach our research in a more structured manner. Let's focus on three things to make our work more reusable:

- Create a repository of reusable prompts.
- Connect to different LLMs.
- Export results.

One goal is to keep everything as simple as possible. Each chapter features full-functioning code that is downloadable from the publisher's website. You'll also find the code snippets for calling LLMs outlined in chapter 8 of the notebook, which is referenced in chapter 9. Let's get started.

### 9.2.1 Prompt repository

By continually analyzing companies, we can develop reusable prompts that can be applied to multiple scenarios. For example, we can ask an LLM about Apple's performance parameters. We can reuse that prompt for Alphabet or Amazon as well. In chapter 8, we learned how to optimize prompts. We can update and refine existing prompts, mapping them to various scenarios.

We can also store prompts in a database to reuse them. Let's explore the simplest possible database structure:

- *ID*—The ID identifies our prompt. Examples of IDs could be porter_5_forces_framework or swot_analysis. The IDs tell us what the prompt is about.
- *Prompt*—The prompt contains the text that is precise enough to elicit the expected answer from the LLM. Take your time to refine the questions, and improve them if the LLMs don't provide the answers you desire. You can also use placeholders in the text that get replaced later.

As every fan of *The Hitchhiker's Guide to the Galaxy* knows, asking the right question isn't always trivial. The key is to build up a solid repository and refine it as needed. For example, this is an elementary prompt:

> As an investor, I'm looking at the company {company}. Provide a Boston Consulting Group (BCG) Framework analysis. Tell me which quadrant the company is in.

The identifier company, enclosed in curly brackets, is a variable that needs to be defined so that we can fill in the variable content into the string using a Python f-string. Take your time to refine and extend this prompt as needed to add more context. We stick to a simple prompt for teaching purposes.

Each prompt can have multiple contexts. For example, the prompt above may be helpful if we're looking for income or growth stocks. It's a generic prompt that helps explore new companies. If we already know the company well, asking an LLM about the quadrant of the BCG framework for a company no longer adds value.

If we keep a vast number of prompts in a database, we can tag them with a context that allows us to find them more easily later. You might reuse prompts based on industries or sectors. In chapter 11, we'll examine catalysts, which are events that can lead to a significant change in share prices. Some prompts might be reusable for specific catalysts, such as earnings calls. The more specific a prompt gets—and remember, the more specific we ask, the more particular answers we get—the fewer scenarios we can use these prompts in.

If we kept a separate table to store tags, we could create an n:m relation in the table. A tag can be associated with multiple prompts, and a prompt can have multiple tags.

If we now want to store prompts and tags in database tables, we can use `create table` statements, as shown in listing 9.1. We stripped these tables to the simplest form possible. This way, you can always fetch prompts from your local database to reuse them for different scenarios. Remember that you need a SQL console connected to a database to execute the Data Definition Language (DDL) statements. For exploratory purposes, SQLite is more than sufficient.

### Listing 9.1 DDL Scripts for creating a prompt repository

```
create table prompt
(
    id      TEXT primary key,
    prompt TEXT not null
);

create table main.tag
(
    tag_name   TEXT not null,
    prompt_id TEXT not null
);
```

We can use these tables in an interactive research scenario. We have our Jupyter Notebook open in our development environment. We might decide to investigate a specific stock, let's say, Apple. Later, we investigate alternative stocks, such as Alphabet. If we have prompts in our database, we can always reload the text of the prompts to send them to the LLMs.

Having that, we can always fetch prompts and send them to an LLM—how we send prompts to an LLM we've shown in the chapter before—and we'll get many answers. We need to store this information in a secure location. Let's explore how we can do that.

#### 9.2.2 Export results

Someone who has worked with various LLM chatbots may be familiar with this situation. You're using multiple LLMs. At some point, all the prompts and answers are dispersed on many platforms. Various questions on different topics are often intermixed, making it challenging to find the past results you want to look up immediately.

One way to prevent that is to store the output in a central repository. In chapter 6, we used Google Sheets to monitor our portfolio. For our research, we use a structured note-taking app.

Notion is a professional note-taking app that enables you to create journals with multiple pages for notes on a single topic, such as investment research. You can filter these notes efficiently by tags and sort them by properties such as last edited time or creation date.

Figure 9.2 shows a Notion journal in which we made two portfolios. At the top, we have a unique ID in the URL. This URL contains an identifier: 1a9bc3d9e2cd809-ca869f99516383ccc. Creating your notebook with the journal will assign a unique identifier to each page in Python, and you'll see it in the URL the moment you share the notebook via the web.

Let's learn how to export content to Notion. First, we need a title for the note. The screenshot displays reference entries, such as INVZ—Initial Investment Thesis. Notion needs a dictionary structure with a title to create a title page. The following method contains a basic template. We pass the title in string form as a method parameter.

## 9.2 Agentic workflows without frameworks

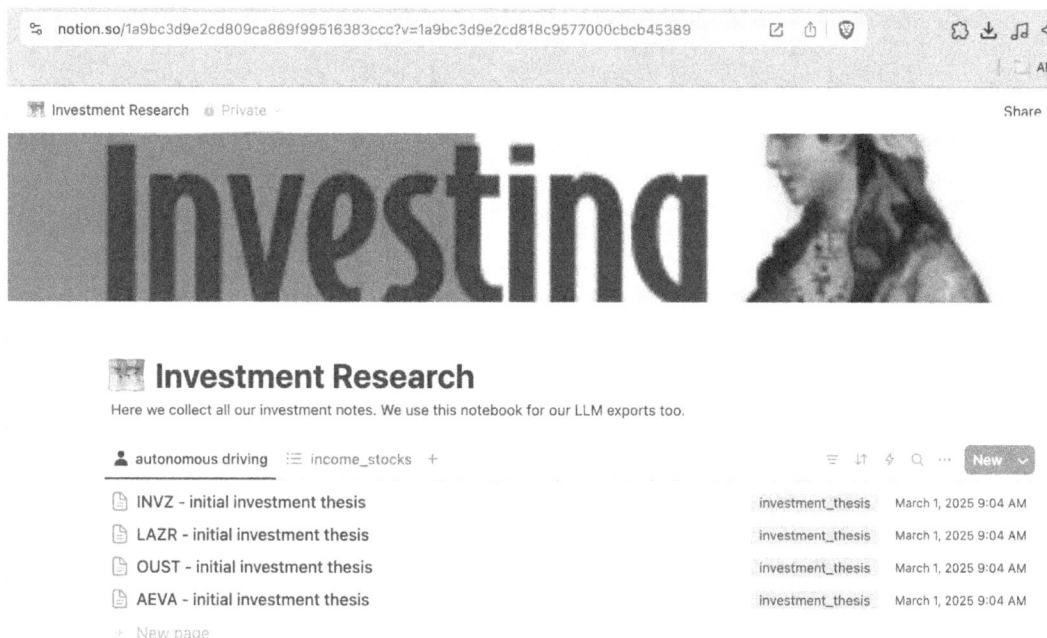

Figure 9.2 A Notion journal with some reference entries. You can use Notion as a unified storage for all responses from multiple LLMs.

Then, we insert the title as a value for the property content below the property text. We also add it as a value for the property `plain_text`:

```
def get_title_property(title: str):
    return {'Name': {'id': 'title',
  'type': 'title',
  'title': [{'type': 'text',
    'text': {'content': title, 'link': None},
    'annotations': {'bold': False,
     'italic': False,
     'strikethrough': False,
     'underline': False,
     'code': False,
     'color': 'default'},
    'plain_text': title,
    'href': None}]}}
```

With the `title` property, we can create pages. As shown in the following code, we trigger a REST call and pass the `title` property as a parameter. We receive a return code and validate that the call has returned a status code of 200, indicating that everything was successful. The parameter `DATABASE_ID` is the unique ID that we collect through the URL, as described at the beginning of this section.

```python
def create_page(title_properties: dict) -> str:
    create_url = "https://api.notion.com/v1/pages"
    payload = {"parent": {"database_id": DATABASE_ID},
               "properties": title_properties}
    res = requests.post(create_url, headers=headers, json=payload)
    if res.status_code == 200:
        print(f"{res.status_code}: Page created successfully")
    else:
        print(f"{res.status_code}: Error during page creation")
    return res.json()["id"]
```

The result is a property ID. This ID refers to the newly created page. With that, we have a new page that we can identify, so we can write content on that page, as shown in the following code. Again, this is done via REST API, and we insert data through a JSON-compatible dictionary structure.

```python
def write_to_page(page_block_id: str, data: dict) -> bool:
    edit_url = f"https://api.notion.com/v1/blocks/{page_block_id}/children"
    res = requests.patch(edit_url, headers=headers, json=data)
    if res.status_code != 200:
        print(f"{res.status_code}: Error during page editing")
        return False
    return True
```

When writing to Notion, it's essential to note that we can only write up to 2,000 characters simultaneously. For this reason, we must first break down the text into parts to write a comprehensive answer. The following method shows this. If a write operation fails, we interrupt the whole process.

```python
def write_chunked(page_block_id, text, chunk_size = 2000):
    for i in range(0, len(text), chunk_size):
        chunk = text[i:i+chunk_size]
        if not write_to_page(page_block_id, create_block(chunk)):
            break
```

The content is again encapsulated in a JSON-compatible dictionary structure covering formatting and other topics. In the preceding code, when we call the `write_to_page` method, we also call the `create_block` method to create this dictionary. We fill in the text into this template by setting a value for the property content:

```python
def create_block(content : str) -> dict:
    return {
        "children": [
            {
                "object": "block",
                "type": "paragraph",
                "paragraph": {
                    "rich_text": [
                        {
                            "type": "text",
                            "text": {
```

```
                    "content": content,
                },
            }
        ]
    },
},
]
}
```

Once this is written, we can embed all the code in a routine to ask a question. Listing 9.2 shows this code that would call LLMs and write the results to Notion. For the note's title, we combine a stock ticker, the current date, the prompt ID, and the LLM used.

Listing 9.2 Submitting a prompt

```
from datetime import datetime
def ask_question(stock_ticker: str, prompt_id: str,
                 prompt_text = None, llm = LLM.OPENAI) -> None:
    date_str = datetime.now().strftime("%Y_%m_%d")
    if stock_ticker:
        properties = get_title_property(
            f"{stock_ticker}-"
            f"{date_str}-{prompt_id}-{llm}")
    else:
        properties = get_title_property(
            f"generic-{date_str}-{question_id}-{llm}")
    page_block_id = create_page(properties)

    if prompt_text is None:
        prompt_text = get_question_by_id(question_id)
    if len(prompt_text) > 0:
        write_chunked(page_block_id, prompt_text)
        write_chunked(page_block_id,
                      get_answer(stock_ticker,
                                 prompt_text,
                                 llm))
```
◁— Gets the title property

◁— We can also pass text directly if we don't want to fetch text from a database.

◁— Writes the prompt first

◁— Writes the answer from the LLM

Figure 9.3 illustrates how a notebook might appear if we continue submitting prompts. The LLMs return answers, and we can perform fact-checking when we open the notes to review the answers provided by the LLMs.

Research is often interactive. With a data science notebook, you have your coding environment from which you send prompts to an LLM. Collecting information from our databases allows us to filter by tags and retrieve prompts by referencing their IDs. The methods in listing 9.3 outline this. You receive all the prompts, along with their IDs, related to a specified topic. In the reference case, the referenced ID is called `earnings_call`.

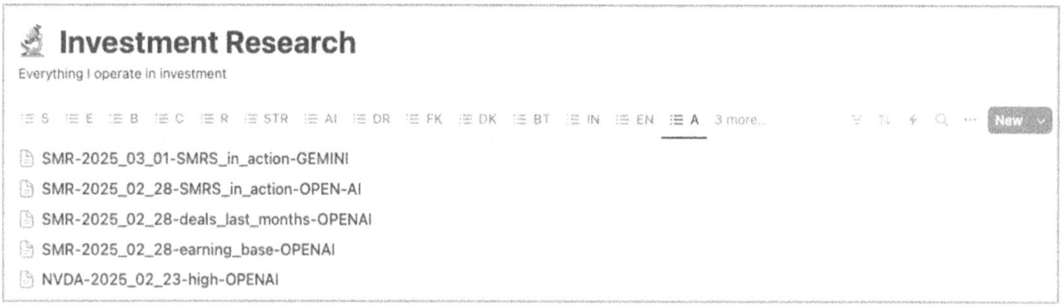

## Investment Research
Everything I operate in investment

≡ S  ≡ E  ≡ B  ≡ C  ≡ R  ≡ STR  ≡ AI  ≡ DR  ≡ FK  ≡ DK  ≡ BT  ≡ IN  ≡ EN  ≡ A  3 more...

- SMR-2025_03_01-SMRS_in_action-GEMINI
- SMR-2025_02_28-SMRS_in_action-OPEN-AI
- SMR-2025_02_28-deals_last_months-OPENAI
- SMR-2025_02_28-earning_base-OPENAI
- NVDA-2025_02_23-high-OPENAI

**Figure 9.3** Reference content of an investment research that stores responses in Notion

**Listing 9.3  Getting all prompts for a topic**

```
engine = create_engine('sqlite:///question.db')
all_questions = pd.read_sql('prompt', engine)
all_prompts = pd.read_sql('context', engine)
all_tags = pd.read_sql('tag', engine)

def get_prompt_by_id(id: str) -> str:         ◁── Gets a prompt by ID
    try:
        return all_prompts[all_prompts["id"] == id]["prompt"].iloc[0]
    except:
        return "No prompt found with that ID"

def get_prompts_per_tag(tag: str):            ◁── Gets all prompts
    all_prompt_tags = all_tags.loc[
        all_tags['tag_name'] == tag,
        'prompt_id'].tolist()
    return all_prompts[all_prompts['id'].isin(all_prompt_tags)]

all_prompts_per_category = get_prompts_per_category("earnings_call")
all_prompts_per_category
```

Then, by calling `get_prompt_by_id("earnings_call")`, you retrieve the prompt text for the `prompt_ID "earnings_call"`, which could be a prompt such as: "An earnings call of the company is ahead. What should I check to decide whether to sell my position or buy more?" Reading from the `all_prompts_per_category` may not be enough, as the prompt texts may be truncated if you display them on the screen.

With that, all you need to do is call the `ask_question` method with the correct parameters, such as stock ticker and prompt ID, and you fill up your notion pages with content. Based on the results, you can seek further details or begin fact-checking.

## 9.3  Framework for AI agents

Instead of a user communicating directly with the LLM, many frameworks provide abstraction and add functionality to facilitate the interaction, such as prompt enhancements and retrieval of augmented generation. If a user authorizes the AI agent, they can access specific resources, such as personal data.

We can examine the features of AI agents, as illustrated in figure 9.1 at the beginning of this chapter. Developers are familiar with the distinctions between no-code and code approaches in various fields of computer science. Data integration is a good example. Some teams integrate data sources by writing code to interact with frameworks such as Apache Kafka. They push data into Kafka topics, which are then distributed to all consumers who have subscribed to that topic. In contrast, other frameworks, such as Apache NiFi, offer a user interface (UI). Users click on a data source, drag it to a destination, and configure details.

Companies often value tools that reduce complexity because they lack sufficient qualified team members with programming skills. However, critics claim that click-and-point tools are also just an abstraction of logic. Frequently, these "no-code tools" miss core functionalities. Perhaps some teams can quickly click themselves into a first demo, but then, when engineers need to put them into production, integrating non-custom functionality takes more time, as if programmers had implemented the solution themselves.

Using AI agents, developers encounter a similar strategic decision. Some frameworks allow engineers to create agents via a UI. One of these frameworks is called n8n. To build a workflow with n8n, you need to register for a user account on the platform, which gives you access to the workflow UI. Users can create workflows on a canvas, connecting them to an input, such as a messenger or a chat window. They can incorporate various services into the workflow, such as transcribing voice to text or invoking LLMs with prompts based on the input. Click-and-drag tools are often easier to grasp by watching videos than by reading books. Numerous interactive tutorials are available that guide you step-by-step in creating your workflow. Let's concentrate on how to build AI agents using programming logic, which is often easier to comprehend in a book.

### 9.3.1 From one-shot prompting to agents

Many videos explain what to click and how to collect the results of the past steps to process further. As this book is titled *Investing for Programmers*, we aim to focus on creating workflows in general using development tools. LangChain is a framework for developing applications that use LLMs. It simplifies the stages of the LLM application life cycle. LangChain incorporates a broad and growing list of providers (https://mng.bz/xZx6).

A provider connects data sources and LLMs. Listing 9.4 shows an example that executes a one-shot prompt using a LangChain module that wraps code around the access to OpenAI's LLMs.

Listing 9.4 Executing a one-shot prompt using LangChain

```
from langchain_openai import ChatOpenAI
OPENAI_KEY = os.getenv("ai.openai.pwd")
llm = ChatOpenAI(
    model="gpt-4o",
```

```
        temperature=0,
        max_tokens=None,
        timeout=None,
        max_retries=2,
        api_key=OPENAI_KEY)
messages = [
    (
        "system",
        investment_persona,
    ),
    ("human", "Provide a SWOT analysis of Google."),
]
ai_msg = llm.invoke(messages)        ◁─── Submits the prompt
ai_msg
```

We implemented the same functionality in chapter 8 using OpenAI's native libraries. We can now explore the integration of other LLMs, such as Anthropic (https://mng .bz/AGXQ), and observe that the code structure is similar.

> **NOTE** In chapter 8, we explained how to create an investment persona. Whenever you use LLMs to analyze investment opportunities, use the opportunity to provide LLMs as much information as possible about yourself.

Python is a language built on convention. If we have collections, the principle is that regardless of the data structure used in the collection, the len() method will always return the number of items in the collection. Now, we also have a unification with LangChain. We can assume that, for instance, no matter which LLM we use, the method invoke() will always send a prompt to the LLM. This also makes it easier to add new LLMs, as with native providers, we would have to learn the specific details. This is a good start, but it's not yet LangChain's primary value proposition.

Let's explore the snippet in listing 9.5. In this code, we integrate Yahoo Finance News into our conversation.

### Listing 9.5 Using LangChain with Yahoo

```
from langchain.agents import AgentType, initialize_agent
from langchain_community.tools.yahoo_finance_news import YahooFinanceNewsTool

tools = [YahooFinanceNewsTool()]
agent_chain = initialize_agent(
    tools,
    llm,  # see listing 9.4
    agent=AgentType.ZERO_SHOT_REACT_DESCRIPTION,
    verbose=True,
)
agent_chain.invoke(
    "What happened today with Microsoft stocks?",   ◁─── Submits the agent
)
```

This code snippet underlines a substantial difference from plain LLM calls. We use agents that connect data sources to an LLM. In the code example, we set the verboseness to `True`. Let's look at the output of the agent. Following is the transcript of the previous listing 9.5, executed in April 2025:

> *Entering new AgentExecutor chain . . .*
>
> *I should check the latest financial news for Microsoft to see what happened today.*
>
> *Action: yahoo_finance_news*
>
> *Action Input: MSFT*
>
> *Observation: Is Microsoft (MSFT) the Best Machine Learning Stock to Buy Now?*
>
> *We recently published a list of the 10 Best Machine Learning Stocks to Buy Now. In this article, we're going to take a look at where Microsoft Corporation (NASDAQ:MSFT) stands against other machine-learning stocks. Grand View Research reported that the global machine-learning market was valued at $36.73 billion in 2022. It's now expected to [ . . .]*
>
> *Microsoft Corporation (MSFT): Still Among "Cleanest" AI Plays*
>
> *We recently published a list of 10 AI Stocks to Watch Amid Market Volatility. In this article, we're going to take a look at where Microsoft Corporation (NASDAQ:MSFT) stands against other AI stocks to watch amid market volatility. The uncertain macroeconomic environment is diminishing investors' readiness to pay high prices for stocks related to [. . .]*
>
> *Thought: Based on the news articles, it seems like Microsoft is still a strong player in the machine learning and AI markets.*
>
> *Final Answer: Microsoft stocks are still performing well in the machine learning and AI sectors.*
>
> *Finished chain.*

As shown in the output, we've instructed LangChain to create an AI agent that explores Yahoo Finance for news and integrates the collected information into research for a given prompt. We can chain more tools together when running our research. LangChain also enables us to incorporate providers into our research using AI agents. We can implement code to access custom data and create custom data providers for AI agents. This makes LangChain a robust framework that can aid in research.

### 9.3.2 Retrieval-augmented generation

We can enhance LLM generation performance by providing additional data that is inaccessible to LLMs during training. Recent data (e.g., data created after LLM training) or data unavailable due to restricted access (e.g., internal corporate data) are good candidates for retrieval-augmented generation (RAG).

The previous example illustrated how to integrate recent data using Yahoo Finance. Pulling information from news resources helps balance missing data after model training. However, countless data sources can be integrated, at least in theory. In chapter 11, we outline some of them, and they are so huge that you don't want to poll them from public web sources during prompting. We need to find a structured way to provide access to additional data, including storing this extra data in databases.

In the following example, we'll add the earnings call transcripts of selected companies to the prompting. If an LLM had been trained some months ago, it wouldn't have had access to data from a recent event in which the executives of a public company informed investors about the latest results. How do we get the earnings call data? Various financial analysis platforms provide transcripts from earnings calls, but the question is whether it's possible to scrape them.

When you have a vast amount of data, you want to store it in containers that allow you to keep this data safe and accessible. We separate work to achieve this goal. One process fetches data from various sources and loads it into a database. Prompt submissions are part of a different approach, in which the LLM uses this database as an extended brain. Let's get our hands dirty.

**LOADING DATA**

We need to fetch data from different sources. We can scrape pages from various financial analysis platforms using a web crawler, fetch information from downloaded documents, or load data via API or databases. Some of this data is also available through public data exchange. As a reference example, you can load company filings from Electronic Data Gathering, Analysis, and Retrieval system (EDGAR) offered by a data marketplace from Amazon Web Services (AWS; https://mng.bz/Z9a9).

Use cases for professional hedge funds and investment firms, which load data from various sources (e.g., many commercial providers) into their data platforms, are outside the scope of this book. Scraping data from multiple platforms poses a risk for a book, as many platforms change their internal structures, and code samples that load data from external web pages may no longer function properly. If you're interested in scraping data, you can explore frameworks such as Beautiful Soup and other libraries that load data from various sources.

Instead, we provide transcripts from earnings calls of companies in the automotive sector as text files for download. Feel free to add data if you want to experiment with the code.

In listing 9.6, we show how to load these text files into memory. While the logic for loading files should be familiar to most programmers, be aware that we add the loaded text to a LangChain-specific data structure to store additional documents for prompt submission.

Listing 9.6 Loading text files into memory

```
from langchain_core.documents.base import Document

all_docs = []
```

```
files = ["pony.txt", "oust.txt", "lazr.txt", "invz.txt", "aeva.txt"]
for f in files:
    file = open(f, "r")
    content = file.read()
    doc = Document(content)         ◁   Loads data into specific
    all_docs.append(doc)                 containers for LangChain
    file.close()
```

Let's provide additional context. In this reference example, we want to explore autonomous driving companies. We can run two different contexts to validate the functionality. In one context, we state that we believe in Light Detection and Ranging (LiDAR) systems; in the other, we state that we prefer companies that don't focus on LiDAR. We'll submit both contexts separately later to validate that the answers differ. We expect different recommendations based on our configuration, such as whether we prefer LiDAR technologies.

Listing 9.7 outlines how to define and add these preferences to the catalog. Note that we need to recreate the data structures to rerun the example with a different context.

### Listing 9.7 Providing additional context

```
generic = """I have a computer science background. I have worked on various
 digital transformation projects for multiple companies. I understand well
 how AI can change companies' businesses. I am looking for stocks of
 companies that might get transformed through AI but have not yet been
 overrun by investors."""

pro_lidar_text = """I believe in the future of autonomous driving.
Autonomous driving needs a LiDAR system. Do not recommend any companies
 that reject LiDAR."""

con_lidar_context = """Please prefer companies that focus on solutions
without LiDAR systems as they are expensive."""

all_docs.append(Document(generic + pro_lidar_text))
```

After executing this script, all the documents have been collected. Let's transform the data to be submitted to an LLM. Because we have a large amount of text in memory, we need to convert it into a format that an LLM can understand.

#### PREPARING DATA

We have data in memory, and to use all the content in RAGs, we need to add it to a vector database. A vector database is a storage container that enables the storage of vector embeddings. All the variable content in our memory must now be mapped as vectors. This helps us orchestrate workflows in which, during a prompt submission, this additional information is evaluated and processed accordingly. We accumulate vast amounts of information in more advanced scenarios and store it in dedicated databases, such as PostgreSQL or MongoDB. We use an in-memory database for this reference example to focus on the use case and not get distracted by data platform management. In listing 9.8, we split the data from the documents into subdocuments.

### Listing 9.8 Chunking data

```
from langchain_text_splitters import RecursiveCharacterTextSplitter

text_splitter = RecursiveCharacterTextSplitter(
    chunk_size=1000,
    chunk_overlap=200,
    add_start_index=True,
)
all_splits = text_splitter.split_documents(all_docs)

print(f"Split blog post into {len(all_splits)} sub-documents.")
```

Once we've split the documents into enough chunks, we need to convert them into embeddings. Each LLM has its standard. Listing 9.9 shows how to add all the chunks into an in-memory vector database using OpenAI embeddings.

### Listing 9.9 Adding all text in an in-memory vector database

```
from langchain_openai import OpenAIEmbeddings
embeddings = OpenAIEmbeddings(model="text-embedding-3-large")
from langchain_core.vectorstores import InMemoryVectorStore
vector_store = InMemoryVectorStore(embeddings)
document_ids = vector_store.add_documents(documents=all_splits)
```

Now that everything is ready and prepared, we need to move to the final stages: submitting prompts and evaluating results. We expect to see different results depending on whether we state that we believe in LiDAR or not, and we also expect some of the content from the RAG to be reflected in the response.

#### CALL

In a RAG, we'll build execution graphs. These involve data structures to help orchestrate workflows. Programmers who have worked with Apache Spark or Apache Airflow are familiar with the directed acyclic graph (DAG) concept. We create a class called Stage that contains variables for the question, context, and response.

We also have methods for two stages. In one stage, we retrieve data from the vector database. Of course, what content we need from the data that we currently hold in memory depends on the question we send as a parameter. Lastly, we need to submit the prompt. Listing 9.10 shows this logic. The methods retrieve and generate represent two separate steps in processing the prompt.

### Listing 9.10 Creating helper structures

```
from langchain_core.documents import Document
from typing_extensions import List, TypedDict
from langchain import hub
prompt = hub.pull("rlm/rag-prompt")
```

```
class State(TypedDict):
    question: str
    context: List[Document]
    answer: str

def retrieve(state: State):
    retrieved_docs = vector_store.similarity_search(state["question"])
    return {"context": retrieved_docs}

def generate(state: State):
    docs_content = "\n\n".join(doc.page_content for doc in state["context"])
    messages = prompt.invoke({"question": state["question"], "context":
     docs_content})
    response = llm.invoke(messages)
    return {"answer": response.content}
```

In the next step, we define a question and initialize the LLM. In this example, we use the GPT-4.1 model from OpenAI:

```
from langchain.chat_models import init_chat_model
llm = init_chat_model("gpt-4.1", model_provider="openai")
question = "Recommend companies in the autonomous driving sector with good"
 " recent earnings."
```

Our inquiry is about autonomous driving. We kept the prompt small to focus on clarity. Normally, you would often provide a longer prompt with more context and detail, as shown in chapter 8.

Listing 9.11 is our last step before execution. This snippet outlines how the orchestration works. We add both steps to a state machine and define the retrieve step as the starting point. The other sequence, generating first and retrieving additional content later, wouldn't make sense. Keep in mind that execution workflows can become more complex with time. In the last line, we call the method to display the execution graph.

### Listing 9.11 Building an execution graph

```
from langgraph.graph import START, StateGraph
from IPython.display import Image, display

graph_builder = (StateGraph(State).add_sequence
                ([retrieve, generate]))              ◁— Adds edges to the graph
graph_builder.add_edge(START, "retrieve")
graph = graph_builder.compile()
display(Image(graph.get_graph().draw_mermaid_png()))  ◁— Displays the execution graph
```

Figure 9.4 outlines the execution graph where we first retrieve and then generate. The execution can become more complicated in more complex scenarios, but two stages are sufficient for this case.

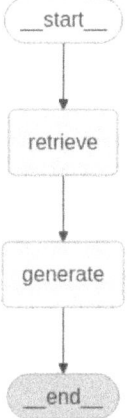

**Figure 9.4** The execution graph from the RAG engines, which contains information retrieval from the RAG and output generation using RAG and LLM data

Lastly, invoke the whole graph in which you submit the prompt with the question. This invocation will also include retrieving information from the vector database:

```
result = graph.invoke({"question": question})
print(f'Answer: {result["answer"]}')
```

The author received the following response when presented with a positive context about LiDAR:

> *Answer: Based on recent strong earnings and leadership in LiDAR technology for autonomous driving, Innoviz is recommended. Innoviz has secured partnerships with key players like Mobileye and integration with NVIDIA's platform, while expanding production to meet rising demand. Additionally, Chinese robotaxi companies using LiDAR technology—with regulatory approvals and commercial fleet operations—are well-positioned, though specific company names aren't given in the provided context.*

We get a recommendation for Innoviz. If we review the earnings call transcript, we'll also find a reference to this partnership with Mobileye.

Now, we examine the opposite scenario, in which we claim we don't prefer LiDAR. The last Mobileye earnings call wasn't included in the supplied documents; however, we can find information on the internet indicating that Mobileye has halted its efforts on LiDAR:

> *Based on the context, Mobileye is a notable company in autonomous driving with strong recent partnerships, OEM programs, and good earnings momentum, focusing on AI-powered solutions that don't rely heavily on expensive LiDAR. The context also notes significant regulatory progress and commercial operation scale among companies with robotaxi services, suggesting strong business fundamentals for leading players in this space. Considering your preference to avoid LiDAR-centric approaches and the need for companies not currently overrun by investors, Mobileye stands out as a promising candidate.*

We can now run agents with many different data sources. This should be done for now, and we can investigate charts and perform technical analysis. Many details in this chapter are based on earlier chapters in which we advocated investing in what we know. In the same way, to receive good answers, we need to know what to ask, which leads to the question of what additional context we need to provide. The final part is submitting the question as a prompt and evaluating the answer.

## *Summary*

- Communication with humans and AI has parallels. You can enhance your communication skills by using the right tools.
- To communicate more effectively, we can gain access to specific information sources that would otherwise be inaccessible, allowing us to strategize more effectively when communicating.
- We can store prompts in a simple database to reuse them later.
- If you want to research special topics, you can collect all prompts in a database and tag them to find them on demand.
- Notion is a note-taking tool that allows you to export all your research to one place.
- Without specialized frameworks to facilitate AI agents, working with LLMs requires a significant amount of custom work. For example, accessing specific data sources for RAG requires writing a substantial amount of code to connect the data to an LLM.
- AI agents help automate and streamline conversations with AI.
- AI agents often have providers for additional data sources, which enables us to orchestrate LLMs to gain new insights.
- N8n is a no-code framework that orchestrates workflows using AI agents.
- LangChain is a framework for developing applications powered by LLMs. It can integrate different data sources into AI agent workflows.
- LangChain streamlines access to LLMs. All calls to invoke prompts are therefore syntactically similar.
- LangChain has an extensive list of existing providers and provides an interface to programmers to add additional providers.
- Using LangChain, we can create AI agents that query recent financial news and then invoke a prompt in an LLM, incorporating the retrieved information into the analysis.
- LangChain provides a mechanism for logging the workflow of AI agents during their execution, offering valuable insights into how these agents operate.
- RAG is an approach to providing an LLM with additional data beyond its training data.

- We can hold additional information for response generation in a vector database. For this, we need to prepare the data by converting it into specific data structures, known as vector embeddings.
- In many complex use cases, we need a data platform such as a RAG database. For simple use cases, an in-memory vector database is fine.
- We can create execution workflows as a graph that orchestrates workflows.

# Charts and technical analysis

**This chapter covers**
- Interpreting patterns in charts
- How to use candlesticks
- Which averages help you assess stocks
- Bollinger Bands, moving average convergence divergence, and moving average ribbons
- Displaying an Ichimoku Cloud
- Using Streamlit for visualization

Imagine being presented with a captivating product—something you never considered but now find yourself intrigued by. The possibilities are endless, whether it's a stunning piece of art, a luxurious property, or an exquisite car. Now, picture that the seller turns to you, eyes glinting with opportunity, and asks, "How much would you offer?"

Imagine you've never bought a similar product. No advisor stands next to you, and you can't ask any search engine or AI chatbot for a reasonable price. Without any historical data or reference, all you can do is guess.

Many potential buyers find this situation distressing. If they overpay, they might regret their purchase for years. However, offering too little can cause issues. A buyer risks offending the seller or showing everyone around them that they are unaware of the market value, which can jeopardize their reputation.

Historical data provide a solid foundation for informed decisions. For instance, if you know the purchase price of neighboring houses, you can at least estimate the price of real estate (though you could still end up with a lousy deal for various reasons). The more data you have, the easier it is to determine if the price is reasonable.

Technical analysis of financial data is, to a large extent, a study of historical price developments. Knowledge about past movements is good. However, it's even better when historical prices are visualized, as many people prefer visuals over numbers in tables. Let's start by looking at charts and how we can interpret them. Afterward, we'll examine specific charts for investment and explore how to visualize information ourselves.

## 10.1 Charts

In previous chapters, we often plotted charts using share prices over time. The idea that charts represent data is, therefore, not a new concept. Once you have price and time, you can plot a chart where the x-axis is usually the time, and the y-axis defines the value of an asset in a currency. Let's examine a chart without context in figure 10.1.

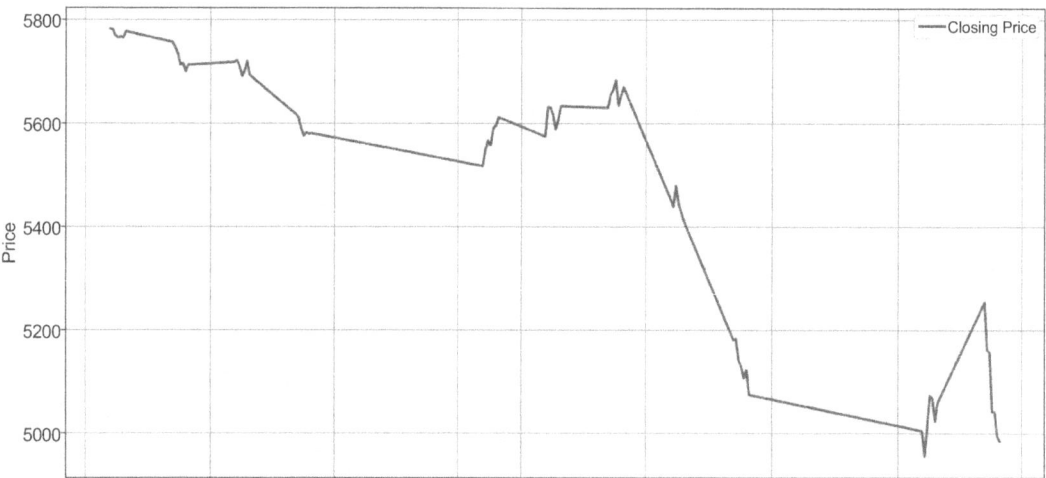

Figure 10.1 A chart without context in which we still must interpret a lot

We can start making assumptions if we look at a chart without context. Knowing that the x-axis represents time and the y-axis represents price, we see that the cost of an asset was relatively stable until approximately the middle of the chart. Then something happened, and we had a sharp decline with minor corrections in between. We can make basic observations without context, but to interpret what was going on, we need details. Let's add some context and examine figure 10.2.

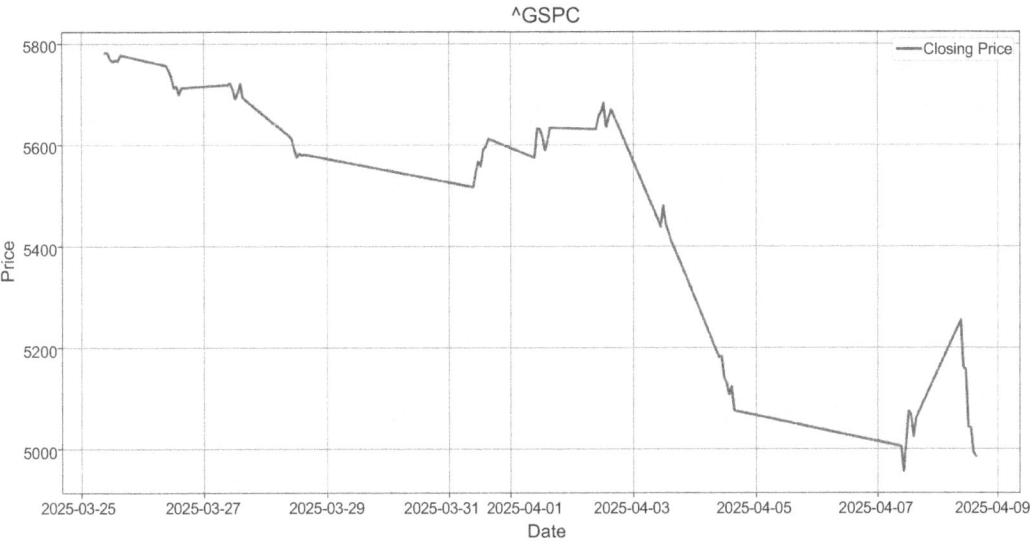

**Figure 10.2** The price development of the S&P 500 (ticker: ^GSPC) after Liberation Day (April 2, 2025), in which President Donald Trump announced a fundamental change in the US tariff strategy

With context, we can give meaning to charts. We understand that we're looking at the S&P 500. We examine a relatively short interval of a few days, as we have data on the S&P 500 since its inception on March 4, 1957.

If we had the data displayed in the chart as a DataFrame, we would have time series data starting from April 1 at a price of around $5,600 and ending slightly below $5,000. We don't know how many data points this DataFrame would hold, as this depends on the update frequency. We'll have 60 times as much data if the data is updated per minute than if it's updated per hour.

The price of the S&P 500 data has fallen by 11.15%. Someone who had a value of $100,000 in an index fund that mirrors the S&P 500 would lose $11,150 in value within five days. This chart appears alarming to conservative investors, who expect the value of their assets to increase. But at the same time, let's look at a chart in figure 10.3.

Someone accustomed to price movements, such as those seen with GameStop stock, might find the changes in the S&P 500 less dramatic. After all, an 11% drawdown at an index doesn't mean the value is likely gone forever. Unless there is a dramatic shift in the global economy, index prices are expected to continue recovering and growing. However, the S&P 500 is an index fund, and comparing it to the share price development of a distressed company is far-fetched. Let's relate the data to other past stock market crashes to understand what falling by more than 10% means in a short time frame. We see in table 10.1 that losses following President Trump's announcement of sweeping tariffs on foreign goods were comparable to those in the aftermath of the Lehman Brothers' collapse.

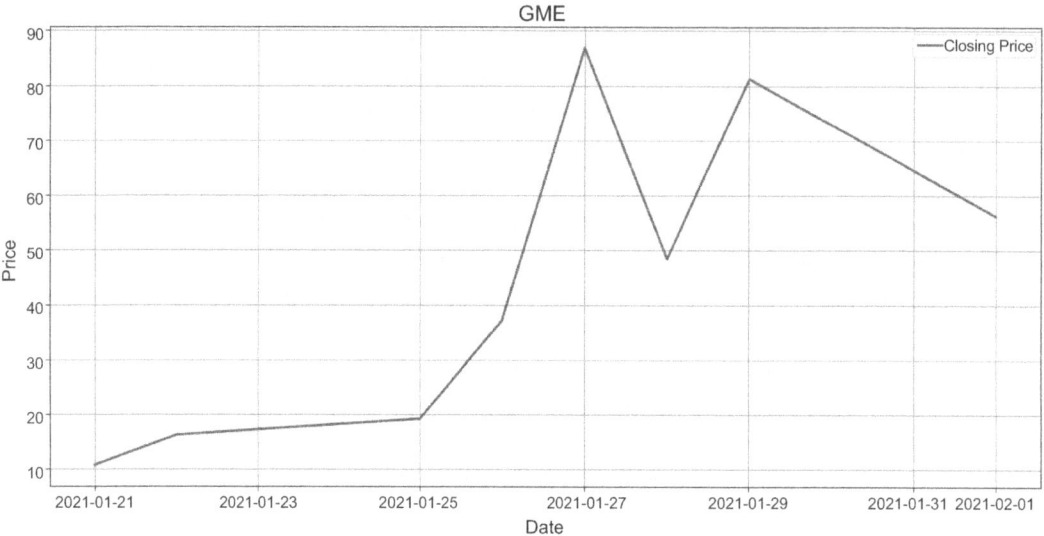

**Figure 10.3** The extreme price development of GameStop is often seen as a case study for volatile share prices. GameStop is a video game retailer whose share price rose after discussions on the subreddit r/wallstreetbets suggested that the stock was undervalued. This resulted in significant losses for hedge funds that had shorted the stock.

Table 10.1 Five most significant drawdowns in the past few decades

| Day | Date | % Change |
| --- | --- | --- |
| Black Monday | October 19, 1987 | −24.57 |
| Black Tuesday | October 20, 1987 | −16.23 |
| Covid-19 pandemic | March 12, 2020 | −13.93 |
| Lehman Brothers' collapse | November 20, 2008 | −12.43 |
| US tariff announcement | April 4, 2025 | −10.53 |

We can also scale out and examine a larger time interval to determine what a drop in share prices signifies. In figure 10.4, we present the S&P 500 data from November 1996.

We see some drawdowns in the chart. We see the dot-com crash, the Lehman Brothers' bankruptcy, COVID, and the start of the Russian invasion of Ukraine. The aftermath of Liberation Day will leave a lasting effect on the chart, one that will remain visible for decades to come. However, even after falling significantly, the S&P 500 remains higher in April 2025 than it was at the beginning of 2024.

Let's look at other charts and focus on single stocks. In figure 10.5, we examine NVIDIA's share price development.

Figure 10.4 The S&P index from November to April 4, 1996, shows various crises in the past, such as the dot-com bubble burst (early 2000), the housing crisis (2008), the COVID-19 pandemic (2020), the assault on Ukraine (2022), and the announcement of tariffs by the United States (2025).

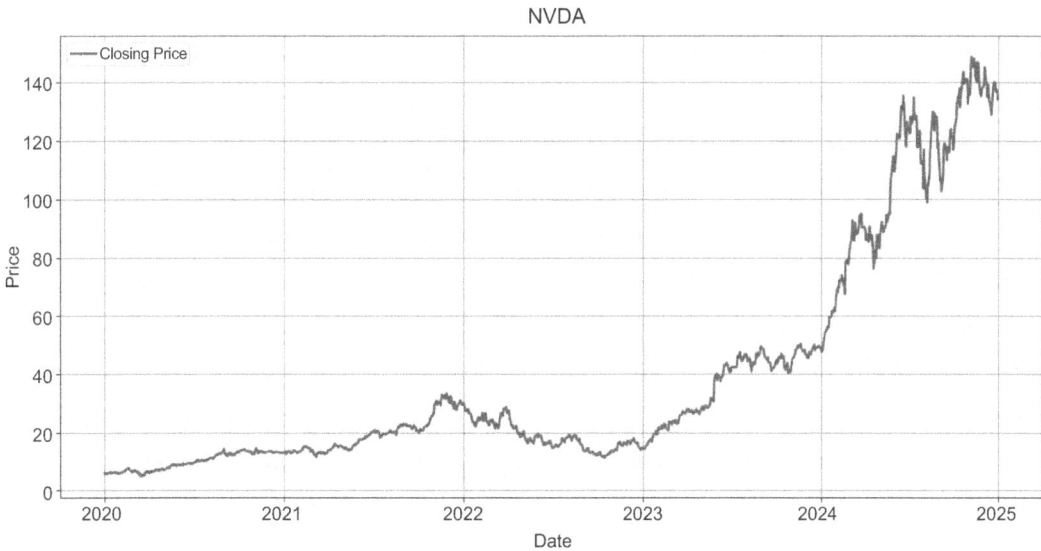

Figure 10.5 NVIDIA's share price data grew by 1787.89% in five years, which is an exceptional result in the stock market's history.

Single stocks are more volatile than indices. A buyer who purchased NVIDIA shares at a price equivalent to $6.65 in 2020 would have made a good decision. After five years, having $120 per share is the fulfillment of every investor's dream.

> **NOTE** Remember that NVIDIA has undergone two stock splits since 2020. If you bought one share of stock in January 2020 for $266, it would have been split into 40 shares.

Technology companies often aim for significant growth, relying heavily on being at the forefront of innovation to outperform competitors. Consequently, they usually exhibit a higher price-to-earnings (P/E) ratio and lower dividend payments, as a significant portion of the earnings is reinvested in R&D. If competitors outperform them, a technology company that doesn't consistently increase its yearly earnings compared to its competitors can be a risky investment.

Figure 10.6 outlines NVIDIA's earnings. As this company grows and generates more revenue, investors have a positive outlook for a company that continues to grow. Even if NVIDIA's P/E ratio is higher today than some of its peers, NVIDIA can be a good asset when calculating potential future growth.

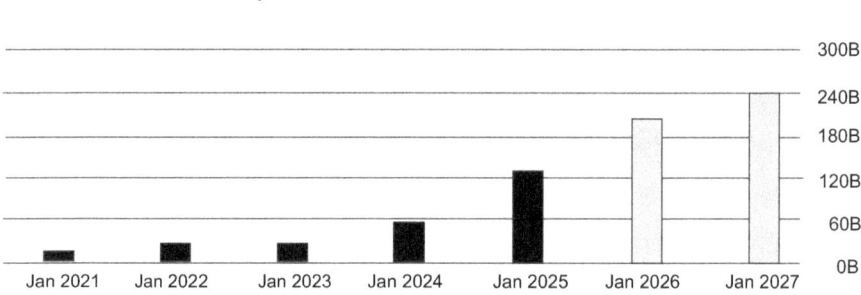

**Figure 10.6** NVIDIA's annual revenue, including estimates for 2026 and 2027 that were reported in January 2025

In chapter 7, our portfolio analysis concluded that, based on historical returns, we should allocate a greater weight to Pfizer and NVIDIA in a portfolio. Let's examine Pfizer in figure 10.7, which tells a different story than NVIDIA's.

If we bought Pfizer shares in 2020, we would have less value today. Pfizer is a high-dividend-paying stock, meaning we would have received annual payments over the years, which helps balance out some of the missing capital appreciation.

The Pfizer chart reflects the history of COVID-19. This is also reflected in its earnings, as shown in figure 10.8.

Earnings are a substantial factor for every company. However, we can't expect constant increases in earnings in every sector. Pfizer investors would have to accept that the earnings during the COVID-19 pandemic's peak can't last forever. Still, they can

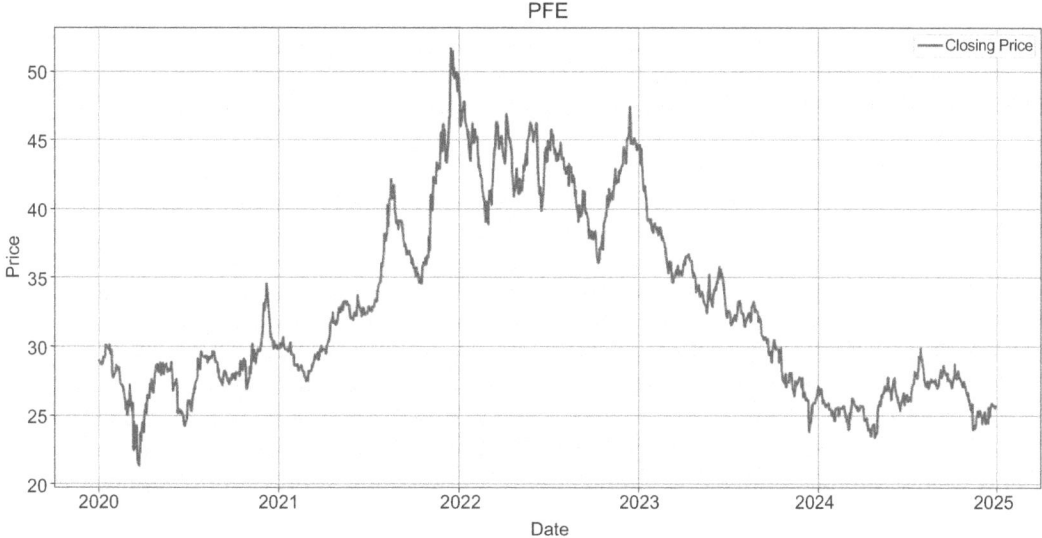

**Figure 10.7** Pfizer shares provided no capital appreciation if you bought shares five years ago, which means that sometimes buying low and selling high doesn't always work out.

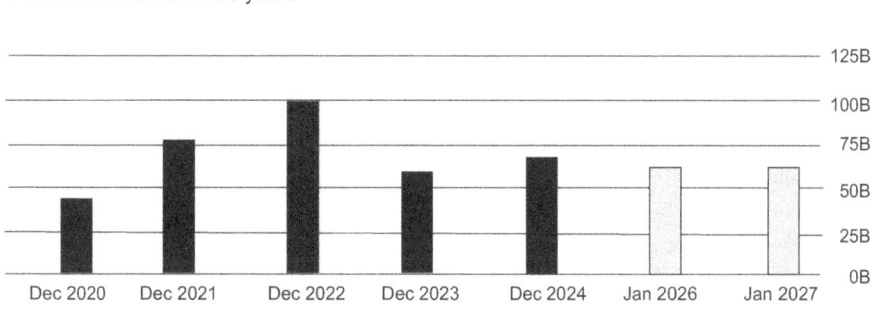

**Figure 10.8** Pfizer had massive earnings during the COVID-19 pandemic, and once it was over, the earnings went back.

also expect Pfizer to continue generating sufficient revenue to pay good dividends and grow at a steady pace.

Earnings and share prices can correlate. Often, a profitable year is reflected in the share price. Investors watch an earnings call, see tremendous results, and buy shares. If the results are disappointing, they sell. Technical analysis also looks at share prices, but the focus is different. Technical analysis tries to discover patterns in price development to forecast share prices based on these patterns. This may sound like superstition, but if everyone believes in the same patterns, these patterns will reappear because some individuals follow these signals, and then many more follow the herd, causing the repeating trend. Let's delve deeper by examining charts and defining these patterns that may influence technical analysts' decisions.

### 10.1.1 Reading charts

Let's examine the charts in figure 10.9. These charts show the price developments of assets over the past five years.

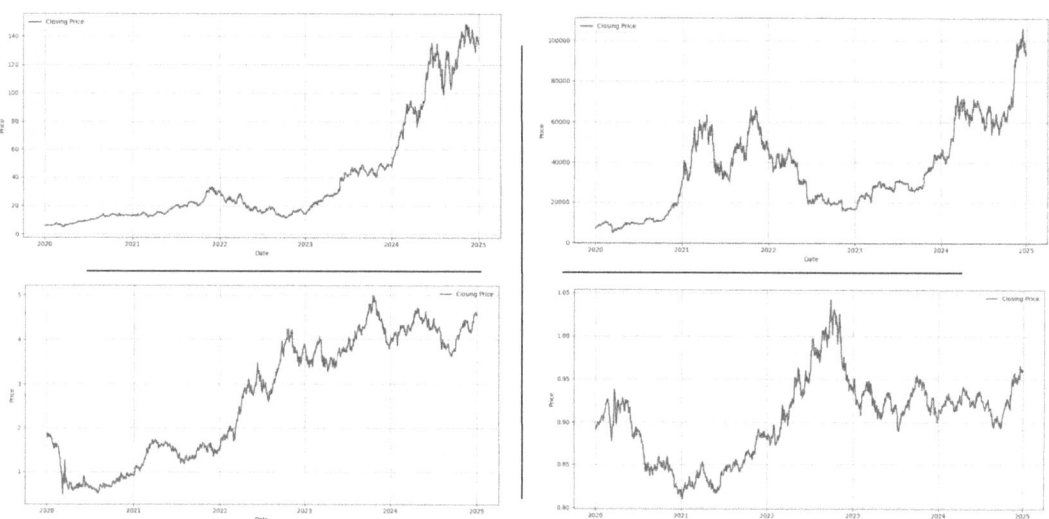

Figure 10.9  Four charts (NVIDIA, Bitcoin, the 10-year USD T-Notes/T-Bond yield interest rate, and the US dollar exchange rate to the euro). Every chart tells a story, and we can assume what was happening.

Some talent shows require candidates to solve challenges. If there were a talent show for investors, one of the challenges could be to ask contestants to identify the company when presented with unlabeled charts. Sort of like *Name That Tune*. Some investors can do that for familiar charts. They might look at Bitcoin and say something like this:

> Do you see these two humps on the left? Remember, this was 2021. The year started so well. In May, I thought I was screwed and then in November I cheered again until . . . well you know the story, Luna, FTX, it was a nightmare for a while.

Now, there's a game show I would watch! Identifying some patterns is a start—even if we don't have names for them yet—because you create stories based on the patterns. You rose to the stars, to fall again, and then you were reborn to rise like a phoenix again! Some stories of share price developments could be dramatized. Let's have a closer look.

> **Universal principles?**
>
> Are there general insights about how prices must move? Let's give it a try. One principle is *mean reversion*: what goes up must go down again, and vice versa. If we see mean reversion as a guiding principle, we're tempted to sell after a massive rally, believing a market correction is inevitable.
>
> Someone who sees *momentum* as a core principle might disagree. If a stock rises, its momentum can continue to increase. Why sell if a streak is ongoing? Although the momentum won't last forever, they will try to ride it as long as possible.
>
> A *contrarian investor* might disagree with that assessment. They might say, "I will lose if I do what the market does. I instead look for something that nobody else does."
>
> Investors hold different and sometimes conflicting beliefs. If a share price increases, a believer in mean reversion and a contrarian might advise selling, while a momentum believer might suggest holding or even continuing to buy. Everyone can't always be right.

### 10.1.2 Patterns

Let's examine asset price changes to see if we can identify similarities. The pattern in the Bitcoin chart, which we previously referred to as humps, can be interpreted as a bearish double top. Look at figure 10.10, which depicts this pattern and reflects share price developments (vertical) over time (horizontal).

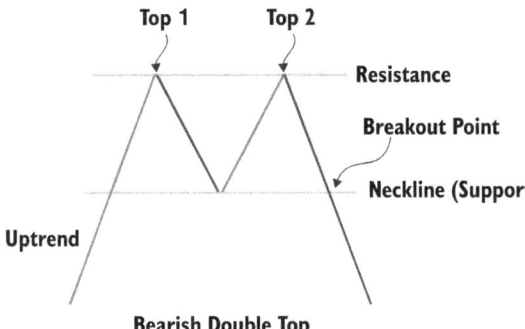

Figure 10.10 The bearish double top is a pattern that, after an uptrend, has two peaks before it goes down again. If traders identify this pattern in time, they can sell or buy accordingly.

First, we have an uptrend. Traders are excited; they see momentum and expect more gains. The asset price will increase as investors see rewards from buying low and selling high, and continue to buy. Various platforms assess the mood of their clients and provide a fear and greed index about specific assets. In this phase, investors' sentiment is characterized by extreme greed.

Then, we reach a point where the mood turns, marked in the chart as Top 1. The reasons for the trend reversal can be manifold, but investors likely examined the fundamentals and judged the asset as overvalued following the price increase. People start to sell, and the mood changes. However, enough people still see potential in that asset and begin buying again at some point. The price goes up again. Then, after the second reversal, the price drops again. But this time, the downtrend continues.

You can look up many chart patterns online or in technical analysis documents. They will find many examples, such as the head-and-shoulders, rising wedge, expanding triangle, triple top, or pennant pattern. The basic idea remains the same: there are up-and-down movements, and a trader attempts to identify patterns based on past experiences to predict what comes next. Each pattern has a bearish and bullish form, as shown in figure 10.11.

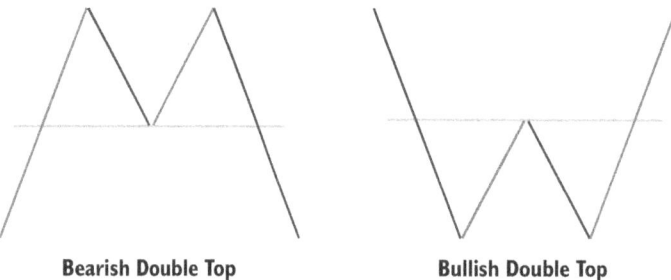

Figure 10.11  A bullish double top and its "twin", the bearish double top. Investors looking up other chart patterns, such as the head and shoulders or rising wedge, will always find bullish or bearish patterns.

The double top is a reversal pattern. The bearish version starts with an uptrend and ends with a downtrend, and vice versa in the bullish version. It's also a continuation pattern. It starts with a trend until it gets into an opposite trend, to turn into its original trend again. Figure 10.12 provides an example of bullish and bearish flag patterns as a reference for a continuation pattern. Again, we start with a trend being disrupted by an opposite trend. Eventually, however, the original trend continues in a continuation pattern.

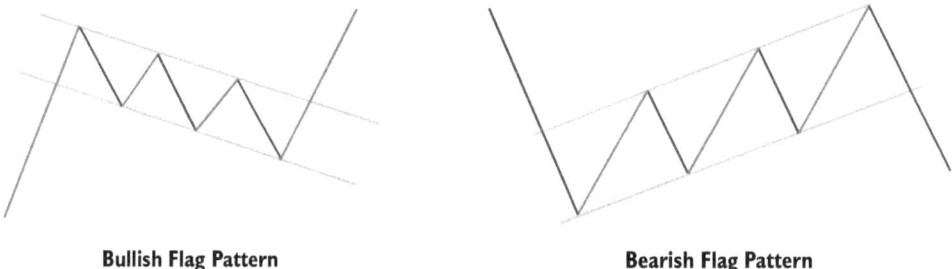

Figure 10.12  The bullish and bearish flag patterns are reference examples for continuation patterns. A temporary initial trend was reversed and continues again in the same direction.

Chart patterns are just templates. "Chart whisperers" have often been wrong in the past. Many of them have misjudged movements, as there is no guarantee that asset prices will always follow the pattern.

When an asset's price falls, analysts often discuss support lines. A *support line* is a price level at which an asset is unlikely to fall. Investors also frequently discuss *resistance lines*, which are high prices that are difficult to break through. Another important term is *breakout*, when a price crosses a support or resistance line.

Support and resistance lines are essential for investors who explore more volatile assets. At the time of writing, the price of 1 Bitcoin is $78,940. Analysts may suggest that we see a support line at $72,000, which is another way of saying that it's unlikely for the price to drop below that level unless an external event occurs.

Although support and resistance lines are an interpretation of data, we must not overlook the psychological effect. Imagine a resistance line at $100,000. You see prices going up and down, and when the price is nearing $100,000, you may hear yourself arguing in your head. The more adventurous you might say: "Come on, buddy! Buy! It's an asset that will always go up in the long run. Today is the day, you'll see." The more cautious you will reply to that, something like: "Investors are rational beings. The price of that asset is already so high, and six digits are huge. While you buy below $100,000, others will sell, and the price will decrease. You'll sit on an asset you can't sell for profit. Better to wait until the price drops." Again, your adventurous part might reply, "What if it crosses the resistance line and never goes back? We must buy now, or it's too late." While knowing current resistance or support lines is essential for traders, long-term investors may ignore them, as their idea is that assets will continue to grow over a long period.

The shorter the time window you aim to hold an asset, the more critical chart patterns become. Short-term traders tend to borrow resources—using leverage—to buy assets. If they don't sell soon, they must pay interest.

Conclusively, charts can help traders and investors decide when it's a good time to buy and sell. Additionally, long-term investors won't ignore them entirely. Let's examine how we can interpret a chart.

### 10.1.3 Interpreting a chart

Many financial analysis platforms such as TradingView, Finviz, and Seeking Alpha provide advanced charting features. They allow you to plot the share prices, and you can add indicators on top of the chart showing price movements. This chapter will show how to plot some of these indicators in later sections using Python. But be aware that the indicators presented in this book, such as moving averages, Bollinger Bands, or Ichimoku Cloud, are a small selection of the existing indicators that advanced charts provide.

Figure 10.13 shows a chart on Finviz.com, which also provides charting functionalities. You can view the chart with the latest data on that asset (NuScale Power Corporation) at https://finviz.com/quote.ashx?t=SMR&p=d. The screenshot is based on data from June 13, 2025.

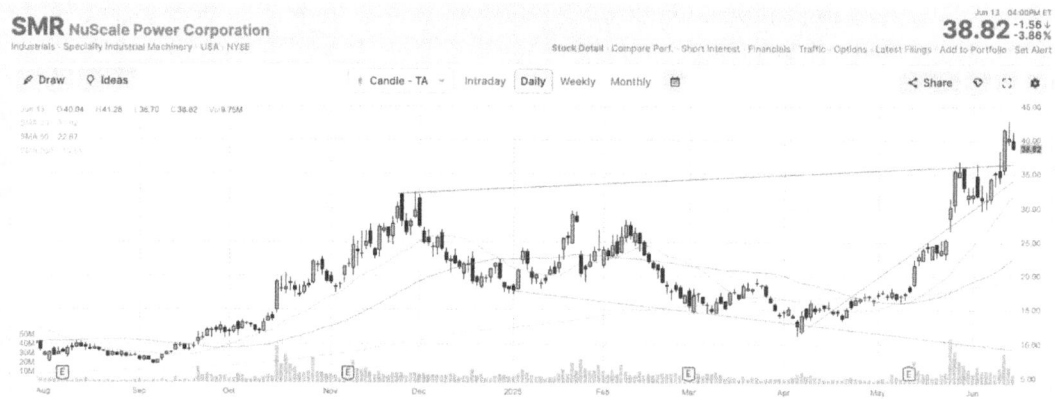

Figure 10.13  A NuScale (SMR) chart provided by Finviz.com shows how quickly we can perceive price movements over a longer time when the details are visualized.

Technical investors attempt to identify bearish and bullish patterns based on such charts. You can even paste screenshots like the previous one into a GenAI chatbot and ask the LLM to recognize patterns. It will return interpretations and, in some cases, even speculate on possible price developments based on signals such as a golden cross in late May, which describes that an SMA 50 crossed above the SMA 200 (we'll investigate simple moving averages [SMAs] later in this chapter).

Some investors argue that the effectiveness of technical analysis hasn't been proven and consider it a form of gambling. Others will tell you they start making money if they are successful, just 51% of the time. Whether you try to leverage price patterns for short-term trading or not, reading charts is also essential for long-term investors, as they tell an important story over time.

An asset has momentum, which is often reflected in patterns on the chart. Time is also an essential aspect of reading a chart. While a share price might decrease in the short term, a long-term trader may not be overly concerned if they still see a long-term upward trend. A short-term trader who has borrowed money to buy leveraged assets must make decisions earlier, as they must pay interest on the borrowed funds.

Technical traders develop algorithms to analyze moving averages, Bollinger Bands, Fibonacci retracements, Elliott waves, and other technical indicators. Many technical investors employ SMA crossover strategies, such as the 200-day SMA versus the 5-day SMA. Let's look at some of these principles to understand what this is all about.

### 10.1.4 Alternative chart types

While we primarily use line charts to visualize the price of an asset over time, investors often employ other chart types as well. Let's explore some of them.

## TREEMAPS

Treemaps have become popular on platforms such as Finviz. They show the growth and fall of prices. Figure 10.14 shows the treemap displayed on Finviz.

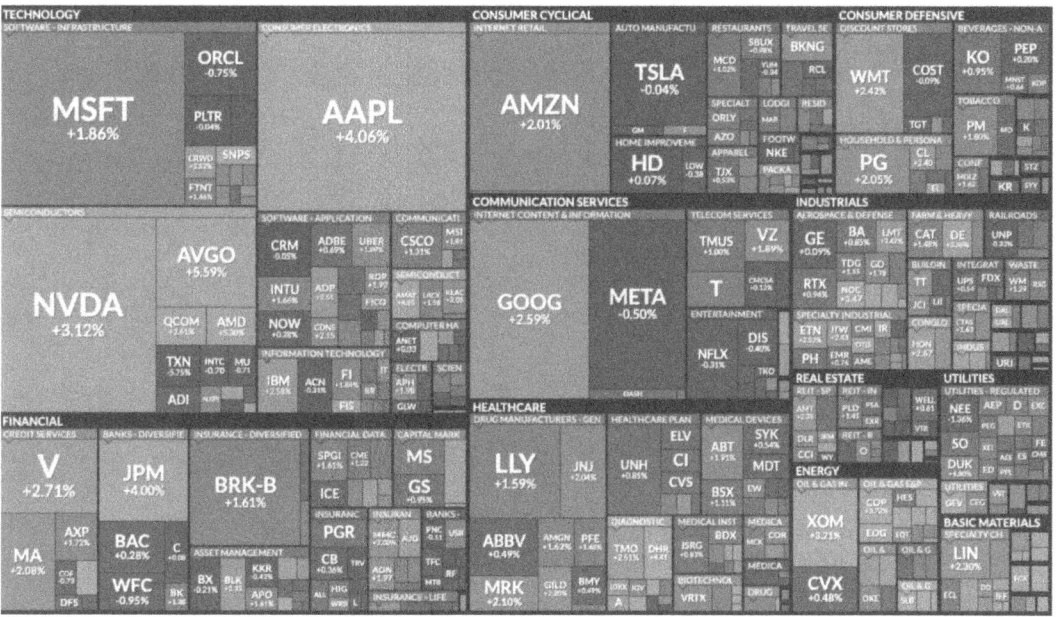

Figure 10.14  A treemap from Finviz gives us an idea about price movement. Check out today's chart (https://finviz.com/map.ashx) to get the latest data, drill down, interactively, and get a better impression of how much you can read through the color scheme.

## BAR CHART

Bar charts can help show the distribution of elements within a category. Again, Finviz provides an excellent example that can be explored at https://finviz.com/groups.ashx. In figure 10.15, we can see which sectors did well within one day. Finviz also provides bar charts that reflect the performance of assets over an extended period.

## HISTOGRAM

Histograms plot the distribution of values for a numeric variable as a series of bars, so we can use them to validate whether the data follows a Gaussian distribution. In chapter 7, we used a histogram in a Monte Carlo simulation to display returns, as shown in figure 10.16. Here, we have them distributed well-balanced over a Gaussian curve.

## SCATTERPLOT

In chapter 8, we used a scatterplot to plot companies. A scatterplot helps to identify interesting assets if you group multiples of them based on various criteria. For example, if we're interested in examining multiple assets based on risk and returns, we can plot them in a scatterplot with risk and return axes, as shown in chapter 8.

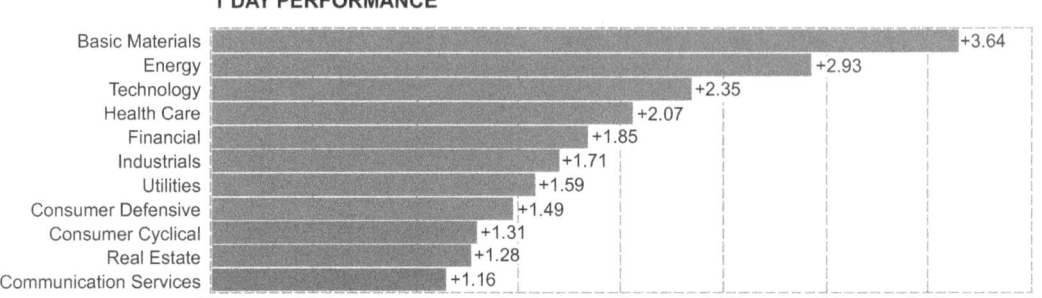

**Figure 10.15** A bar chart showing the distribution of growth by sector within a day. Bar charts are effective for illustrating the distribution of elements within a group.

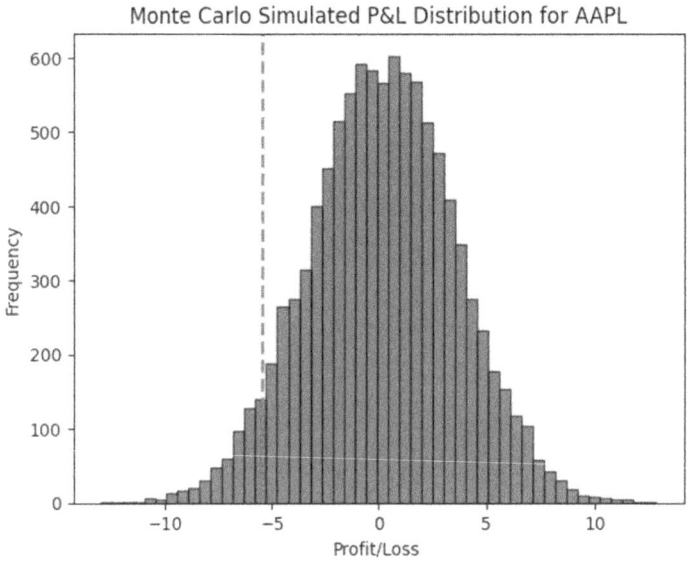

**Figure 10.16** This shows a histogram of Apple's returns over time, indicating that the returns of Apple follow a normal distribution, which, in other words, means there's no need to worry about the stock's performance.

We again display the figure from chapter 8 in figure 10.17 to immediately illustrate the value of a scatterplot. We see three outliers. The dot on the far left represents an asset that has lost significant value. If we hovered over the dot, we would know that it's Moderna, a capital-intensive business that is, among other things, affected by high federal interest rates. The topmost dot represents Super Micro Computer, a semiconductor company that had been in turmoil due to its failure to report on time, which caused its share price to plummet. On the far right, we have Palantir, whose high returns are also reflected in its P/E ratio, as indicated by a review of that ratio.

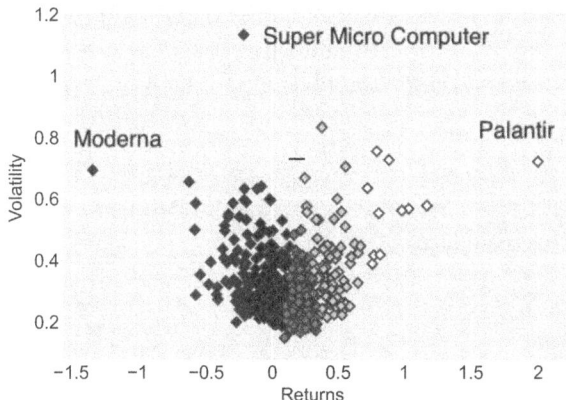

Figure 10.17  A scatterplot that categorizes stocks by volatility and returns

## 10.2 Using charts to interpret price changes

We learned how charts can help us gain faster insights than viewing the raw data. In a sense, charts are a shortcut to data analysis. Now, we shift our focus slightly toward analyzing price movements by putting them into context, which is essential for some investment and trading strategies.

At the beginning of this chapter, we highlighted that a price tag without additional knowledge and context can be confusing. Something we want to buy has an intrinsic value, also called the real value. The essential pattern in trading goods that existed already before the advent of money was to get a better value in goods exchange. This universal principle also applies to securities: we can make good or bad deals depending on the price we pay to acquire an asset.

When studying fundamentals, as we did in the previous chapters, we examine a company's details to determine whether an asset has lost or gained value. Efficient market theorists, such as Eugene Fama, say that assets are priced approximately at their worth unless you're an insider and know things the rest of the investors can't know. Some experts disagree with the efficient market theory, as some investors have repeatedly beaten the market.

By analyzing fundamentals, you determine what you believe the company is worth. You investigate changes in balance sheets and other documents to hypothesize whether an asset is undervalued or overvalued based on changes within the company. Analyzing price development in charts is a different approach, often called technical analysis. In this aspect, you examine price developments over time concerning what the market thinks the company is worth to determine trends, so you time your purchases accordingly. Let's get started.

### 10.2.1 Candlesticks

Candlestick charts visualize price movements in financial markets. They provide insights into market sentiment and show how prices fluctuate within a given time frame.

A candlestick chart is like a time series plot, but enhanced with additional information about a stock, cryptocurrency, or other financial asset's *open, high, low,* and *close* (OHLC) prices. Let's look at the anatomy of candlesticks to see how they work.

#### ANATOMY OF A CANDLESTICK CHART

Figure 10.18 shows NVIDIA's candlestick chart for three trading days with each candlestick representing a day in this chart. Time is scalable, meaning we can view it in terms of hours or months in such a chart.

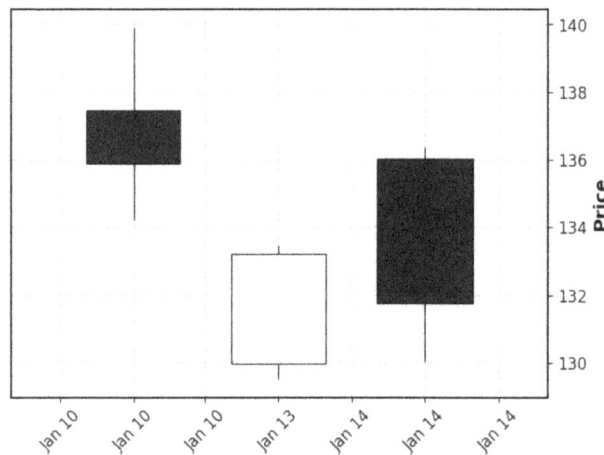

Figure 10.18  This candlestick diagram references three trading days of NVIDIA, from which we deduce price movements. Days 1 and 3 ended with a lower closing price than the opening price, and we can also see that on Day 3, the price was more volatile than on the preceding days.

Candlesticks use different schemata. On most platforms, the schema is represented by green and red colors. White and black are also common for other use cases, such as in print media like this book. If the candlestick is green or white, it means that, within the specified period—one day in our example—the closing price is higher than the opening price, indicating a bullish movement. If the closing price is lower than the opening price, the body is red or black, indicating a bearish movement (the price has decreased). If you're interested in seeing charts as examples, you can explore platforms such as Finviz (https://finviz.com) or TradingView (www.tradingview.com), where you can drill down into charts and zoom in on specific days to examine details. It's also often helpful to study charts of companies you know, as you can usually see how investors reacted to specific catalysts affecting your company (see chapter 11).

Figure 10.19 shows the anatomy of a candlestick. The height of the candle's body represents the difference between the opening and closing prices. The wicks, also known as shadows, represent the highest and lowest prices reached during the trading period, as depicted by a candle. The upper wick extends from the top of the body to the highest point, and the lower wick extends from the bottom to the lowest point.

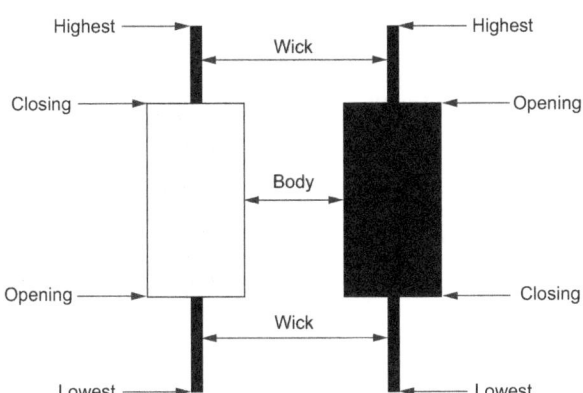

Figure 10.19 The anatomy of a bullish (white) and bearish (black) candlestick

Knowing all of this and referring to figure 10.18 shown earlier, the share price began at $138 on January 10th. It rallied up during the day until it reached $140, but it also fell at some point to a bit above $134, to end a bit below $136.

To create a plot similar to the figure 10.19, we need the mplfinance library, a Python library for financial data visualization. We load data from NVIDIA and plot it as shown in listing 10.1. We get the same result as in figure 10.6 earlier.

Listing 10.1 Creating candlestick charts

```
import mplfinance as mpf
import pandas as pd

import yfinance as yf
ticker = "NVDA"
data = yf.Ticker(ticker).history(start="2025-01-10", end="2025-01-15")
df = pd.DataFrame(data).dropna()
mpf.plot(df, type='candle', style='charles', title='Candlestick Chart')
```

Now, let's examine candlestick patterns in more detail to understand how we can interpret their price movements. For that, we need to examine multiple consecutive days.

## CANDLESTICK PATTERNS

Candlestick patterns enable traders and investors to interpret price action quickly. We can detect market trends, reversals, and continuation patterns by analyzing multiple candles, such as the following:

- Long wicks indicate rejection and support of certain price levels.
- Small bodies suggest indecision in the market.
- Large bodies indicate strong momentum.

Some patterns are commonly used to predict price movements, as shown in figure 10.20:

- *Doji*—The opening and closing prices are almost the same, forming a small body, which signals market indecision.
- *Hammer*—A small body with a long lower wick indicates a potential reversal after a downtrend.
- *Engulfing*—A large candle that completely engulfs the previous one signals a substantial shift in momentum.

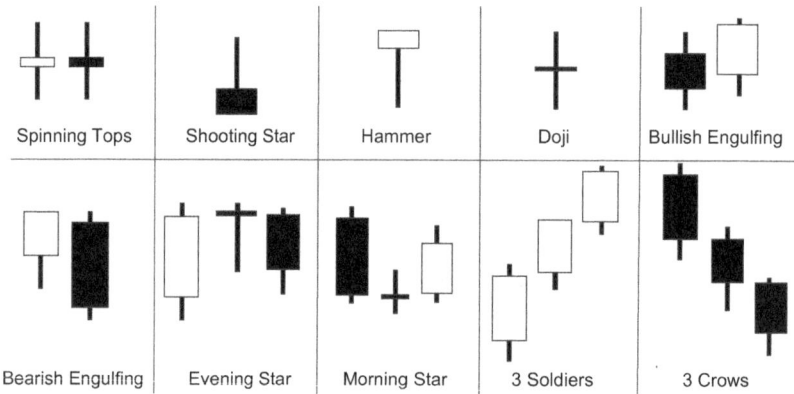

Figure 10.20 Various candlestick patterns in which we can describe the behavior of the market. In addition to the Doji, Hammer, and Engulfing patterns, we can see the volatility of prices. You immediately realize that candles with long bodies represent high volatility, whereas candles with multiple short bodies represent a calm market situation.

Using the terminology from the figure, we can describe the patterns. A Spinning Top is a pattern in which, on two consecutive days, we experience high price volatility during the trading day but end up with a Doji. As another example, a Shooting Star is a pattern that has a high volatility during the day, and then the closing price is lower than the opening price. Being able to give the patterns names facilitates discussions about trends with other investors.

Now that we know how to interpret candlesticks, we can investigate averages over multiple periods to gain a deeper understanding of the share price development. Let's discuss that next.

### 10.2.2 Charts based on averages

At the beginning of the chapter, we highlighted the importance of data about past purchases. Imagine an item listed for $100. Knowing that similar items have been sold for $80 on average will lead you to consider it differently than knowing that the item is usually sold for $120.

When working with shares with frequent price changes, we must examine price developments over an extended period. In addition to highs and lows, one central benchmark is the average price: you have three numbers—let's take 1, 2, and 3—and everyone with basic math skills knows that the average is 2. Let's explore some more complex scenarios.

Let's take the closing price of a stock for $x$ days and calculate the average by adding all values and dividing them by the total number of values. If we look at changes over time, we set a window (say 20 days) and calculate the average. When we add a new value to an existing set of 20 days, we remove the oldest value from the set. This is that simple moving average (SMA) that we mentioned earlier in the chapter.

We might wonder if it's efficient to weigh all numbers the same. Would it not make sense to weigh the more recent values higher than the oldest ones? For this reason, other average calculation formulas incorporate weighting, such as the *exponential moving average (EMA), weighted moving average (WMA),* and *Hull moving average (HMA)*, which we explore in this chapter. The goal is to smooth price data and identify trends earlier. As different average calculations have different goals, they target different scenarios.

In listing 10.2, we create a data set for demonstration and then apply the SMA and EMA. The EMA weights the later values more. We define a set of random data and use the algorithms.

#### Listing 10.2 Calculating SMA and EMAs

```
import pandas as pd

data = {
    "Date": pd.date_range(start="2023-01-01", periods=10),
    "Price": [10, 11, 12, 13, 14, 15, 16, 17, 18, 19],
}
df = pd.DataFrame(data)

window_size = 3
df['SMA'] = df['Price'].rolling(
    window=window_size).mean()
df['EMA'] = df['Price'].ewm(
    span=window_size, adjust=False).mean()
```

- `df['SMA'] = df['Price'].rolling(window=window_size).mean()` ◁── SMA is the unweighted mean of the last N values.
- `df['EMA'] = df['Price'].ewm(span=window_size, adjust=False).mean()` ◁── EMA gives more weight to recent values.

Looking at the results, the EMA returns a slightly higher result (17.003906) for the mean of 16, 17, and 18 than 17, which would be the result of SMA based on these numbers. These differences don't seem significant unless you consider large transactions. If you trade millions, it will have a considerable effect. Let's compare data using historical share prices and add the remaining two average calculations.

> **NOTE** We'll use an option to limit floating-point numbers behind the decimal point, using the following parameter to enhance visualization: `pd.options .display.float_format = '{:,.2f}'.format`.

The WMA also weights averages, but unlike the EMA, it does this linearly, balancing some of the differences between the EMA and SMA. The HMA uses the WMA as a base to smooth out the extra by adding half the time window and the square root of the time window in the calculation. If you're interested in the details, you can look up the math; in brief, the formula is HMA > WMA > EMA > SMA. The further to the left, the more sensitive our calculations are to recent changes. Let's look at the Python implementation in the following code:

```
def weighted_moving_average(prices, window):
    weights = np.arange(1, window + 1)
    return prices.rolling(window).apply(
        lambda x: np.dot(x, weights) / weights.sum(), raw=True)

def hull_moving_average(prices, window):
    half_window = int(window / 2)
    sqrt_window = int(np.sqrt(window))
    wma_half = weighted_moving_average(prices, half_window)
    wma_full = weighted_moving_average(prices, window)
    hma = weighted_moving_average(2 * wma_half - wma_full, sqrt_window)
    return hma
```

Now that everything is defined, let's load data from NVIDIA for 2024 and compare the results. In the following code, we load the data and add all averages of the closing prices to the DataFrame.

```
import yfinance as yf
ticker = "NVDA"
data = yf.Ticker(ticker).history(start="2024-01-01", end="2024-12-31")
averages = pd.DataFrame(data).dropna()
averages.reset_index(inplace=True)

def add_averages(close, window_size):
    close['SMA'] = close['Close'].rolling(window=window_size).mean()
    close['EMA'] = close['Close'].ewm(span=window_size, adjust=False).mean()
    close['WMA'] = weighted_moving_average(close['Close'], window_size)
    close['HMA'] = hull_moving_average(close['Close'], window_size)
    return close[['Date', 'Close', 'SMA', 'EMA', 'WMA', 'HMA']]
```

Examining the data, we observe that the larger the window we use, the more not a number (NaN) values we encounter at the beginning of the DataFrame. We'll confirm that each average has slightly different values. Let's extract a single entry and look at it. In table 10.2, we display the average for a 3-day window on February 2, 2024. In the row below, we show the average for a 20-day time window on the same day.

## 10.2 Using charts to interpret price changes

Table 10.2 Multiple averages for the same day, each with a different time window

| Window (days) | Closing | SMA | EMA | WMA | HMA |
|---|---|---|---|---|---|
| 3 | 66.14 | 63.55 | 64.29 | 64.33 | 67.96 |
| 20 | 66.14 | 58.33 | 58.83 | 60.60 | 64.19 |

Examining the EMA, WMA, and HMA, we can conclude that the more recent data is weighted, the closer the results will be to the closing price of the last day. The SMA is further away from the closing price. We can also conclude that the SMA reacts more slowly to price changes than other moving averages. This doesn't have to be negative; if we look for long-term trends, recent spikes wouldn't bother us. We can sum up with the following conclusions:

- SMA is the best for long-term trend analysis.
- EMA is suitable for short-term trading strategies that require quicker reactions.
- WMA offers a balance between EMA and SMA, emphasizing recent prices.
- HMA is the most effective approach for detecting rapid trends.

We can also create another hypothesis. Regardless of which moving average we use, we can also employ different time windows, which provide us with distinct insights. Let's look at that next.

#### MOVING AVERAGE RIBBONS

*Moving average ribbons* visualize trend strengths: narrow ribbons indicate consolidation, and wide ribbons show strong trends. In listing 10.3, which plots moving average ribbons, we use six windows: 10, 20, 30, 40, 50, and 60.

Listing 10.3 Plotting moving average ribbons

```
import yfinance as yf
import matplotlib.pyplot as plt

ticker = "NVDA"
df = yf.Ticker(ticker).history(start="2024-01-1", end="2025-01-1")
df.reset_index(inplace=True)

periods = [10, 20, 30, 40, 50, 60]
for period in periods:                                      ⎫  Creates different
    df[f"SMA_{period}"] = df["Close"].rolling(              ⎬  windows
        window=period).mean()                               ⎭

plt.figure(figsize=(12, 6))
plt.plot(df["Date"], df["Close"], label="Price", color="black",
    linewidth=1.5)
for period in periods:
    plt.plot(df["Date"], df[f"SMA_{period}"], label=f"SMA {period}")
plt.title("Moving Average Ribbon")
plt.xlabel("Date")
plt.ylabel("Price")
```

```
plt.legend()
plt.grid()
plt.show()
```

The results are shown in figure 10.21. We observe fewer movements in May and October, indicating that the price has been more stable than at other times, where the ribbons are more spread out.

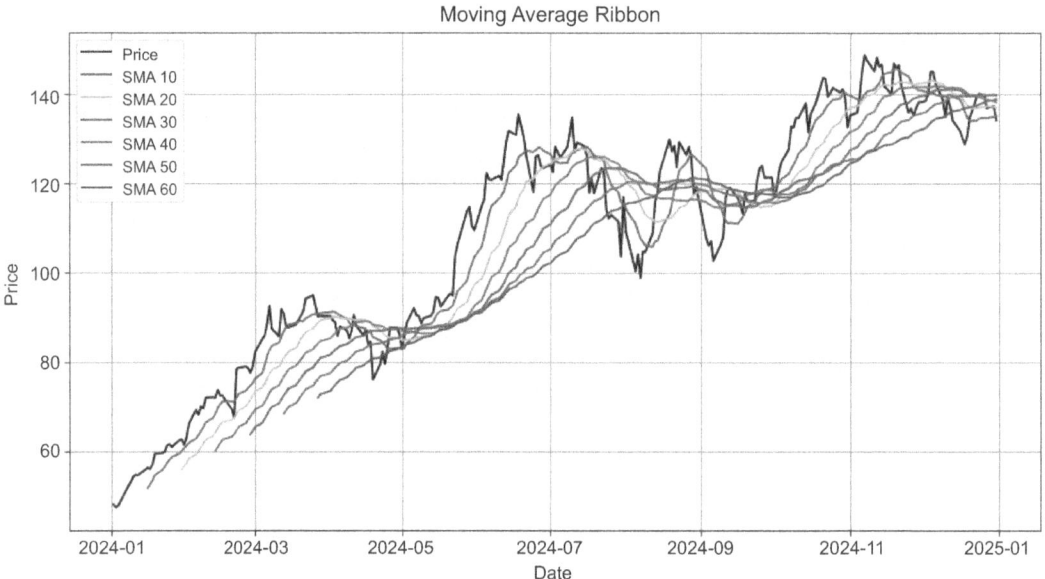

Figure 10.21   Moving average ribbons that contract around 2024-05 and 2024-10, indicating that the market was consolidating at that time

> **NOTE** We'll explore multiple SMA trading strategies in chapter 11. In that chapter, we'll also examine optimal time windows for trading strategies and investigate whether standard parameters, such as the SMA 50 versus the SMA 200, are optimal.

Let's look at Bollinger Bands next to understand better how we can show overbought or oversold conditions more clearly.

**BOLLINGER BANDS**

*Bollinger Bands* is a popular technical analysis tool that measures price volatility and identifies overbought or oversold conditions in a security. They use the following parameters:

- *Middle band*—This is a 20-period SMA, representing the average price over the chosen period. The default value is 20, and traders can adjust it. Too high or too low values risk being overly sensitive or not responsive enough to trading signals.

- *Upper band*—This equals the middle band plus two times the standard deviation of price, representing a level often seen as overbought or a resistance area.
- *Lower band*—This equals the middle band minus two times the standard deviation of price, representing a level typically considered oversold or a support area.

Let's use Python code to plot Bollinger Bands and then interpret them. We collect technical data from a stock and calculate the bands with the parameters defined in listing 10.4. We first load stock tickers. Then, we define 20 as the default window and calculate the necessary values for the bands described in the preceding list. Lastly, we plot the Bollinger Bands.

**Listing 10.4 Plotting Bollinger Bands**

```
import yfinance as yf
import pandas as pd
import matplotlib.pyplot as plt

ticker = "NVDA"
data = yf.download(ticker, start="2024-01-01")

window = 20
std_dev_factor = 2
data['SMA'] = data['Close'].rolling(
    window=sma_window_length).mean()
rolling_std = data['Close'].rolling(
    window=sma_window_length).std()
data['rf'] = (rolling_std * std_dev_factor)
data['upper'] = data['SMA'] + data['rf']
data['lower'] = data['SMA'] - data['rf']

plt.figure(figsize=(12, 6))
plt.plot(data.index, data['Close'], label="Close Price", color="blue",
linewidth=1)
plt.plot(data.index, data['SMA'], label=f"{window}-Day SMA",
color="orange", linewidth=1.5)
plt.plot(data.index, data['upper'], label="Upper Bollinger Band",
color="green", linestyle="--", linewidth=1)
plt.plot(data.index, data['lower'], label="Lower Bollinger Band",
color="red", linestyle="--", linewidth=1)

plt.title(f"Bollinger Bands for {ticker} (20-day window)", fontsize=14)
plt.xlabel("Date", fontsize=12)
plt.ylabel("Price", fontsize=12)
plt.legend()
plt.grid(alpha=0.3)
plt.show()
```

Calculates the bands

Figure 10.22 shows the Bollinger Bands. The plot represents all the lines we've created based on the preceding formulas. Now, we should see more evident upper and lower barriers.

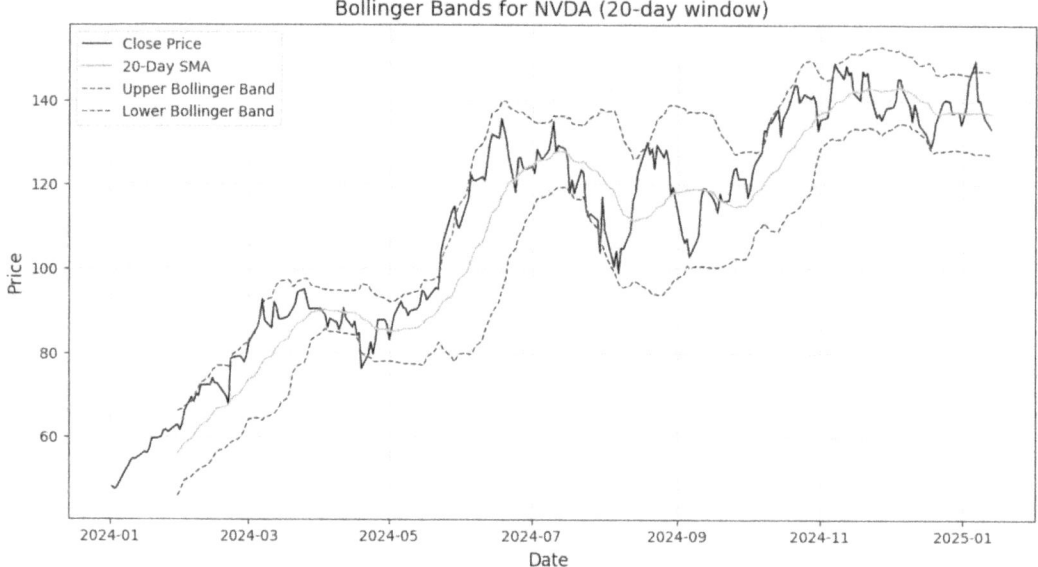

Figure 10.22  The Bollinger Bands for NVIDIA provide insight into potential days to buy or sell shares.

Bollinger Bands expand during periods of high volatility and contract during periods of low volatility. Around August 2024, the closing price also exhibited significant fluctuations. Typically, following periods of high volatility, we experience a phase of contraction, indicating a consolidation period and a potential breakout.

Prices tend to stay within the band. We attempt to identify moments when it deviates, which signals price action, potential trend continuation, or reversal. In late April 2024, the share price was below 80 and crossed the lower band, signaling a possible buy opportunity. At the same time, around 2024-06, we have a sell signal. While buying in April 2024 would have led to profits, the sell signal in June 2024 would have resulted in losses if we hadn't identified this as a strong uptrend, which likely would have rendered the sell signal obsolete.

In chapter 11, we'll test strategies using backtesting. But let's move forward to the next indicator.

#### Moving Average Convergence Divergence (MACD)

*The Moving Average Convergence Divergence (MACD)* is a momentum-based technical indicator used to spot potential buying or selling opportunities in the market. It analyzes the relationship between two moving averages of a share price: the short-term and long-term moving averages. Let's examine the details of MACDs. As we can see, we use different window sizes or periods to detect buy or sell signals:

- *MACD line*—The difference between a short-term EMA and a long-term EMA. Commonly, the 12-period EMA is subtracted from the 26-period EMA.

- *Signal line*—A nine-period EMA of the MACD line, which is a trigger for buy or sell signals.
- *Histogram*—A visual representation of the difference between the MACD and signal lines. When the histogram is above 0, the MACD line is above the signal line, indicating bullish momentum. Conversely, when it's below 0, bearish momentum is indicated.

Let's examine the code in listing 10.5. In the `calculate_macd` method, we calculate the `EMA_12` and `EMA_26` based on the close price. With that, we get the MACD and, consequently, the signal line. After calculating the MACD parameter, we plot the MACD chart using the method `plot_macd`.

### Listing 10.5 Moving Average Convergence Divergence

```
import pandas as pd
import matplotlib.pyplot as plt

def calculate_macd(data, short_window=12, long_window=26, signal_window=9):
    data['EMA_12'] = data['Close'].ewm(
        span=short_window, adjust=False).mean()
    data['EMA_26'] = data['Close'].ewm(
        span=long_window, adjust=False).mean()              Calculates the
    data['MACD'] = data['EMA_12'] - data['EMA_26']          MACD parameter
    data['Signal_Line'] = data['MACD'].ewm(
        span=signal_window, adjust=False).mean()
    return data

def plot_macd(data):
    plt.figure(figsize=(12,6))
    plt.plot(data.index, data['MACD'], label='MACD', color='blue')
    plt.plot(data.index, data['Signal_Line'],
      label='Signal Line', color='red')
    plt.bar(data.index, data['MACD'] - data['Signal_Line'],
      label='Histogram', color='gray', alpha=0.5)
    plt.legend(loc='best')
    plt.title('MACD Indicator')
    plt.xlabel('Date')
    plt.ylabel('MACD Value')
    plt.grid()
    plt.show()

import yfinance as yf
ticker = "NVDA"
df = yf.Ticker(ticker).history(start="2024-01-01")
df = calculate_macd(df)
plot_macd(df)
```

We obtain the data from NVIDIA in a chart, as shown in figure 10.23. We can then examine historical buy and sell signals.

Buy and sell signals are identified by crossover signals. We have a bullish signal when the MACD line crosses above the signal line. We see them before March 2024

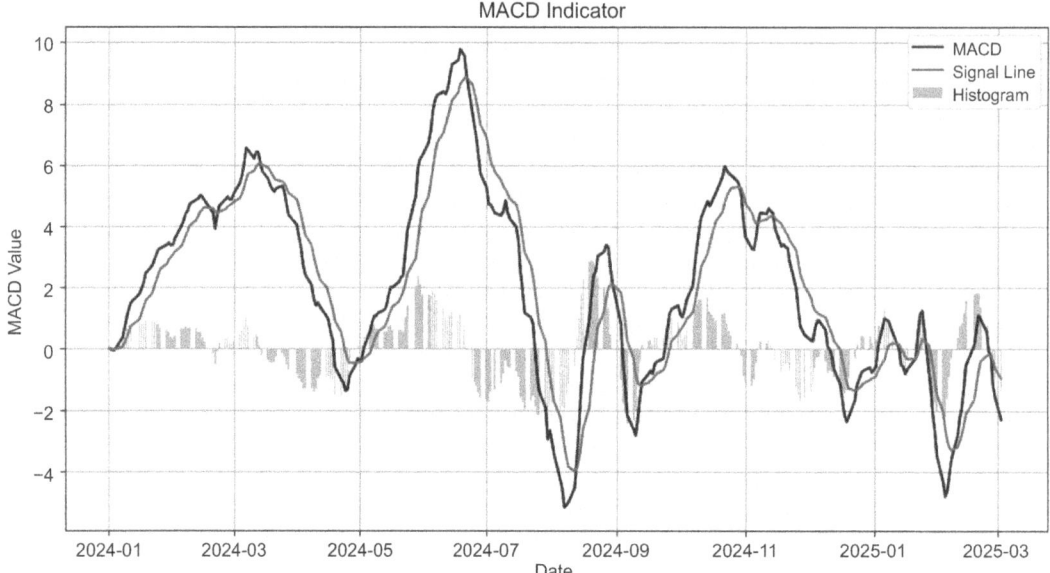

Figure 10.23  Shows the MACD for NVIDIA closing prices. Whenever a signal line crosses the MACD, a trading signal is generated.

and again in May 2024. A bearish signal occurs when the MACD line crosses below the signal line. This indicates downward momentum and may suggest a potential selling opportunity, particularly near or around April 2024. We also need to examine the zero-line crossings and conclude that the sentiment was more bearish in March 2025 than in March 2024.

The larger the histogram bars grow, the more it suggests increasing momentum in the current trend. Shrinking bars indicate weakening momentum, which might hint at an impending reversal.

Understanding MACD can be particularly useful if you build or use algorithmic trading systems. While MACD is a powerful tool, it's not foolproof. It may produce false signals in choppy or sideways markets. For confirmation, it's best used with other indicators or fundamental analysis.

In chapter 11, we'll also examine how we can back-test such strategies and how much money we would have made or lost if we had used this strategy for buying or selling. Let's explore the next technical indicator.

### 10.2.3  Ichimoku Cloud

The Ichimoku Cloud (or just Ichimoku) is a charting technique used in technical analysis that provides a comprehensive view of price action by incorporating trend, momentum, and support and resistance levels in a single chart. Unlike SMAs or candlesticks, the Ichimoku offers a multidimensional approach to understanding market conditions.

**NOTE** The Ichimoku Cloud often uses Japanese terms for its key elements. They have been omitted from this book for clarity and brevity. You can look them up on Investopedia or similar sites.

Although it may appear complex initially, breaking it down into its components makes it much easier to understand. The Ichimoku consists of five key elements:

- *Conversion line*—A short-term moving average that reacts quickly to price changes
- *Baseline*—A medium-term trend line used as a momentum and trend direction
- *Leading span A*—Forms the first boundary of the cloud, acting as dynamic support or resistance
- *Leading span B*—Forms the second boundary of the cloud
- *Lagging span*—Helps confirm trends by comparing the current price to past prices

We adjust the time windows for the averages accordingly. The conversion line has a lower window (nine days), and the baseline has longer time windows. We also use the base and conversion lines to calculate other lines, as demonstrated in the code.

Let's implement the Ichimoku using Python and Matplotlib in listing 10.6. We reload the NVIDIA data, calculate all parameters, and then plot them.

**Listing 10.6 Creating an Ichimoku**

```python
import yfinance as yf
import matplotlib.pyplot as plt
ticker = "NVDA"
data = yf.Ticker(ticker).history(start="2024-01-10", end="2025-01-15")
df = pd.DataFrame(data).dropna()
df.reset_index(inplace=True)

df["ConversationLine"] = (df["Close"].rolling(
    window=9).max() + df["Close"].rolling(
    window=9).min()) / 2
df["BaseLine"] = (df["Close"].rolling(
    window=26).max() + df["Close"].rolling(
    window=26).min()) / 2
df["SpanA"] = ((df["ConversationLine"]
    + df["BaseLine"]) / 2).shift(26)
df["SpanB"] = ((df["Close"].rolling(
    window=52).max() + df["Close"].rolling(
    window=52).min()) / 2).shift(26)
df["LaggingSpan"] = df["Close"].shift(-26)

plt.figure(figsize=(12, 6))
plt.plot(df.index, df["Close"], label="Close Price", color="black")
plt.plot(df.index, df["ConversationLine"], label="ConversationLine",
color="red")
plt.plot(df.index, df["BaseLine"], label="BaseLine", color="blue")
plt.fill_between(df.index, df["SpanA"], df["SpanB"],
    where=df["SpanA"] >= df["SpanA"], color="lightgreen", alpha=0.5)
plt.fill_between(df.index, df["SpanA"], df["SpanB"],
    where=df["SpanA"] < df["SpanB"], color="lightcoral", alpha=0.5)
```

Calculates the parameter for the Ichimoku

```
plt.plot(df.index, df["LaggingSpan"], label="LaggingSpan", color="purple",
    linestyle="dotted")

plt.title("Ichimoku Cloud")
plt.legend()
plt.show()
```

Now, let's look at the plot results in figure 10.24. We can see that we had essentially a bullish momentum, as evidenced by the many green (light gray in grayscale) clouds.

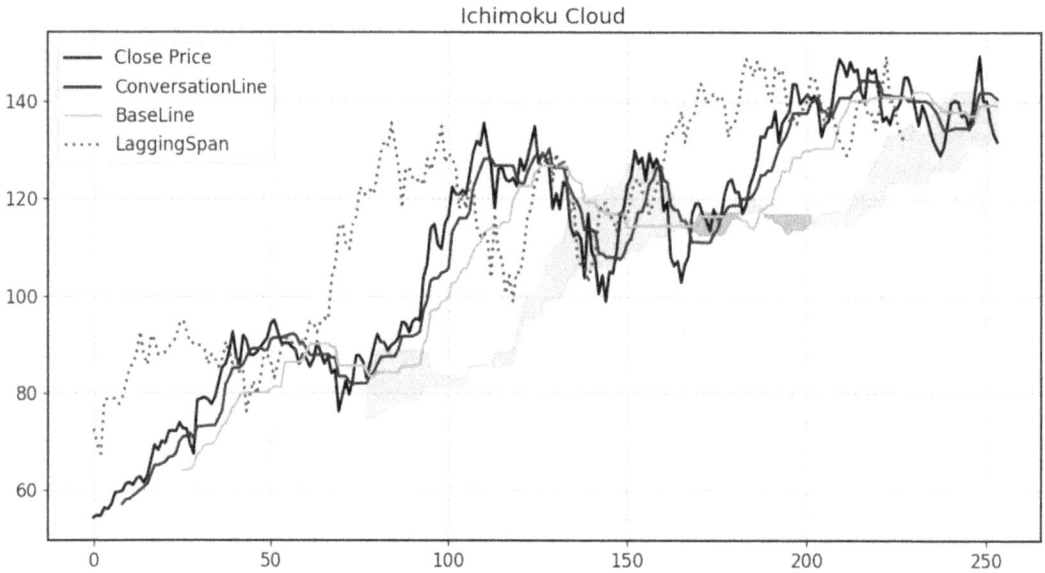

Figure 10.24 An Ichimoku for NVIDIA closing prices indicating multiple bullish moments

The space between spans A and B forms the Ichimoku Cloud, and green (light gray in grayscale) means that span A is above span B. It's a bullish signal. If span B is above span A, the cloud is red (dark gray in grayscale), a bearish signal.

The cloud acts as support in an uptrend and resistance in a downtrend. We can use them to identify trends:

- If the price is above the cloud, the market is in an uptrend.
- If the price is below the cloud, the market is in a downtrend.
- If the price is inside the cloud, the market is in a consolidation phase (uncertainty).

We can also look for buy and sell signals:

- *Bullish signal (Buy)*—When the conversion line crosses above the baseline while the price is above the cloud

- *Bearish signal (Sell)*—When the conversion line crosses below the baseline while the price is below the cloud

The cloud acts as support in uptrends and resistance in downtrends. A thicker cloud suggests stronger support or resistance, making it harder for the price to break through.

## 10.3 Visualization with Streamlit

In certain situations, it can be beneficial to visualize results online. Although some of you may have experience with advanced web technologies, others may not want to delve into a powerful but complex solution. We need a technology that keeps visualization simple and straightforward.

One way to quickly generate web UIs is to use the Streamlit library, which can be installed as a Python package. Streamlit allows us to define web controls, and once we execute the Python files, it generates a local web page. Note that we use traditional Python files in the following example (ending with the .py extension), not the data science notebooks used throughout the rest of the book.

Listing 10.7 provides a simple example of plotting returns. We have multiple predefined tickers and define input controls to collect the start and end times of the plot. The code's logic checks whether one or more stocks have been selected. If we have the data, we calculate the returns and plot a line chart.

**Listing 10.7  Displaying returns with Streamlit**

```
import streamlit as st
import pandas as pd
import yfinance as yf
st.title("Finance Dashboard")

tickers = ('TSLA', 'AAPL', 'MSFT', 'ETH-USD', 'BTC-USD')
dropdown = st.multiselect("Select Ticker", tickers)

start = st.date_input('Start Date', pd.to_datetime('2024-01-01'))
end = st.date_input('End Date', pd.to_datetime('today'))

def relativeret(df):
    rel = df.pct_change()
    cumret = (1+rel).cumprod() -1
    cumret = cumret.fillna(0)
    return cumret

if len (dropdown) > 0:
    df = relativeret(yf.download(dropdown, start=start, end=end))['Close']
    st.header(f"Returns of {dropdown}")
    st.line_chart(df)
```

We start the Streamlit website by calling the Streamlit application on the command line using the syntax `streamlit run <pythonfile>`. We need to open our web browser and follow the directions in the command line to view a figure similar to the one displayed in figure 10.25.

# Finance Dashboard

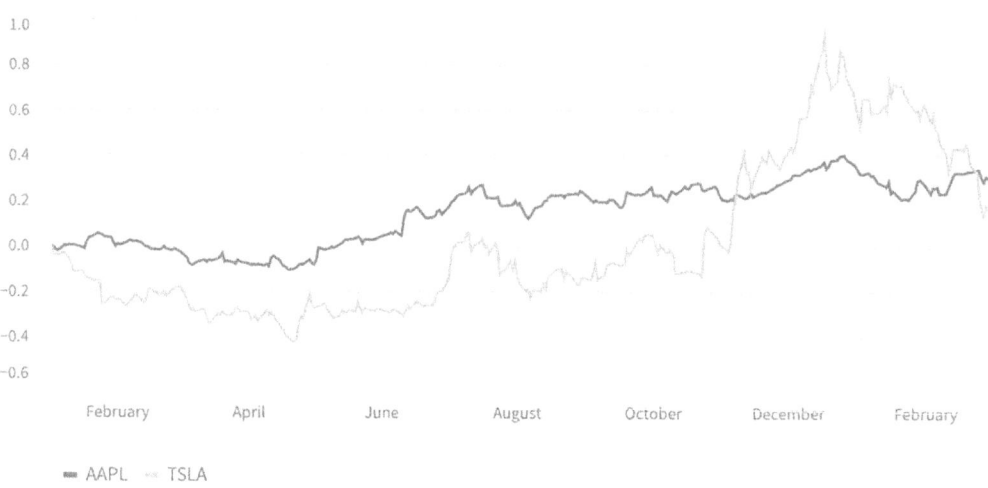

Figure 10.25  The returns of Apple and Tesla in a chart rendered on a website by Streamlit

Now that we understand the principles of Streamlit, we can plot moving average ribbons, Bollinger Bands, MACDs, and candlesticks. In the code shown in listing 10.8, we use select boxes instead of multi-select controls, as in the previous examples, because we'll always examine one company at a time. Be aware that this listing omits the logic for Bollinger Bands, MACDs, and moving average ribbons, as it's identical to the code previously shown in the listings and has been incorporated into methods. The complete code for this chapter, as well as the code for the other chapters, is available for download from the Manning site for this book. We added the technique to display a plot from the Streamlit library, mplfinance, for the candles. As with mplfinance, you need to pass a specific parameter, `returnfig=True`, so that the plots can be plotted correctly. To display a selected chart, we pass a method parameter to the method and call it to create the plot, which will then be plotted.

**Listing 10.8  Streamlit Technical Analysis**

```python
import streamlit as st
import pandas as pd
import yfinance as yf
import matplotlib.pyplot as plt
import mplfinance as mpf

st.title("Technical Analysis")

ptype = ('NONE', 'MA', 'BOLL', 'MACD', 'CANDLE', 'CLOUD')
tickers = ('TSLA', 'AAPL', 'MSFT', 'ETH-USD', 'BTC-USD')
dropdown = st.selectbox("Select Ticker", tickers)
plot = st.selectbox("Select Plot", ptype)
start = st.date_input('Start Date', pd.to_datetime('2024-01-01'))
end = st.date_input('End Date', pd.to_datetime('today'))

def bollinger(data):
    pass

def macd(data):
    pass

def ma(data):
    pass

def cloud(data):
    pass

def candle(data):
    fig, ax = mpf.plot(data, type='candle', style='charles',figsize=(15,10), title='Candlestick Chart', returnfig=True)
    return fig

def plot_ta(title: str, method):        # Method to plot
    st.header(title)                    # the chart
    plt = method(df)
    st.pyplot(plt)

if len(dropdown) > 0 and plot != 'NONE':
    df = yf.Ticker(dropdown).history(start=start, end=end)
    match(plot):
        case 'BOLL':
            plot_ta("Bollinger bands", bollinger)
        case 'MA':
            plot_ta("Moving Average Ribbons", ma)
        case 'MACD':
            plot_ta("MACD", macd)
        case 'CANDLE':
            plot_ta("CANDLE", candle)
        case 'CLOUD':
            plot_ta("CLOUD", cloud)
```

In figure 10.26, we can see a reference example of the result using Bollinger Bands. If you run the Streamlit application downloadable from the GitHub repository for this book, you'll also be able to plot other charts.

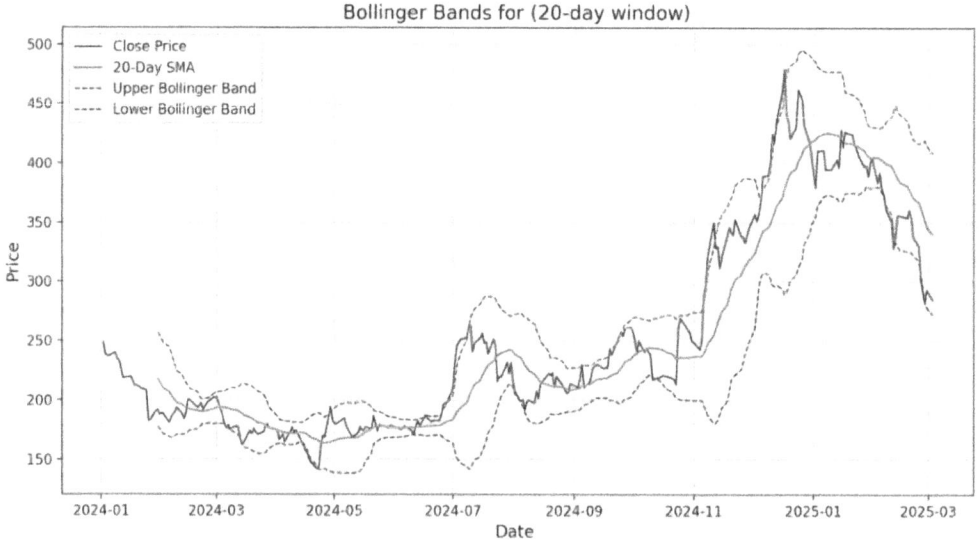

Figure 10.26  **A Streamlit web page displaying Bollinger Bands**

To sum it all up, even if you're not a technical trader who identifies buy or sell opportunities based on chart patterns, charts can help you understand better how share prices are evolving. You can use charts to identify potential weak points in your portfolio and combine this analysis with a reevaluation of your investment thesis for the stock.

## *Summary*

- Every chart tells a story. If you plot the share price development of an asset, you'll also see the effect of catalysts—events that propel significant changes in asset prices.
- You need to put price movements into context. For some asset classes, you expect more or less volatility than for others.
- You can look for patterns in a chart to predict future development.
- Patterns, such as the double top, serve as a reference example. These patterns can reveal a trend, but identifying them can be tricky, as they are merely templates of the past.
- Chart patterns can be categorized into two main groups: reversals and continuations. The first follows a trend and then reverses it; the second continues to follow a trend.
- Treemaps of a full stock market, popularized by platforms such as Finviz, provide a comprehensive overview of all constituents within the stock market.
- Bar charts allow the display of the distribution of participants in a group. You can visualize the assets within an exchange-traded fund (ETF) weighted by their size.
- Histograms are ideal for plotting daily returns. If their returns follow a Gaussian distribution, everything is in order.
- Scatterplots can be used to detect specific assets within a group of assets.
- Candlesticks provide insights into market trends and movements during the period represented by a candle.
- A candlestick body represents the price difference between the security's opening and closing prices. The wicks of a candlestick identify the maximum and minimum price during a trading day.
- We can identify patterns across multiple trading days using candlesticks and name trends. Some prominent patterns in candlesticks that identify trends are Doji (opening and closing prices are almost the same), Hammer (possible reversal after a downtrend), and Engulfing (a substantial shift in momentum).
- You can calculate averages in many ways; some approaches weigh values differently:
  - Use simple moving averages (SMAs) for long-term trend analysis.
  - Use exponential moving averages (EMAs) for momentum and recent changes.
  - Use weighted moving averages (WMAs) for fast-moving signals.
  - Use Hull moving averages (HMAs) for lag reduction with smoothness.

- Moving average ribbons are a way to plot multiple moving averages with different time windows over the closing price of a stock.
- If moving average ribbons contract, we can identify a consolidation in the share price.
- Use Bollinger Bands to analyze volatility and price extremes, as they can be easily detected when they cross the upper and lower bands plotted in the chart.
- Moving average convergence divergence (MACD) measures the relationship between two moving averages of a share price. Use MACD for momentum and crossovers.
- Traders look for crossovers in such charts, as they serve as trading signals to buy or sell stocks.
- Streamlit is an excellent way for Python programmers to visualize content on a web page without needing to learn web programming.

# Algorithmic trading

### This chapter covers
- Quantitative analysis
- Testing strategies using backtesting
- Catalysts as game changers
- The difference between exchanges and brokers
- Executing orders with Python
- Order types and modalities

Now that you've mastered technical analysis with charts, this chapter introduces algorithms for trading strategies, transforming raw insights into actions. This step is the culmination of everything we've covered: collecting data, analyzing ratios and charts, assessing risks, and integrating machine learning (ML) and large language models (LLMs). We'll bring it all together and outline scenarios for applying it.

Various scenarios affect trading strategies. Some algorithms perform better in bull markets than bear markets, or vice versa. Catalysts are specific moments that signal more volatility in the market, which can be an opportunity or risk. We'll review catalysts from a trading perspective.

In the third part of this chapter, we'll demonstrate how to place orders programmatically using Interactive Brokers and Alpaca. We'll explore different order types, parameters, and their implications, learning how to apply them effectively.

## 11.1 Nonfinancial data

In chapter 3, we categorized data for financial analysis. In chapters 4 and 5, we conducted ad hoc research to build portfolios. Then, we showed how to monitor our portfolio, explored ML and LLM applications, and analyzed charts. As shown in figure 11.1, three data sources, including their update frequencies, are used to create data models and algorithms for trading decisions. The efficient market theory says that an asset price represents the knowledge of all investors, and therefore, individual investors can't beat the market in the long run. But what if we get insights that nobody else or only a few investors have? We won't likely find these hidden gems of knowledge in fundamental or technical data, as investors have tried to explore financial data for decades. Let's focus on the nonfinancial data, as this category is the newest source for insights, and not everyone might have explored all possibilities.

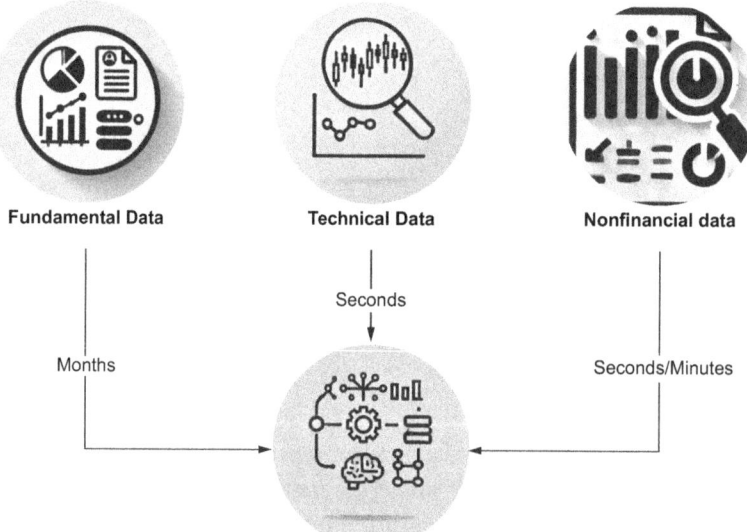

Figure 11.1 Three types of data flow can lead to insights, and nonfinancial data, being the newest of them, is especially interesting.

Let's explore how much data has changed the investment approach to understand how nonfinancial data has added a new flavor to investment and trading strategies. Many investors have read about investment basics from books about Warren Buffett, who often refers to his mentor, Benjamin Graham, as the father of sophisticated investment techniques. If we read classic books by Graham such as *Security Analysis* or *The Intelligent Investor*, we can imagine a young Warren Buffett getting his information from newspapers and seeing him and his partner, Charlie Munger, making deals in person with other investors in the pre-information age. We can hardly imagine an investment legend such as Warren Buffett in front of a Bloomberg terminal studying data or exploring Python scripts using an Integrated Development Environment (IDE).

Films such as *Wall Street* or *The Big Short* can also influence perceptions of the investment profession. These films feature computers already in use for trading. Many documentaries and movies also illustrate an era when the internet was a game changer, allowing us to respond to fast-moving signals that would have taken earlier investors significantly more time to uncover.

The time between Warren Buffett's early years (think of investing without computers) and trading stocks around the financial crisis in 2008 (think of investors looking at a screen at green or red charts) shows how digitalization changed for investors. What may be less obvious is how much has changed since the early information age. In the millennium years, it was unimaginable that one person's statement in the media could cause share prices in the world to fall or rise by more than 10%.

The effect on share prices after President Donald Trump changed US tariff policies has confronted everyone with a new reality: data originating outside the world of finance—social media posts can, after all, be collected in real time and added to trading algorithms as a decision factor—sometimes affects share prices more than financial data. In the future, we might screen social media for significant messages like we study charts for investment decisions.

Social media data is just one subcategory of the generic nonfinancial data category. Let's explore more categories of nonfinancial data to help us gain insights about possible share price movements. When exploring different categories of nonfinancial data, we'll discover that one difference between financial and nonfinancial data is that different categories of nonfinancial data sources have different relevance for various sectors and industries. Social media data is, in most cases, more relevant to consumer-oriented companies than companies that focus on business-to-business (B2B) solutions. This separates nonfinancial from financial data sources because the latter includes sources that everyone must provide. In other words, serious investors might skip social media analysis but not numbers in the balance sheets.

> **Structured trend analysis**
>
> Controversial topics make some debaters' blood boil. Let's take nuclear energy as a reference. Opponents claim that building nuclear power plants takes a long time and is costly. They also warn about the dangers of atomic meltdowns and raise concerns that nuclear waste threatens future generations. Proponents of nuclear energy praise the constant flow of energy as an addition to the volatile energy from renewables and advocate for the energy density of nuclear power plants.

> *(continued)*
>
> If you put opponents and proponents in a room, the chances are high that debates will be heated. Those who fight for their cause want to win debates, either out of years-long conviction that has blinded them or because they represent a lobby. You might not gain any meaningful insights if you listen to debates.
>
> Investors can explore trends instead by using nonfinancial data: How many new nuclear power plants are being built? How many papers about nuclear energy have been written? What do research papers say about the future energy demands of data centers? How do the prices of companies on the stock exchange that focus on nuclear energy change? Collecting that information is feasible and can be added as a factor to algorithms.

### 11.1.1 Big data by example

Beyond fundamentals and technicalities, additional data sources will broaden our perspective on asset investability. This exploration leads to many different data sources and use cases, which we can group by sectors and industries. They are more complex to use than the data that is available out of the box. An overview of the possibilities of enriching data models with financial data can still be beneficial, as access to rare data in a treasury may be the differentiator that determines profit or loss.

> **Is big data equal to a big company?**
>
> Many data sources can help us gain valuable insights. For example, satellite imagery or data from telecommunications providers can reveal movement trends. But does this mean we need to be part of a large corporation to access such data?
>
> Not necessarily. Some datasets are available for purchase through marketplaces such as AWS Data Exchange or Snowflake Marketplace. If you're a programmer developing analytical models, selected paid external data sources can be useful. However, because we don't want to require you to subscribe to commercial data services, this section remains more theoretical than others in this book.

Investment management company Renaissance Technologies (RenTech) started collecting data early, which may be one reason for its success. Still, we shouldn't collect data for the sake of collecting data. We need to develop an investment thesis, and once we've explored all the fundamentals, we need to consider what additional information is required to validate our thesis. Next, we examine how to obtain the data.

We can hypothesize that Google's share price will soar in the upcoming years due to Waymo. Some may even speculate that Waymo's success will affect Google like the iPhone did Apple. We can read up on articles stating that Waymo could become a cash cow. But articles are just one-time opinions. We need to find data sources that prove the growing importance of Waymo:

- Hard facts on the number of drives per week
- Rollouts of new Waymo services to new cities
- Reduced number of reports on robotaxi accidents

Let's see how we can collect this information. The sections are intended to give you some ideas on how to add specific details to your models. In some cases, this also means investing in external data sources, as many insights might not be available through free data sources.

#### MEDIA

We get most of the media information from the web. We can collect information from various sources, such as social media, traditional media, and blog posts, using crawlers and APIs. We can also transcribe video data to text.

We can learn more about trends using a vast pool of information on Waymo: Is Waymo mentioned more often over time? In what context is Waymo mentioned? How positive was the mood when people talked about Waymo? Are the deployments to new cities on time?

> **NOTE** Human emotions are a category of nonfinancial data. The CBOE Volatility Index (VIX) is a popular measure of the stock market's expectation of volatility based on S&P 500 index options. There are many engaging scenarios matching sentiments in the media with price changes from that index.

#### MOVEMENT DATA

We can use geolocation and movement data to explore what is happening in an area. Using satellite and webcam images, we can count objects, such as different car brands on the streets, if we have computer vision skills. Knowing the growth rate of Waymo cars in certain areas will give us additional insights into their overall success.

You might wonder if collecting and analyzing "exotic data" is worth the additional effort. Even with the vast amount of satellite data available, running computer vision algorithms and training models to identify specific objects correctly requires significantly more effort than exploring mainstream data.

The efficient market theory says that the share prices of one company represent the total information available to all investors. Engineers who find ways to collect and analyze data not available to everyone may have a way to get a competitive advantage as investors. Never underestimate the value of "underrepresented" data.

#### DEMOGRAPHIC DATA

Demographic data tells you about the demands of a population. As a long-term investor, you see more demand for hearing aids than for skateboards if statistics tell you that the population in an area is aging.

The demand for Waymo services may follow demographic developments. Autonomous driving can be popular with teenagers who aren't allowed to drive themselves, and it can even be an incentive for them to postpone a driver's license if they start using robotaxis. Think also about handicapped and older adults who might face challenges driving themselves.

One core thesis is that using robotaxis is part of a mindset shift, and that we can detect this mindset shift in people. If we evaluate the data, we can gain insight into the behavior of target groups.

## 11.2 Catalysts

In finance, a *catalyst* is a trigger that propels the price of a stock dramatically up or down. Earning reports, new analyst ratings on stocks, product announcements, legislative changes, lawsuits, mergers and acquisitions, bankruptcy declarations, and the involvement of activist investors are good examples.

A catalyst is an opportunity to buy or sell positions when we expect the share price to change more than usual. Anyone interested in quantitative or algorithmic trading may focus on specific catalysts and build models specifically created for them.

### 11.2.1 Mergers and acquisitions

Nothing lasts forever, and everything with a beginning also has an end. In business as in life, growth is followed by maturity, saturation, and eventually decline. Some see the cycle of life and rebirth even as a philosophical principle far beyond business. One principle is that, in the end, everything is just a transformation. Figure 11.2 outlines a business life cycle with multiple phases. Imagine a company that has a stunning product idea. As it enters the market, many customers want to own that product, and this company grows and reaches maturity.

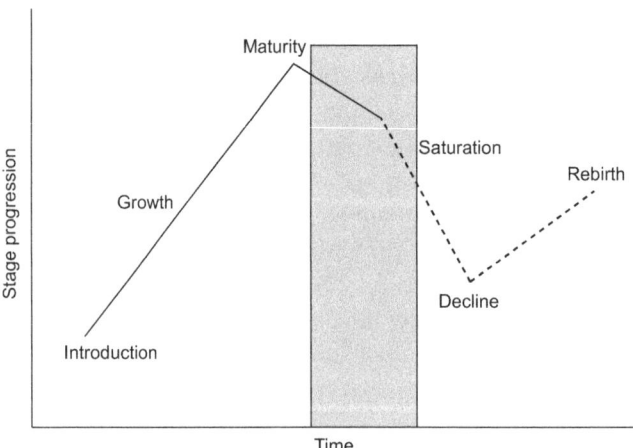

Figure 11.2 How companies might evolve. The shaded area marks a window of opportunity. A merger or acquisition can rescue a company in decline.

Many companies face competitors over time unless they have a strong economic moat. New rivals enter the market, and at some point, the sales growth of key products starts to slow down. Everyone is clear that without a new hit, the company will be unable to keep up with its past performance.

Some companies may lack the resources to revive themselves in a market saturated with competitors. Maybe they've lost too much money to have a proper R&D budget for the next big thing in their products and services. In the corporate world, *mergers and acquisitions (M&A)* are one strategy to prevent decline if you don't have enough resources to reinvent yourself. The executives may see a chance for an early revival by joining forces with another company, either by merging or by acquisition.

The idea of a merger is *1 + 1 = 3*; that is, the combined entity with all possible synergies is more potent than the sum of its parts. By merging two companies with complementary products, they expand their offerings and streamline operations. An acquisition is more one-sided: a larger company absorbs a smaller one, integrating it into its structure, for example, Microsoft acquiring GitHub while keeping it distinct within its corporate structure.

For investors, M&A events represent both opportunities and risks. When a company is announced to be acquired, its stock price often surges, benefiting existing shareholders. If two public companies merge, investors might see long-term value creation. Most mergers look excellent on paper, but what happens when two distinct corporate cultures, operational systems, and management styles clash? What if employees resist the integration? Not all M&As deliver the expected value; some even destroy shareholder wealth instead of creating it.

> **NOTE** An investor might assume that the executives will prevent a merger if they believe a cultural mismatch exists. For some executives, an exit is a successful end of an era, and all the troubles will be passed on to a successor. Therefore, whether all executives involved in a merger or acquisition always have altruistic goals in mind is doubtful.

We can build models that focus on M&As and try to determine the key parameters that indicate success or failure. In the preceding section, we talked about nonfinancial data. Many data sources tell us if an M&A is successful. We can, for instance, analyze sentiment data in blog posts and comments. We might find the insights we need if we can access data from LinkedIn, Glassdoor, or other providers of employees' sentiment.

### 11.2.2 Companies in distress

"Cigar butt investing" is an investment strategy famously associated with Warren Buffett's early years, inspired by his mentor Benjamin Graham. It's like finding a discarded cigar on the ground, taking one last free puff, and throwing it away. It's a hazardous approach, and Warren Buffett abandoned it. Still, there's an opportunity to make money.

You need to find cheap, discarded assets. You look for deeply undervalued companies, often ignored or struggling, but still have some potential. You buy the stock at a deep discount, wait for a slight rebound, and then sell at a profit. Once the market recognizes the company's fair value and the stock price rises slightly, sell it before its deeper problems surface.

This strategy is like hacking together an old repository to get a quick fix—it can work, but it's risky, inefficient, and not a long-term plan. You look for companies that are close to bankruptcy and explore all the data to find out if there's a way this company can be bought or rebound. Figure 11.3 shows the workflow of a company in distress. The later an investor gets involved, the more risk they face.

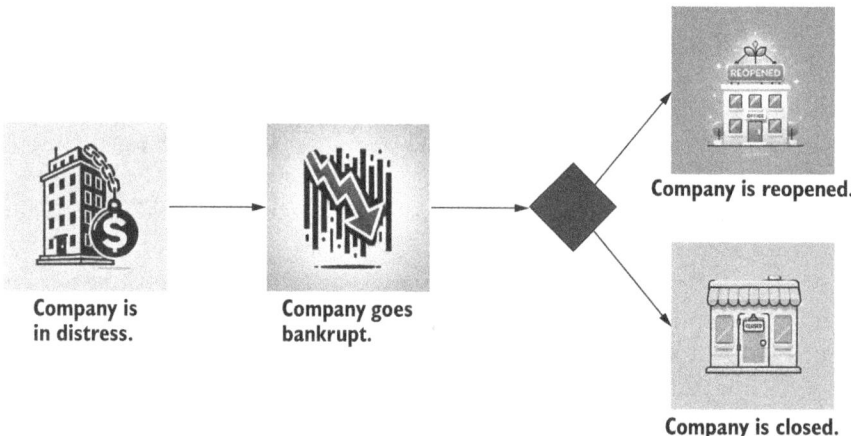

Figure 11.3  The workflow of a company in distress and its possible turnaround depending on its assets

You can look for companies that filed for bankruptcy. Some may have a *stalking horse agreement*, which is a binding purchase agreement between a seller (often in bankruptcy or financial distress) and an initial bidder. This agreement sets the floor price and terms for an asset sale in a competitive bidding process, ensuring the asset isn't sold for too little. Many shareholders might want to liquidate their positions because of a bankruptcy, fearing they could lose everything. If you believe that a company in distress is interesting enough and that competitors are interested in acquiring it, you can buy when the share price is at its bottom and try your luck. Just be aware that this can go wrong, even with intensive research, and you might lose these assets completely.

> **WARNING**  You'll find some examples of companies that went bankrupt yet managed a turnaround, generating huge gains for risk-taking investors. Just keep in mind, these cases are rare—in most bankruptcies, equity is wiped out as creditors assume ownership.

### 11.2.3  Earnings calls

Every company has quarterly earnings calls, during which executives discuss the past quarter. Depending on the company, stocks can move quite a lot. The central question is whether the company met its earnings expectations. If so, how big was the surprise, positive or negative? Executives might also discuss many topics during earnings calls besides earnings. Taking the transcript of an earnings call and running a sentiment analysis can be insightful.

One way to prepare for earnings calls is to start researching a few days before. For example, you should explore when executives last acquired or sold their shares, which could indicate a possible move. You can also find many online reports about new or closed deals of that company to predict an *earnings surprise*, which refers to diverging from the expected earnings.

One question is whether to trigger an order during an earnings call or beforehand. You can imagine that some investors might listen to the call for insights on prepared orders to buy and sell; when a message indicates possible price movements, they will place an order. So, if you have a strong intuition, you can buy or sell in advance.

> **Earning calls strategies**
>
> If you're bold, consider a leveraged purchase ahead of likely significant price movements. If your broker allows leverage of, let's say, $500,000, and you bet on a share that rises by 10%, you'll earn $50,000 in a day. However, you could also evaporate $50,000 in one day if the price decreases by 10%. Many investors advise against leveraged orders, even if they feel confident about the company's performance. After all, the market is unpredictable. NVIDIA has made numerous record-earning calls, yet investors remain cautious, fearing that NVIDIA might be overvalued; if the gains fall short of expectations, they may still decide to sell.
>
> Another way of approaching earnings calls is to trade options instead of shares. They provide leverage with lower up-front costs. If you buy options, your risk is clearly defined, as you know in detail what you spend on your premium. You can also use specific option strategies to net on increased volatility without predicting the exact direction of the stock's move.
>
> Primarily, if you focus on small and midsize companies, where more volatile and more surprising developments are possible, trading options can feel like casino-style gambling.

### 11.2.4 Disasters

The COVID-19 pandemic was a game changer on the stock market. The shares of many companies fell rapidly. There were notable exceptions, however. Examining biotech companies such as Moderna and Pfizer reveals significant profits, as evidenced by their share price history.

With every disaster, there are winners and losers. Natural catastrophes, such as wildfires and hurricanes—we'll see more of them thanks to climate change—may challenge businesses, such as insurance companies. Companies that produce solutions to mitigate catastrophes, such as companies that help with early wildfire detection, will benefit. Wars challenge the economies of countries that are involved, directly or indirectly. Looking at the share prices of Rheinmetall, a German defense industry company, underscores that there are also beneficiaries of wars.

You can generate profits by addressing potential upcoming disasters early. You can use momentum or long-term strategies. To clarify the difference, let's consider wildfires as an example. As a long-term investor, you buy shares of companies that help prevent or mitigate wildfires. As climate change worsens, new disasters will boost demand for these solutions. With momentum investing, you can short sell insurance stocks before a major catastrophe happens. Predicting disasters is difficult. Any entrepreneur who can develop such an innovative system will likely get even wealthier by selling their services to governments.

### 11.2.5 Interest rate changes

The relationship between the federal interest rate and the share prices may be one of new investors' most overlooked parameters. We can learn a lot from the past. Alan Greenspan was a Federal Reserve (aka Fed) director who aimed to keep the interest rate low. If the federal interest rate is low, companies can borrow money cheaply, leading to more investments and lower unemployment. Side effects of low interest rates can be manias—some might remember the subprime mortgage crisis of 2008, which was partly also triggered by the availability of cheap money, and higher inflation.

The Fed policies around COVID-19 are a good lesson about the effect of interest rates on share prices. Biotech companies focusing on research, such as Moderna, show a clear picture. During COVID, Moderna did well thanks to high earnings, but the interest rates went up to curb inflation. The share prices of capital-intensive companies, including Moderna, struggled after the pandemic.

One strategy is buying capital-intensive shares when interest rates are high but share prices are low. When the Fed lowers interest rates, the shares of capital-intensive companies will likely go up. There's a big catch, though. Some capital-intensive companies that haven't secured a stable cash inflow are at risk of bankruptcy during high interest rates.

> **NOTE** If you're a freelancer programmer, you might have noticed that you receive more offers on average when interest is low. Companies prefer not to spend money when borrowing is expensive. LLM prompts such as "What is the outlook for freelancers to get new gigs based on the current economic situation, and when will it improve?" can be used for deeper research.

## 11.3 Trading algorithms

By continuously screening for data spikes—such as shifts in public sentiment or unusual price movements—we can establish rule-based trading strategies:

- If X happens, we buy.
- If Y happens, we sell.

The key is defining what X and Y are. X and Y must be quantifiable, as an algorithm must determine if the buy or sell event has been reached.

Before hunting for X and Y, let's first focus on validating results. Any programmer familiar with test-driven development (TDD) understands the importance of defining validation criteria before implementing logic. Even the most sophisticated strategies risk being unreliable or misleading without a solid validation framework.

### 11.3.1 Backtesting

Backtesting evaluates trading strategies using historical data. Let's illustrate this concept with an example. In the chapter on technical analysis, we explored moving averages and observed that a simple moving average (SMA) crossover can serve as a buy or sell signal. This strategy involves calculating two SMAs with different time windows based on a stock's closing price:

- When the shorter-period SMA crosses above the longer-period SMA, it signals a buy.
- When it crosses below, it signals a sell.

Let's test this strategy with historical prices. To begin, we need generic methods. The first step is adding SMA calculations to a DataFrame of historical prices. As we'll use SMAs with different time windows within a DataFrame, we must also validate if the SMA with a specific time window has already been added, as shown in the following snippet:

```
def add_sma(df: pd.DataFrame, lower: int, upper: int) -> pd.DataFrame:
    if f'sma_{lower}' not in df.columns:
        df[f'sma_{lower}'] = df.Close.rolling(lower).mean()
    if f'sma_{upper}' not in df.columns:
        df[f'sma_{upper}'] = df.Close.rolling(upper).mean()
    return df
```

Let's explore the backtesting method shown in Listing 11.1. We pass a DataFrame containing historical data loaded from a yfinance ticker object. Additionally, we specify parameters for the lower and upper periods of the SMAs and the number of shares to trade. We define a Boolean parameter to trigger a buy order on the first trading day to make tests more comparable with other results.

> **NOTE** In this backtesting strategy, we'll sell or buy a predefined number of shares. After one signal, we wait for a reverse signal as the following action, and we don't trigger the same signal twice in a row. We can repeat the same orders in intervals, including short selling for advanced scenarios. We can also adjust the number of shares to trade. But let's keep things simple.

**Listing 11.1  Backtest**

```
def backtest(df: pd.DataFrame, lower: int, upper: int, shares : int,
   buy_first_day = False) -> pd.DataFrame:
      schema={'date': 'datetime64[ns]', 'action': 'str', 'cash_movement':
'float64'}
      results = pd.DataFrame(columns=schema.keys()).astype(schema)
```

```
        if buy_first_day:
            results.loc[len(results)] = [df["Date"].iloc[0], "Buy",
df["Close"].iloc[0] * shares * -1]
            waiting_for_bear = True
        else:
            waiting_for_bear = False

    for index, row in df.iterrows():
        if not waiting_for_bear:
            if row[f"sma_{lower}"] > row[f"sma_{upper}"]:
                results.loc[len(results)] = [row.Date, "Buy",
                    row.Close * shares * -1]
                waiting_for_bear = True
        if waiting_for_bear:
            if row[f"sma_{lower}"] < row[f"sma_{upper}"]:
                results.loc[len(results)] = [row.Date,
                                             "Sell",
                                             row.Close * shares]
                waiting_for_bear = False
    if waiting_for_bear:
        results.loc[len(results)] = [df["Date"].iloc[-1], "Sell",
df["Close"].iloc[-1] * shares]
    return results
```

Let's run some tests. We want to use a fixed amount of money in a target currency as a benchmark to compare the performance of different stocks. We calculate the number of stocks to buy from this initial investment sum. The higher the share price, the fewer shares we would buy.

We need a baseline to measure our strategy's success: the difference between the shares bought on the first day of the plan and those sold on the last day of the strategy. We also need to account for transaction costs. If we spend $1 for one transaction, we can subtract the number of transactions from the total gains of our SMA strategy. If an SMA strategy leads to better results than this, it's successful.

### Does company outlook matter?

In the following reference example, we start backtesting with NVIDIA. One argument could be that using NVIDIA might not be a good choice, as NVIDIA has been one of the most successful companies in recent years. Would it make more sense to use a company whose performance is cyclical?

We'll look at more companies in this chapter, but starting with a successful one helps us establish a baseline. People who follow long-term investment strategies try to pick companies with a good outlook based on strong past earnings and economic moats. Traditional long-term investors don't touch their investments for years. So, what does it mean if we learn that with a trading strategy, we can make the returns of a company that already provides good returns even better?

> We'll contrast this strategy of using NVIDIA with other companies and then see if we can develop a more generic idea of whether trading algorithms make sense. One small spoiler alert: the answer is—as you might have expected—it depends. For decades, traders and investors have debated whether sophisticated trading strategies lead to better investment results, and so far, there's no clear winner in this debate.

We'll execute a test for NVIDIA using $1,000 and calculate 10 years of data. In this first test scenario shown in listing 11.2, we take 10 trading days for a lower SMA window and 20 trading days for the upper time window.

Listing 11.2 Executing a single backtest

```
def run_single_backtest(ticker: str, cash, start_date: str, end_date: str,
transaction_costs = 1) -> pd.DataFrame:
    df = load_data(ticker, start_date, end_date)
    shares = round(cash / df["Close"][0])
    print(f"Shares: {shares}. start price: {df["Close"][0]}. end price: "
        f"{df["Close"].iloc[-1]}. to beat: {df["Close"].iloc[-1]*shares -
                                            df["Close"][0]*shares -
                                            transaction_costs}")
    df = add_sma(df, 10, 20)
    res = backtest(df, 10, 20, shares, True)
    gain = res['cash_movement'].sum()
    gain = gain - transaction_costs * len(res['cash_movement'])
    print(f"Gains: {gain})")
    return df
results_nvda
 = run_single_backtest("NVDA", 1000, "2015-01-01", "2025-01-01")
```

Looking into the console output, we can buy 2,070 shares on January 1, 2015. We calculate that this leads to a performance to beat of $276,980, which is quite impressive for 10 years. There's a small caveat, though, that we need to highlight: NVIDIA went through stock splits. This means the initial NVIDIA stocks at the beginning of January 1, 2015, didn't cost $0.48.

Running this simulation, it turns out that an SMA10/SMA20 crossover strategy is unsuccessful. We would have made $177,960 in 10 years, clearly below $276,980.

Let's see if we can do better with other time window parameters. To do this, let's create a DataFrame that provides parameter combinations:

```
x = pd.DataFrame(np.arange(10, 210, 10))
test_params = pd.merge(x,x,how='cross')
test_params.columns = ['sma_lower','sma_upper']
test_params = test_params[test_params.sma_lower < test_params.sma_upper]
```

We can now adjust the method to run the same test with various time windows, starting with 10 (the lowest) and 200 (the highest). Listing 11.3 shows the same logic as with single runs, just with a `for` loop in between that uses all configurations.

### Listing 11.3 Executing multiple backtests

```
def run_multiple_backtests(ticker, investment_sum = 1000):
    schema={'lower': 'int64', 'upper': 'int64', 'gain': 'float64'}
    results = pd.DataFrame(columns=schema.keys()).astype(schema)
    df = load_data(ticker, start_date)
    shares = round(investment_sum / df["Close"][0])
    print(f"Shares: {shares}. start price: {df["Close"][0]}. end price: "
        f"{df["Close"].iloc[-1]}. to beat: {df["Close"].iloc[-1]*shares -
            df["Close"][0]*shares}")
    for n,m in test_params.values:
        df = add_sma(df, n, m)
        res = backtest(df, n, m, shares)
        gain = res['change'].sum()
        results.loc[len(results)] = [n, m, gain]
    sorted_results = results.sort_values(by='gain', ascending=False)
    return sorted_results
ticker = "NVDA"res_nvda = run_multiple_backtests(ticker,
    investment_sum = 1000)
res_nvda
```

While we learned that a setup using SMA10 and SMA20 doesn't beat the baseline for our initial test, a different setup does. Table 11.1 shows the five best results for NVIDIA. With a maximum of $309,821.27, we can beat the strategy of buying low on the first trading day and selling high later.

Table 11.1 The results of various SMA crossover strategies for 10 years of NVIDIA historical share prices

| SMA low window | SMA high window | Gains ($) |
|:---:|:---:|:---:|
| 90 | 120 | 309,821.27 |
| 100 | 110 | 301,097.67 |
| 60 | 160 | 300,504.11 |
| 50 | 110 | 298,242.05" |
| 50 | 180 | 297,201.84" |

Let's test this code with other company data. As we show in table 11.2, this strategy worked four out of five times using the best parameters. Again, there are some uncertainties. If on the first trading day—when the algorithm needs to purchase shares—the share prices were at a peak but were at a low on the selling day, we might have a distorted result.

An SMA crossover strategy doesn't beat the baseline for every asset. It's also essential to highlight that, depending on the brokers we use, we might need to adjust the transaction costs per order. One parameter that we haven't touched at all is taxation. Every time you sell, you create capital appreciation, which can be taxable depending on your residency.

Table 11.2 The results of running the backtests with shares of some companies

| Ticker | Lower SMA | Upper SMA | Gain ($) | To beat |
|---|---|---|---|---|
| KO | 100 | 110 | 664 | 1,042 |
| MMM | 120 | 190 | 810 | 310 |
| PFE | 110 | 180 | 1243.55 | 312.55 |
| AAPL | 160 | 170 | 10,136.21 | 9258.81 |
| MSFT | 80 | 140 | 10,240.63 | 9514.61 |

**NOTE** If you prefer to code less, you might look at platforms such as WorldQuant BRAIN. These platforms often provide data and a scripting language to define alpha candidates based on logic, such as our if statements in the code. Users can also trigger automated backtests. For some, their approach looks like shooting with cannons at data. From a pool of potential candidates, select well-defined buy and sell conditions and test them until you find conditions that have been successful in the past. Compute or license costs may apply when using these platforms.

In the next section, we'll also address another detail that can affect the outcome of these backtests. In these backtests, we buy using the close price, but the question is the price we might get. Stock prices are volatile during the day, and there's always a spread between the ask and bid price, meaning we might not get the theoretically best price.

In the next section, we'll explore how to buy and sell stocks at a minimum price using limit orders. Before we go into the details of orders, let's close the topic of algorithmic trading by looking into complex rules.

### 11.3.2 Complex trading signals

To illustrate basic algorithmic trading, we used an SMA crossover strategy to find profitable trading signals. Let's explore alternative trading signals to decide whether to buy or sell shares.

We use two clauses in our Python code to decide whether to buy or sell shares. If we replace if row[f"sma_{lower}"] > row[f"sma_{upper}"] with a method isBuySignal(args), and exchange the clause to sell in the same way, we can host a more complex logic to evaluate buy and sell decisions.

We can screen data for trading signals daily or even in a shorter time. These signals don't have to be related directly to the company whose shares we trade. We might also evaluate indicators that indicate geopolitical challenges (e.g., if a president announces another round of tariffs, we might be inclined to sell assets that would be affected by it). Let's define quantifiable trading signals as method declarations as reference examples. These trading signals can also be combined with technical indicators such as the SMA:

- `def price_movement_score(assets: list)` #—If the assets in the parameters move positively, return a buy signal; otherwise, return a sell signal.
- `def keyword_score(channels: list, keywords: list, upper, lower)` #—If the score surpasses the upper threshold, buy; if it's below the lower threshold, sell.
- `def insider_score()` #—This calculates a score based on insider trades (institutional investors or executives of a company buying or selling shares).

**NOTE** Investors trading with cryptocurrency can group cryptocurrency owners by the number of tokens they hold as the blockchain is a public data source that identifies holders with an ID. If traders who own a lot of tokens unstake them, they are likely to sell them, which can be a strong sell signal.

We can collect and combine multiple scores from signals such as the preceding examples via a scorecard for decision-making. The precondition for each score is that it's quantifiable and comparable with earlier results.

> **Comparable parameters and historical data**
>
> Using natural language processing, we can create sentiment scores for keywords from text we collect from different sources. We can use a web crawler or APIs to collect the content. Therefore, we can also determine how moods change if we keep parsing the same sources over time. What yields a result one day can yield one another day as well.
>
> However, media sources change over time. We might even lose access to some and gain access to new ones. The challenge is that the pool from which we collect data changes over time; therefore, comparing new results with past results will be more complex.

We can experiment with different signal combinations and use backtesting algorithms to see which combination of signals leads to the best results. Of course, we can also collect the signals in an analytical data set, each signal represented in a column, and using historical data, we can run supervised ML algorithms to train the model for good trading strategies. As mentioned, ML algorithms have a high risk of overfitting, and past results don't always guarantee future results.

**CAUTION** Traders need to be aware of potential costs during trading. *Slippage* is the difference between where the computer signaled the entry and exit for a trade and where actual clients, with actual money, entered and exited the market using the computer's signals. In addition, transaction costs might add up if we have frequent orders, and we must never forget that there's a spread for each trade.

We can increase the complexity by using parameters other than trading signals. For instance, we can adjust the number of shares to trade based on decision parameters. If we have a higher risk tolerance, we can allow leverage to buy shares, meaning we would borrow money to execute a transaction and use short-sell strategies.

Entering advanced trading strategies using algorithms can be compared to entering professional boxing and the ability to challenge every fighter without restrictions. With a lot of training, you can win fights and get rich. But otherwise, if you end up a bold lightweight amateur boxer challenging a heavyweight champion, you can have regrets.

## 11.4 Orders

Let's examine orders, as we want to trigger orders automatically using Python. We'll first discuss the difference between exchanges and brokers, and then we'll explore the two brokers' APIs.

### 11.4.1 Exchanges vs. brokers

Figure 11.4 outlines what we've learned so far. Exchanges sell assets. With direct access to an exchange, we can purchase from the source. However, we usually need a broker to execute orders and hold our shares in the stock and bond markets. A stockbroker is an intermediary between investors and exchanges.

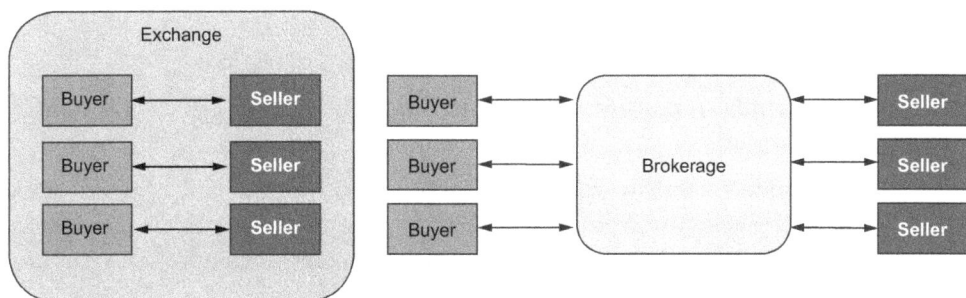

Figure 11.4  On an exchange, sellers and buyers can interact directly. A broker is an entity between a buyer and a seller. A broker usually facilitates trading on one or more exchanges.

Stockbrokers differ by the number of exchanges they support. They will likely support popular US exchanges such as the NYSE or NASDAQ. Most will also support other popular exchanges such as the DAX, London, or Nikkei. But what about emerging markets? Not every broker supports every stock exchange from every country. Conditions might differ for each exchange, which includes data actuality (some data is provided with delays) and fees.

A crypto exchange differs fundamentally from a stock market exchange. For example, following are some characteristics of a stock market exchange:

- Stock market exchanges are highly regulated marketplaces where investors buy and sell shares of public companies.

- A public company is listed on a primary stock exchange. For example, NVIDIA is listed on the NASDAQ in the United States, which is regulated by the Securities and Exchange Commission (SEC).
- Companies may also be traded on secondary stock exchanges—for instance, NVIDIA shares can be traded on Frankfurt/Xetra—but investors globally can trust that NVIDIA must comply with US regulations and undergo independent audits required by its primary listing.

In contrast, *crypto exchanges* are mostly private companies, often incorporated in tax havens or jurisdictions with light financial oversight. As a result, individual governments typically can't enforce the same regulatory protections as they do for public companies. Investor protection is weak: users may have little legal recourse if an exchange misuses customer funds or fails to maintain proper accounting.

Some countries require crypto exchanges to establish local legal entities to serve their citizens (e.g., within the European Union or Japan), introducing a degree of governance and investor protection. However, the risk remains high, particularly for global exchanges that operate in lightly regulated environments. Many investors have lost substantial funds by trusting unregulated platforms or chasing speculative gains.

The core function of a crypto exchange is to provide an online platform that enables the trading of cryptocurrencies. Their APIs handle the following:

- Placing and matching trades
- Storing digital assets (custody)
- Signing transactions on the underlying blockchains of each supported cryptocurrency

Unlike public company stocks, which are listed on a limited number of exchanges, cryptocurrencies are typically available on most major crypto exchanges. This makes them globally liquid but also subject to fragmented regulation and varying levels of operational quality.

> **High-frequency trading**
>
> *High-frequency trading (HFT)* uses algorithms and advanced technology to execute a high volume of trades in fractions of a second, profiting from small price inefficiencies or arbitrage opportunities. If done right, a trader can benefit from tiny price movements and liquidity provisions repeated thousands of times daily. The success depends a lot on the sophistication of the algorithms, the low-latency infrastructure, and the co-location near stock exchanges. There's a constant operational risk.
>
> You might be fascinated with technology, so it can be helpful to know that HFT exists. However, getting involved in this form of trading also means upgrading infrastructure. Even Python libraries might be too slow to outperform competitors.

### 11.4.2 Order modifiers

Think of the market as an asynchronous system where tasks are queued. You select the execution logic by creating an order object and submitting it. The parameters you pass to that object, such as asking for immediate execution or execution at a specific price, might adjust the performance.

In this section, we look at order types and order modalities, giving you more insights into executing orders so they meet your investment goals. Let's start with order types.

**ORDER TYPES**

Orders can be categorized based on their execution triggers, as described in table 11.3. We can either execute them at once or at a specific price.

Table 11.3  Different order types when buying or selling assets

| Order type | Description |
|---|---|
| Market order | A market order is the "just do it now" approach. It tells a system to buy or sell immediately at the current market price. If we had to shape it into a method, we would use a signature such as executeTradeImmediately(ticker, amount). We pass the ticker and the amount to the system, and the transaction will be executed next. |
| Limit order | Sometimes, we prefer an order to be executed if a price reaches a certain level. This is the domain of the limit order. In a code analogy, we can see it as executeTradeWhen(price <= targetPrice): If the price reaches the target price threshold, execute the trade. |
| Stop order | Stop orders, also known as stop-loss orders, help to manage risks. You can create stop orders to protect yourself against losses. They trigger a market order when a price falls below a given level. Translated to code, it would be a method such as triggerTradeWhen(price <= stopPrice). |
| | Imagine you hold shares at $100 and are afraid that a catalyst may hit the market and your stock may plummet. If you make a stop-loss order at $90, your stocks will automatically be sold when they fall below $90. |
| Stop-limit order | A stop-limit order triggers a limit order when a price is reached. As a combination of stop and limit orders, we can define this method as follows: triggerLimitTradeWhenPriceBetween(limitPrice, stopPrice). |
| | This order carries a risk that the market may move too quickly, leaving your position unsold. Imagine, like in the stop order example, you hold $100. You can make a stop-limit order with a limit price of $89 and a stop price of $90. If the falls from $91 directly to $88, the sell order wouldn't be triggered in a stop-limit order. If then the price went up again to $89.50, the order would be triggered. |
| Trailing stop | Like a self-adjusting algorithm, this order type follows the stock's price movement by a set margin. If the stock price rises, the stop price adjusts; if the stock falls by a set amount, the order is triggered: adjustStopPriceDynamically(trailAmount). |
| | If the price rises, the stop price moves up. If it drops $5 from the peak, it sells. |

#### ORDER MODALITIES

Order modalities are parameters for executing orders, as described in table 11.4. They can be parameters for every order type introduced earlier.

Table 11.4  Order modalities for order types

| Order modality | Description |
| --- | --- |
| Fill or kill (FOK) | When you've bought shares in the past, you might have observed that not all orders are fulfilled at once. Sometimes, you have more than one transaction. The FOK order ensures that the entire order is fulfilled immediately or gets aborted. |
| Good 'til canceled (GTC) | Orders are usually only valid during a trading day. An order submitted with the GTC modality stays active until it's executed or canceled manually. GTC orders are especially valuable for stop-loss orders. Combining a stop-loss order with a GTC ensures that you never go below a certain point, protecting yourself from the effects of a market crash. |
| | GTC doesn't mean "forever." Different brokers set different time limits until a GTC order expires. These expiration time frames are usually between 0 and 90 days after investors placed the orders. Be sure to explore the modalities of your brokers. |

### 11.4.3 Executing orders

Let's use Python APIs to execute orders using Interactive Brokers and Alpaca. We examined both brokers in chapter 6, so we won't explain them again here.

#### INTERACTIVE BROKERS

In chapter 6, we mentioned that we needed to start a local application called the Trader Workstation to use a Python API for Interactive Brokers. The Python API connects to this workstation and executes read operations through this application. We can also buy and sell shares through this connection. The following snippet shows the code to connect to the Interactive Broker's Trader Workstation app:

```
from ib_insync import *
util.startLoop()
ib = IB()
ib.connect()
```

Let's execute orders after connecting to the platform. In the following code, we must pass the parameters about the stock we want to look at to create a contract object:

```
import pandas as pd

def get_data(market_data):
    print(f"Market Data: {market_data.ask}")
    print(f"askSize: {market_data.askSize}")
    print(f"marketPrice: {market_data.marketPrice()}")
    print(f"marketPrice: {market_data.time}")

contract_apple = Stock("AAPL", "SMART", "USD")
market_data = ib.reqMktData(contract_apple)
get_data(market_data)
```

After that, we collect the market data for the shares. The market data also contains the ask price we must pay to purchase the asset. Remember, there's always a tiny spread between ask (buying) and bid (selling) prices, as this is how brokers make money.

Finally, it's also possible to place market orders. Brokers execute market orders using the current market price. Some investors believe that market orders are fine when you need to be fast and expect the price to only go in one direction:

```
order = MarketOrder(action = "BUY", totalQuantity = 1)
trade = ib.placeOrder(contract_apple, order)
```

A limit order allows an investor to define a minimum cost to buy or sell. In the following code, we execute a limit order with a price of $200. Suppose an investor believes that a share price will fluctuate during the day. In that case, it's often recommended not to buy at the first possible opportunity but rather to buy at a price that is likely to be good during the trading day:

```
order = LimitOrder(action = "BUY", totalQuantity = 1, lmtPrice = 200)
trade = ib.placeOrder(contract, order)
```

One detail of how Interactive Brokers tries to differentiate itself from many other brokers is the number of exchanges this broker supports. As a user of Interactive Brokers, you need to be aware that there are also paid subscriptions for premium services. For some markets, you'll get delayed data without these premium services.

### ALPACA

In chapter 6, we introduced Alpaca as a broker. This broker is developer-friendly and has good APIs. We set the client up using the following code to get an object representing your trading account:

```
from alpaca.trading.client import TradingClient
from alpaca.trading.requests import GetAssetsRequest

k = get_secret("broker.alpaca.key")
s = get_secret("broker.alpaca.secret")

trading_client = TradingClient(k, s, paper=True)
account = trading_client.get_account()
```

Before we start trading, let's parse tradable assets on this platform. The following snippets define search parameters to look for US equity on the NASDAQ exchange whose status is active:

```
from alpaca.trading.enums import AssetClass, AssetExchange, AssetStatus
search_params = GetAssetsRequest(asset_class=AssetClass.US_EQUITY,
    exchange=AssetExchange.NASDAQ, status=AssetStatus.ACTIVE)

assets = trading_client.get_all_assets(search_params)
print(f"{len(assets)} found")
```

Depending on the execution time, you might get different results. When writing this book, this method returns 4,772 tradable stocks.

> **NOTE** In this code, we use the parameter `paper=True`. This setting means that trades are executed in Alpaca only on paper. If you were to remove this parameter, you would trade for real.

Let's find out if a specific stock is tradable by obtaining an asset from the client and then calling the method `tradable` (when writing this book, NuScale Power Corporation [SMR] was tradable):

```
trading_asset = trading_client.get_asset("SMR")

if trading_asset.tradable:
    print(f'We can trade {asset}.')
```

To be able to buy shares, let's find out how much we have to pay per share by getting the asking price. The `ask_price` is a variable of an object that the client returns:

```
from alpaca.data import StockHistoricalDataClient
from alpaca.data.requests import StockLatestQuoteRequest
stock_client = StockHistoricalDataClient(k, s)
quote = StockLatestQuoteRequest(symbol_or_symbols="SMR")
latest_multisymbol_quotes = stock_client.get_stock_latest_quote(quote)
latest_ask_price = latest_multisymbol_quotes[symbol].ask_price
print(latest_ask_price)
```

Let's look at how to execute a market order to buy or sell an asset at the market price. In the following snippet, we execute it as a FOK as specified with the parameter `time_in_force`:

```
from alpaca.trading.requests import OrderRequest
from alpaca.trading.enums import OrderSide, TimeInForce, OrderType

order_request = OrderRequest(
            symbol="SMR",
            qty = 2,
            side = OrderSide.BUY,
            type = OrderType.MARKET,
            time_in_force = TimeInForce.FOK
            )
new_order  = trading_client.submit_order(
            order_data=order_request
            )
```

We can also trigger limit orders using Alpaca, which allows an investor to set a minimum price for buying or selling. In the following snippet, we add a `time_in_force` parameter that validates this order until it's executed or canceled by the user:

```
from alpaca.trading.requests import LimitOrderRequest

limit_order_data = LimitOrderRequest(
                symbol="SMR",
                limit_price=8,
                notional=2,
                side=OrderSide.BUY,
                time_in_force=TimeInForce.GTC
                )
limit_order = trading_client.submit_order(
            order_data=limit_order_data
```

## *Summary*

- The efficient market theory assumes that we can't beat the market because the price results from all the information available to investors.
- Nonfinancial data can be an untapped resource for learning details about assets that other investors don't yet know. It can contain hidden information to beat the market.
- Data such as media, geolocation data, demographics, or trends might tell you much about additional insights that can be added as factors to a model.
- Nonfinancial data isn't as openly available as financial data, which must be reported for public companies. However, you can purchase access to nonfinancial data on some marketplaces.
- A catalyst in equity markets is something that propels the price of a stock dramatically up or down. Catalysts include mergers and acquisitions (M&A), bankruptcy filings, earnings calls, disasters, and interest rate changes.
- M&A means that two companies join forces. Such a big event often creates bigger movements in share prices. Being able to predict successful M&As can be rewarding.
- Bankruptcy is also a profit opportunity if existing shareholders panic and sell their shares too fast. However, it's a considerable risk to bet on a bankrupt company's turnaround. If a stalking horse agreement (a buyer's commitment to buy the resources at a minimum price if an auction doesn't yield a higher price) is in place, risks are lower.
- Every publicly traded company has quarterly earnings calls, during which the executives report on the company's performance. Missing or surpassing the earnings estimates can cause substantial shifts in stock prices.
- Disasters, such as wars and natural catastrophes, affect share prices. Some companies make more profits when disasters happen. Buying shares of them at the beginning of a calamity or selling them before a disaster ends can be a strategy to make profits.
- The Federal Reserve interest (or its equivalent in other countries) defines the interest rate at which it lends money to borrowers. Capital-intensive companies—those that need more external investments to be successful—are more affected by interest rate changes.

- Investing in low-priced capital-intensive companies can be beneficial before the Fed reduces the rate. However, some capital-intensive companies face bankruptcy risks if the interest rates are high.
- You can define algorithmic trading strategies, which you define when you buy and when you sell.
- Backtesting is a way to test buy and sell the strategies you created by validating them using historical data.
- Even if your backtesting strategy is successful, past results don't guarantee future results.
- A simple moving average (SMA) crossover strategy extracts buy and sell signals based on two SMAs with different time windows. SMA crossover strategies don't always return better results than "buy low and sell high" strategies.
- We can add more complex rules to evaluate buy-and-sell decisions in algorithms. Factors are the criteria we might consider for decision-making.
- While we can use Python to program trading algorithms and backtest them, some platforms offer this as a service so that customers don't need coding experience.
- A trader buys assets through a broker, who will purchase them from an exchange. Brokers hold assets in the name of a holder.
- A trader can buy crypto assets directly from an exchange.
- Exchanges and brokers charge commissions per order.
- A market order is to be transacted immediately at the current price.
- A limit order is an order executed at a specific price. The order is canceled if the price isn't reached during a trading day.
- A stop order triggers an order when the share price exceeds a defined stop price.
- A stop limit triggers an order executed when the share price is between a minimum (limit price) and a maximum (stop price).
- A trailing stop order adjusts the stop price. It moves with the market price and is triggered by sharp changes.
- Fill or kill (FOK) is a parameter that determines whether an entire order is executed. The broker won't execute the order in parts.
- Good 'til canceled (GTC) is a parameter for an order that doesn't expire. The person who created it can either execute or cancel it. Some brokers will still mark GTC orders as expired if they aren't executed over an extended period.
- If you set a stop order with a GTC, you can prevent yourself from significant losses when the market collapses.

# Private equity: Investing in start-ups

**This chapter covers**
- Investing in start-ups
- Seeing a start-up's evolution from pre-seed to Series C
- Comparing venture funds, angel syndicates, and sovereign wealth funds
- Addressing valuation, dilution, and scoring

Many programmers contemplate starting a start-up at some point. Even if you haven't considered creating one, you've likely had friends who have. Ambitious development teams can produce impressive products with minimal up-front costs, especially when working without salaries, but eventually, finances become a critical topic of discussion.

Working purely for equity, however, isn't always enough to create a product. Some team members require immediate cash flow to meet living expenses, so salaries or invoicing for their contributions is necessary. While cloud providers may offer attractive starter packages, they typically don't provide unlimited free resources. Additionally, acquiring and servicing clients incurs extra costs.

In this chapter, we turn the tables for those of you considering launching a start-up. Rather than examining start-ups from a programmer's perspective—focused on attracting investors and meeting their expectations—we'll adopt the investor's viewpoint, assessing start-ups from a top-down, scenario-based approach. By investing money in a start-up, an investor receives a portion of the company in return, commonly referred to as equity. As this ownership isn't traded on a public market like a stock exchange, ownership in a start-up is referred to as private equity. Let's delve into how investors evaluate opportunities in private equity that comes from investing money in a start-up.

## 12.1 From idea to initial public offering

Investors have developed a model that illustrates the growth of start-ups, beginning with pre-seed and seed funding and progressing through various stages of development until an initial public offering (IPO). Each stage has specific challenges based on the start-up's evolution. Let's explore these phases. The goal of the subsequent sections is to view them from an investor's perspective and highlight the differences from a founder's perspective.

### 12.1.1 The first minimum viable product (pre-seed)

Imagine your friend Fred finally decides to take the plunge. He's been discussing his start-up idea for months, and now he's ready to create a *minimum viable product (MVP)* to validate it. Fred is committed to programming the backend and business logic, while his cofounder, Lin, a seasoned corporate professional like him, focuses on the frontend.

Neither expects a salary, but they have genuine expenses—such as cloud services, marketing, and sales—that they don't want to shoulder alone. They reached out to family and potential investors. The investors declined, citing high risk, but family members contributed enough to assist with some of the costs.

Now, you meet them and pose the critical questions: How much cash do you need to advance your MVP? And more importantly, what's in it for me if I provide you with at least part of the necessary funds?

If you recognize the potential in Fred and Lin's start-up ideas, you may have a self-serving reason to invest. In 1981, a venture capitalist invested $1 million in a company for a 10% stake in the equity. This company went public in March 1986. Today, that investment would be worth billions of dollars. The company was Microsoft.

Of course, nobody can predict that Fred and Lin will step into the shoes of Bill Gates and Paul Allen, but let's consider a scenario. What if you invested $10,000 for a 10% equity stake, and later someone else invested millions for an additional 10%? Even if Fred and Lin were "just" acquired in five years, this check could transform into life-changing wealth. This is the fundamental power of early-stage investing—recognizing potential before the world does. But before you write that check, let's discuss how to evaluate such opportunities.

> **Don't mistake pre-seed start-ups for lottery tickets**
>
> For pre-seed start-ups, it's tempting to take the easy route when asked for investment. Consider this typical response:
>
> > *Instead of investing money, I'd rather contribute my time and advice. No worries, I don't expect a payment, but if I land a client and help with the basics, maybe you can throw some equity my way?*
>
> Now, let's reframe this. Imagine you buy an old house that needs serious renovations. A friend offers to help but wants 10% ownership in return. Or, another analogy, you have a baby, and another friend offers occasional babysitting, expecting to be named a godparent.
>
> When approached for pre-seed investments, offering advice or minimal efforts for equity is like trying to buy a lottery ticket. The chances of betting on a unicorn are as low as winning the jackpot, but it still feels tempting to try one's luck occasionally. The problem is that it just doesn't work this way.
>
> Start-ups demand full commitment. To be part of the journey, you need *skin in the game*—either capital or sustained, mission-critical effort. The latter is tricky to measure: one friend might work for months and contribute nothing valuable, while another might deliver a game-changing feature in a day.
>
> Money, however, is clear-cut. The size of their checks easily compares to investors' contributions. Everyone understands the risk—if the start-up fails, the investor loses money. That risk justifies compensation. But expecting a meaningful stake simply for offering occasional advice? That's wishful thinking.

At the pre-seed stage, personal relationships frequently influence investment decisions. Founders typically approach friends and family first, not only for financial support but also for their endorsement of the vision.

Your perception of the founders plays a crucial role in shaping your understanding of them. Maybe you see Fred as a dreamer who has frequently misjudged situations. You know he has a family and can't just quit his job. How long can he sustain working nights before reality forces him to give up? Or maybe Fred is that rare genius who can make anything happen—the person you'd regret not backing.

Additionally, the perception of the start-up's business model can differ if you're an investor rather than a founder. As a founder, you're naturally more likely to be biased. You may have seen a market from the perspective of someone who has the desire to create something. Regardless, if you want to get rich or change the world, exploring your idea is different from exploring someone else's. You can be hooked on a "why." Perhaps as a founder, you believe in your start-up because you see your development skills as superior to others, or you believe in a yearlong observation that gradually completes a puzzle into a full picture of what the world needs. As an investor, you have a different perspective. Your focus is likely on the business model. The first question isn't how to create a product—it's how likely your investment will gain value. Your observation is narrower on questions such as network effects, scalability, and revenue growth opportunities, so you don't need to worry as much about the details to get there. If you were a founder before and then became an investor, you'll likely be surprised at how your focus changes.

Pre-seed investment is the ultimate high-risk, high-reward game. In many cases, it's just enough cash to get the founders started. Sure, if your start-up founder turns out to be the next Steve Jobs, Bill Gates, or Jeff Bezos, your small check could be life-changing. But statistically, the odds aren't in your favor.

Most of the time, you'll never see that money again. So, the real question is this: Are you betting on a vision or just funding a friend's expensive hobby?

> **The reality of first start-ups and incubators**
>
> If you're young and working on your first start-up, the odds are stacked against you. Most first-time founders fail. Many investors consider a founder's track record of failures a badge of experience. Failure isn't just common—it's expected.
>
> This is where incubators come in. An incubator program is designed to help founders turn an idea into a viable business. They provide office space, mentorship, and resources to help young, ambitious teams "incubate" their start-ups.
>
> A typical incubator welcomes all kinds of founders—some with promising ideas and others who will soon realize their idea isn't viable or that start-up life isn't for them. Over a few intensive weeks or months, start-ups experience highs and lows, setbacks, and breakthroughs. However, the harsh reality is that most incubated start-ups will still fail.
>
> Incubators aren't free to run. They require funding, which can come from multiple sources:
>
> - *Government grants and public funding*—Governments often provide financing for incubators to stimulate innovation.
> - *Corporate sponsorships*—Large companies sponsor incubators to stay close to innovation.
> - *Universities and research institutions*—Many incubators are affiliated with universities, helping students commercialize their research.
> - *Venture capitalists and angel investors*—Some incubators are backed by investors looking for early-stage deal flow.
> - *Membership and service fees*—Some incubators charge start-ups for participation.
> - *Equity stakes*—Many incubators take a small equity percentage in exchange for resources.
>
> For founders, an incubator can be an invaluable learning experience. But for investors? Backing incubator-stage start-ups is a high-risk game—one that requires patience, deep pockets, or a willingness to lose money in search of the next big success story.

### 12.1.2 Validating the business model (seed)

Imagine receiving an invitation to join the panel to judge the final presentations of an incubation program. You find yourself among experienced investors, many of whom have business backgrounds rather than technical ones. If you had looked at their LinkedIn profiles, you would have noticed a common theme—advisory roles, connections with influential leaders, and proud mentions of their experiences with Fortune 100 companies. They speak a different language from the programmers you're used to. They throw around terms such as *venture growth*, highlighting their speaking engagements and subtly (or not) displaying their networks.

The event begins. One by one, start-ups pitch their ideas, following a format that has been drilled into them by their mentors. They know they must discuss TAM, SAM, and SOM (see the NOTE box), as well as other metrics that investors expect to hear. Some pitches are promising, some are uninspiring, and some are downright painful to watch.

> **NOTE** TAM, SAM, and SOM aren't long-lost relatives of Donald Duck. The total addressable market (TAM) represents the global potential market for a product, whereas the serviceable available market (SAM) refers to the audience the product could reach. A serviceable obtainable market (SOM) is the portion of the addressable market that a business is likely to own. One challenge for investors is often the speculative nature of the numbers that start-up founders provide, which typically lack supporting evidence.

Now, the tables have turned. Founders are trying to impress *you*, and suddenly, you see things in a different light. Before you asked angels for investment, you had all the questions other angels might have had about your start-up.

> **The pitch**
>
> The first presenter focuses solely on himself. His team consists of a group of people executing his vision. He believes he has built something amazing and is passionate about his product. But what if you gave him a substantial amount of money? Would his arrogance drive the team away? If no one challenges him, would he crash and burn his one-person show?
>
> Another team takes the stage, but its pitch is filled with uncertainty. Their voices rise at the end of every sentence as if they constantly question themselves. There's nervous laughter, hesitation, and zero confidence. Imagine Rocky Balboa's victory pose—then picture the exact opposite. That's them. Deep down, they don't believe they deserve investment, and you can feel it.
>
> Another founder tries to tell an elaborate story but loses the audience within the first minute. Even the incubator instructors look confused. You watch, waiting for clarity, but it never comes. At the end of the pitch, you still have no idea what the product does or who the customers are. Trying too hard to be impressive often backfires.

> *(continued)*
>
> Then comes a team that nails its pitch. Their business model makes sense, the market is there, and their growth strategy is solid. This could work. If it goes viral, they could acquire thousands of customers overnight. But then they demo the product, and as an engineer, you can tell right away that they still have a long way to go to have even an MVP. The vision is there, but can they execute?
>
> This is the reality of incubator-stage start-ups. Many won't make it past this stage. Some have potential but still lack key elements. A few might have paying customers—real validation—but they still need to prove they can scale their operations effectively.
>
> From an investor's point of view, you need to make up your mind fast. You invest not just in a product but also in people. And even if you shortlist two or three out of an incubator's cohort, you still need to decide if you want to risk the money you would give them.

At the pre-seed stage, investments are often made by personal friends, family, and close connections who believe in a founder's vision. At the seed stage, the interactions are almost exclusively business-related. Investors want traction, real customers, and a scalable business model. Seed-stage start-ups need the following:

- First customers to validate demand
- First hires to expand capacity
- Proof that an MVP can be replicated at scale

At this point, investors aren't just betting on an idea—they're assessing whether emerging businesses can grow into something big.

> **Accelerator**
>
> You're not in a seed phase unless you've built an MVP and proven serious about turning it into a reality. One of the most significant differences between pre-seed and seed is formal incorporation. You may still operate informally at the pre-seed stage with no formal legal entity in place. However, once you reach the seed stage—especially if you want to invoice clients—you need to establish a company. Incorporation is no longer optional, whether it's an LLC, C-Corp, or another structure.
>
> For many founders, the seed phase is a turning point. Should you quit your day job? If you haven't already, now is the time to decide whether to commit to a full-time role. The seed stage is, therefore, not just about getting investment—it's about speed. You don't want to waste months dragging out an acceleration program or endless fundraising while working a day job. You need to move fast to do the following:
>
> - Start acquiring real customers
> - Prove that your early-stage product gets attention in the market
> - Scale operations to a point where more significant investors take you seriously

> When you have paying customers and a plan to scale further, you're no longer just "working on a start-up idea"—you're running a business. Investors now look at your traction, execution speed, and ability to scale. The question isn't "Is this a great idea?" but "Is this a company that can grow fast and generate returns?"

### 12.1.3 Scaling a start-up: The shift to institutional investment

As a start-up grows, the risk of failure decreases, but at the same time, the funding requirements increase. While individual investors can still back pre-seed and seed rounds, later-stage start-ups require institutional investors to fuel their growth.

Once past the early stages, founders want to focus on their business, but raising money is an art. It requires access to a network of high-net-worth individuals, venture capital (VC) firms, and investment institutions specializing in scaling start-ups.

You might attract investors without going through an investment firm if you're already a known celebrity or industry leader. But for most start-ups, funding isn't just about the money—it's about the network, expertise, and structured investment process that firms provide. Investment firms aren't just check-writers; they act as agents for the start-up, helping with the following:

- *Legal and accounting aspects*—Ensuring investments are appropriately structured and booked
- *Business strategy*—Connecting start-ups with the right talent, advisors, and partners
- *Future fundraising*—Laying the groundwork for later-stage funding rounds

Start-ups follow distinct funding stages, each with a different focus. Let's look at them next.

#### SERIES A: SCALING THE BUSINESS MODEL

The company has not only hired employees but also acquired its first customers, learning how to manage them and continuously provide value. The focus is on refining the business model and scaling the product.

For founders, this is a crucial phase. They must work a lot, and there's still a considerable risk of failure; most likely, the big VC firms aren't yet interested in you. Most Series A companies aren't profitable yet. Investors prioritize growth over profits at this stage. Companies with a higher burn rate—spending their investments more quickly—are especially pressured to advance to the next stage rapidly.

#### SERIES B: SCALING OPERATIONS AND MARKET EXPANSION

The start-up has a solid foundation and proven business model. The leaders shift their focus to expanding into new markets and optimizing monetization. The company's style is evolving. From founders who do everything, the start-up establishes hierarchies and responsibilities.

However, working in a Series B start-up is still demanding. You have more precise goals and more apparent competitive strategies because you've discovered what works in the market and what doesn't. You also know your real competitors on the market, and you need to incentivize your team to work hard to stay ahead.

Investors still prioritize growth, but managing burn rate has become increasingly critical. Investors still accept that the company isn't yet profitable, but they expect to see a clear path to profitability.

**SERIES C: MARKET DOMINATION AND ACQUISITIONS**

When you reach Series C, you should have a stable niche in the market and be regarded as a key player there. In some exceptional cases, especially when your start-up is in a blue ocean market, being a market leader is the key to becoming a unicorn.

The company aims to expand internationally, enhance its technology, and acquire other start-ups. However, the primary goal is still a successful exit. In that case, an exit means that an industry giant acquires the start-up or the start-up goes public through an IPO, which means it becomes a publicly traded company and is listed on the stock market. Investors will benefit significantly from this, as their investment has been successful, and they can reap the rewards.

### 12.1.4 Exits: The final transition

For many developers, discussing start-ups with venture capitalists or serial entrepreneurs can be a valuable and eye-opening experience. Unlike traditional businesses that grow organically, start-ups backed by investors are built with an exit in mind from day one. The term *exit* is often thrown around, but it can mean different things:

- A high-profile acquisition by a larger company
- An IPO that lists the start-up's shares on a public exchange
- A smaller-scale acquisition that occurs when another company acquires a start-up
- A shutdown, which technically is still an exit

A successful exit is selling the company at a profit or transferring ownership to become a publicly traded company. Commonly, every founder celebrates every form of exit, but the successful ones do so more extensively. An exit means that you've started a business and ended it. A shutdown without an acquisition or a fire sale of the start-up is, strictly speaking, an unsuccessful exit, and investors will lose money. However, from a different perspective, taking the risk and becoming a founder is a strong commitment, and many factors—including pure luck—influence how a company will ultimately exit. Therefore, unsuccessful exits—some founders may use the term *successfully failed*—can be a badge of honor for founders. Many investors will value founders who have had only unsuccessful exits more than first-time founders who haven't had any exits. Table 12.1 summarizes the four types of exits, along with a reference scenario, to help us understand what was happening.

Table 12.1  Types of exits (successful and unsuccessful)

| Exit | Reference scenario | Returns |
| --- | --- | --- |
| IPO | Company A is a Series C company. After long talks and planning with investment bankers, they finally announce their IPO. After the IPO, an investor can trade his ownership on the stock market. | High |
| Acquisition | Company B is sold to an industry giant for billions. Direct investors are paid out and make a huge profit. Limited partners (LPs) get their profits minus carry fee and their initial investment paid out. | High |
| Fire sale | Company C is a company in distress but can sell itself to another company. Unlike a successful acquisition, in a fire sale, the buyer's investment is largely to pay off debts. The investors won't receive their full investment back. | Partial |
| Shutdown | Company D is a company in distress but shut down. Unlike in the fire sale, no company wants to acquire the company. Maybe some equipment, such as computers and office equipment, can be liquidated, but investors will likely not receive any money. | None |

But why is an exit so important? Investing in private equity means locking up money for years. Unlike stocks, which can be sold at any time, VC investments are typically illiquid. Investors take extreme risks, and many start-ups fail. Therefore, when a start-up exits successfully, the returns must be substantial to compensate for the failures and inflation. This explains the pressure for speed. For founders, it's essential to understand why hardly any venture capitalist wants to invest in a company that is growing slowly and is already profitable. After all, the dividends are small, and a return on investment over many years isn't what they have signed up for. A company with slow growth expectations doesn't attract the attention of buyers.

If a start-up has no viable business model—something that is often unknown in advance—investors want to fail it quickly so they can refocus their attention on those start-ups with a viable business model. Investors who have enjoyed collaborating with the founding team that reached a later stage might even tell the founders to bring a new horse instead of riding a dead one. A fail-fast culture demands that time be minimized to achieve results and, in some cases, that we be able to try again soon.

From an investor's point of view, if you want to get into VC, you need to shift your mindset. You need to ask different questions, such as these:

- Who has acquired similar start-ups before?
- Who would buy this start-up? (Can this company become attractive to Google, Amazon, Microsoft, Meta, or another giant?)
- Is the start-up building something that fills a real gap that someone will want once it has scaled?
- Is the team valuable?

The last item highlights another practice, known as *acqui-hire*. Some investors might understand that your start-up won't be the one that builds a product to become a market leader. However, at the same time, they recognize an immense shortage of qualified engineers, and a large company may pay millions to secure top engineers on its payroll.

> **NOTE** Often, it doesn't require building a highly profitable start-up, but rather solutions that can become highly profitable in the right hands. For some companies, a start-up with a solid product and capable engineers in a future market, such as quantum computing, can be highly valuable even if it generates no profits.

## 12.2 Investment vehicles

First, let's ask the maybe most fundamental question when deciding whether to invest in start-ups: If you have money, why bet on such a risky venture as start-ups? Blue-chip stocks and diversified exchange-traded funds (ETFs) provide steady growth, dividends, and low risk. And as we've seen in this book, you can hardly go wrong with an index fund. After all, there's a high chance that you'll lose your entire investment in a start-up if it fails (and statistics indicate that 90% of them do).

---

**A deeper dive into private equity**

Private equity refers to investments in privately held companies. While start-ups are the primary focus of private equity investments, investors may also invest in established, private businesses that aren't start-ups. The goal of private equity investments is to acquire a significant stake in target companies, transform them, and benefit from the resulting value increase. The company's ownership is defined in the cap table, which outlines the owners and their shares.

Suppose a company is successful and consequently more highly valued than before. The value of private equity shares usually grows far more in percentage than those invested in large public companies. One reason can relate to the efficient market theory. While the markets have extensive information about public companies, new private companies are largely unknown to investors, and this means their information can't yet be priced.

High rewards come with high risks. If a start-up fails, the money invested is likely gone. Valuation and your eventual return are vague for a long time. Critics see private equity as a form of high and illiquid investment, meaning, unlike stocks in a public company, you can't sell your stocks at any time for a relatively predictable price. So, why do it if you can achieve relatively safe gains by keeping your money in a 10-year index fund?

While institutional investors have, of course, learned to manage risks, for private investors, the primary motivation is often finding the one outlier in a batch of start-ups that are otherwise doomed to fail within the next two to three years. Everything is rooted in the same confidence in buying public stock—you believe you see something others don't see.

Microsoft went public on March 13, 1986, for $21 per share. Through a stock split, that single share would now be equivalent to 288 shares. As of January 31, 2024, one share purchased at the IPO would be worth nearly $120,000. But if you had invested in Microsoft before it went public, you would get one share for even less than $21, and you can calculate many scenarios of how much money you could have made by being one of the first investors in such a company.

Someone needs to bring the next Microsoft to the stock exchange. If we imagine that all venture capitalists disappeared overnight, there would be no new businesses in the market to challenge the status quo. The countrywide innovation cycle would slow down because talented individuals with great ideas would no longer receive funding. A short window of opportunity often exists to launch a new concept in the market. If you're too slow, the opportunity is lost. There's no way innovation at scale can exist without VC.

> **Innovation and corporate business**
>
> Google acquired YouTube in 2005, and Meta acquired WhatsApp in 2014. A fair question is why don't these cash-rich companies build these solutions themselves? Given their talent and funding, wouldn't developing a new messenger or video-sharing platform in-house be easier?
>
> The reality is that many R&D teams of companies focus on refining existing products rather than developing new ones that might disrupt their market. But there's also a practical reason: if only 1 in 100 start-ups manages to be exceptional, an industry giant with superior resources might improve those odds—but even if 5 out of 100 start-ups build stunning products, the company still wastes significant resources. Cash may not even be the constraint, but engineering talent is.
>
> Moreover, corporate engineers often prioritize work-life balance. A start-up demands relentless dedication—something an internal team may struggle to match. Frequently, the founder's commitment to creating something extraordinary can't be matched by any salary. So, while billion-dollar acquisitions might seem extravagant, they often make financial sense when you run the numbers.

Overall, we understand that if we find a future unicorn—a start-up valued at over a billion dollars—there is likely no other investment category in the world that offers returns comparable to those of an investment in a unicorn. For some angels, searching for potentially strong early-stage start-ups may still feel like playing the lottery, but the industry has evolved. Angels often form syndicates to evaluate promising start-ups together, thereby reducing their overall risk of failure. Increasingly, public funds are available for early-stage start-ups as countries recognize that this investment can yield significant returns. Even if founders can't use the pre-seed or seed funding received from a sovereign fund or public investment program, young engineers who strive for success learn valuable lessons along the way, enhancing their worth in the job market.

They may outperform their peers when entering a corporate job with their skills. Let's examine the investment vehicles in detail.

### 12.2.1 Venture capital

Venture capitalists typically focus on start-ups in later stages—Series A, B, and beyond—where risks are lower and returns are still high. However, there are exceptions, such as incubators affiliated with elite universities, where the chances of discovering the next unicorn are significantly higher.

When discussing top-tier venture capitalists, specific names dominate the market, including Sequoia, Andreessen Horowitz (aka AH Capital Management, LLC, or a16z), Accel, Benchmark, Tiger Global, SoftBank, and many more. Be aware that smaller, emerging venture funds are also available.

Let's say you have a five- or six-digit investment amount in your account and want to get in on the next WhatsApp-style deal. Why not simply contact one of these venture capitalists and secure a position? Bad news: it doesn't work that way.

VCs primarily work with institutional investors, including pension funds, sovereign wealth funds, university endowments, and ultra-high-net-worth individuals (e.g., billionaires, rather than retail investors). If you're a billionaire, exceptions might be made. Otherwise, they won't take your call.

The good news is that fund managers run VC funds for large private investors. So, you might not call Sequoia directly and tell them you have some bucks to spare for one specific company, but you can look for pooled investments and find someone who collects investments from wealthy private investors. The minimum investment size is typically $100,000 or more, and it can sometimes exceed millions. There's an annual management fee, most are about 2%. There's a carry fee of 20%, which is a fee that is only paid on profits. If your investment generates $100,000 in profits, $20,000 is allocated to the venture capitalist. You receive the remaining $80,000, minus the initial investment and management fees. Figure 12.1 illustrates this flow of money in a simplified fashion. Remember that every fund will have more limited partners (LPs); in most cases, a fund invests in multiple start-ups. You should also be aware that more than one fund can invest in the same start-up.

Venture funds invest in multiple start-ups in parallel. Some of these companies will be in Series C rounds. Every fund manager will ensure that the founders make a substantial commitment to an exit. After all, fund managers will be pressured by investors, who want to see results for their 2% annual management fees. In most cases, investors will encounter some exits along the way, as the fund typically contains multiple start-ups.

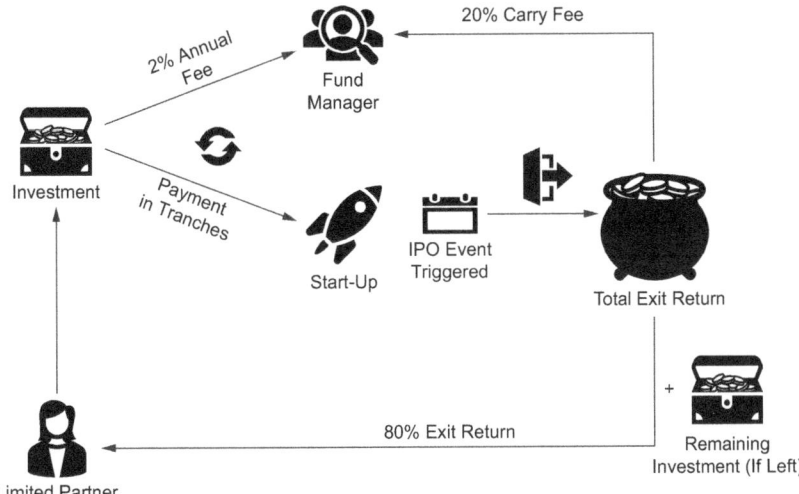

**Figure 12.1** In the simplified money flow, 80% of the profits and your investment, minus the annual fees, will be returned to you.

### 12.2.2 Angel networks

Investing in VC funds requires a substantial amount of capital. But what do you do if you can't afford the minimum ticket size? Does this imply that your chances of investing in a unicorn are slim unless you engage with them during the pre-seed and seed funding stages before institutional investors are on board?

While later-stage start-ups require significantly higher investments, it's still possible to invest in them even with a smaller wallet. Angel investors can form a syndicate. In a syndicate, a seasoned lead investor identifies a start-up opportunity. The syndicate negotiates the terms and determines the amount of capital to raise from LPs.

Angel investors don't have the same reach as established venture capitalists, who often have access to start-up incubators located near elite universities. They can rarely pool investors into a fund. However, angel investors often have a strong network and frequently collaborate with serial investors who cofound start-ups.

> **NOTE** One typical network of angels is a diaspora from a particular country. For example, Armenia has a vast diaspora, especially in California. Many Armenians living in the United States with accumulated capital are attracted to invest in start-ups where the founders are in Armenia. This way, they can combine two things: making money and helping the country they originated from.

So, let's say an angel has negotiated a deal with a start-up in which he wants to invest. The angel might be willing to invest $10,000, $50,000, or $100,000. However, a start-up needs more than that. The angel negotiates a deal with the start-up. The parameters of this deal include the desired check size, the timing of when the money is needed, and the amount of equity the investing entity would receive for that money.

The angel negotiating the deal connects with other angels through a network to become a lead investor in a jointly established *Special Purpose Vehicle (SPV)*. An SPV is a legal entity, typically an LLC, created for a specific investment purpose. In VC, SPVs pool multiple investors into a single entity to invest in a start-up. Instead of each LP appearing on the start-up's cap table, the SPV is the only investor listed, simplifying legal and administrative processes. Therefore, the lead investor's role is to act as an agent (see figure 12.2). He provides capital to the start-up and must manage all the formalities associated with it.

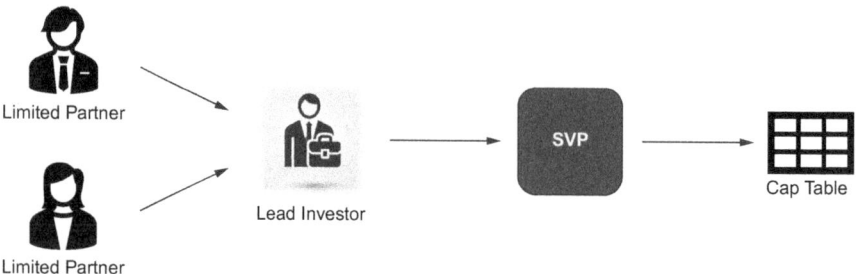

Figure 12.2 A lead investor's job is to represent all investors when forming an SVP that will be registered on a start-up's cap table.

Investors who join the SPV are referred to as LPs within that SPV. Being an LP in the SPV means that, as an individual, you don't own equity in the start-up, but you do have a stake in the SPV. The SPV will be listed in the start-up cap table.

You can search for companies on platforms such as AngelList as an individual investor. You can also reach out to other angels on platforms such as LinkedIn. Angel investors often create a one-pager summarizing the investment opportunity. In this one-pager, you'll find a summary of the company and its value proposition. You'll learn about their story, what made them successful, who the leaders are, and what they want to achieve. The one-pager will outline economic moats and active users, as well as share insights about the management team.

Sometimes, if you approach angels, this one-pager looks more like a sales pitch. The angel list will share details about earlier investment rounds, as they will want to demonstrate that you're not the first to believe in the start-up. The goal is typically an acquisition or an IPO, and the angel syndicate will share success stories of how an industry giant acquired a similar start-up with a comparable product in the past. This suggests that a successful exit can result in billions.

Like a VC, a syndicate looks for a minimum check size. If you exceed this size, you typically increase it in 10k steps. Each round has a closing, meaning the opportunity is gone if you decide too late.

A lead investor, who bears most of the work and expenses to set up the deal, needs to earn a return on their investment. In a VC, you have an annual management fee of

2%. However, with an investment in a single start-up, a yearly charge can become a challenge. Imagine that this start-up needs many years to go public, paying 2% interest nibbles away at much of your investment yearly. For this reason, syndicates often request a one-time payment. This can be around a $7,000 one-time pro rata charge. These charges cover all the expenses of a lead investor, as they also need to incur costs for contracts, travel expenses, and other related expenses to finalize the deal. Rarely is everything done with a quick online call; creating an agreement takes time and experience.

A lead investor who creates a syndicate wants to benefit from the start-up's success. As with venture capitalists, a lead investor often requests a carry fee of 20%. The same rules apply as with VCs in that a carry fee is a charge on profits—no profit, no charge.

> **Founders**
>
> There is a thought experiment commonly attributed to Warren Buffett, which he presented to his students. Imagine you could choose a classmate and receive 50% of that person's future earnings for the rest of your life. Warren Buffett also flipped the questions and asked students to short (bet against) a different classmate, meaning they would have to pay 50% of that person's future earnings. Who would they pick, and why?
>
> This thought experiment can be perfectly attributed to investing in start-ups. Most of what start-ups eventually achieve depends on their founders. If you're required to put skin in the game, you must also ponder what makes someone successful. It might not be intelligence, but traits such as work ethic, integrity, leadership, and resilience.
>
> Some go even further. They say that founders aren't just something to invest in when evaluating a start-up, but *the* key thing. Ultimately, these founders present a business model that will make the venture valuable. Perhaps whenever an investor met Steve Jobs, Bill Gates, Jeff Bezos, and other successful founders, it was hard to say if their ideas would truly bear fruit, as, at that time, nobody knew if personal computers, operating systems, or e-commerce platforms would be successful on the market.

### 12.2.3 Sovereign wealth funds

Some countries' leaders establish Sovereign Wealth Funds (SWFs), state-owned investment funds that manage national wealth. Typically, these funds are sourced from government surpluses, revenues from commodities (e.g., oil, gas, and minerals), or foreign exchange reserves.

These funds can be valuable resources for start-ups. A country lacking natural resources requires investments to establish a start-up ecosystem that can compete internationally. Alternatively, consider petrostates that derive their wealth from oil and gas. These nations often seek to diversify their income sources, as the profits from oil and gas are inevitably finite.

Like VCs, it's rare for individual investors to contribute to an SWF. However, many SWFs focus on developing a start-up ecosystem. You can explore start-ups created through an SWF and engage where it makes sense. From an investor's point of view, you can explore which ecosystems sovereign funds invest in and if you can contribute as well.

## 12.3 Assessing start-ups

Some investment decisions follow gut feelings. A charismatic and energized founder who is determined to do something great can be a decisive factor for an investment decision. After all, a saying goes that you invest as much in people as in the product. And as the start-ups have no history, and founders can't guarantee that their ideas will be successful, how else can we decide but based on instinct?

However, there are various ways to use programming to make educated decisions. We look at some of them in this section.

### 12.3.1 Valuation

Valuing start-ups is different from valuing established companies. Traditional valuation methods, such as price-to-earnings (P/E) ratios or Enterprise Value (EV), rely on stable cash flows and profits. However, many start-ups aren't yet profitable and may have negative cash flow. Instead, investors rely on methods such as:

- *Comparable company analysis (CCA)*—Comparing similar start-ups' valuations
- *Precedent transactions*—Looking at past acquisitions of similar companies
- *VC method*—Estimating exit value based on expected returns
- *Discounted cash flow (DCF)*—Projecting future cash flows based on present value

None of these methods can be used out of the box. We can't apply the CCA method unless we have data on enough start-ups. Using expected returns as a basis is a risky approach. Almost every founder claims impressive figures, and without a critical review, start-ups might be overvalued. Due diligence can be expensive and complicated, as start-ups often lack the sophisticated accounting standards and accounting history of established companies.

While the DCF appears to be the most reliable method, we must still be aware that revenue growth is uncertain, and we continue to face high burn rates and variable expenses. In addition, in the early stages, the business models are often unproven. If it's still unclear how a company generates its revenue, how can we accurately forecast its future cash flow?

> **NOTE** Some start-ups try to do something utterly different, unlike anything that exists on the market. Consider geoengineering solutions to reverse climate change, which involve partly experimental approaches. While such cases require somewhat speculative models, investors still can define business models and estimate potential revenues. They add a markup for the risks of the idea not working.

Despite these challenges, DCF can provide a structured approach to estimating a start-up's intrinsic value. Start-ups typically face high early-stage risk, so discount rates often

## 12.3 Assessing start-ups

range from 20% to 50%, which is significantly higher than those used for established businesses.

Let's build a DCF model in Python, assuming a start-up expects to grow its revenue and eventually reach positive cash flow. We need to set up some assumptions:

- Revenue grows at 30% annually.
- Expenses reduce over time as the start-up scales (10%).
- Terminal value accounts for the long-term value after Year 5.
- The discount rate is 40%, which means you reduce this percentage from the final value to cover the risks.

The cash flow is calculated yearly as revenue minus expenses. Let's look at listing 12.1 for the DCF. We first define the assumptions. Then, we use these inputs to project future earnings and return the results.

### Listing 12.1 DCF using Python

```
import numpy as np

years = 5
initial_revenue = 500_000            ◁  Sets the assumption, such as Forecast period,
growth_rate = 0.3                       Initial revenue ($), 30% annual growth, Initial
initial_expense = 700_000               expense ($), Expenses decrease by 10% per
expense_reduction = 0.1                 year, High discount rate due to risk (40%)
discount_rate = 0.4

cash_flows = []
for t in range(1, years + 1):
    revenue = initial_revenue * (1 + growth_rate) ** t   ◁  Calculates future
    expense = initial_expense *                             cash flow
              (1 - expense_reduction) ** t
    cash_flow = revenue - expense
    cash_flows.append(cash_flow)

terminal_growth_rate = 0.05
terminal_value = cash_flows[-1] *        ◁  Terminal value using the
                 (1 + terminal_growth_rate) /    perpetuity growth model
                 (discount_rate -                with a long-term 5%
                  terminal_growth_rate)          growth assumption

discounted_cash_flows = [
cf / (1 + discount_rate) ** (t+1)
for t, cf in enumerate(cash_flows)]          ◁
discounted_terminal_value = terminal_value / (
1 + discount_rate                                 Discounts cash
) ** years                                   ◁    flows to present
startup_valuation = sum(                          value
discounted_cash_flows
) + discounted_terminal_value                ◁
print(f"Estimated Startup Valuation: ${startup_valuation:,.2f}")
```

Unfortunately, inputting some numbers and receiving a precise number doesn't always work. Formulas can become more complex than that. People may negotiate about the parameters. Some might argue that because a specific start-up operates in a high-risk industry, it should have a higher discount rate. Others might say that some figures in the planning documents are too speculative to yield substantial results.

In general, it's difficult to quantify all possible risks. What if the principal founder leaves? What if a corporate giant suddenly brings a similar product to the market? What if there are macroeconomic shifts or unexpected tariffs that affect the world economy?

For many early-stage start-ups, valuation is merely a means to assign a numerical value to a company. Every founder wants to impress others with good numbers. As hardly anyone will acquire an early-stage start-up, nobody denies founders the right to boast about their creativity in front of other founders.

When a start-up seeks to raise money and negotiations with investors begin, the valuation serves as a baseline for further discussion. Then, the market will decide what investors are ready to spend.

### 12.3.2 Dilution

Start-ups can raise multiple funding rounds at each stage of development. They can raise money through debt (borrowing money) or equity (selling ownership). Raising money through equity leads to *dilution*: preexisting owners will own fewer shares after an investment round unless they participate in the investment round themselves.

A founding round doesn't mean the value of an earlier round decreases; if the company's overall value increases, it also means that the value per share is increasing. After all, they use this money to enter new markets and acquire new clients. Let's outline this in a simplified scenario:

1 Fred and Lin started a company and issued 1,000,000 shares, with a 50/50 split.
2 An investor offers $500,000 for 25% of the company in a seed round.
3 To give the investor 25% equity, the company issues 333,333 new shares, increasing the total number of shares to 1,333,333.
4 Fred and Lin successfully acquire clients with this capital, increasing their overall valuation and the value per share.

Mark Zuckerberg started Facebook with 100% ownership. By the time of its IPO in 2012, his stake was just over 28%. Despite dilution, Facebook was worth $104 billion at the IPO, making Zuckerberg's ownership worth billions. Dilution isn't always bad—owning a smaller percentage of a highly valuable company is often better than owning 100% of a struggling one. Let's use sample data to model dilution across multiple funding rounds in Python.

> **NOTE** Some founders almost sabotage themselves with the idea that if they sell shares of their company, they will lose control over the product. If a founder is passionate about their product and expects a vision to be created

## 12.3 Assessing start-ups

in all the details as they imagine it, they might risk failure. Successful founders are deeply passionate about their business model.

Start-ups can't treat funding rounds as an infinite moneymaking machine. Not only do owners' stakes decrease, but investors who buy themselves in want to see a business that increases its earnings and is on the trajectory to profitability without requiring constant new investment rounds.

Let's look at listing 12.2, which shows dilution. We use artificial data to demonstrate how the ownership percentage decreases.

### Listing 12.2 Calculating dilution

```python
import pandas as pd

total_shares = 1_000_000
founder_shares = 500_000

funding_rounds = [
    ("Seed", 500_000, 25),
    ("Series A", 2_000_000, 20),
    ("Series B", 10_000_000, 15),
    ("Series C", 50_000_000, 10)
]

dilution_data = []

for round_name, investment, equity_given in funding_rounds:
    new_shares = (total_shares *
                  (equity_given /
                  (100 - equity_given)))
    total_shares += new_shares
    founder_ownership = (founder_shares /
                        total_shares) * 100
    dilution_data.append([round_name,
                         investment,
                         int(total_shares),
                         round(founder_ownership, 2)])

df = pd.DataFrame(dilution_data,
                columns=["Round", "Investment ($)", "Total Shares",
"Founder Ownership (%)"])
df
```

- Sets parameters ownership details, funding rounds
- Calculates dilution

This sample illustrates that with each subsequent funding round, the total number of shares increases, while founder ownership decreases. Even though dilution happens, the start-up raises millions, fueling growth. Earlier investors and founders will own less over time, but their shares will be worth more.

### 12.3.3 Scoring

Statistics indicate that only a small percentage of start-ups survive. As this book is about investing for programmers, and investing in start-ups is part of a comprehensive investment strategy, the question arises whether we can use programming skills to determine which start-up has a better chance of survival.

The smaller the start-up, the lower the chances of gaining significant insights through financial valuation. Let's see if we can score start-ups through nonfinancial parameters as well.

The following subsections list the potential factors to consider in this evaluation. Some of the insights we can get through large language models (LLMs). Other data is also available from platforms such as LinkedIn or Crunchbase. In the following categories, we describe the insights that can be obtained and outline the possible steps a programmer can take to retrieve the information.

#### INCUBATOR AND ACCELERATOR

Each incubator or accelerator has a success rate. The more start-ups originating from them succeed, the better. Investors who narrow their search parameters only to integrate successful incubators or accelerators increase their chances of success. They might focus on start-up programs affiliated with elite universities. We can ask LLMs to provide us with a list of successful incubators and accelerators and use this information as weighted model parameters.

#### FOUNDERS AND ADVISORS

We can profile start-up founders and score them on various parameters. We can examine their overall experience in the businesses for which they plan to create their next start-up, and review where they studied and with whom they have previously worked. We're also interested in their experience as founders and would like to know if they have had exits before.

We can gather a wealth of information about founders on LinkedIn or other platforms that contain data on professional achievements. We can also see if skills are missing in a founder team. It's also helpful to examine the company's advisors. In many cases, advisors with a solid track record on boards are a good sign.

#### EXISTING INVESTORS

If we know who has already invested in that company, we can build a scorecard by rating the existing investors based on their success rate. Platforms such as Crunchbase provide data on start-ups and their investors. Based on this, we can develop a scoring system that incorporates certain parameters, for example, the volume of past investments. We then score investors based on factors such as size, success rates, and other similar criteria.

#### CLIENTS AND STRATEGIC PARTNERSHIPS

If we know who their clients are, we can also forecast potential growth scenarios for start-ups. In many cases, collecting data about client collaborations would require access to confidential contracts, making it a topic of negotiation rather than a technical one.

Often, start-ups form strategic partnerships to expand and market their products. If a start-up collaborates with a major player in its field, this adds value. Still, both client relations and strategic partnerships are complex to rate, as many aspects are challenging to measure because various contracts and other documents related to collaborations may not contain commitments from both sides, but rather statements of intention.

### COUNTRY OF ORIGIN

Unicorns get their name because they are rare. Some countries attempt to breed unicorns, while others are less invested in this endeavor. You can look up the number of unicorns by country and the number of unicorns per million people. Countries such as Israel, for instance, do well.

There's a catch if you look for "start-up nations." Some start-up teams may originate from one country but incorporate in another due to tax reasons and access to markets. It's no surprise that many founders of Delaware C corporations aren't US residents. Still, knowing the country of origin of a start-up team can be one item on a scorecard.

### DOMAIN

Trends that dictate the focus of start-ups often depend on technological breakthroughs. In the early 2000s, numerous innovations enabled the creation of more advanced web pages, which we later referred to as Web 2.0. Start-up teams that were capable of adopting these technologies faster than their competitors had the potential to become hugely successful.

Following the release of the iPhone, numerous companies emerged to develop mobile apps. At the time of writing this book, if you look up start-up ideas, hardly anyone would recommend that you build apps. Now, the world is seeking innovations in quantum computing, AI, nuclear energy, improved storage technologies, and carbon capture. The times of consumer apps are over.

Domains can also be scored by risk. Think of domains in the early stages, such as geoengineering, in which you look for large-scale interventions to fix the climate or new nuclear reactor types. If companies in risky fields succeed, the rewards are higher.

### REGULATION

Think of two categories of start-ups: a biotech company that researches new mRNA vaccines and an IT company that builds a new messenger platform that incorporates AI. We don't need to guess which of these two start-ups will face heavy regulation and which one won't. More regulations mean more risk.

### ECONOMIC MOAT

Let's stick with the example from the previous subsection and imagine the biotech company is successful, creating a new type of vaccine. Who faces more risks through competition? The IT company that builds a new messenger platform doesn't have much room to defend itself from competitors. If a new start-up creates a better messenger platform, it might still fail. However, a successful biotech start-up, which has likely patented its products that contributed to its success, can't be easily displaced from its success by a competitor. An economic moat isn't always easy to quantify, but we can evaluate companies within their respective industries and explore various parameters to assess this key factor.

### CAPITAL INTENSITY AND BURN RATE

While we stick to our previous example, we can also take them as a reference for capital intensity and burn rate. The biotech company is likely capital-intensive. A significant amount of money is required for a lab and a minimum staff size. They would also have to spend a considerable amount of money on equipment and likely hire patent lawyers and officers who are well-versed in regulations, ensuring that all trials run smoothly. Compare this to IT companies that need budgets for notebooks and some cloud services to get started. They often need to spend money on licenses, as many tools are open source.

Capital intensity is often also expressed using a metric called *burn rate*, which refers to the amount a start-up spends in a given period. Start-ups with a high burn rate and a lengthy path to profitability are inherently risky.

### BUSINESS MODEL

First-time founders might wonder what app to build. Experienced founders may wonder how to monetize their business model. As investors, we can adopt a more informed approach to evaluate business models, as our destiny doesn't depend on them, which makes it easier to differentiate between the product being created and its monetization.

### NETWORK EFFECT

Investors such as Peter Thiel view the network effect as essential. Facebook, for example, is a product that started small and focused on a specific scenario. However, with a blue ocean market ahead of them, they were able to scale worldwide, as suddenly everyone gravitated toward a product that allowed them to present themselves to the world.

Perhaps it's harder today to build a new social media platform, as the market is already saturated. However, every investor dreams of finding a product that not everyone has, but where it's certain that it's only a matter of time until everyone wants it.

### INDIVIDUAL NORTH STAR METRICS

You can ask a founder the question, "What is the one metric you keep screening and that will make you smile once it reaches a certain milestone?" For a social media company, it might be 1 million subscribers. For a company selling products, the customer acquisition costs might be below $x$ USD.

Each domain may have a different North Star Metric. If you find these metrics, you can likely monitor their chance of a breakthrough over time.

## *Summary*

- Investing in start-ups may be the riskiest investment, but it can pay off tremendously if the venture is successful.
- Some experts in venture capital (VC) say you invest more in people and business models, and less in the product.
- Start-ups progress through distinct stages, each with specific investment requirements:
  - Pre-seed start-ups often serve as a reference point for founders with an idea who are working on a minimum viable product (MVP) to demonstrate the product's potential.
  - Seed start-ups are companies that aim to transform a successful MVP into a full-fledged product that can be sold to customers.
  - Series A companies typically have paying customers; their primary role is to develop and refine a working product for the mass market or to meet the advanced requirements of customers.
  - Series B companies must retain their existing customers and strive to expand into new markets.
  - Series C companies have gained some market dominance and primarily strive for a successful exit, typically through an acquisition or an initial public offering (IPO).
- Most founders view unsuccessful exits as badges of honor, which can help attract more investments.
- VC-backed start-ups don't exist to grow slowly. If a company takes VC, the goal is to get acquired or go public.
- Retail investors can't directly invest in a prominent VC's likely next unicorn, but if you have enough capital, you can still gain exposure to private equity through VC funds.
- There are various start-up valuation methods. DCF values start-ups based on their future expected cash flows, which are discounted for risk.
- Investors and fund managers of a VC firm expect a start-up to work hard toward achieving an exit.
- Angel syndicates are alternatives to VCs and enable investors with smaller check sizes to invest in start-ups.
- A lead investor of an angel syndicate commonly incorporates a special purpose vehicle (SPV) that, when invested in a start-up, is added to a start-up's cap table.
- VCs don't just look at DCF; they compare it to market trends and past acquisitions.
- Each funding round adds new shares, reducing existing ownership percentages. This is known as dilution, and it's an inevitable consequence in venture-backed start-ups.
- You can use data and programming skills to score start-ups on nonfinancial aspects.

- For a scoring model of start-ups, you can explore parameters such as the success chance based on the incubator/accelerator, founders, existing investors, clients, strategic partnerships, country of origin, domain, regulations, economic moats, capital intensity, burn rate, business model, network effect, and individual North Star Metrics.

# 13
# The road goes ever on and on

**This chapter covers**
- Getting advice
- Realizing knowledge alone doesn't make you a financial advisor
- Being a digital nomad to get you closer to financial freedom
- Preventing irrational decisions with control measures
- Seeing index funds as the safest choice after all

Congratulations! You made it this far. In this final chapter, we explore possible next steps in your journey to use your programming skills to make wise investment decisions. Some of the discussion is about behavioral finance, as managing yourself is often a central criterion for success. It will complete your view, allowing you to begin your journey.

## 13.1 Getting advice

Imagine embarking on a journey to a distant country with a different culture, having prepared for it only by reading books. If you're a frequent traveler, you know that in some countries, you'll encounter situations that no travel guide can prepare you for. It's the same with investment. Books don't provide financial advice on how to deal with specific situations. Investments are time-sensitive. Even if a writer had a good idea about a purchase decision at the time of writing, the decision criteria might have changed when the reader reads that information. This book aims to equip you with the techniques to assess financial assets. The decision to invest—or not—must ultimately be yours.

If you're new to investing, not knowing what you don't know is a risk. In this book, we introduced the Dunning-Kruger effect, which underlines that people new to a field often overestimate their skills. Some new and overconfident investors learn some lessons the hard way. The question is whether the hours of frustration and the loss of money are worth it.

Learning lessons through low-stakes investing can be a good start. You can invest only a minimal amount of money in riskier assets to build experience gradually until you're ready for bigger stakes. If you've never consulted a financial or tax advisor, consider doing so before making significant investments. Ensure that any advisor you choose has the necessary experience and credentials.

Additionally, Reddit and other social media platforms are excellent resources for seeking advice and obtaining a peer review of investment ideas. Just be cautious; some "experts" on social media, who confidentially recommend you make bold moves to get rich fast, may be affected by the Dunning-Kruger effect when offering guidance. Always be aware that there are also many scammers on social media. As usual, the more people you ask, the more opinions you get, and the more chances you have that critical thinking helps you develop a good strategy.

Taxation is another crucial factor that investors shouldn't ignore. Specific strategies may optimize your returns depending on your citizenship and tax residency. Even if an investment appears outstanding based on fundamental analysis, tax-efficient alternatives sometimes offer better overall returns.

This book explores how large language models (LLMs) can serve as powerful research assistants. Using LLMs to determine what to ask the human tax consultant might make sense. However, AI often lacks full context and can make mistakes. If you provide basic details about your citizenship, tax residency, and income, AI may suggest strategies you can validate with a professional financial advisor, such as reducing withholding taxes.

Many experts have opinions on how and when AI chatbots replace human advisors or when the advice of an AI is tough to beat. Remember that AI is trained on data created by humans, so it's likely that some specific strategies you might come up with can be unique. By building your Retrieval-Augmented Generations (RAGs) with investor-related information on fields that interest you, optimizing prompts, and using AI agents to orchestrate workflows, you can have one LLM validate the results of other LLMs. This approach offers no limits to creativity in using AI. And chances are good that with every new model that is released, you see more sophistication and fewer hallucinations.

Some developers who shared their experiences about vibe coding sessions, where they let AI create code, found one big behavioral problem: they "get lazy" to solve problems themselves. Instead of examining the code to identify areas for improvement, they write a single prompt, submit it, do something else in the meantime, such as checking social media, and then check the results. When the AI-generated code doesn't work well, they copy and paste the error message and submit another prompt. Many programmers conclude that they often could have created some solutions faster if they hadn't used AI (while also admitting that no human can be faster than any AI to write code in some situations, so context matters). One AI-related piece of advice is to beware of falling into the trap of relying on AI for everything. The more advanced they get, the more tempting it will be.

## 13.2 Stay curious

In this book, we emphasize the importance of investing in businesses we understand. One way to become a better investor is to stay curious and learn as much as possible about companies. Research them, learn about their operations, and speak with people who have experience with them. Many audiobooks and podcasts explain how the investment world operates, offering numerous insights that can inform your investment decisions.

Sometimes, you meet new people and aren't sure what to discuss. Take this chance to learn more about a profession. With that knowledge, you can conduct your research and gather significant expertise to answer questions from others in a similar field. One important trait is having active listening skills, which helps make your interview partner feel more comfortable sharing about their work.

## 13.3 Alpha hunter

After reading this book, you might feel tempted to create alpha portfolios that outperform the market and sell your strategies to clients. Before pitching your ideas to friends and family, consider this: even highly experienced investors with strong financial backgrounds make mistakes and lose money. Giving direct investment advice can damage relationships.

Even if you become skilled at evaluating assets—something we've demonstrated is possible for those with strong analytical abilities—you must face a hard truth: proving financial success requires effort and time. While you can showcase back-tested statistics and historical simulations, what truly matters to fund managers, banks, and clients is whether you have skin in the game. When you demonstrate consistent performance over the years and explain how you achieved it, serious investors may start paying attention.

Regardless of your approach, expect one common question: "With so many established investment firms—BlackRock, Berkshire Hathaway, Vanguard—boasting decades of data and proven strategies, why do *you* believe you can do better?" If you can't deliver a convincing answer that stands up to experts in the field, it's probably not time to launch your start-up.

One alternative to going solo is forming an investment group. Collaborating with others enables peer reviews, which strengthens your skills and credibility. Additionally, various platforms enable you to share insights, and some even offer monetization options, allowing investors to subscribe to your group for a fee.

If you intend to charge others for financial services, be sure to also review the regulations in your country. While it's okay to weigh out the best investment opportunities among friends, reaching out to potential clients to charge them for your advice is a business, and this business, in most countries, requires a license. Before attempting to monetize, always verify the regulations of your local market regarding the requirements for being a financial advisor.

## 13.4 Nomadism

Some readers may approach this book as a step toward achieving financial freedom, perhaps even as a means to escape the constraints of corporate jobs and pursue a more fulfilling life. For those living in high-cost countries, digital nomadism can be a significant milestone on that journey.

Being a digital nomad isn't just about exploring new places, meeting people, and having adventures. It can also mean lowering your living costs and tax burden. As a programmer, you have the unique advantage of location independence, whether building your start-up or working with multiple clients remotely.

As mentioned earlier, consulting a knowledgeable tax advisor can help you determine whether relocating to a country with a digital nomad program is financially beneficial. Some countries offer attractive tax incentives, including reduced income tax and capital gains tax, which can make such a move a significant step toward financial independence.

However, there are challenges to consider. Your citizenship may affect the ease with which you can obtain a visa. Many countries with digital nomad programs aim to protect local businesses from unfair competition, which often means you're only permitted to work for clients outside your new country of residence.

Freelancers should also be mindful of corporate policies. While many companies support remote work, some exclude certain countries as locations for fulfillment. You sign a contract, try to log in from your notebook on the corporate network, and you're suddenly blacklisted because your IP address doesn't match. You can prevent that beforehand by ensuring that your client is okay if you work from your new country of residence.

While lower living costs and favorable tax rates can be appealing, be aware of the potential effect of inflation and currency fluctuations. The value of some local currencies has sharply declined over time, potentially eroding your purchasing power. However, as you've gained some financial literacy in this book, you can also assess the risks by studying the Forex charts.

If you're freelancing, building a strong online presence is essential. Platforms such as Upwork, Toptal, and LinkedIn can help you showcase your expertise, attract clients, and establish a sustainable remote career.

If you plan to work as a remote consultant to earn money as an investor, remember the basic lessons learned in this book about interest rates. When the interest rates of a central bank are high, borrowing money is more expensive. Thus, starting your career as a freelancer is easier when interest rates are low and more projects are on the market.

## 13.5 Activist investing

In chapter 2, we noted that younger generations, who have many years ahead of them, tend to be more concerned about environmental, social, and governance (ESG) issues than earlier generations. Organizational frameworks, such as diversity, equity, and inclusion (DEI) or "my country first," have also gained influence. While some may prefer to ignore them to avoid painful debates with evangelists of each side, we must acknowledge that we're experiencing a growing divide between political standpoints that may also influence the investment decisions of many individuals and even organizations.

Many consumers are value-driven and don't purchase products from companies that fail to share their ethical concerns. But what about investment? Most of this book was about how to increase your wealth through investing. Would you buy shares of a company you dislike but whose share price growth outlook is excellent? As getting richer may not be everyone's top priority, we need to ask the following: Can individual investors affect a company's success through their investment decisions? How much money would a single investor need to invest to influence the fate of a company?

The financial world has seen activist investors such as Carl Icahn and Bill Ackman, who buy significant stakes in companies—often 10% or more—to influence board decisions. However, the average private investor's equity in firms is usually statistically insignificant, and they won't significantly affect corporate strategy, even if they invest their entire wealth in one company.

So, unless you're a billionaire, it's doubtful that a CEO of the Magnificent Seven will call you to thank you for your investment. However, as we've seen in chapter 12 on private equity and start-up investment, the smaller a company is, the greater the effect single investors can have. You might face a dilemma though even if you acquire enough shares to push for change in a company for ethical reasons. Suppose the company profits significantly from controversial, but legal, actions. If you become a leading investor and get a seat on the board, you can change the business approach. However, investing in a company to cut its primary income is akin to climbing a large tree to cut off the branch you're sitting on.

Perhaps only the ultra-wealthy have the privilege of investing in groundbreaking technologies that can reshape industries. But, as societal values evolve, ethical investing may become an increasingly powerful force that shapes markets in ways we're only beginning to understand.

In his Yale Financial Markets course, Professor Robert F. Shiller indicated that investors may have a moral duty to improve their environment. As you become more prosperous, you should become more invested in philanthropic projects. However, if changing the world is your ultimate goal, remember that some entrepreneurs have taken it too far, committing fraud in the name of effective altruism. Never forget that investing is a business first. You need to excel at it if you hope to make even a slight change in the world.

## 13.6 Measures of control

Whether you follow this book's advice to stay cautious or take a more aggressive approach, you may eventually invest significant money in assets. In one extreme scenario, you experience rapid gains, fueling confidence and leading you to start planning your early retirement. However, overconfidence often leads to costly mistakes. Countless books warn about cognitive biases and market risks, yet some investors downplay them, investing *heavily* without considering the potential downside. You may think you're brighter than others and ignore all the warnings. When reality strikes, the consequences can be severe. Imagine someone who quits their job, declaring themselves financially free, only to face unexpected losses. In extreme cases, they may find themselves returning to their former employer and asking HR to reverse their resignation to stay financially afloat.

### 13.6.1 Checks and balances

Minor miscalculations can compound into significant problems. One way to mitigate these risks is by implementing *checks and balances* in your decision-making process.

One example of checks and balances comes in the form of *peer reviews*. Discussing strategies with experienced investors who can challenge your views can provide valuable insights. Some investors often feel compelled to make investments quickly because they fear that an opportunity will pass. Some refer to this as FOMO, or the fear of missing out. Still, often it makes sense to wait with a buy order. Meet with a friend and explain why you want to buy the shares. The more you need to justify your actions with arguments, the more you'll discover if you're on to something. The more you engage with brilliant, critical thinkers who offer different perspectives, the better equipped you'll be to make sound financial decisions and avoid costly pitfalls.

Another practical approach is conducting *regular retrospectives* to assess past investment decisions and refine future strategies. For that, you need to write down why you invested in an asset. Then, you continue to review your decision, and even after you've sold your asset, you may still refer to your notes. Sometimes, you might have to accept that you must learn a lesson to improve. But this again means that you likely prevented yourself from making a mistake twice.

One practice that many investors do is to document everything. We may refer to this as an investment diary. For every decision they make, they document the exact reasons for doing so and the associated expectations. If they review their choices a few months or years later, they can reassess the situation and apply the lessons learned. Based on these learnings, many investors follow principles and strict rule sets for their investment decisions.

### 13.6.2 Gain distance

Some investors take a thoughtful approach, carefully analyzing decisions and considering long-term outcomes. However, once they invest, they step back and check in only occasionally to ensure things are on track.

However, maintaining this level of detachment becomes possible if you own a limited number of assets. Having an over-diversified portfolio with maybe a hundred assets or more is a challenge. If you reach a point where you no longer remember why you invested in a particular company—or worse, if you see a stock ticker in your portfolio and have to look up what company it belongs to—you may have lost control over your investments.

A better strategy is to focus on a manageable number of businesses you *understand well*. Investing in companies you can track and evaluate is more effective than cluttering your portfolio with assets that sounded exciting at the time. Simplification leads to better decision-making and stronger conviction in your investments.

Another essential part is to not make decisions based on strong emotions. In an era where you can make investment decisions 24/7 from anywhere, it also means you can create a buy order at a party while drinking with a friend who shares an outstanding investment opportunity, promising a 10x return because the company is excellent. A hangover might not be the worst thing you wake up with.

### 13.6.3 Programmer's journey

This book is for programmers and data analysts who are new to the world of investing. It bridges the gap between your technical expertise and financial concepts, showing you how to apply your analytical skills to achieve better investment outcomes. The examples provided are intentionally straightforward, allowing you to run them on a standard notebook or a simple cloud setup.

For those seeking a greater challenge, your programming skills open the door to more sophisticated applications in quantitative finance. While this book focuses on the fundamentals, you can explore advanced models on your own. For instance, you could experiment with time series forecasting using AutoRegressive Integrated Moving Average (ARIMA) models or delve into complex quantitative finance theories.

If you have access to significant computational resources, you might even explore high-frequency trading (HFT), an area where speed and algorithmic complexity provide a competitive edge. This field is dominated by hedge funds and specialized investment firms that dedicate massive resources to forecasting market movements and executing trades in fractions of a second.

### 13.6.4 Playing it safe

As a final observation, my conclusion is the same in all my journeys. In discussions about efficient market theory, many individuals claim to beat the market. Some individuals brag about staggering results with speculative trades, often backed by "bro advice" or vague technical analysis.

Many of these "star traders" have a story about their huge gains, but they won't tell you how much they lost on the way. And if you check in years later, often they tell you that they stopped trading without wanting to give you a reason why.

At the same time, you read about investors who got rich and where it's proven that they beat the market. You might want to study people such as Warren Buffett, Peter Lynch, and George Soros. Like the book *Outliers: The Story of Success* by Malcolm Gladwell (Little Brown and Company, 2008), which examines individuals who excel with extraordinary business performance, you should investigate whether the same pattern exists.

Some believe that following principles helps people make the best decisions when stressed and emotional. Investor Ray Dalio wrote a book, *Principle: Life and Work* (Avid Reader Press, 2017), about this. Many investors spend considerable time researching their assets. One principle is to make rational decisions and learn from mistakes.

Some individuals have become rich in emerging markets. The crypto market is one of them, but consider Russia in the 1990s when the country was effectively up for grabs. After the collapse of the Soviet Union and the transition to capitalism, the Russian state rapidly privatized industries through programs such as the "voucher privatization" and "loans-for-shares" schemes. In the chaos, well-connected and often ruthless businessmen were able to acquire state-owned assets—particularly in natural resources, energy, and banking—at a fraction of their value. A small group of these individuals became immensely wealthy and came to be known as Russia's oligarchs.

Investors in emerging markets often face fewer challenges in finding suitable investment opportunities; however, they must also be cautious to avoid being tricked or scammed. Emerging markets can be roller-coaster rides. Not everyone is in for the long ride. Some people want to avoid the stress. One way to do that is to pick an index or world fund. Select one that is tax-optimized for you and proceed. You spend your time relaxing and occasionally return to your portfolio.

In Shiller's Yale Financial Markets course mentioned earlier, he recommends allocating 80% of your money to index funds and reserving 20% for stocks. Success grows with an understanding of the business you invest in. If you start there and consistently outperform the other 80%, you can still adjust the ratio.

When you do your own research about index funds—or even world funds, that distribute all the positions on assets worldwide—you'll also find a lot of other people giving the same advice: put everything in an index fund, come back in some years, and you'll be happy with the results. What an index fund doesn't do, however, is find the growth potential in businesses that you understand well and that can outperform the market, as shown in this book.

Lastly, ensure that investing doesn't interfere with your life. You might be off track if you spend most of your day just tracking prices and watching what goes up or down. After all, if you strive for freedom by becoming an investment prodigy, remember that you're not truly free if the desire to live independently consumes all of your time and energy. In the end, in the wise words of Gandalf in J.R.R. Tolkien's *The Lord of the Rings*, "All we have to decide is what we do with the time that is given to us."

## Summary

- Seeking advice before making significant investments is almost always a wise decision.
- Discussing potential investments with a friend and charging clients for your advice are distinct actions. For the latter, you likely need a business license.
- Staying curious about businesses is one way to accumulate a wealth of knowledge, enabling sound investment decisions over time.
- Becoming a digital nomad enables you to pick countries with favorable tax conditions. Some countries may not have taxes on capital appreciation.
- Become aware that your investment also supports a company. Sometimes, you might not want to support specific companies, even if you might benefit financially.
- The smaller the company, the more effect your investment has.
- You can become your own most significant obstacle to getting rich if you act irrationally. Establish checks and balances to minimize the effect of strong emotions.
- You can document every investment decision and then later use a retrospective to find potential learnings to improve your investment process.
- Occasionally, it helps to take a step back and reevaluate situations with a clear mind.
- Many investors claim that new investors are best off with an index or world fund.
- Patience and a stoic mindset may be the key ingredients to achieving wealth in the long run.

# *appendix*
# *Setting up the environment*

Some of you may prefer cloud services, while others of you prefer to use your own devices. Many programmers are familiar with specific tools to replace the ones shown in the book, allowing them to choose their final configuration independently. In this appendix, we list options for each category. We'll demonstrate how to integrate cloud services, manage source code, select development environments, and export data.

To work with financial assets, you'll need to register with a broker or exchange. In this book, I'll demonstrate using Alpaca, Interactive Brokers, and Binance. You're free to use other providers, but in that case, you'll need to handle data access and integration on your own. Be aware that because these are platforms that host financial data, they require some extra security procedures such as a Know Your Customer (KYC) process. Suppose you feel uncomfortable with using a broker as a backend, or your broker doesn't support remote access through an API. In that case, you can always create a small relational database that contains tables with all your positions.

This appendix highlights only the basic actions, but doesn't explain all the details required for possible environments. For detailed instructions on setting up a framework or service for your specific environment, do some web research or consult a large language model (LLM).

## A.1 Python

Python is the lingua franca of data analytics. It provides key data structures and features to facilitate efficient data analysis. Since its beginnings in the 1990s, Python has developed a growing library of tools that excel in all aspects of data exploration, including data retrieval and visualization.

## A.1 Python

Many operating systems come with a preinstalled Python version. You can use this Python installation locally or create a virtual environment for your exploration. Most experts recommend the latter because it allows you to install as many custom libraries as you want and update each library without risking conflicts with other libraries for different use cases.

In this book, we use Python 3.13, the latest version available at the time of writing. The Python community provides new versions every year. As Python is mature, functional changes that remove backward compatibility are rare. In most cases, the exercises should run with slightly older or newer versions of the programming language. You can determine your Python version by running the following command in the console:

```
Python --version
```

If you don't have a Python interpreter installed, follow the instructions on www.python.org to set up your Python environment. You can also check the availability of the package manager pip on your system, which allows you to install libraries for data exploration. For example, you can install these three libraries, which we frequently use in this book, in this way:

```
pip install yfinance pandas numpy
```

This book relies heavily on the pandas and matplotlib libraries in most samples. If you still have a lot to learn about using Python or these two libraries, we recommend catching up before delving into programming examples.

> **NOTE** Developers can port the code in this book to other languages if they offer similar libraries to Python. Just don't underestimate the effort required, as some libraries, such as a port of yfinance, might not be available for every language.

We list the libraries used in this book in table A.1. Be aware that for some of these tools, you need to register on a platform and get API keys.

Table A.1 Python libraries used in this book by chapter

| Library | Link | Chapter | Key required |
|---|---|---|---|
| python-dotenv | https://pypi.org/project/python-dotenv/ | 3 | No |
| yfinance | https://pypi.org/project/yfinance/ | 3 | No |
| pandas | https://pypi.org/project/pandas/ | 3 | No |
| NumPy | https://pypi.org/project/numpy/ | 3 | No |
| matplotlib | https://pypi.org/project/matplotlib/ | 3 | No |

Table A.1 Python libraries used in this book by chapter *(continued)*

| Library | Link | Chapter | Key required |
|---|---|---|---|
| finviz | https://pypi.org/project/finviz/ | 3 | Yes |
| openbb | https://pypi.org/project/openbb/ | 3 | Yes |
| alpha-vantage | https://pypi.org/project/alpha-vantage/ | 3 | Yes |
| eodhd | https://pypi.org/project/eodhd/ | 3 | Yes |
| pytrends | https://pypi.org/project/pytrends/ | 4 | No |
| Alpaca-py | https://pypi.org/project/alpaca-py/ | 6 | Yes |
| ib_insync | https://pypi.org/project/ib-insync/ | 6 | No |
| python_binance | https://pypi.org/project/python-binance/ | 6 | Yes |
| SQLAlchemy | https://pypi.org/project/SQLAlchemy/ | 6 | No |
| CurrencyConverter | https://pypi.org/project/CurrencyConverter/ | 6 | No |
| scikit-learn | https://pypi.org/project/scikit-learn/ | 8 | No |
| statsmodels | https://pypi.org/project/statsmodels/ | 8 | No |
| openai | https://pypi.org/project/openai/ | 8 | Yes |
| google-genai | https://pypi.org/project/google-genai/ | 8 | Yes |
| google-generativeai | https://pypi.org/project/google-generativeai/ | 8 | Yes |
| anthropic | https://pypi.org/project/anthropic/ | 8 | Yes |
| transformers | https://pypi.org/project/transformers/ | 8 | No |
| langchain | https://pypi.org/project/langchain/ | 9 | No |
| Langchain-community | https://pypi.org/project/langchain-community/ | 9 | No |
| Langchain-openai | https://pypi.org/project/langchain-openai/ | 9 | Yes |
| Langchain-core | https://pypi.org/project/langchain-core/ | 9 | No |
| mplfinance | https://pypi.org/project/mplfinance/ | 10 | No |
| streamlit | https://pypi.org/project/streamlit/ | 10 | No |

## A.2 Secrets manager

The most crucial section of the whole setup is securing API keys and secrets. An unauthorized person who gets access to them can cause harm. For that reason, we need to protect them as much as possible. Listing A.1 uses the python-dotenv library to load secret keys from a file named .env.

### Listing A.1 Using python-dotenv

```
import os
import requests
from dotenv import load_dotenv

load_dotenv()

NOTION_TOKEN = os.getenv("doc.notion.api")
DATABASE_ID = os.getenv("doc.notion.db")
```

Suppose the .env file in the directory where the code is executed contains key-value pairs assigning values to the keys doc.notion.api and doc.notion.db. In that case, the library loads the values and later assigns them to variables. We can apply these concepts to all keys that we want to load, including usernames and passwords.

Be aware that python-dotenv is just a minimum-security measure and helps you to separate hardcoded API keys from the source code. We can use a secrets manager, which takes security even one step further. If someone runs code locally on their computer, they can use HashiCorp Vault. In addition, there are custom solutions for each environment. If you're using a Mac, take a look at the keyring library. Be sure to invest some time in exploring the best way to secure your keys as much as possible based on your environment.

## A.3 Source code repository

The choice of a remote git server, such as GitHub or GitLab, doesn't make a difference. Both solutions do the job, and deciding which one to use depends on personal preference.

While we don't need to explain to programmers the benefits of a source code repository, and most programmers will be able to create their own repositories, we need to highlight the risk of accidentally committing API keys in plain text. Some remote git repositories offer features to detect if keys are pushed to a server by mistake, and you can also use private Git repositories to mitigate the possible impact of pushing keys by accident. We can't stress enough that the best protection for your keys is to prevent them from leaving your secured environment from the beginning.

> **NOTE** When using API keys to trade on financial platforms, it's always better to be safe than sorry. If you feel that there's even the slightest risk that an unauthorized party could gain access to the keys, change them. All platforms offer methods to make access keys invalid.

One way to prevent a file from being uploaded to a remote cloud repository is to add the file names containing the keys, such as the .env file, as shown previously, to the list of files your source code repository will ignore. A git-add will check the content of a .gitignore file and ignore all files and directories that match the patterns specified in the file.

## A.4 Development environment

In this book, we use Jupyter Notebooks. A Jupyter Notebook is an interactive environment that executes code in single cells. It can be run in its native environment, Jupyter, or a hosted setup using an Integrated Development Environment (IDE). What makes Jupyter Notebooks unique is that they provide an interactive environment. You can execute code in one cell and use the results of earlier executions in a different cell. This interactivity offers flexibility and is particularly well-suited for research-oriented approaches. Let's explore some of the typical environments.

### A.4.1 Anaconda

Jupyter can be installed as a Python standalone library using the pip package manager. However, developers can use Jupyter when it's integrated into a development environment. Figure A.1 illustrates a Jupyter Notebook running in Anaconda, an open source data science and AI platform that supports Python and R programming languages.

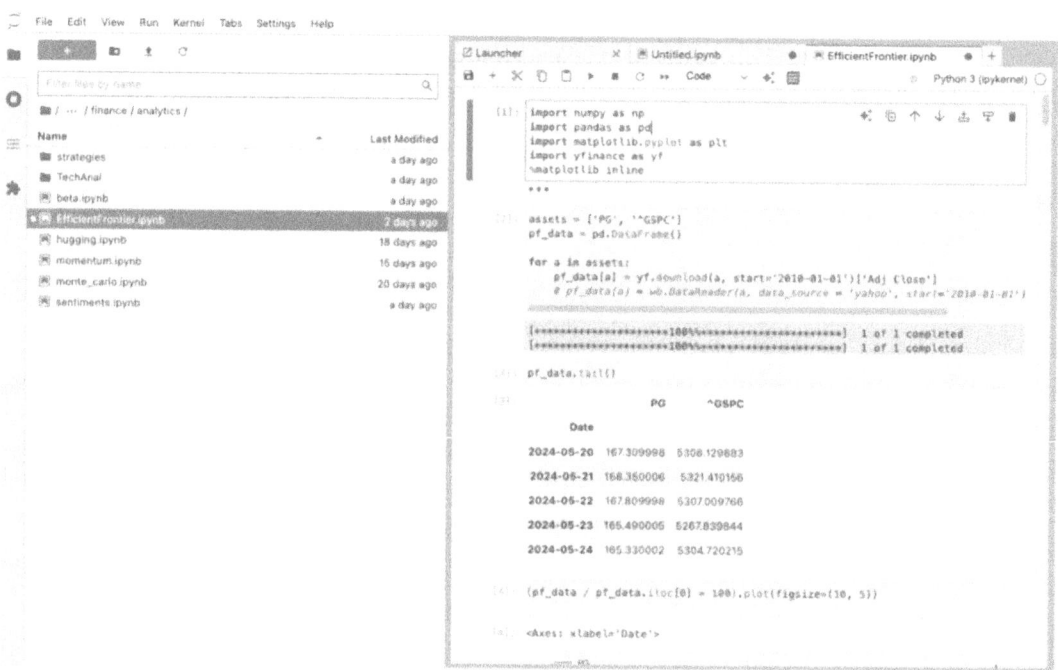

Figure A.1  A Jupyter Notebook running in Anaconda in a web browser

Anaconda provides an entire environment for data scientists, including the package manager conda, which follows similar principles to pip. Refer to the installation routine on the Anaconda web page (https://mng.bz/Rwoa).

## A.4 Development environment

Many cloud-hosted environments offer notebooks, including AWS Sagemaker, Azure Machine Learning, Google Colab, and JetBrains Datalore. Developers who don't want to install anything in their local environment can use these hosted environments.

### A.4.2 Visual Studio Code

Visual Studio Code (VS Code), shown in figure A.2, is a standard IDE that runs on most operating systems provided by Microsoft. It's also trendy among Mac and Linux users because it's free and offers many functionalities. Download and install VS Code for your operating system based on the vendor's instructions at https://mng.bz/15BR.

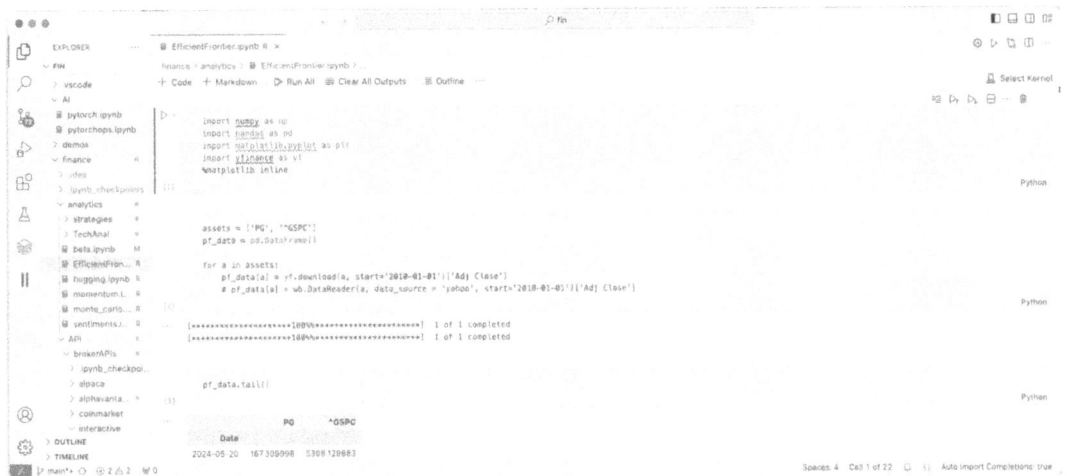

**Figure A.2** The VS Code environment with Jupyter Notebooks

### A.4.3 PyCharm

Many developers prefer PyCharm, an IDE specifically designed for Python programmers (figure A.3). PyCharm offers numerous features of interest to Python programmers. It's available in a paid pro edition and a free community edition. The producer JetBrains also provides other useful developer tools, such as DataGrip, to manage SQL databases.

Install PyCharm according to the vendor's instructions. PyCharm Pro isn't required, but it can facilitate some programming activities.

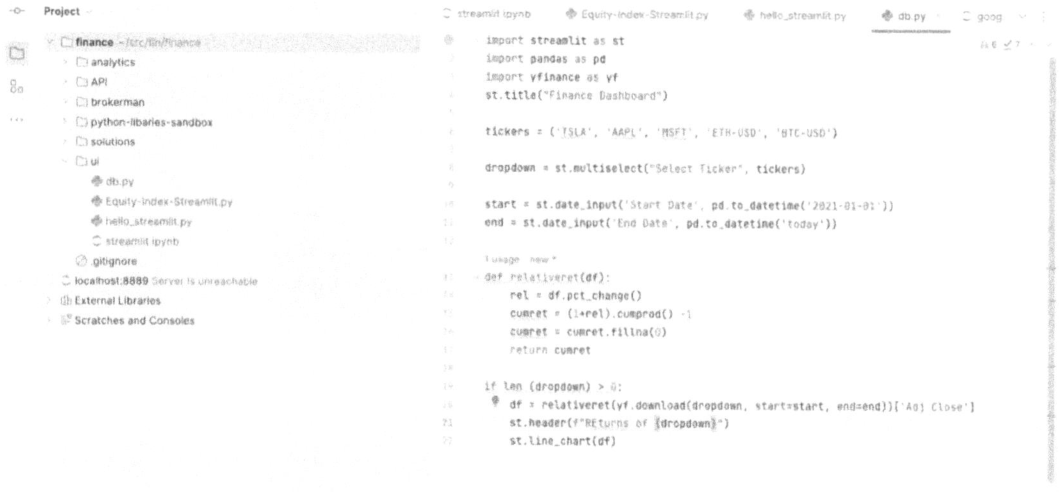

**Figure A.3** PyCharm with Jupyter Notebooks

## A.5 Cloud

This book demonstrates how to access and store financial data using databases and APIs securely. In the examples, we run data science notebooks on a local system. Alternatively, you can execute everything in cloud services that allow hosting Jupyter Notebooks.

Some programmers shy away from using one of the big cloud providers because they need to follow a KYC process and provide credit card information for registration, and not everyone feels comfortable doing this for private projects. For each service you use locally, you can replace it with a cloud-based option. Besides options hosted on large cloud providers, there are likely free versions from smaller providers that don't require any credit card information.

### A.5.1 Database

The first item to replace, if you want to get more advanced, is likely the SQLite database we use in this book, which is excellent for explanatory scenarios. For more advanced scenarios, there are limitations, however. One reference database provider that allows you to use a simple database setup without a credit card is Supabase.

We can use all forms of relational databases hosted on cloud providers. Of course, cloud developers must also be familiar with opening access ports and setting up and configuring databases in the cloud. Every cloud provider has extensive material on how to do this.

This book uses the SQL Alchemy library to read and write database data. A developer, therefore, only needs to replace the connection string if they want to change the backend.

## A.5.2 Cloud secrets managers

Users who use a public cloud can also use the secrets managers provided by these platforms. We can then use these libraries from Python scripts or command-line tools. Listing A.2 shows how to use the Boto3 library to access AWS Secrets Manager. Each big cloud provider has its own secrets management solution. Pick the one you like best.

**Listing A.2 Accessing AWS Secret Manager using Boto3**

```
client = boto3.client('secretsmanager')
try:
    response = client.get_secret_value(SecretId=secret_name)
    secret = json.loads(response['SecretString'])
    return secret
except Exception as e:
    print(f"Error retrieving secret: {e}")
    return None
```

While the secret manager solutions from public cloud providers are secure, keep in mind that cloud providers offer more sophisticated features to minimize risks. Cloud endpoints may, for instance, accept only requests from limited IP ranges if security is configured accordingly.

## A.6 Export and documentation

In this book, we export data to note-taking platforms such as Notion or Google Sheets. Both frameworks allow export with keys. You can access these services by creating an account for each of them.

You can replace these two platforms with all kinds of alternatives. The recommendation is to use a centralized repository to store all research and responses from LLMs, as this allows you to have a structured study. If you want to reassess a decision you've made some time ago based on an LLM response, you can also use that response and submit it as part of a prompt to ask an LLM if it still agrees with the original assessment.

## A.7 LLMs

Ever since LLMs went mainstream in IT, vendors have been racing to release versioned models to capture market share. We use four LLMs in this book:

- Anthropic
- OpenAI
- Google Gemini
- AdaptLLM/finance-chat

Using frameworks such as LangChain, we unify the API and don't have to manage multiple vendor APIs. What we still need to prepare for is generating accounts on the platforms, obtaining access keys, and occasionally purchasing a minimum number of credits. The detailed process of creating accounts and creating keys is out of this book's scope. LLM chatbots typically do a great job explaining how to create an account on their platform and generate API keys, which can be used in Python.

## A.8 Brokers and exchanges

We use brokers for stocks and bonds, and we use exchanges for stocks. Chapter 11 explains the difference between these categories. In this book, we use three platforms to trade assets and gather data from them:

- *Interactive Brokers*—A long-established international broker with a tremendous amount of functionality
- *Alpaca*—A developer-first broker with innovative APIs
- *Binance*—A well-known cryptocurrency exchange

As many different brokers and exchanges are available worldwide, we must be aware that every financial platform requires a KYC process, which requires customers to provide proof of their identity. This procedure is for your protection as investors. Verified users who must authenticate to use a system are less likely to attempt fraud.

While two platforms use API keys to authenticate, Interactive Brokers takes a different approach. Interactive Brokers uses a local installation of a tool called Trader Workstation (TWS) to connect with a Python API. Sometimes, you need to configure the API access with the TWS. Interactive Brokers provides information tailored to your operating system.

# index

## A

accelerator, explained 302–303
accounting 20–27
   balance sheet 25
   FCF (free cash flow) 26
   income statement 22–25
accredited investors 5
actively managed ETFs 4
activist investing 325
AdaptLLM/finance-chat model 207
ADAS (Advanced Driver-Assistance System) 81
ADRs (American Depositary Receipts) 71, 132
AEB (Euronext Amsterdam) 132
AI agents 11, 216
   agentic workflows without frameworks 222–228
   framework for 228–237
   requirements 217–222
AI (artificial intelligence) 181
   prompt engineering 208–213
alert, price 220
algorithmic trading 273
   catalysts 278–282
   nonfinancial data 274–278
   orders 289–294
Alpaca
   extracting data 128
   orders 293

Alpha Vantage 73
Anaconda 334
analytical investors
   programmers as 16–17
   risks and rewards 15
angel networks 309–311
angel or venture capital investments 7
annual payout 108
ARIMA (AutoRegressive Integrated Moving Average) models 192, 327
asset monitor 123
   architecture 124–126
   enriching data 130–131
   extracting data 127–129
   processing assets 131–139
   spreadsheets 126
assets 2–8
   bonds 4
   choosing 8
   cryptocurrency 5
   derivatives 6
   ETFs (exchange-traded funds) 4
   forex (foreign exchange) market 5
   funds 5
   other assets 7
   private equity 6
   stocks 3
asset-specific risk 147
automated trading 12

autonomous driving 80
   ethics and security 81
   known brands 82–84
AWS (Amazon Web Services) 232
AWS Data Exchange 276

## B

B2B (business-to-business) companies 69, 275
backtesting 283–287
balance sheet 25, 58
bar charts 251
BCG (Boston Consulting Group) Framework 106, 164, 223
bearish hypothesis 24
behavioral finance 182
big data 276–278
   big companies 276
   demographic data 277
   media 277
   movement data 277
*Big Short, The* (film) 275
bikeshedding 146
blockchain 6
Bollinger Bands 260–262
bonds 4, 112–116, 137
breakout 249
brokers
   exchanges 338
   orders 289
Buffett, Warren 30, 275

bullish hypothesis 22
burn rate 45, 318
business model, validating 301–302
buying overperformers 177

## C

candlesticks 254–256
   anatomy of candlestick chart 254
   patterns 256
CapEx (capital expenses) 26
capitalization 32
cash-secured put 162
catalysts 278–282
   disasters 281
   distressed companies 279
   earnings calls 281
   events 165
   interest rate changes 282
   mergers and acquisitions 278
CGA (comparable company analysis) 312
CDOs (collateralized debt obligations) 116
CDS (credit default swap) 116
CFA (Chartered Financial Analyst) 113
charts 239–253
   alternative chart types 250–251
   interpreting 249
   interpreting price changes with 253–267
   patterns 247–249
   reading 246
   Streamlit 267–271
classification approach 183
Coca-Cola Company 108
code generation 201
collecting data, commercial libraries 67
complex trading signals 287–289
contrarian investor 247
correlation 153–156
coupon payments 113
coupons 4
covered call 161
credit risk 4

credit spread 163
cryptocurrencies 5, 138
crypto exchanges 290
curiosity 323
current ratio 34
cycles, economic, sectors and 30

## D

DAG (directed acyclic graph) 234
Dalio, Ray 328
data
   call 234–237
   collecting, commercial libraries 67
   exporting 337
   extracting 127–129
   financial data 53–54
   loading 232
   preparing 234
database, cloud 336
DATABASE_ID parameter 225
data collection 52
   Alpha Vantage 73
   EODHD 71
   financial analysis platforms 54–56
   Finviz 69
   libraries 76
   notebooks 57
   OpenBB 75
   yfinance 57–66
data science, notebooks 57
day trading 12
DCA (dollar-cost averaging) 158
DCF (discounted cash flow) method 37, 312
DDL (Data Definition Language) 125, 223
debt 36
D/E (debt-to-equity) ratio 36, 61
DEI (diversity, equity, and inclusion) 325
demographic data 277
derivatives 6, 159–163
development environment 334
   Anaconda 334
   PyCharm 335
   VS Code 335

dilution 45, 314
direct investment 7
disasters 281
distressed companies 279
diversification 163
dividends 40, 106–112
   growth 109
   payout frequency 108
   yield 108
documentation 337
*Domain-Driven Design* (Evans) 19
Dunning-Kruger effect 322

## E

earnings 36
   calls 281
   surprise 281
EBIT (Earnings Before Interest and Taxes) 36
economic cycles, sectors and 30
economic moat 84, 107
EDGAR (Electronic Data Gathering, Analysis, and Retrieval system) 232
efficient market theory 193
EMA (exponential moving average) 257
environments 330
   cloud 336–337
environment setup 332–333
EPS (earnings per share) 33, 36, 87
equity, defined 3
ESG (environmental, social, and governance) 45, 194, 325
   factors 141
ETFs (exchange-traded funds) 4, 62, 125, 135–137, 209, 306
Euronext Amsterdam (AEB) 132
Evans, Eric 19
EV (Enterprise Value) 312
exchanges
   ledgers and 117
   orders 289
exits 304–306
exporting data 337
external assessments 46–49
   ratings 47
   target prices 48

## F

face value 114
factors 183
FCF (free cash flow) 26, 37
features, defined 188
finance chat 206–208
financial data 53–54
Finviz platform 55, 69
float, defined 44
fluctuations 146
FMCW (frequency-modulated continuous wave) 85
forex (foreign exchange) market 5
founders 311
FRED (Federal Reserve Economic Data) 167
FSE (Frankfurt Stock Exchange) 132
FullRatio 33
fundamental analysis, yfinance 58–61
fundamental data 53
funding stages 303–304
funds, types of 5
futures, defined 160

## G

GAAP (Generally Accepted Accounting Principles) 20
Gemini 182, 204
GenAI (Generative AI) 11, 68
  machine learning vs. 198–201
  practical use of 201–208
GICS (Global Industry Classification Standard) 28
Gladwell, Malcolm 328
Graham, Benjamin 275
growth investing 13, 105
growth portfolios 78
  investment thesis 79–84
  LiDAR market 85–95
  ongoing analysis 97–101

## H

hedge funds 5
hedging 15, 160–165
  derivatives 160–163
  diversification 163
  pair trading 163
  risk pairing 164
HFT (high-frequency trading) 12, 158, 290, 328
histograms 251, 263
HMA (Hull moving average) 257
Hugging Face 182

## I

Ichimoku Cloud 264–267
IDE (Integrated Development Environment) 275, 334
IFRS (International Financial Reporting Standards) 21
income investing 13
income portfolios 105
  bonds 112–116
  dividends 106–112
  early retirement 121
  staking 117–120
income statement 22–25
incubators 300
indenture 113
industry classification 28–32
  influences on GICS sectors 28
  sectors and economic cycles 30
insider transactions 44
*Intelligent Investor, The* (Graham) 275
Interactive Brokers
  extracting data 129
  orders 292
interest rate changes 282
investing 19
  activist investing 325
  analytical investor 1
  approaches to 8–14
  journey 2
  measures of control 326–329
investment advice 323
investment essentials
  debt 36
  industry classification 28–32
  liquidity 34
  metrics and ratios 33
  ownership 44–45
  profitability 40
  sustainability 45
  valuation 37
investment thesis 79–84
  challenging the idea 81–84
  starting with an idea 79
  your investment thesis 84
iron condor 162
iShares MSCI World ETF (URTH) 121
ISIN (International Securities Identification Number) 138
ITM (in the money) 162

## K

K-means clustering 185
KYC (Know Your Customer) process 157, 330

## L

labels 188
large-cap 32
leverage 159
liabilities 25
libraries 76
LiDAR (Light Detection and Ranging) 82, 84, 233
LiDAR market
  debt 91–92
  management 92
  picking candidates 86–88
  price development 88–91
  projected earnings 94–95
  technology and partnership 92–94
liquidity 26, 34
LLMs (large language models) 68, 81, 169, 181, 273, 316, 322, 330, 337
  as research assistants 201–203
  integrating into code 203–208
logarithmic returns 65
long position 12
lower band 261
LSE (London Stock Exchange) 58

## M

M&A (mergers and acquisitions) 278
MACD line 262
MACD (Moving Average Convergence Divergence) 262–264
margin of safety 158
market capitalization 37
market risk 147
Markowitz-efficient portfolio 170–174
matplotlib library 331
maturation date 113
max_tokens parameter 205
MCPs (model context protocols) 222
mean metric 66
mean reversion 247
media 97, 277
mega-cap 32
merge_fin_data function 132
merge_value_into_df function 136
metrics 33
micro-cap 32
mid-cap 32
middle band 260
mining 118
ML (machine learning) 28, 54, 181–182, 273
  generative AI vs. 198–201
  market challenges 192–195
  narrowing scope 197
  supervised learning 188–192
  technical challenges 195–196
  unsupervised learning 184–187
moats, economic 108
Monte Carlo simulation 151
movement data 277
moving average ribbons 259
mplfinance library 255
MPT (modern portfolio theory) 170
Munger, Charlie 275
mutual funds 5
MVP (minimum viable product) 298–300

## N

NaN (not a number) values 258
NAV (net asset value) 5, 136
navPrice ratio 136
negligence 157
news sentiment analysis 100
NLP (natural language processing) 198
nomadism 324
nonfinancial data 54, 274–278
  big data 276–278
nonfinancial risks 202
notebooks 57
NYSE (New York Stock Exchange) 58

## O

one-shot prompting 229–231
OpenAI 182, 203
OpenBB 75
operational design domain 93
OpEx (operating expenses) 26
options, types of 6, 160
orders 289–294
  exchanges vs. brokers 289
  executing 292–294
  modifiers 291–292
OTM (out of the money) 162
outliers, defined 183
*Outliers* (Gladwell) 328
out of the money (OTM) 162
overfitting 195
ownership 44
  stock-based compensation and dilution 45

## P

pair trading 163
pandas library 331
par value 114
passively managed ETFs 4
patterns 247–249
payment modalities 113
payout ratio 42, 109
PEG (price/earnings-to-growth) ratio 38
P/E (price-to-earnings) ratio 10, 20, 33, 38, 135, 312
pip package manager 331
pitching, explained 301–302
portfolios 13
  growth investing 13
  income investing 13
  value investing 13
PoS (Proof-of-Stake) consensus mechanism 119
PoW (Proof-of-Work) consensus mechanism 118
premium, defined 6
price-to-book ratio 39
price-to-sales ratio 39
principal, defined 4
*Principle: Life and Work* (Dalio) 328
private equity 6
  investing in start-ups 298–306
  investment vehicles 306–312
profitability 40
prompt engineering 208–213
  investor profile 208–210
  using prompts to find companies to invest in 211–213
put option 6
PyCharm 335
PyPI (Python Package Index) 71
Python 330–332
  libraries and APIs 331
python_binance API 138

## Q

qualitative research 11
quantitative research 10
Quant Rating 47
quarterly_ identifier 59
quick ratio 34

## R

R&D (research and development) 22
RAG databases 221
RAG (Retrieval-Augmented Generation) 217
RAG (retrieval-augmented generation) 231–237
  call 234–237
  loading data 232
  preparing data 234
RAGs (Retrieval-Augmented Generations) 212, 323

random walk 193
ratings 47
ratios, defined 33
rebalancing 176–179
   Shiller P/E ratio 174
regression 183
REITs (real estate investment trusts) 13, 43, 111
RenTech (Renaissance Technologies) 197, 276
residence of company 109
resilience 159
resistance lines 249
retirement, early 121
ride-hailing services 82
risk-averse investor 208
risk avoidance 157–159
risk management 143
   generating risk profiles for individual stocks 150–156
   hedging 160–165
   human factor 156–160
   nonfinancial risk 165–169
   portfolio optimization 169–179
   ukemi 144–150
risk pairing 164
risk profiles, generating for individual stocks 150–156
   correlation 153–156
   VaR 150–153
risk rating 113
risks 95–97
   and rewards 15
   falling into obsolescence 96
   globalization and conflicts 97
   squashed by industry giants 96
ROA (return on assets) 40
ROE (return on equity) 40

## S

SA Analyst Rating 47
SAM (serviceable available market) 301
SBC (stock-based compensation) 45
scaling start-ups 303–304
scatterplots 251

scheduled event 220
scoring
   business model 318
   capital intensity and burn rate 318
   clients and strategic partnerships 316
   country of origin 317
   domain 317
   economic moat 318
   existing investors 316
   founders and advisors 316
   incubator and accelerator 316
   individual North Star Metrics 318
   network effect 318
   regulation 317
Scrum 157
secrets managers 332, 337
sector risk 147
*Security Analysis* (Graham) 275
selling underperformers 177
shareholder equity 25
Shiller P/E ratio 174
short selling 12, 159
short-term trading 12
signal line 263
simple returns 65
slippage 288
small-cap 32
SMA (simple moving average) 257, 283
SMEs (small and midsize enterprises) 32
SMRs (Small Modular Reactors) 164
Snowflake Marketplace 276
SOM (serviceable obtainable market) 301
source code repository 333
spreadsheets 126
SPV (Special Purpose Vehicle) 310
SREs (site reliability engineers) 146
Stage class 234
staking 117–120
   affordable options 119
   ledgers and exchanges 117
   mining and 118
stalking horse agreement 280

start-ups 297–306
   accelerator 302
   assessing 312–318
   exits 304–306
   incubators 300
   investment vehicles 306–312
   minimum viable product (MVP) 298–300
   pitching 301
   scaling 303–304
   validating business model 301–302
std (standard deviation) 66, 153
stock price prediction 190
stocks 3, 131–135
   generating risk profiles for individual stocks 150–156
stock screeners 55
stock worksheet 134
stop-loss orders 144
   in practice 145
Streamlit 267–271
strike price 6
successfully failed 304
summarizing documents 201
supervised learning 183, 188–192
   building analytical datasets 188–190
   stock price prediction 190
support line 249
sustainability 45–46
swaps, defined 160
SWFs (Sovereign Wealth Funds) 311
swing trading 12
SWOT (strengths, weaknesses, opportunities, and threats) analysis 81–84
systemic risk 146

## T

TAM (total addressable market) 301
target prices 48
taxes 145
TDD (test-driven development) 144, 283
technical analysis 150, 239
   yfinance 61–66
technical data 53

temperature parameter 204–205
tenbaggers 32
time value of money 22
TMO (Thermo Fisher
    Scientific) 111
trading
    algorithmic 12
    asset monitors 12
    brokers and exchanges 338
trading algorithms 282–289
    backtesting 283–287
    complex trading signals 287–289
transaction costs 145
treemaps 251
trend analysis 98
TWS (Trader Workstation) 129, 338

## U

UI (user interface) 54
ukemi 144–150
    risk classification 146–148

risk measurement 148–150
    stop-loss 144
underfitting 195
unsupervised learning 183–187
unsystematic risk 147
upper band 261
URTH (iShares MSCI World ETF) 121
user query 220

## V

V2X (vehicle-to-everything) communication 83
valuation 37, 312–314
value investing 13, 105
vanilla bond 113
variance metric 66
VaR (value at risk) 150–153
var (variance) 153
venture capital 308
VIX (CBOE Volatility Index) 277

volatility 195
VOO (Vanguard S&P 500 ETF) 121
VR (virtual reality) 16
VS Code (Visual Studio Code) 335
VSE (Vienna Stock Exchange) 132

## W

*Wall Street* (film) 275
Wall Street Rating 47
WMA (weighted moving average) 257

## Y

yfinance 57–66
    fundamental analysis 58–61
    library 56
    limitations of 66
    technical analysis 61–66